The Kaggle Book

Data analysis and machine learning for competitive data science

Konrad Banachewicz

Luca Massaron

BIRMINGHAM—MUMBAI

The Kaggle Book

Copyright © 2022 Packt Publishing

Producer: Tushar Gupta

Acquisition Editor – Peer Reviews: Saby Dsilva

Project Editor: Parvathy Nair

Content Development Editor: Lucy Wan

Copy Editor: Safis Editing

Technical Editor: Karan Sonawane

Proofreader: Safis Editing

Indexer: Sejal Dsilva

Presentation Designer: Pranit Padwal

First published: April 2022

Production reference: 3141022

Published by Packt Publishing Ltd.
Livery Place
35 Livery Street
Birmingham
B3 2PB, UK.

ISBN 978-1-80181-747-9

www.packt.com

Foreword

I had a background in econometrics but became interested in machine learning techniques, initially as an alternative approach to solving forecasting problems. As I started discovering my interest, I found the field intimidating to enter: I didn't know the techniques, the terminology, and didn't have the credentials that would allow me to break in.

It was always my dream that Kaggle would allow people like me the opportunity to break into this powerful new field. Perhaps the thing I'm proudest of is the extent to which Kaggle has made data science and machine learning more accessible. We've had many Kagglers go from newbies to top machine learners, being hired at places like NVIDIA, Google, and OpenAI, and starting companies like DataRobot.

Luca and Konrad's book helps make Kaggle even more accessible. It offers a guide to both how Kaggle works, as well as many of the key learnings that they have taken out of their time on the site. Collectively, they've been members of Kaggle for over 20 years, entered 330 competitions, made over 2,000 posts to Kaggle forums, and shared over 100 notebooks and 50 datasets. They are both top-ranked users and well-respected members of the Kaggle community.

Those who complete this book should expect to be able to engage confidently on Kaggle – and engaging confidently on Kaggle has many rewards.

Firstly, it's a powerful way to stay on top of the most pragmatic developments in machine learning. Machine learning is moving very quickly. In 2019, over 300 peer reviewed machine learning papers were published per day. This volume of publishing makes it impossible to be on top of the literature. Kaggle ends up being a very valuable way to filter what developments matter on real-world problems – and Kaggle is useful for more than keeping up with the academic literature. Many of the tools that have become standard in the industry have spread via Kaggle. For example, XGBoost in 2014 and Keras in 2015 both spread through the community before making their way into industry.

Secondly, Kaggle offers users a way to "learn by doing." I've heard active Kagglers talk about competing regularly as "weight training" for machine learning. The variety of use cases and problems they tackle on Kaggle makes them well prepared when they encounter similar problems in industry. And because of competition deadlines, Kaggle trains the muscle of iterating quickly. There's probably no better way to learn than to attempt a problem and then see how top performers tackled the same problem (it's typical for winners to share their approaches after the competition).

So, for those of you who are reading this book and are new to Kaggle, I hope it helps make Kaggle less intimidating. And for those who have been on Kaggle for a while and are looking to level up, I hope this book from two of Kaggle's strongest and most respected members helps you get more out of your time on the site.

Anthony Goldbloom
Kaggle Founder and CEO

Contributors

About the authors

Konrad Banachewicz holds a PhD in statistics from Vrije Universiteit Amsterdam. During his period in academia, he focused on problems of extreme dependency modeling in credit risk. In addition to his research activities, Konrad was a tutor and supervised master's students. Starting from classical statistics, he slowly moved toward data mining and machine learning (this was before the terms "data science" or "big data" became ubiquitous).

In the decade after his PhD, Konrad worked in a variety of financial institutions on a wide array of quantitative data analysis problems. In the process, he became an expert on the entire lifetime of a data product cycle. He has visited different ends of the frequency spectrum in finance (from high-frequency trading to credit risk, and everything in between), predicted potato prices, and analyzed anomalies in the performance of large-scale industrial equipment.

As a person who himself stood on the shoulders of giants, Konrad believes in sharing knowledge with others. In his spare time, he competes on Kaggle ("the home of data science").

I would like to thank my brother for being a fixed point in a chaotic world and continuing to provide inspiration and motivation. Dzięki, Braciszku.

Luca Massaron is a data scientist with more than a decade of experience in transforming data into smarter artifacts, solving real-world problems, and generating value for businesses and stakeholders. He is the author of bestselling books on AI, machine learning, and algorithms. Luca is also a Kaggle Grandmaster who reached no. 7 in the worldwide user rankings for his performance in data science competitions, and a **Google Developer Expert (GDE)** in machine learning.

My warmest thanks go to my family, Yukiko and Amelia, for their support and loving patience as I prepared this new book in a long series.

My deepest thanks to Anthony Goldbloom for kindly writing the foreword for this book and to all the Kaggle Masters and Grandmasters who have so enthusiastically contributed to its making with their interviews, suggestions, and help.

Finally, I would like to thank Tushar Gupta, Parvathy Nair, Lucy Wan, Karan Sonawane, and all of the Packt Publishing editorial and production staff for their support on this writing effort.

About the reviewer

Dr. Andrey Kostenko is a data science and machine learning professional with extensive experience across a variety of disciplines and industries, including hands-on coding in R and Python to build, train, and serve time series models for forecasting and other applications. He believes that lifelong learning and open-source software are both critical for innovation in advanced analytics and artificial intelligence.

Andrey recently assumed the role of Lead Data Scientist at *Hydroinformatics Institute* (H2i.sg), a specialized consultancy and solution services provider for all aspects of water management. Prior to joining H2i, Andrey had worked as Senior Data Scientist at IAG InsurTech Innovation Hub for over 3 years. Before moving to Singapore in 2018, he worked as Data Scientist at TrafficGuard.ai, an Australian AdTech start-up developing novel data-driven algorithms for mobile ad fraud detection. In 2013, Andrey received his doctorate degree in Mathematics and Statistics from Monash University, Australia. By then, he already had an MBA degree from the UK and his first university degree from Russia.

In his spare time, Andrey is often found engaged in competitive data science projects, learning new tools across R and Python ecosystems, exploring the latest trends in web development, solving chess puzzles, or reading about the history of science and mathematics.

Dr. Firat Gonen is the Head of Data Science and Analytics at Getir. Gonen leads the data science and data analysis teams delivering innovative and cutting edge Machine Learning projects. Before Getir, Dr. Gonen was managing Vodafone Turkey's AI teams. Prior to Vodafone Turkey, he was the Principal Data Scientist at Dogus Group (one of Turkey's largest conglomerates). Gonen holds extensive educational qualifications including a PhD degree in NeuroScience and Neural Networks from University of Houston and is an expert in Machine Learning, Deep Learning, Visual Attention, Decision-Making & Genetic Algorithms with over more than 12 years in the field. He has authored several peer-review journal papers. He's also a Kaggle Triple GrandMaster and has more than 10 international data competition medals. He was also selected as the 2020 Z by HP Data Science Global Ambassador.

About the interviewees

We were fortunate enough to be able to collect interviews from 31 talented Kagglers across the Kaggle community, who we asked to reflect on their time on the platform. You will find their answers scattered across the book. They represent a broad range of perspectives, with many insightful responses that are as similar as they are different. We read each one of their contributions with great interest and hope the same is true for you, the reader. We give thanks to all of them and list them in alphabetical order below.

Abhishek Thakur, who is currently building AutoNLP at Hugging Face.

Alberto Danese, Head of Data Science at Nexi.

Andrada Olteanu, Data Scientist at Endava, Dev Expert at Weights and Biases, and Z by HP Global Data Science Ambassador.

Andrew Maranhão, Senior Data Scientist at Hospital Albert Einstein in São Paulo.

Andrey Lukyanenko, Machine Learning Engineer and TechLead at MTS Group.

Bojan Tunguz, Machine Learning Modeler at NVIDIA.

Chris Deotte, Senior Data Scientist and Researcher at NVIDIA.

Dan Becker, VP Product, Decision Intelligence at DataRobot.

Dmitry Larko, Chief Data Scientist at H2O.ai.

Firat Gonen, Head of Data Science and Analytics at Getir and Z by HP Global Data Science Ambassador.

Gabriel Preda, Principal Data Scientist at Endava.

Gilberto Titericz, Senior Data Scientist at NVIDIA.

Giuliano Janson, Senior Applied Scientist for ML and NLP at Zillow Group.

Jean-François Puget, Distinguished Engineer, RAPIDS at NVIDIA, and the manager of the NVIDIA Kaggle Grandmaster team.

Jeong-Yoon Lee, Senior Research Scientist in the Rankers and Search Algorithm Engineering team at Netflix Research.

Kazuki Onodera, Senior Deep Learning Data Scientist at NVIDIA and member of the NVIDIA KGMON team.

Laura Fink, Head of Data Science at Micromata.

Martin Henze, PhD Astrophysicist and Data Scientist at Edison Software.

Mikel Bober-Irizar, Machine Learning Scientist at ForecomAI and Computer Science student at the University of Cambridge.

Osamu Akiyama, Medical Doctor at Osaka University.

Parul Pandey, Data Scientist at H2O.ai.

Paweł Jankiewicz, Chief Data Scientist & AI Engineer as well as Co-founder of LogicAI.

Rob Mulla, Senior Data Scientist at Biocore LLC.

Rohan Rao, Senior Data Scientist at H2O.ai.

Ruchi Bhatia, Data Scientist at OpenMined, Z by HP Global Data Science Ambassador, and graduate student at Carnegie Mellon University.

Ryan Chesler, Data Scientist at H2O.ai.

Shotaro Ishihara, Data Scientist and Researcher at a Japanese news media company.

Sudalai Rajkumar, an AI/ML advisor for start-up companies.

Xavier Conort, Founder and CEO at Data Mapping and Engineering.

Yifan Xie, Co-founder of Arion Ltd, a data science consultancy firm.

Yirun Zhang, final-year PhD student at King's College London in applied machine learning.

Join our book's Discord space

Join the book's Discord workspace for a monthly *Ask me Anything* session with the authors:

https://packt.link/KaggleDiscord

Table of Contents

Preface

Having competed on Kaggle for over ten years, both of us have experienced highs and lows over many competitions. We often found ourselves refocusing our efforts on different activities relating to Kaggle. Over time, we devoted ourselves not just to competitions but also to creating content and code based on the demands of the data science market and our own professional aspirations. At this point in our journey, we felt that our combined experience and still-burning passion for competitions could really help other participants who have just started, or who would like to get inspired, to get hold of the essential expertise they need, so they can start their own journey in data science competitions.

We then decided to work on this book with a purpose:

- To offer, in a single place, the best tips for being competitive and approaching most of the problems you may find when participating on Kaggle and also other data science competitions.

- To offer enough suggestions to allow anyone to reach at least the Expert level in any Kaggle discipline: Competitions, Datasets, Notebooks, or Discussions.

- To provide tips on how to learn the most from Kaggle and leverage this experience for professional growth in data science.

- To gather in a single source the largest number of perspectives on the experience of participating in competitions, by interviewing Kaggle Masters and Grandmasters and listening to their stories.

In short, we have written a book that demonstrates how to participate in competitions successfully and make the most of all the opportunities that Kaggle offers. The book is also intended as a practical reference that saves you time and effort, through its selection of many competition tips and tricks that are hard to learn about and find on the internet or on Kaggle forums. Nevertheless, the book doesn't limit itself to providing practical help; it also aspires to help you figure out how to boost your career in data science by participating in competitions.

Please be aware: this book doesn't teach you data science from the basics. We don't explain in detail how linear regression or random forests or gradient boosting work, but how to use them in the best way and obtain the best results from them in a data problem. We expect solid foundations and at least a basic proficiency in data science topics and Python usage from our readers. If you are still a data science beginner, you need to supplement this book with other books on data science, machine learning, and deep learning, and train up on online courses, such as those offered by Kaggle itself or by MOOCs such as edX or Coursera.

If you want to start learning data science in a practical way, if you want to challenge yourself with tricky and intriguing data problems and simultaneously build a network of great fellow data scientists as passionate about their work in data as you are, this is indeed the book for you. Let's get started!

Who this book is for

At the time of completion of this book, there are 96,190 Kaggle novices (users who have just registered on the website) and 67,666 Kaggle contributors (users who have just filled in their profile) enlisted in Kaggle competitions. This book has been written for all of them and for anyone else wanting to break the ice and start taking part in competitions on Kaggle and learning from them.

What this book covers

Part 1: Introduction to Competitions

Chapter 1, Introducing Kaggle and Other Data Science Competitions, discusses how competitive programming evolved into data science competitions. It explains why the Kaggle platform is the most popular site for these competitions and provides you with an idea about how it works.

Chapter 2, Organizing Data with Datasets, introduces you to Kaggle Datasets, the standard method of data storage on the platform. We discuss setup, gathering data, and utilizing it in your work on Kaggle.

Chapter 3, Working and Learning with Kaggle Notebooks, discusses Kaggle Notebooks, the baseline coding environment. We talk about the basics of Notebook usage, as well as how to leverage the GCP environment, and using them to build up your data science portfolio.

Chapter 4, Leveraging Discussion Forums, allows you to familiarize yourself with discussion forums, the primary manner of communication and idea exchange on Kaggle.

Part 2: Sharpening Your Skills for Competitions

Chapter 5, Competition Tasks and Metrics, details how evaluation metrics for certain kinds of problems strongly influence the way you can operate when building your model solution in a data science competition. The chapter also addresses the large variety of metrics available in Kaggle competitions.

Chapter 6, Designing Good Validation, will introduce you to the importance of validation in data competitions, discussing overfitting, shake-ups, leakage, adversarial validation, different kinds of validation strategies, and strategies for your final submissions.

Chapter 7, Modeling for Tabular Competitions, discusses tabular competitions, mostly focusing on the more recent reality of Kaggle, the Tabular Playground Series. Tabular problems are standard practice for the majority of data scientists around and there is a lot to learn from Kaggle.

Chapter 8, Hyperparameter Optimization, explores how to extend the cross-validation approach to find the best hyperparameters for your models – in other words, those that can generalize in the best way on the private leaderboard – under the pressure and scarcity of time and resources that you experience in Kaggle competitions.

Chapter 9, Ensembling with Blending and Stacking Solutions, explains ensembling techniques for multiple models such as averaging, blending, and stacking. We will provide you with some theory, some practice, and some code examples you can use as templates when building your own solutions on Kaggle.

Chapter 10, Modeling for Computer Vision, we discuss problems related to computer vision, one of the most popular topics in AI in general, and on Kaggle specifically. We demonstrate full pipelines for building solutions to challenges in image classification, object detection, and image segmentation.

Chapter 11, Modeling for NLP, focuses on the frequently encountered types of Kaggle challenges related to natural language processing. We demonstrate how to build an end-to-end solution for popular problems like open domain question answering.

Chapter 12, Simulation and Optimization Competitions, provides an overview of simulation competitions, a new class of contests gaining popularity on Kaggle over the last few years.

Part 3: Leveraging Competitions for Your Career

Chapter 13, Creating Your Portfolio of Projects and Ideas, explores ways you can stand out by showcasing your work on Kaggle itself and other sites in an appropriate way.

Chapter 14, Finding New Professional Opportunities, concludes the overview of how Kaggle can positively affect your career by discussing the best ways to leverage all your Kaggle experience in order to find new professional opportunities.

To get the most out of this book

The Python code in this book has been designed to be run on a Kaggle Notebook, without any installation on a local computer. Therefore, don't worry about what machine you have available or what version of Python packages you should install.

All you need is a computer with access to the internet and a free Kaggle account. In fact, to run the code on a Kaggle Notebook (you will find instructions about the procedure in *Chapter 3*), you first need to open an account on Kaggle. If you don't have one yet, just go to www.kaggle.com and follow the instructions on the website.

We link out to many different resources throughout the book that we think you will find useful. When referred to a link, explore it: you will find code available on public Kaggle Notebooks that you can reuse, or further materials to illustrate concepts and ideas that we have discussed in the book.

Download the example code files

The code bundle for the book is hosted on GitHub at https://github.com/PacktPublishing/The-Kaggle-Book. We also have other code bundles from our rich catalog of books and videos available at https://github.com/PacktPublishing/. Check them out!

Download the color images

We also provide a PDF file that has color images of the screenshots/diagrams used in this book. You can download it here: https://static.packt-cdn.com/downloads/9781801817479_ColorImages.pdf.

Conventions used

There are a few text conventions used throughout this book.

CodeInText: Indicates code words in text, database table names, folder names, filenames, file extensions, pathnames, dummy URLs, user input, and Twitter handles. For example; " The dataset will be downloaded to the Kaggle folder as a .zip archive – unpack it and you are good to go."

A block of code is set as follows:

```
from google.colab import drive
drive.mount('/content/gdrive')
```

Any command-line input or output is written as follows:

```
I genuinely have no idea what the output of this sequence of words will be
- it will be interesting to find out what nlpaug can do with this!
```

Bold: Indicates a new term, an important word, or words that you see on the screen, for example, in menus or dialog boxes. For example: " The specific limits at the time of writing are **100 GB per private dataset** and a **100 GB total** quota."

 Further notes, references, and links to useful places appear like this.

 Tips and tricks appear like this.

Get in touch

Feedback from our readers is always welcome.

General feedback: Email feedback@packtpub.com, and mention the book's title in the subject of your message. If you have questions about any aspect of this book, please email us at questions@packtpub.com.

Errata: Although we have taken every care to ensure the accuracy of our content, mistakes do happen. If you have found a mistake in this book, we would be grateful if you would report this to us. Please visit http://www.packtpub.com/submit-errata, selecting your book, clicking on the **Errata Submission Form** link, and entering the details.

Piracy: If you come across any illegal copies of our works in any form on the Internet, we would be grateful if you would provide us with the location address or website name. Please contact us at copyright@packtpub.com with a link to the material.

If you are interested in becoming an author: If there is a topic that you have expertise in and you are interested in either writing or contributing to a book, please visit http://authors.packtpub.com.

Share your thoughts

Once you've read *The Kaggle Book*, we'd love to hear your thoughts! Scan the QR code below to go straight to the Amazon review page for this book and share your feedback.

https://packt.link/r/1-801-81747-2

Your review is important to us and the tech community and will help us make sure we're delivering excellent quality content.

Download a free PDF copy of this book

Thanks for purchasing this book!

Do you like to read on the go but are unable to carry your print books everywhere? Is your eBook purchase not compatible with the device of your choice?

Don't worry, now with every Packt book you get a DRM-free PDF version of that book at no cost.

Read anywhere, any place, on any device. Search, copy, and paste code from your favorite technical books directly into your application.

The perks don't stop there, you can get exclusive access to discounts, newsletters, and great free content in your inbox daily

Follow these simple steps to get the benefits:

1. Scan the QR code or visit the link below

https://packt.link/free-ebook/9781801817479

2. Submit your proof of purchase
3. That's it! We'll send your free PDF and other benefits to your email directly

Part I

Introduction to Competitions

1

Introducing Kaggle and Other Data Science Competitions

Data science competitions have long been around and they have experienced growing success over time, starting from a niche community of passionate competitors, drawing more and more attention, and reaching a much larger audience of millions of data scientists. As longtime competitors on the most popular data science competition platform, Kaggle, we have witnessed and directly experienced all these changes through the years.

At the moment, if you look for information about Kaggle and other competition platforms, you can easily find a large number of meetups, discussion panels, podcasts, interviews, and even online courses explaining how to win in such competitions (usually telling you to use a variable mixture of grit, computational resources, and time invested). However, apart from the book that you are reading now, you won't find any structured guides about how to navigate so many data science competitions and how to get the most out of them – not just in terms of score or ranking, but also professional experience.

In this book, instead of just packaging up a few hints about how to win or score highly on Kaggle and other data science competitions, our intention is to present you with a guide on how to compete better on Kaggle and get back the maximum possible from your competition experiences, particularly from the perspective of your professional life. Also accompanying the contents of the book are interviews with Kaggle Masters and Grandmasters. We hope they will offer you some different perspectives and insights on specific aspects of competing on Kaggle, and inspire the way you will test yourself and learn doing competitive data science.

By the end of this book, you'll have absorbed the knowledge we drew directly from our own experiences, resources, and learnings from competitions, and everything you need to pave a way for yourself to learn and grow, competition after competition.

As a starting point, in this chapter, we will explore how competitive programming evolved into data science competitions, why the Kaggle platform is the most popular site for such competitions, and how it works.

We will cover the following topics:

- The rise of data science competition platforms
- The Common Task Framework paradigm
- The Kaggle platform and some other alternatives
- How a Kaggle competition works: stages, competition types, submission and leaderboard dynamics, computational resources, networking, and more

The rise of data science competition platforms

Competitive programming has a long history, starting in the 1970s with the first iterations of the **ICPC**, the **International Collegiate Programming Contest**. In the original ICPC, small teams from universities and companies participated in a competition that required solving a series of problems using a computer program (at the beginning, participants coded in FORTRAN). In order to achieve a good final rank, teams had to display good skills in team working, problem solving, and programming.

The experience of participating in the heat of such a competition and the opportunity to stand in a spotlight for recruiting companies provided the students with ample motivation and it made the competition popular for many years. Among ICPC finalists, a few have become renowned: there is *Adam D'Angelo*, the former CTO of Facebook and founder of Quora, *Nikolai Durov*, the co-founder of Telegram Messenger, and *Matei Zaharia*, the creator of Apache Spark. Together with many other professionals, they all share the same experience: having taken part in an ICPC.

After the ICPC, programming competitions flourished, especially after 2000 when remote participation became more feasible, allowing international competitions to run more easily and at a lower cost. The format is similar for most of these competitions: there is a series of problems and you have to code a solution to solve them. The winners are given a prize, but also make themselves known to recruiting companies or simply become famous.

Typically, problems in competitive programming range from combinatorics and number theory to graph theory, algorithmic game theory, computational geometry, string analysis, and data structures. Recently, problems relating to artificial intelligence have successfully emerged, in particular after the launch of the **KDD Cup**, a contest in knowledge discovery and data mining, held by the **Association for Computing Machinery's (ACM's) Special Interest Group (SIG)** during its annual conference (https://kdd.org/conferences).

The first KDD Cup, held in 1997, involved a problem about direct marketing for lift curve optimization and it started a long series of competitions that continues today. You can find the archives containing datasets, instructions, and winners at https://www.kdd.org/kdd-cup. Here is the latest available at the time of writing: https://ogb.stanford.edu/kddcup2021/. KDD Cups proved quite effective in establishing best practices, with many published papers describing solutions, techniques, and competition dataset sharing, which have been useful for many practitioners for experimentation, education, and benchmarking.

The successful examples of both competitive programming events and the KDD Cup inspired companies (such as Netflix) and entrepreneurs (such as *Anthony Goldbloom*, the founder of Kaggle) to create the first data science competition platforms, where companies can host data science challenges that are hard to solve and might benefit from crowdsourcing. In fact, given that there is no golden approach that works for all the problems in data science, many problems require a time-consuming approach that can be summed up as *try all that you can try*.

In fact, in the long run, no algorithm can beat all the others on all problems, as stated by the **No Free Lunch** theorem by David Wolpert and William Macready. The theorem tells you that each machine learning algorithm performs if and only if its hypothesis space comprises the solution. Consequently, as you cannot know beforehand if a machine learning algorithm can best tackle your problem, you have to try it, testing it directly on your problem before being assured that you are doing the right thing. There are no theoretical shortcuts or other holy grails of machine learning – only empirical experimentation can tell you what works.

For more details, you can look up the No Free Lunch theorem for a theoretical explanation of this practical truth. Here is a complete article from Analytics India Magazine on the topic: https://analyticsindiamag.com/what-are-the-no-free-lunch-theorems-in-data-science/.

Crowdsourcing proves ideal in such conditions where you need to test algorithms and data transformations extensively to find the best possible combinations, but you lack the manpower and computer power for it. That's why, for instance, governments and companies resort to competitions in order to advance in certain fields:

- On the government side, we can quote DARPA and its many competitions surrounding self-driving cars, robotic operations, machine translation, speaker identification, fingerprint recognition, information retrieval, OCR, automatic target recognition, and many others.

- On the business side, we can quote a company such as Netflix, which entrusted the outcome of a competition to improve its algorithm for predicting user movie selection.

The Netflix competition was based on the idea of improving existing collaborative filtering. The purpose of this was simply to predict the potential rating a user would give a film, solely based on the ratings that they gave other films, without knowing specifically who the user was or what the films were. Since no user description or movie title or description were available (all being replaced with identity codes), the competition required entrants to develop smart ways to use the past ratings available. The grand prize of US $1,000,000 was to be awarded only if the solution could improve the existing Netflix algorithm, Cinematch, above a certain threshold.

The competition ran from 2006 to 2009 and saw victory for a team made up of the fusion of many previous competition teams: a team from Commendo Research & Consulting GmbH, *Andreas Töscher* and *Michael Jahrer*, quite renowned also in Kaggle competitions; two researchers from AT&T Labs; and two others from Yahoo!. In the end, winning the competition required so much computational power and the ensembling of different solutions that teams were forced to merge in order to keep pace. This situation was also reflected in the actual usage of the solution by Netflix, who preferred not to implement it, but simply took the most interesting insight from it in order to improve its existing Cinematch algorithm. You can read more about it in this Wired article: `https://www.wired.com/2012/04/netflix-prize-costs/`.

At the end of the Netflix competition, what mattered was not the solution per se, which was quickly superseded by the change in business focus of Netflix from DVDs to online movies. The real benefit for both the participants, who gained a huge reputation in collaborative filtering, and the company, who could transfer its improved recommendation knowledge to its new business, were the insights that were gained from the competition.

The Kaggle competition platform

Companies other than Netflix have also benefitted from data science competitions. The list is long, but we can quote a few examples where the company running the competition reported a clear benefit from it. For instance:

- The insurance company Allstate was able to improve its actuarial models built by their own experts, thanks to a competition involving hundreds of data scientists (`https://www.kaggle.com/c/ClaimPredictionChallenge`)
- As another well-documented example, General Electric was able to improve by 40% on the industry-standard performance (measured by the root mean squared error metric) for predicting arrival times of airline flights, thanks to a similar competition (`https://www.kaggle.com/c/flight`)

The Kaggle competition platform has to this day held hundreds of competitions, and these two are just a couple of examples of companies that used them successfully. Let's take a step back from specific competitions for a moment and talk about the Kaggle company, which is the common thread through this book.

A history of Kaggle

Kaggle took its first steps in February 2010, thanks to *Anthony Goldbloom*, an Australian trained economist with a degree in Economics and Econometrics. After working at Australia's Department of the Treasury and the Research department at the Reserve Bank of Australia, Goldbloom interned in London at The Economist, the international weekly newspaper on current affairs, international business, politics, and technology. At The Economist, he had occasion to write an article about big data, which inspired his idea to build a competition platform that could crowdsource the best analytical experts to solve interesting machine learning problems (`https://www.smh.com.au/technology/from-bondi-to-the-big-bucks-the-28yearold-whos-making-data-science-a-sport-20111104-1myq1.html`). Since the crowdsourcing dynamics played a relevant part in the business idea for this platform, he derived the name *Kaggle*, which recalls by rhyme the term *gaggle*, a flock of geese, the goose also being the symbol of the platform.

After moving to Silicon Valley in the USA, his Kaggle start-up received $11.25 million in Series A funding from a round led by Khosla Ventures and Index Ventures, two renowned venture capital firms. The first competitions were rolled out, the community grew, and some of the initial competitors came to be quite prominent, such as *Jeremy Howard*, the Australian data scientist and entrepreneur, who, after winning a couple of competitions on Kaggle, became the President and Chief Scientist of the company.

Jeremy Howard left his position as President in December 2013 and established a new start-up, `fast.ai` (`www.fast.ai`), offering machine learning courses and a deep learning library for coders.

At the time, there were some other prominent Kagglers (the name indicating frequent participants of competitions held by Kaggle) such as *Jeremy Achin* and *Thomas de Godoy*. After reaching the top 20 global rankings on the platform, they promptly decided to retire and to found their own company, DataRobot. Soon after, they started hiring their employees from among the best participants in the Kaggle competitions in order to instill the best machine learning knowledge and practices into the software they were developing. Today, DataRobot is one of the leading companies in developing AutoML solutions (software for automatic machine learning).

The Kaggle competitions claimed more and more attention from a growing audience. Even Geoffrey Hinton, the "godfather" of deep learning, participated in (and won) a Kaggle competition hosted by Merck in 2012 (`https://www.kaggle.com/c/MerckActivity/overview/winners`). Kaggle was also the platform where *François Chollet* launched his deep learning package Keras during the *Otto Group Product Classification Challenge* (`https://www.kaggle.com/c/otto-group-product-classification-challenge/discussion/13632`) and *Tianqi Chen* launched XGBoost, a speedier and more accurate version of gradient boosting machines, in the *Higgs Boson Machine Learning Challenge* (`https://www.kaggle.com/c/higgs-boson/discussion/10335`).

Besides Keras, François Chollet has also provided the most useful and insightful perspective on how to win a Kaggle competition in an answer of his on the Quora website: `https://www.quora.com/Why-has-Keras-been-so-successful-lately-at-Kaggle-competitions`.

Fast iterations of multiple attempts, guided by empirical (more than theoretical) evidence, are actually all that you need. We don't think that there are many more secrets to winning a Kaggle competition than the ones he pointed out in his answer.

Notably, François Chollet also hosted his own competition on Kaggle (`https://www.kaggle.com/c/abstraction-and-reasoning-challenge/`), which is widely recognized as being the first general AI competition in the world.

Competition after competition, the community revolving around Kaggle grew to touch one million in 2017, the same year as, during her keynote at Google Next, *Fei-Fei Li*, Chief Scientist at Google, announced that Google Alphabet was going to acquire Kaggle. Since then, Kaggle has been part of Google.

Today, the Kaggle community is still active and growing. In a tweet of his (`https://twitter.com/antgoldbloom/status/1400119591246852096`), Anthony Goldbloom reported that most of its users, other than participating in a competition, have downloaded public data (Kaggle has become an important data hub), created a public Notebook in Python or R, or learned something new in one of the courses offered:

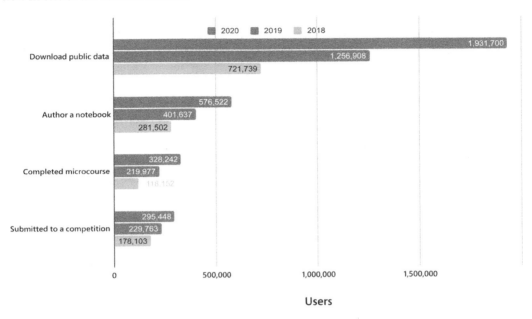

Figure 1.1: A bar chart showing how users used Kaggle in 2020, 2019, and 2018

Through the years, Kaggle has offered many of its participants even more opportunities, such as:

- Creating their own company
- Launching machine learning software and packages
- Getting interviews in magazines (`https://www.wired.com/story/solve-these-tough-data-problems-and-watch-job-offers-roll-in/`)
- Writing machine learning books (`https://twitter.com/antgoldbloom/status/745662719588589568`)
- Finding their dream job

And, most importantly, learning more about the skills and technicalities involved in data science.

Other competition platforms

Though this book focuses on competitions on Kaggle, we cannot forget that many data competitions are held on private platforms or on other competition platforms. In truth, most of the information you will find in this book will also hold for other competitions, since they essentially all operate under similar principles and the benefits for the participants are more or less the same.

Although many other platforms are localized in specific countries or are specialized only for certain kinds of competitions, for completeness we will briefly introduce some of them, at least those we have some experience and knowledge of:

- **DrivenData** (https://www.drivendata.org/competitions/) is a crowdsourcing competition platform devoted to social challenges (see https://www.drivendata.co/blog/intro-to-machine-learning-social-impact/). The company itself is a social enterprise whose aim is to bring data science solutions to organizations tackling the world's biggest challenges, thanks to data scientists building algorithms for social good. For instance, as you can read in this article, https://www.engadget.com/facebook-ai-hate-speech-covid-19-160037191.html, Facebook has chosen DrivenData for its competition on building models against hate speech and misinformation.

- **Numerai** (https://numer.ai/) is an AI-powered, crowdsourced hedge fund based in San Francisco. It hosts a weekly tournament in which you can submit your predictions on hedge fund obfuscated data and earn your prizes in the company's cryptocurrency, Numeraire.

- **CrowdANALYTIX** (https://www.crowdanalytix.com/community) is a bit less active now, but this platform used to host quite a few challenging competitions a short while ago, as you can read from this blog post: https://towardsdatascience.com/how-i-won-top-five-in-a-deep-learning-competition-753c788cade1. The community blog is quite interesting for getting an idea of what challenges you can find on this platform: https://www.crowdanalytix.com/jq/communityBlog/listBlog.html.

- **Signate** (https://signate.jp/competitions) is a Japanese data science competition platform. It is quite rich in contests and it offers a ranking system similar to Kaggle's (https://signate.jp/users/rankings).

- **Zindi** (https://zindi.africa/competitions) is a data science competition platform from Africa. It hosts competitions focused on solving Africa's most pressing social, economic, and environmental problems.

- **Alibaba Cloud** (`https://www.alibabacloud.com/campaign/tianchi-competitions`) is a Chinese cloud computer and AI provider that has launched the **Tianchi Academic competitions**, partnering with academic conferences such as SIGKDD, IJCAI-PRICAI, and CVPR and featuring challenges such as image-based 3D shape retrieval, 3D object reconstruction, and instance segmentation.
- **Analytics Vidhya** (`https://datahack.analyticsvidhya.com/`) is the largest Indian community for data science, offering a platform for data science hackathons.
- **CodaLab** (`https://codalab.lri.fr/`) is a French-based data science competition platform, created as a joint venture between Microsoft and Stanford University in 2013. They feature a free cloud-based notebook called Worksheets (`https://worksheets.codalab.org/`) for knowledge sharing and reproducible modeling.

Other minor platforms are CrowdAI (`https://www.crowdai.org/`) from *École Polytechnique Fédérale de Lausanne* in Switzerland, InnoCentive (`https://www.innocentive.com/`), Grand-Challenge (`https://grand-challenge.org/`) for biomedical imaging, DataFountain (`https://www.datafountain.cn/business?lang=en-US`), OpenML (`https://www.openml.org/`), and the list could go on. You can always find a large list of ongoing major competitions at the Russian community Open Data Science (`https://ods.ai/competitions`) and even discover new competition platforms from time to time.

 You can see an overview of running competitions on the `mlcontests.com` website, along with the current costs for renting GPUs. The website is often updated and it is an easy way to get a glance at what's going on with data science competitions across different platforms.

Kaggle is always the best platform where you can find the most interesting competitions and obtain the widest recognition for your competition efforts. However, picking up a challenge outside of it makes sense, and we recommend it as a strategy, when you find a competition matching your personal and professional interests. As you can see, there are quite a lot of alternatives and opportunities besides Kaggle, which means that if you consider more competition platforms alongside Kaggle, you can more easily find a competition that might interest you because of its specialization or data.

In addition, you can expect less competitive pressure during these challenges (and consequently a better ranking or even winning something), since they are less known and advertised. Just expect less sharing among participants, since no other competition platform has reached the same richness of sharing and networking opportunities as Kaggle.

Introducing Kaggle

At this point, we need to delve more deeply into how Kaggle in particular works. In the following paragraphs, we will discuss the various aspects of the Kaggle platform and its competitions, and you'll get a flavor of what it means to be in a competition on Kaggle. Afterward, we'll come back to discuss many of these topics in much more detail, with more suggestions and strategies in the remaining chapters of the book.

Stages of a competition

A competition on Kaggle is arranged into different steps. By having a look at each of them, you can get a better understanding of how a data science competition works and what to expect from it.

When a competition is launched, there are usually some posts on social media, for instance on the Kaggle Twitter profile, `https://twitter.com/kaggle`, that announce it, and a new tab will appear in the Kaggle section about **Active Competitions** on the **Competitions** page (`https://www.kaggle.com/competitions`). If you click on a particular competition's tab, you'll be taken to its page. At a glance, you can check if the competition will have prizes (and if it awards points and medals, a secondary consequence of participating in a competition), how many teams are currently involved, and how much time is still left for you to work on a solution:

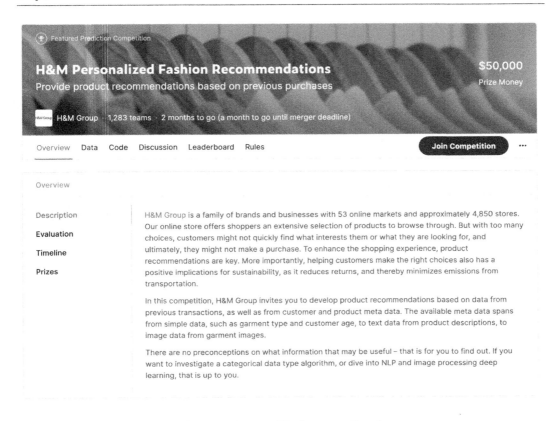

Figure 1.2: A competition's page on Kaggle

There, you can explore the **Overview** menu first, which provides information about:

- The topic of the competition
- Its evaluation metric (that your models will be evaluated against)
- The timeline of the competition
- The prizes
- The legal or competition requirements

Usually the timeline is a bit overlooked, but it should be one of the first things you check; it doesn't tell you simply when the competition starts and ends, but it will provide you with the **rule acceptance deadline**, which is usually from seven days to two weeks before the competition closes. The rule acceptance deadline marks the last day you can join the competition (by accepting its rules). There is also the **team merger deadline**: you can arrange to combine your team with another competitor's one at any point before that deadline, but after that it won't be possible.

The **Rules** menu is also quite often overlooked (with people just jumping to **Data**), but it is important to check it because it can tell you about the requirements of the competition. Among the key information you can get from the rules, there is:

- Your eligibility for a prize
- Whether you can use external data to improve your score
- How many submissions (tests of your solution) a day you get
- How many final solutions you can choose

Once you have accepted the rules, you can download any data from the **Data** menu or directly start working on **Kaggle Notebooks** (online, cloud-based notebooks) from the **Code** menu, reusing code that others have made available or creating your own code from scratch.

If you decide to download the data, also consider that you have a **Kaggle API** that can help you to run downloads and submissions in an almost automated way. It is an important tool if you are running your models on your local computer or on your cloud instance. You can find more details about the API at `https://www.kaggle.com/docs/api` and you can get the code from GitHub at `https://github.com/Kaggle/kaggle-api`.

If you check the Kaggle GitHub repo closely, you can also find all the Docker images they use for their online notebooks, Kaggle Notebooks:

Figure 1.3: A Kaggle Notebook ready to be coded

At this point, as you develop your solution, it is our warm suggestion not to continue in solitude, but to contact other competitors through the **Discussion** forum, where you can ask and answer questions specific to the competition. Often you will also find useful hints about specific problems with the data or even ideas to help improve your own solution. Many successful Kagglers have reported finding ideas on the forums that have helped them perform better and, more importantly, learn more about modeling in data science.

Once your solution is ready, you can submit it to the Kaggle evaluation engine, in adherence to the specifications of the competition. Some competitions will accept a CSV file as a solution, others will require you to code and produce results in a Kaggle Notebook. You can keep submitting solutions throughout the competition.

Every time you submit a solution, soon after, the leaderboard will provide you with a score and a position among the competitors (the wait time varies depending on the computations necessary for the score evaluation). That position is only roughly indicative, because it reflects the performance of your model on a part of the test set, called the **public test set**, since your performance on it is made public during the competition for everyone to know.

Before the competition closes, each competitor can choose a number (usually two) of their solutions for the final evaluation.

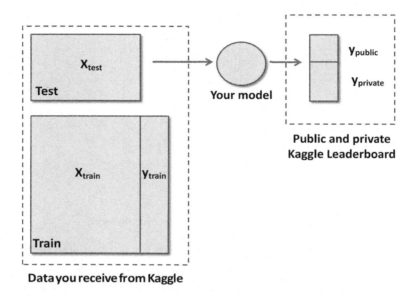

Data you receive from Kaggle

Figure 1.4: A diagram demonstrating how data turns into scores for the public and private leaderboard

Only when the competition closes, based on the models the contestants have decided to be scored, is their score on another part of the test set, called the **private test set**, revealed. This new leaderboard, the private leaderboard, constitutes the final, effective scores for the competition, but it is still not official and definitive in its rankings. In fact, the Kaggle team will take some time to check that everything is correct and that all contestants have respected the rules of the competition.

After a while (and sometimes after some changes in the rankings due to disqualifications), the private leaderboard will become official and definitive, the winners will be declared, and many participants will unveil their strategies, their solutions, and their code on the competition discussion forum. At this point, it is up to you to check the other solutions and try to improve your own. We strongly recommend that you do so, since this is another important source of learning in Kaggle.

Types of competitions and examples

Kaggle competitions are categorized based on *competition categories*, and each category has a different implication in terms of how to compete and what to expect. The type of data, difficulty of the problem, awarded prizes, and competition dynamics are quite diverse inside the categories, therefore it is important to understand beforehand what each implies.

Here are the official categories that you can use to filter out the different competitions:

- Featured
- Masters
- Annuals
- Research
- Recruitment
- Getting Started
- Playground
- Analytics
- Community

Featured are the most common type of competitions, involving a business-related problem from a sponsor company and a prize for the top performers. The winners will grant a non-exclusive license of their work to the sponsor company; they will have to prepare a detailed report of their solution and sometimes even participate in meetings with the sponsor company.

There are examples of Featured competitions every time you visit Kaggle. At the moment, many of them are problems relating to the application of deep learning methods to unstructured data like text, images, videos, or sound. In the past, tabular data competitions were commonly seen, that is, competitions based on problems relating to structured data that can be found in a database. First by using random forests, then gradient boosting methods with clever feature engineering, tabular data solutions derived from Kaggle could really improve an existing solution. Nowadays, these competitions are run much less often, because a crowdsourced solution won't often be much better than what a good team of data scientists or even AutoML software can do. Given the spread of better software and good practices, the increase in result quality obtainable from competitions is indeed marginal. In the unstructured data world, however, a good deep learning solution could still make a big difference. For instance, pre-trained networks such as BERT brought about double-digit increases in previous standards for many well-known NLP task benchmarks.

Masters are less common now, but they are private, invite-only competitions. The purpose was to create competitions only for experts (generally competitors ranked as Masters or Grandmasters, based on Kaggle medal rankings), based on their rankings on Kaggle.

Annuals are competitions that always appear during a certain period of the year. Among the Annuals, we have the Santa Claus competitions (usually based on an algorithmic optimization problem) and the *March Machine Learning Mania* competition, run every year since 2014 during the US College Basketball Tournaments.

Research competitions imply a research or science purpose instead of a business one, sometimes for serving the public good. That's why these competitions do not always offer prizes. In addition, these competitions sometimes require the winning participants to release their solution as open-source.

Google has released a few Research competitions in the past, such as *Google Landmark Recognition 2020* (https://www.kaggle.com/c/landmark-recognition-2020), where the goal was to label famous (and not-so-famous) landmarks in images.

Sponsors that want to test the ability of potential job candidates hold **Recruitment** competitions. These competitions are limited to teams of one and offer to best-placed competitors an interview with the sponsor as a prize. The competitors have to upload their CV at the end of the competition if they want to be considered for being contacted.

Examples of Recruitment competitions have been:

- The *Facebook Recruiting Competition* (https://www.kaggle.com/c/FacebookRecruiting); Facebook have held a few of this kind
- The *Yelp Recruiting Competition* (https://www.kaggle.com/c/yelp-recruiting)

Getting Started competitions do not offer any prizes, but friendly and easy problems for beginners to get accustomed to Kaggle principles and dynamics. They are usually semi-permanent competitions whose leaderboards are refreshed from time to time. If you are looking for a tutorial in machine learning, these competitions are the right places to start, because you can find a highly collaborative environment and there are many Kaggle Notebooks available showing you how to process the data and create different types of machine learning models.

Famous ongoing **Getting Started** competitions are:

- *Digit Recognizer* (https://www.kaggle.com/c/digit-recognizer)

- *Titanic — Machine Learning from Disaster* (https://www.kaggle.com/c/titanic)
- *House Prices — Advanced Regression Techniques* (https://www.kaggle.com/c/house-prices-advanced-regression-techniques)

Playground competitions are a little bit more difficult than the Getting Started ones, but they are also meant for competitors to learn and test their abilities without the pressure of a fully-fledged Featured competition (though in Playground competitions sometimes the heat of the competition may also turn quite high). The usual prizes for such competitions are just swag (an acronym for "Stuff We All Get," such as, for instance, a cup, a t-shirt, or socks branded by Kaggle; see https://www.kaggle.com/general/68961) or a bit of money.

One famous Playground competition is the original *Dogs vs. Cats* competition (https://www.kaggle.com/c/dogs-vs-cats), where the task is to create an algorithm to distinguish dogs from cats.

Mentions should be given to **Analytics** competitions, where the evaluation is qualitative and participants are required to provide ideas, drafts of solutions, PowerPoint slides, charts, and so on; and **Community** (previously known as InClass) competitions, which are held by academic institutions as well as Kagglers. You can read about the launch of the Community competitions at https://www.kaggle.com/product-feedback/294337 and you can get tips about running one of your own at https://www.kaggle.com/c/about/host and at https://www.kaggle.com/community-competitions-setup-guide.

Parul Pandey

https://www.kaggle.com/parulpandey

We spoke to Parul Pandey, Kaggle Notebooks Grandmaster, Datasets Master, and data scientist at H2O.ai, about her experience with Analytics competitions and more.

What's your favorite kind of competition and why? In terms of techniques and solving approaches, what is your specialty on Kaggle?

I really enjoy the Data Analytics competitions, which require you to analyze the data and provide a comprehensive analysis report at the end. These include the Data Science for Good competitions (DS4G), sports analytics competitions (NFL etc.), and the general survey challenges. Unlike the traditional competitions, these competitions don't have a leaderboard to track your performance compared to others; nor do you get any medals or points.

On the other hand, these competitions demand end-to-end solutions touching on multi-faceted aspects of data science like data cleaning, data mining, visualizations, and conveying insights. Such problems provide a way to mimic real-life scenarios and provide your insights and viewpoints. There may not be a single best answer to solve the problem, but it gives you a chance to deliberate and weigh up potential solutions, and imbibe them into your solution.

How do you approach a Kaggle competition? How different is this approach to what you do in your day-to-day work?

My first step is always to analyze the data as part of EDA (exploratory data analysis). It is something that I also follow as part of my work routine. Typically, I explore the data to look for potential red flags like inconsistencies in data, missing values, outliers, etc., which might pose problems later. The next step is to create a good and reliable cross-validation strategy. Then I read the discussion forums and look at some of the Notebooks shared by people. It generally acts as a good starting point, and then I can incorporate things in this workflow from my past experiences. It is also essential to track the model performance.

For an Analytics competition, however, I like to break down the problem into multiple steps. For instance, the first part could be related to understanding the problem, which may require a few days. After that, I like to explore the data, followed by creating a basic baseline solution. Then I continue enhancing this solution by adding a piece at a time. It might be akin to adding Lego bricks one part at a time to create that final masterpiece.

Tell us about a particularly challenging competition you entered, and what insights you used to tackle the task.

As I mentioned, I mostly like to compete in Analytics competitions, even though occasionally I also try my hand in the regular ones too. I'd like to point out a very intriguing Data Science for Good competition titled Environmental Insights Explorer (https://www.kaggle.com/c/ds4g-environmental-insights-explorer). The task was to use remote sensing techniques to understand environmental emissions instead of calculating emissions factors from current methodologies.

What really struck me was the use case. Our planet is grappling with climate change issues, and this competition touched on this very aspect. While researching for my competition, I was amazed to find the amount of progress being made in this field of satellite imagery and it gave me a chance to understand and dive more deeply into the topic. It gave me a chance to understand how satellites like Landsat, Modis, and Sentinel worked, and how they make the satellite data available. This was a great competition to learn about a field I knew very little about before the competition.

In your experience, what do inexperienced Kagglers often overlook? What do you know now that you wish you'd known when you first started?

I will cite some of the mistakes that I made in my initial years on Kaggle.

Firstly, most of the newbies think of Kaggle as a competitions-only platform. If you love competitions, there are plenty here, but Kaggle also has something for people with other specialties. You can write code and share it with others, indulge in healthy discussions, and network. Curate and share good datasets with the community. I initially only used Kaggle for downloading datasets, and it was only a couple of years ago that I actually became active. Now when I look back, I couldn't have been more wrong. A lot of people get intimidated by competitions. You can first get comfortable with the platform and then slowly start participating in the competitions.

Another important thing that I would like to mention is that many people work in isolation, lose motivation, and quit. Teaming up on Kaggle has many unseen advantages. It teaches you to work in a team, learn from the experiences, and work towards a common goal in a limited time frame.

Do you use other competition platforms? How do they compare to Kaggle?

While most of my current time is spent on Kaggle, in the past I have used Zindi, a data science competition platform focused on African use cases. It's a great place to access datasets focused on Africa. Kaggle is a versatile platform, but there is a shortage of problem statements from different parts of the world. Of late, we have seen some diversified problems too, like the recently held chaii competition—an NLP competition focusing on Indian languages. I believe similar competitions concentrating on different countries will be helpful for the research and the general data science community as well.

Cross-sectional to this taxonomy of Kaggle competitions, you also have to consider that competitions may have different formats. The usual format is the so-called **Simple format** where you provide a solution and it is evaluated as we previously described. More sophisticated, the **two-stage competition** splits the contest into two parts, and the final dataset is released only after the first part has finished and only to the participants of the first part. The two-stage competition format has emerged in order to limit the chance of some competitors cheating and infringing the rules, since the evaluation is done on a completely untried test set that is available for a short time only. Contrary to the original Kaggle competition format, in this case, competitors have a much shorter amount of time and much fewer submissions to figure out any useful patterns from the test set.

For the same reason, the **Code** competitions have recently appeared, where all submissions are made from a Kaggle Notebook, and any direct upload of submissions is disabled.

For Kagglers at different stages of their competition careers, there are no restrictions at all in taking on any kind of competition. However, we have some suggestions against or in favor of the format or type of competition depending on your level of experience in data science and your computational resources:

- For complete beginners, the **Getting Started** or the **Playground** competitions are good places to begin, since you can easily get more confident about how Kaggle works without facing high competitive pressure. That being said, many beginners have successfully started from Featured and Research competitions, because being under pressure helped them to learn faster. Our suggestion is therefore to decide based on your learning style: some Kagglers need to learn by exploring and collaborating (and the Getting Started or the Playground competitions are ideal for that), others need the heat of a fast-paced competition to find their motivation.

- For **Featured** and **Research** competitions, also take into account that these competitions are often about fringe applications of AI and machine learning and, consequently, you often need a solid background or the willingness to study all the relevant research in the field of application of the competition.

Finally, keep in mind that most competitions require you to have access to computational resources that are often not available to most data scientists in the workplace. This can turn into growing expenses if you use a cloud platform outside the Kaggle one. **Code** competitions and competitions with time or resource limitations might then be the ideal place to spend your efforts, since they strive to put all the participants on the same resource level.

Submission and leaderboard dynamics

The way Kaggle works seems simple: the test set is hidden to participants; you fit your model; if your model is the best in predicting on the test set, then you score highly and you possibly win. Unfortunately, this description renders the inner workings of Kaggle competitions in an overly simplistic way. It doesn't take into account that there are dynamics regarding the direct and indirect interactions of competitors, or the nuances of the problem you are facing and of its training and test set.

Explaining the Common Task Framework paradigm

A more comprehensive description of how Kaggle works is actually given by Professor *David Donoho*, professor of statistics at Stanford University (`https://web.stanford.edu/dept/statistics/cgi-bin/donoho/`), in his paper *50 Years of Data Science*. It first appeared in the *Journal of Computational and Graphical Statistics* and was subsequently posted on the *MIT Computer Science and Artificial Intelligence Laboratory* (see `http://courses.csail.mit.edu/18.337/2015/docs/50YearsDataScience.pdf`).

Professor Donoho does not refer to Kaggle specifically, but to all data science competition platforms. Quoting computational linguist *Mark Liberman*, he refers to data science competitions and platforms as being part of a **Common Task Framework (CTF)** paradigm that has been silently and steadily progressing data science in many fields during the last decades. He states that a CTF can work incredibly well at improving the solution of a problem in data science from an empirical point of view, quoting the Netflix competition and many DARPA competitions as successful examples. The CTF paradigm has contributed to reshaping the best-in-class solutions for problems in many fields.

A CTF is composed of **ingredients** and a **secret sauce**. The **ingredients** are simply:

1. A publicly available dataset and a related prediction task
2. A set of competitors who share the common task of producing the best prediction for the task
3. A system for scoring the predictions by the participants in a fair and objective way, without providing hints about the solution that are too specific (or limiting them, at least)

The system works the best if the task is well defined and the data is of good quality. In the long run, the performance of solutions improves by small gains until it reaches an asymptote. The process can be sped up by allowing a certain amount of sharing among participants (as happens on Kaggle by means of discussions, and sharing Kaggle Notebooks and extra data provided by the datasets found in the Datasets section). According to the CTF paradigm, competitive pressure in a competition suffices to produce always-improving solutions. When the competitive pressure is paired with some degree of sharing among participants, the improvement happens at an even faster rate – hence why Kaggle introduced many incentives for sharing.

This is because the **secret sauce** in the CTF paradigm is the competition itself, which, within the framework of a practical problem whose empirical performance has to be improved, always leads to the emergence of new benchmarks, new data and modeling solutions, and in general to an improved application of machine learning to the problem posed by the competition. A competition can therefore provide a new way to solve a prediction problem, new ways of feature engineering, and new algorithmic or modeling solutions. For instance, deep learning did not simply emerge from academic research, but it first gained a great boost because of successful competitions that signaled its efficacy (we have already mentioned, for instance, the Merck competition, won by _Geoffrey Hinton's_ team: https://www.kaggle.com/c/MerckActivity/overview/winners).

Coupled with the open software movement, which allows everyone access to powerful analytical tools (such as Scikit-learn, TensorFlow, or PyTorch), the CTF paradigm brings about even better results because all competitors are on the same level at the start. On the other hand, the reliance of a solution to a competition on specialized or improved hardware can limit achievable results, because it can prevent competitors without access to such resources from properly participating and contributing directly to the solution, or indirectly by exercising competitive pressure on the other participants. Understandably, this is the reason why Kaggle started offering cloud services free to participants of its competitions, the Kaggle Notebooks we will introduce in the _Computational resources_ section. It can flatten some differences in hardware-intense competitions (as most deep learning ones are) and increase the overall competitive pressure.

Understanding what can go wrong in a competition

Given our previous description of the CTF paradigm, you may be tempted to imagine that all a competition needs is to be set up on a proper platform, and good results such as positive involvement for participants and outstanding models for the sponsor company will automatically come in. However, there are also things that can go wrong and instead lead to a disappointing result in a competition, both for the participants and the institution running it:

- Leakage from the data
- Probing from the leaderboard (the scoring system)
- Overfitting and consequent leaderboard shake-up
- Private sharing

You have **leakage** from data when part of the solution can be retraced in the data itself. For instance, certain variables could be posterior to the target variable, so they reveal something about it. This happens in fraud detection when you use variables that are updated _after_ a fraud happens, or in sales forecasting when you process information relating to the effective distribution of a product (more distribution implies more requests for the product, hence more sales).

Another issue could be that the training and test examples are ordered in a predictable way or that the values of the identifiers of the examples hint at the solution. Examples are, for instance, when the identifier is based on the ordering of the target, or the identifier value is correlated with the flow of time and time affects the probability of the target.

Such solution leakage, sometimes named *golden features* by competitors (because getting a hint of such nuances in the data can turn into gold prizes for the participants), invariably leads to a solution that is not reusable. This also implies a sub-optimal result for the sponsor, but they at least are able to learn something about leaking features that can affect solutions to their problem.

Another problem is the possibility of **probing a solution** from the leaderboard. In this situation, you can take advantage of the evaluation metrics shown to you and snoop the solution by repeated submission trials on the leaderboard. Again, in this case the solution is completely unusable in different circumstances. A clear example of this happened in the competition *Don't Overfit II*. The winning participant, *Zachary Mayers*, submitted every individual variable as a single submission, gaining information about the possible weight of each variable that allowed him to estimate the correct coefficients for his model (you can read Zach's detailed solution here: https://www. kaggle.com/c/dont-overfit-ii/discussion/91766). Generally, time series problems, or other problems where there are systematic shifts in the test data, may be seriously affected by probing, since they can help competitors to successfully define some kind of *post-processing* (like multiply- ing their predictions by a constant) that is most suitable for scoring highly on the *specific* test set.

Another form of leaderboard snooping (that is, getting a hint about the test set and overfitting to it) happens when participants rely more on the feedback from the public leaderboard than their own tests. Sometimes this turns into a complete failure of the competition, causing a wild shake-up – a complete and unpredictable reshuffling of the positions on the final leaderboard. The winning solutions, in such a case, may turn out to be not so optimal for the problem or even just dictated by chance. This has led to the diffusion of techniques analyzing the potential gap between the training set and the public test set. This kind of analysis, called **adversarial testing**, can provide insight about how much to rely on the leaderboard and whether there are features that are so different between the training and test set that it would be better to avoid them completely.

For an example, you can have a look at this Notebook by *Bojan Tunguz*: https://www.kaggle. com/tunguz/adversarial-ieee.

Another kind of defense against leaderboard overfitting is choosing safe strategies to avoid submitting solutions that are based too much on the leaderboard results. For instance, since (typically) two solutions are allowed to be chosen by each participant for final evaluation, a good strategy is to submit the best performing one based on the leaderboard, and the best performing one based on your own cross-validation tests.

In order to avoid problems with leaderboard probing and overfitting, Kaggle has recently introduced different innovations based on Code competitions, where the evaluation is split into two distinct stages, as we previously discussed, with participants being completely blind to the actual test data so they are forced to consider their own local validation tests more.

Finally, another possible distortion of a competition is due to **private sharing** (sharing ideas and solutions in a closed circle of participants) and other illicit moves such as playing through multiple accounts or playing in multiple teams and stealing ideas. All such actions create an asymmetry of information between participants that can be favorable to a few and detrimental to most. Again, the resulting solution may be affected because sharing has been imperfect during the competition and fewer teams have been able to exercise full competitive pressure. Moreover, if these situations become evident to participants (for instance, see https://www.kaggle.com/c/ashrae-energy-prediction/discussion/122503), it can lead to distrust and less involvement in the competition or subsequent competitions.

Computational resources

Some competitions pose limitations in order to render feasible solutions available to production. For instance, the *Bosch Production Line Performance* competition (https://www.kaggle.com/c/bosch-production-line-performance) had strict limits on execution time, model file output, and memory limit for solutions. Notebook-based (previously known as Kernel-Only) competitions, which require both training and inference to be executed on the Kaggle Notebooks, do not pose a problem for the resources you have to use. This is because Kaggle will provide you with all the resources you need (and this is also intended as a way to put all participants on the same start line for a better competition result).

Problems arise when you have competitions that only limit the use of Notebooks to inference time. In these cases, you can train your models on your own machine and the only limit is then at test time, on the number and complexity of models you produce. Since most competitions at the moment require deep learning solutions, you have to be aware that you will need specialized hardware, such as GPUs, in order to achieve a competitive result.

Even in some of the now-rare tabular competitions, you'll soon realize that you need a strong machine with quite a number of processors and a lot of memory in order to easily apply feature engineering to data, run experiments, and build models quickly.

Standards change rapidly, so it is difficult to specify a standard hardware that you should have in order to compete at least in the same league as other teams. We can get hints about the current standard by looking at what other competitors are using, either as their own machine or a machine on the cloud.

For instance, HP launched a program where it awarded an HP Z4 or Z8 to a few selected Kaggle participants in exchange for brand visibility. For instance, a Z8 machine has up to 72 cores, 3 TB of memory, 48 TB of storage (a good share by solid storage hard drive standards), and usually dual NVIDIA RTX as the GPU. We understand that this may be a bit out of reach for many; even renting a similar machine for a short time on a cloud instance such as Google's GCP or Amazon's AWS is out of the discussion, given the expenses for even moderate usage.

 The cloud costs for each competition naturally depend on the amount of data to process and on the number and type of models you build. Free credit giveaways in Kaggle competitions for both GCP and AWS cloud platforms usually range from US $200 to US $500.

Our suggestion, as you start your journey to climb to the top rankings of Kaggle participants, is therefore to go with the machines provided free by Kaggle, Kaggle Notebooks (previously known as Kaggle Kernels).

Kaggle Notebooks

Kaggle Notebooks are versioned computational environments, based on Docker containers running in cloud machines, that allow you to write and execute both scripts and notebooks in the R and Python languages. Kaggle Notebooks:

- Are integrated into the Kaggle environment (you can make submissions from them and keep track of what submission refers to what Notebook)
- Come with most data science packages pre-installed
- Allow some customization (you can download files and install further packages)

The basic Kaggle Notebook is just CPU-based, but you can have versions boosted by an NVIDIA Tesla P100 or a TPU v3-8. TPUs are hardware accelerators specialized for deep learning tasks.

Though bound by a usage number and time quota limit, Kaggle Notebooks give you access to the computational workhorse to build your baseline solutions on Kaggle competitions:

Notebook type	CPU cores	Memory	Number of notebooks that can be run at a time	Weekly quota
CPU	4	16 GB	10	Unlimited
GPU	2	13 GB	2	30 hours
TPU	4	16 GB	2	30 hours

Besides the total runtime, CPU and GPU notebooks can run for a maximum of 12 hours per session before stopping (TPU notebooks for just 9 hours) meaning you won't get any results from the run apart from what you have saved on disk. You have a 20 GB disk saving allowance to store your models and results, plus an additional scratchpad disk that can exceed 20 GB for temporary usage during script running.

In certain cases, the GPU-enhanced machine provided by Kaggle Notebooks may not be enough. For instance, the recent *Deepfake Detection Challenge* (`https://www.kaggle.com/c/deepfake-detection-challenge`) required the processing of data consisting of around 500 GB of videos. That is especially challenging because of the 30-hour time limit of weekly usage, and because of the fact that you cannot have more than two machines with GPUs running at the same time. Even if you can double your machine time by changing your code to leverage the usage of TPUs instead of GPUs (which you can find some guidance for easily achieving here: `https://www.kaggle.com/docs/tpu`), that may still not prove enough for fast experimentation in a data-heavy competition such as the *Deepfake Detection Challenge*.

For this reason, in *Chapter 3, Working and Learning with Kaggle Notebooks*, we are going to provide you with tips for successfully coping with these limitations to produce decent results without having to buy a heavy-performing machine. We are also going to show you how to integrate Kaggle Notebooks with GCP or, alternatively, in *Chapter 2, Organizing Data with Datasets*, how to move all your work into another cloud-based solution, Google Colab.

Teaming and networking

While computational power plays its part, only human expertise and ability can make the real difference in a Kaggle competition. For a competition to be handled successfully, it sometimes requires the collaborative efforts of a team of contestants. Apart from Recruitment competitions, where the sponsor may require individual participants for a better evaluation of their abilities, there is typically no restriction against forming teams. Usually, teams can be made up of a maximum of five contestants.

Teaming has its own advantages because it can multiply efforts to find a better solution. A team can spend more time on the problem together and different skills can be of great help; not all data scientists will have the same skills or the same level of skill when it comes to different models and data manipulation.

However, teaming is not all positive. Coordinating different individuals and efforts toward a common goal may prove not so easy, and some suboptimal situations may arise. A common problem is when some of the participants are not involved or are simply idle, but no doubt the worst is when someone infringes the rules of the competition – to the detriment of everyone, since the whole team could be disqualified – or even spies on the team in order to give an advantage to another team, as we mentioned earlier.

In spite of any negatives, teaming in a Kaggle competition is a great opportunity to get to know other data scientists better, to collaborate for a purpose, and to achieve more, since Kaggle rules do reward teams over lonely competitors. In fact, for smaller teams you get a percentage of the total that is higher than an equal share. Teaming up is not the only possibility for networking in Kaggle, though it is certainly more profitable and interesting for the participants. You can also network with others through discussions on the forums, or by sharing Datasets and Notebooks during competitions. All these opportunities on the platform can help you get to know other data scientists and be recognized in the community.

There are also many occasions to network with other Kagglers outside of the Kaggle platform itself. First of all, there are a few Slack channels that can be helpful. For instance, **KaggleNoobs** (https://www.kaggle.com/getting-started/20577) is a channel, opened up in 2016, that features many discussions about Kaggle competitions. They have a supportive community that can help you if you have some specific problem with code or models.

There are quite a few other channels devoted to exchanging opinions about Kaggle competitions and data science-related topics. Some channels are organized on a regional or national basis, for instance, the Japanese channel **Kaggler-ja** (http://kaggler-ja-wiki.herokuapp.com/) or the Russian community **Open Data Science Network** (https://ods.ai/), created in 2015, which later opened also to non-Russian speaking participants. The Open Data Science Network doesn't offer simply a Slack channel but also courses on how to win competitions, events, and reporting on active competitions taking place on all known data science platforms (see https://ods.ai/competitions).

Aside from Slack channels, quite a few local meetups themed around Kaggle in general or around specific competitions have sprung up, some just on a temporary basis, others in a more established form. A meetup focused on Kaggle competitions, usually built around a presentation from a competitor who wants to share their experience or suggestions, is the best way to meet other Kagglers in person, to exchange opinions, and to build alliances for participating in data science contests together.

In this league, a mention should be given to **Kaggle Days** (`https://kaggledays.com/`), built by *Maria Parysz* and *Paweł Jankiewicz*. The Kaggle Days organization arranged a few events in major locations around the world (`https://kaggledays.com/about-us/`) with the aim of bringing together a conference of Kaggle experts. It also created a network of local meetups in different countries, which are still quite active (`https://kaggledays.com/meetups/`).

Paweł Jankiewicz

`https://www.kaggle.com/paweljankiewicz`

We had the opportunity to catch up with Paweł about his experiences with Kaggle. He is a Competitions Grandmaster and a co-founder of LogicAI.

What's your favourite kind of competition and why? In terms of techniques and solving approaches, what is your specialty on Kaggle?

Code competitions are my favourite type of competition because working in a limited environment forces you to think about different kinds of budgets: time, CPU, memory. Too many times in previous competitions I needed to utilize even up to 3-4 strong virtual machines. I didn't like that in order to win I had to utilize such resources, because it makes it a very uneven competition.

How do you approach a Kaggle competition? How different is this approach to what you do in your day-to-day work?

I approach every competition a little bit differently. I tend to always build a framework for each competition that allows me to create as many experiments as possible. For example, in one competition where we needed to create a deep learning convolutional neural network, I created a way to configure neural networks by specifying them in the format C4-MP4-C3-MP3 (where each letter stands for a different layer). It was many years ago, so the configuration of neural networks is probably now done by selecting the backbone model. But the rule still applies. You should create a framework that allows you to change the most sensitive parts of the pipeline quickly.

Day-to-day work has some overlap with Kaggle competitions in terms of modeling approach and proper validation. What Kaggle competitions taught me is the importance of validation, data leakage prevention, etc. For example, if data leaks happen in so many competitions, when people who prepare them are the best in the field, you can ask yourself what percentage of production models have data leaks in training; personally, I think 80%+ of production models are probably not validated correctly, but don't quote me on that.

Another important difference in day-to-day work is that no one really tells you how to define the modeling problem. For instance:

1. *Should the metric you report or optimize be RMSE, RMSLE, SMAPE, or MAPE?*
2. *If the problem is time-based, how can you split the data to evaluate the model as realistically as possible?*

And these are not the only important things for the business. You also must be able to communicate your choices and why you made them.

Tell us about a particularly challenging competition you entered, and what insights you used to tackle the task.

The most challenging and interesting was the Mercari Price Prediction *Code competition. It was very different from any other competition because it was limited to 1 hour of computation time and only 4 cores with 16 GB of memory. Overcoming these limitations was the most exciting part of the challenge. My takeaway from this competition was to believe more in networks for tabular data. Before merging with my teammate Konstantin Lopukhin (*https://www.kaggle.com/lopuhin*), I had a bunch of complicated models including neural networks, but also some other boosting algorithms. After merging, it turned out that Konstantin was using only one architecture which was very optimized (number of epochs, learning rate). Another aspect of this competition that was quite unique was that it wasn't enough to just average solutions from the team. We had to reorganize our workflow so that we had a single coherent solution and not something quickly put together. It took us three weeks to combine our solutions together.*

In your experience, what do inexperienced Kagglers often overlook? What do you know now that you wish you'd known when you first started?

Software engineering skills are probably underestimated a lot. Every competition and problem is slightly different and needs some framework to streamline the solution (look at https://github.com/bestfitting/ instance_level_recognition and how well their code is organized). Good code organization helps you to iterate faster and eventually try more things.

> ## What's the most important thing someone should keep in mind or do when they're entering a competition?
>
> *The most important thing is to have fun.*

Performance tiers and rankings

Apart from monetary prizes and other material items, such as cups, t-shirts, hoodies, and stickers, Kaggle offers many immaterial awards. Kagglers spend a whole lot of time and effort during competitions (not to mention in developing the skills they use to compete that are, in truth, quite rare in the general population). The monetary prizes usually cover the efforts of the top few Kagglers, if not only the one in the top spot, leaving the rest with an astonishing number of hours voluntarily spent with little return. In the long term, participating in competitions with no tangible results may lead to disaffection and disinterest, lowering the competitive intensity.

Hence, Kaggle has found a way to reward competitors with an honor system based on medals and points. The idea is that the more medals and the more points you have, the more relevant your skills are, leaving you open for opportunities in your job search or any other relevant activity based on your reputation.

First, there is a **general leaderboard**, that combines all the leaderboards of the individual competitions (https://www.kaggle.com/rankings). Based on the position they attain in each competition, Kagglers are awarded some number of points that, all summed together, provide their ranking on the general leaderboard. At first glance, the formula for the scoring of the points in a competition may look a bit complex:

$$\left[\frac{100000}{\sqrt{N_{teammates}}} \right] * [Rank^{-0.75}] * [\log_{10}(1 + \log_{10}(N_{teams}))] * [e^{-t/500}]$$

Nevertheless, in reality it is simply based on a few ingredients:

- Your rank in a competition
- Your team size
- The popularity of the competition
- How old the competition is

Intuitively, ranking highly in popular competitions brings many points. Less intuitively, the size of your team matters in a non-linear way. That's due to the inverse square root part of the formula, since the proportion of points you have to give up grows with the number of people involved.

It is still quite favorable if your team is relatively small (2, max 3 people) due to the advantage in wits and computational power brought about by collaboration.

Another point to keep in mind is that points decay with time. The decay is not linear, but as a rule of thumb keep in mind that, after a year, very little is left of the points you gained. Therefore, glory on the general leaderboard of Kaggle is ephemeral unless you keep on participating in competitions with similar results to before. As a consolation, on your profile you'll always keep the highest rank you ever reach.

More longer-lasting is the medal system that covers all four aspects of competing in Kaggle. You will be awarded medals for Competitions, Notebooks, Discussion, and Datasets based on your results. In Competitions, medals are awarded based on your position on the leaderboard. In the other three areas, medals are awarded based on the upvotes of other competitors (which can actually lead to some sub-optimal situations, since upvotes are a less objective metric and also depend on popularity). The more medals you get, the higher the ranks of Kaggle mastery you can enter. The ranks are **Novice**, **Contributor**, **Expert**, **Master**, and **Grandmaster**. The page at `https://www.kaggle.com/progression` explains everything about how to get medals and how many and what kinds are needed to access the different ranks.

Keep in mind that these ranks and honors are always relative and that they do change in time. A few years ago, in fact, the scoring system and the ranks were quite different. Most probably in the future, the ranks will change again in order to keep the higher ones rarer and more valuable.

Criticism and opportunities

Kaggle has drawn quite a few criticisms since it began. Participation in data science competitions is still a subject of debate today, with many different opinions out there, both positive and negative.

On the side of negative criticism:

- Kaggle provides a false perception of what machine learning really is since it is just focused on leaderboard dynamics
- Kaggle is just a game of hyperparameter optimization and ensembling many models just for scraping a little more accuracy (while in reality overfitting the test set)
- Kaggle is filled with inexperienced enthusiasts who are ready to try anything under the sun in order to get a score and a spotlight in hopes of being spotted by recruiters
- As a further consequence, competition solutions are too complicated and often too specific to a test set to be implemented

Many perceive Kaggle, like many other data science competition platforms, to be far from what data science is in reality. The point the critics raise is that business problems do not come from nowhere and you seldom already have a well-prepared dataset to start with, since you usually build it along the way based on refining business specifications and the understanding of the problem at hand. Moreover, many critics emphasize that Kagglers don't learn or excel at creating *production-ready* models, since a winning solution cannot be constrained by resource limits or considerations about technical debt (though this is not always true for all competitions).

All such criticism is related, in the end, to how Kaggle standings can be compared to other kinds of experience in the eyes of an employer, especially relative to data science education and work experience. One persistent myth is that Kaggle competitions won't help to get you a job or a better job in data science, and that they do not put you on another plane compared to data scientists that do not participate at all.

Our stance on this is that it is a misleading belief that Kaggle rankings do not have an automatic value beyond the Kaggle community. For instance, in a job search, Kaggle can provide you with some very useful competencies in modeling data and problems and effective model testing. It can also expose you to many techniques and different data/business problems, beyond your actual experience and comfort zone, but it cannot supplement you with everything you need to successfully place yourself as a data scientist in a company.

You can use Kaggle for learning (there is also a section on the website, Courses, devoted to just learning) and for differentiating yourself from other candidates in a job search; however, how this will be considered varies considerably from company to company. Regardless, what you learn on Kaggle will invariably prove useful throughout your career and will provide you a hedge when you have to solve complex and unusual problems with data modeling; by participating in Kaggle competitions, you build up strong competencies in modeling and validating. You also network with other data scientists, which can get you a reference for a job more easily and provide you with another way to handle difficult problems beyond your skills, because you will have access to other people's competencies and opinions.

Hence, our opinion is that Kaggle functions in a more indirect way to help you in your career as a data scientist, in a variety of different ways. Of course, sometimes Kaggle will help you to be contacted directly as a job candidate based on your successes, but more often Kaggle will provide you with the intellectual skills and experience you need to succeed, first as a candidate and then as a practitioner.

In fact, after playing with data and models on Kaggle for a while, you'll have had the chance to see enough different datasets, problems, and ways to deal with them under time pressure that when faced with similar problems in real settings you'll be skilled in finding solutions quickly and effectively.

This latter opportunity for a skill upgrade is why we were motivated to write this book in the first place, and what this book is actually about. You won't find a guide purely on how to win or score highly in Kaggle competitions, but you absolutely will find a guide about how to compete better on Kaggle and how to get the most back from your competition experiences.

Use Kaggle and other competition platforms in a smart way. Kaggle is not a *passepartout* – being first in a competition won't assure you a highly paid job or glory beyond the Kaggle community. However, consistently participating in competitions is a card to be played smartly to show interest and passion in your data science job search, and to improve some specific skills that can differentiate you as a data scientist and not make you obsolete in front of AutoML solutions.

If you follow us through this book, we will show you how.

Summary

In this starting chapter, we first discussed how data science competition platforms have risen and how they actually work, both for competitors and for the institutions that run them, referring in particular to the convincing CTF paradigm as discussed by Professor David Donoho.

We illustrated how Kaggle works, without forgetting to mention other notable competition platforms and how it could be useful for you to take on challenges outside Kaggle as well. With regards to Kaggle, we detailed how the different stages of a competition work, how competitions differ from each other, and what resources the Kaggle platform can offer you.

In the next few chapters, we will begin to explore Kaggle in more detail, starting with how to work with Datasets.

Join our book's Discord space

Join the book's Discord workspace for a monthly *Ask me Anything* session with the authors:

`https://packt.link/KaggleDiscord`

2

Organizing Data with Datasets

In his story *The Adventure of the Copper Beeches*, Arthur Conan Doyle has Sherlock Holmes shout *"Data! Data! Data! I cannot make bricks without clay."* This mindset, which served the most famous detective in literature so well, should be adopted by every data scientist. For that reason, we begin the more technical part of this book with a chapter dedicated to data: specifically, in the Kaggle context, leveraging the power of the Kaggle Datasets functionality for our purposes.

In this chapter, we will cover the following topics:

- Setting up a dataset
- Gathering the data
- Working with datasets
- Using Kaggle Datasets in Google Colab
- Legal caveats

Setting up a dataset

In principle, any data you can use you can upload to Kaggle (subject to limitations; see the *Legal caveats* section later on). The specific limits at the time of writing are **100 GB per private dataset** and a **100 GB total** quota. Keep in mind that the size limit per single dataset is calculated uncompressed; uploading compressed versions speeds up the transfer but does not help against the limits. You can check the most recent documentation for the datasets at this link: https://www.kaggle.com/docs/datasets.

Kaggle promotes itself as a "home of data science" and the impressive collection of datasets available from the site certainly lends some credence to that claim. Not only can you find data on topics ranging from oil prices to anime recommendations, but it is also impressive how quickly data ends up there. When the emails of *Anthony Fauci* were released under the *Freedom of Information Act* in May 2021 (`https://www.washingtonpost.com/politics/interactive/2021/tony-fauci-emails/`), they were uploaded as a Kaggle dataset a mere 48 hours later.

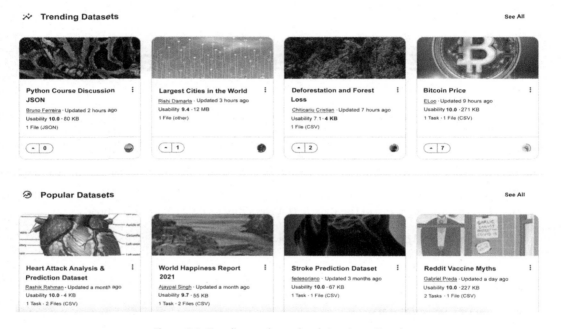

Figure 2.1: Trending and popular datasets on Kaggle

Before uploading the data for your project into a dataset, make sure to check the existing content. For several popular applications (image classification, NLP, financial time series), there is a chance it has already been stored there.

For the sake of this introduction, let us assume the kind of data you will be using in your project is not already there, so you need to create a new dataset. When you head to the menu with three lines on the left-hand side and click on **Data**, you will be redirected to the **Datasets** page:

Figure 2.2: The Datasets page

When you click on **+ New Dataset,** you will be prompted for the basics: uploading the actual data and giving it a title:

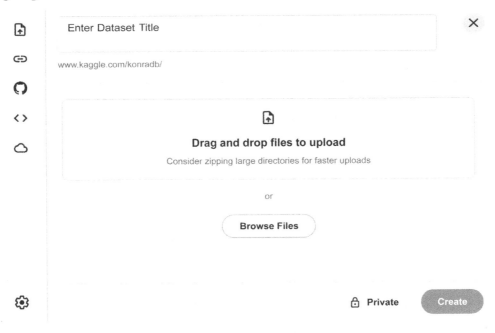

Figure 2.3: Entering dataset details

The icons on the left-hand side correspond to the different sources you can utilize for your dataset. We describe them in the order they are shown on the page:

- Upload a file from a local drive (shown in the figure)
- Create from a remote URL
- Import a GitHub repository
- Use output files from an existing Notebook
- Import a Google Cloud Storage file

An important point about the GitHub option: This feature is particularly handy when it comes to experimental libraries. While frequently offering hitherto unavailable functionality, they are usually not included in the Kaggle environment, so if you want to use such a library in your code, you can import it as a dataset, as demonstrated below:

1. Go to **Datasets** and click **+ New Dataset**.
2. Select the GitHub icon.
3. Insert the link to the repository, as well as the title for the dataset.
4. Click on **Create** at the bottom right:

Figure 2.4: Dataset from GitHub repository

Next to the **Create** button, there is another one marked **Private**. By default, any dataset you create is private: only you, its creator, can view and edit it. It is probably a good idea to leave this setting at default at the dataset creation stage and only at a later stage make it public (available to either a select list of contributors, or everyone).

Keep in mind that Kaggle is a popular platform and many people upload their datasets – including private ones – so try to think of a non-generic title. This will increase the chance of your dataset actually being noticed.

Once you have completed all the steps and clicked **Create**, voilà! Your first dataset is ready. You can then head to the **Data** tab:

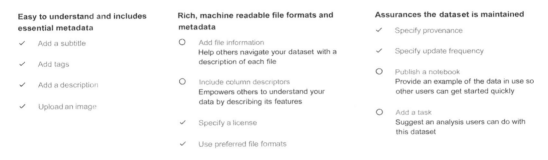

Figure 2.5: The Data tab

The screenshot above demonstrates the different information you can provide about your dataset; the more you do provide, the higher the **usability index**. This index is a synthetic measure summarizing how well your dataset is described. Datasets with higher usability indexes appear higher up in the search results. For each dataset, the usability index is based on several factors, including the level of documentation, the availability of related public content like Notebooks as references, file types, and coverage of key metadata.

In principle, you do not have to fill out all the fields shown in the image above; your newly created dataset is perfectly usable without them (and if it is a private one, you probably do not care; after all, you know what is in it). However, community etiquette would suggest filling out the information for the datasets you make public: the more you specify, the more usable the data will be to others.

Gathering the data

Apart from legal aspects, there is no real limit on the kind of content you can store in the datasets: tabular data, images, text; if it fits within the size requirements, you can store it. This includes data harvested from other sources; tweets by hashtag or topic are among the popular datasets at the time of writing:

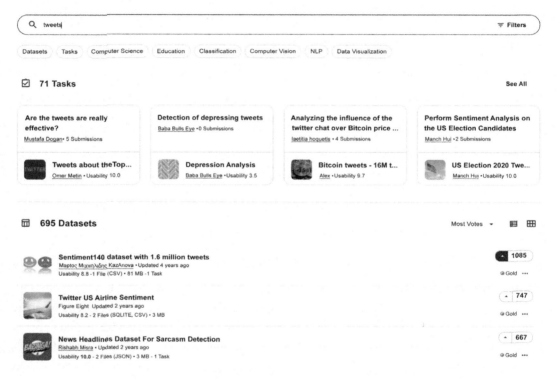

Figure 2.6: Tweets are among the most popular datasets

Discussion of the different frameworks for harvesting data from social media (Twitter, Reddit, and so on) is outside the scope of this book.

Andrew Maranhão

https://www.kaggle.com/andrewmvd

We spoke to Andrew Maranhão (aka Larxel), Datasets Grandmaster (number 1 in Datasets at time of writing) and Senior Data Scientist at the Hospital Albert Einstein in São Paulo, about his rise to Datasets success, his tips for creating datasets, and his general experiences on Kaggle.

What's your favourite kind of competition and why? In terms of techniques and solving approaches, what is your specialty on Kaggle?

Medical imaging is usually my favourite. It speaks to my purpose and job. Among medical competitions, NLP is language-bound, tabular data varies widely among hospitals, but imaging is mostly the same, so any advancement in this context can bring about benefits for many countries across the world, and I love this impact potential. I also have a liking for NLP and tabular data, but I suppose this is pretty standard.

Tell us about a particularly challenging competition you entered, and what insights you used to tackle the task.

In a tuberculosis detection in x-ray images competition, we had around 1,000 images, which is a pretty small number for capturing all the manifestations of the disease. I came up with two ideas to offset this:

1. *Pre-train on external data of pneumonia detection (~20k images), as pneumonia can be mistaken for tuberculosis.*

2. *Pre-train on multilabel classification of lung abnormalities (~600k images) and use grad-CAM with a simple SSD to generate bounding box annotations of classification labels.*

In the end, a simple blend of these two achieved 22% more compared to the result that the second-place team had. It happened at a medical convention, with about 100 teams participating.

You have become a Dataset Grandmaster and achieved the number 1 rank in Datasets. How do you choose topics and find, gather, and publish data for your datasets on Kaggle?

This is a big question; I'll try to break it down piece by piece.

1. *Set yourself a purpose*

   The first thing that I have in mind when choosing a topic is the reason I am doing this in the first place.

   When there is a deeper reason underneath, great datasets just come off as a result, not as a goal in itself. Fei Fei Li, the head of the lab that created ImageNet, revealed in a TED talk that she wanted to create a world where machines would be able to reason and appreciate the world with their vision in the same way her children did.

   Having a purpose in mind will make it more likely that you'll engage and improve over time, and will also differentiate you and your datasets. You can certainly live off tabular data on everyday topics, though I find that unlikely to leave a lasting impact.

2. *A great dataset is the embodiment of a great question*

   If we look at the greatest datasets in current literature, such as ImageNet and others, we can see some common themes:

   - *It is a daring, relevant question with great potential for all of us (scientific or real-world application)*
   - *The data was well collected, controlled for quality, and well documented*
   - *There is an adequate amount of data and diversity for our current hardware*
   - *It has an active community that continuously improves the data and/or builds upon that question*

   As I mentioned before, I feel that asking questions is a primary role of a data scientist and is likely to become even more prominent as automated machine and deep learning solutions advance. This is where datasets can certainly exercise something unique to your skillset.

3. *Create your process for success, rather than only pursuing success for the sake of success*

   Quality far overshadows quantity; you only need 15 datasets to become a Grandmaster and the flagship datasets of AI are few and well made.

I have thrown away as many datasets as I have published. It takes time, and it is not a one and done type of thing as many people treat it – datasets have a maintenance and continuous improvement side to them.

One thing that is very often overlooked is supporting the community that gathers around your data. Notebooks and datasets are mutual efforts, so supporting those who take the time to analyze your data goes a long way for your dataset too. Analyzing their bottlenecks and choices can give directions as to what pre-processing steps could be done and provided, and also the clarity of your documentation.

All in all, the process that I recommend starts with setting your purpose, breaking it down into objectives and topics, formulating questions to fulfil these topics, surveying possible sources of data, selecting and gathering, pre-processing, documenting, publishing, maintaining and supporting, and finally, improvement actions.

For instance, let's say that you would like to increase social welfare; you break it down into an objective, say, racial equity. From there, you analyze topics related to the objective and find the Black Lives Matter movement. From here, you formulate the question: how can I make sense of the millions of voices talking about it?

This narrows down your data type to NLP, which you can gather data for from news articles, YouTube comments, and tweets (which you choose, as it seems more representative of your question and feasible). You pre-process the data, removing identifiers, and document the collection process and dataset purpose.

With that done, you publish it, and a few Kagglers attempt topic modeling but struggle to do so because some tweets contain many foreign languages that create encoding problems. You support them by giving them advice and highlighting their work, and decide to go back and narrow the tweets down to English, to fix this for good.

Their analysis reveals the demands, motivations, and fears relating to the movement. With their efforts, it was possible to break down millions of tweets into a set of recommendations that may improve racial equity in society.

4. *Doing a good job is all that is in your control*

    Ultimately, it is other people that turn you into a Grandmaster, and votes don't always translate into effort or impact. In one of my datasets, about Cyberpunk 2077, I worked on it for about 40 hours total and, to this day, it is still one of my least upvoted datasets.

    But it doesn't matter. I put in the effort, I tried, and I learned what I could — that's what is in my control, and next week I'll do it again no matter what. Do your best and keep going.

Are there any particular tools or libraries that you would recommend using for data analysis/machine learning?

Strangely enough, I both recommend and unrecommend libraries. LightGBM is a great tabular ML library with a fantastic ratio of performance to compute time, CatBoost can sometimes outperform it, but it comes at the cost of increased compute time, during which you could be having and testing new ideas. Optuna is great for hyperparameter tuning, Streamlit for frontends, Gradio for MVPs, Fast API for microservices, Plotly and Plotly Express for charts, PyTorch and its derivatives for deep learning.

While libraries are great, I also suggest that at some point in your career you take the time to implement it yourself. I first heard this advice from Andrew Ng and then from many others of equal calibre. Doing this creates very in-depth knowledge that sheds new light on what your model does and how it responds to tuning, data, noise, and more.

In your experience, what do inexperienced Kagglers often overlook? What do you know now that you wish you'd known when you first started?

Over the years, the things I wished I realized sooner the most were:

1. *Absorbing all the knowledge at the end of a competition*
2. *Replication of winning solutions in finished competitions*

In the pressure of a competition drawing to a close, you can see the leaderboard shaking more than ever before. This makes it less likely that you will take risks and take the time to see things in all their detail. When a competition is over, you don't have that rush and can take as long as you need; you can also replicate the rationale of the winners who made their solutions known.

If you have the discipline, this will do wonders for your data science skills, so the bottom line is: stop when you are done, not when the competition ends. I have also heard this advice from an Andrew Ng keynote, where he recommended replicating papers as one of his best ways to develop yourself as an AI practitioner.

Also, at the end of a competition, you are likely to be exhausted and just want to call it a day. No problem there; just keep in mind that the discussion forum after the competition is done is one of the most knowledge-rich places on Planet Earth, primarily because many rationales and code for winning solutions are made public there. Take the time to read and study what the winners did; don't give into the desire to move on to something else, as you might miss a great learning opportunity.

Has Kaggle helped you in your career? If so, how?

Kaggle helped my career by providing a wealth of knowledge, experience and also building my portfolio. My first job as a data scientist was largely due to Kaggle and DrivenData competitions. All throughout my career, I studied competition solutions and participated in a few more. Further engagement on Datasets and Notebooks also proved very fruitful in learning new techniques and asking better questions.

In my opinion, asking great questions is the primary challenge faced by a data scientist. Answering them is surely great as well, although I believe we are not far from a future where automated solutions will be more and more prevalent in modeling. There will always be room for modeling, but I suppose a lot of work will be streamlined in that regard. Asking great questions, however, is far harder to automate – if the question is not good, even the best solution could be meaningless.

Have you ever used something you have done in Kaggle competitions in order to build your portfolio to show to potential employers?

Absolutely. I landed my first job as a data scientist in 2017 using Kaggle as proof of knowledge. To this day, it is still a fantastic CV component, as educational backgrounds and degrees are less representative of data science knowledge and experience than a portfolio is.

A portfolio with projects with competitions shows not just added experience but also a willingness to going above and beyond for development, which is arguably more important for long-term success.

Do you use other competition platforms? How do they compare to Kaggle?

I also use DrivenData and AICrowd. The great thing about them is that they allow organizations that don't have the same access to financial resources, such as start-ups and research institutions, to create competitions.

Great competitions come from a combination of great questions and great data, and this can happen regardless of company size. Kaggle has a bigger and more active community, and the hardware they provide, coupled with the data and Notebook capabilities, make it the best option; yet both DrivenData and AICrowd introduce just as interesting challenges and allow for more diversity.

What's the most important thing someone should keep in mind or do when they're entering a competition?

Assuming your primary goal is development, my recommendation is that you pick a competition on a topic that interests you and a task that you haven't done before. Critical sense and competence require depth and diversity. Focusing and giving your best will guarantee depth, and diversity is achieved by doing things you have not done before or have not done in the same way.

Working with datasets

Once you have created a dataset, you probably want to use it in your analysis. In this section, we discuss different methods of going about this.

Very likely, the most important one is starting a Notebook where you use your dataset as a primary source. You can do this by going to the dataset page and then clicking on **New Notebook**:

Figure 2.7: Creating a Notebook from the dataset page

Once you have done this, you will be redirected to your **Notebook** page:

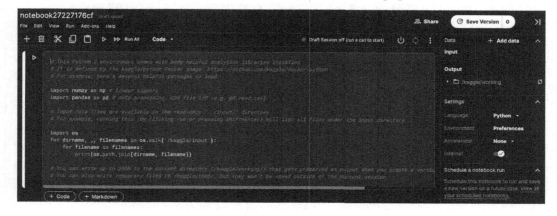

Figure 2.8: Starting a Notebook using your dataset

Here are a few pointers around this:

- The alphanumeric title is generated automatically; you can edit it by clicking on it.
- On the right-hand side under **Data**, you see the list of data sources attached to your Notebook; the dataset I selected can be accessed under `../input/` or from `/kaggle/input/`.
- The opening block (with the imported packages, descriptive comments, and printing the list of available files) is added automatically to a new Python Notebook.

With this basic setup, you can start to write a Notebook for your analysis and utilize your dataset as a data source. We will discuss Notebooks at greater length in *Chapter 4, Leveraging Discussion Forums*.

Using Kaggle Datasets in Google Colab

Kaggle Notebooks are free to use, but not without limits (more on that in *Chapter 4*), and the first one you are likely to hit is the time limit. A popular alternative is to move to Google Colab, a free Jupyter Notebook environment that runs entirely in the cloud: `https://colab.research.google.com`.

Even once we've moved the computations there, we might still want to have access to the Kaggle datasets, so importing them into Colab is a rather handy feature. The remainder of this section discusses the steps necessary to use Kaggle Datasets through Colab.

The first thing we do, assuming we are already registered on Kaggle, is head to the account page to generate the **API token** (an access token containing security credentials for a login session, user identification, privileges, and so on):

1. Go to your account, which can be found at `https://www.kaggle.com/USERNAME/account`, and click on **Create New API Token**:

Figure 2.9: Creating a new API token

A file named kaggle.json containing your username and token will be created.

2. The next step is to create a folder named `Kaggle` in your Google Drive and upload the `.json` file there:

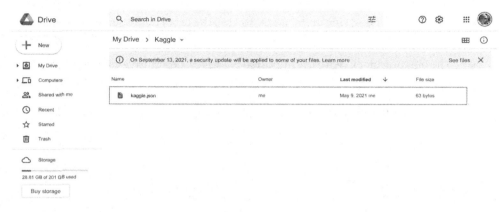

Figure 2.10: Uploading the .json file into Google Drive

3. Once done, you need to create a new Colab notebook and mount your drive by running the following code in the notebook:

```
from google.colab import drive
drive.mount('/content/gdrive')
```

4. Get the authorization code from the URL prompt and provide it in the empty box that appears, and then execute the following code to provide the path to the `.json` config:

```
import os

# content/gdrive/My Drive/Kaggle is the path where kaggle.json is
# present in the Google Drive
os.environ['KAGGLE_CONFIG_DIR'] = "/content/gdrive/My Drive/Kaggle"

# change the working directory
%cd /content/gdrive/My Drive/Kaggle

# check the present working directory using the pwd command
```

5. We can download the dataset now. Begin by going to the dataset's page on Kaggle, clicking on the three dots next to **New Notebook**, and selecting **Copy API command**:

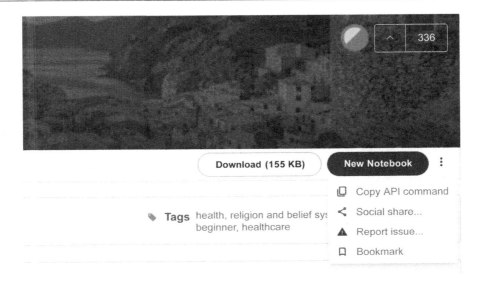

Figure 2.11: Copying the API command

6. Run the API command to download the Dataset (readers interested in details of the commands used can consult the official documentation: `https://www.kaggle.com/docs/api`):

    ```
    !kaggle datasets download -d ajaypalsinghlo/world-happiness-
    report-2021
    ```

7. The dataset will be downloaded to the `Kaggle` folder as a `.zip` archive – unpack it and you are good to go.

As you can see from the list above, using a Kaggle dataset in Colab is a straightforward process – all you need is an API token, and making the switch gives you the possibility of using more GPU hours than what is granted by Kaggle.

Legal caveats

Just because you can put some data on Kaggle does not necessarily mean that you should. An excellent example would be the *People of Tinder* dataset. In 2017, a developer used the Tinder API to scrape the website for semi-private profiles and uploaded the data on Kaggle. After the issue became known, Kaggle ended up taking the dataset down. You can read the full story here: `https://www.forbes.com/sites/janetwburns/2017/05/02/tinder-profiles-have-been-looted-again-this-time-for-teaching-ai-to-genderize-faces/?sh=1afb86b25454`.

In general, before you upload anything to Kaggle, ask yourself two questions:

1. **Is it allowed from a copyright standpoint?** Remember to always check the licenses. When in doubt, you can always consult `https://opendefinition.org/guide/data/` or contact Kaggle.

2. **Are there privacy risks associated with this dataset?** Just because posting certain types of information is not, strictly speaking, illegal, doing so might be harmful to another person's privacy.

The limitations speak to common sense, so they are not too likely to hamper your efforts on Kaggle.

Summary

In this chapter, we introduced Kaggle Datasets, the standardized manner of storing and using data in the platform. We discussed dataset creation, ways of working outside of Kaggle, and the most important functionality: using a dataset in your Notebook. This provides a good segue to our next chapter, where we focus our attention on Kaggle Notebooks.

Join our book's Discord space

Join the book's Discord workspace for a monthly *Ask me Anything* session with the authors:

`https://packt.link/KaggleDiscord`

3

Working and Learning with Kaggle Notebooks

Kaggle Notebooks – which until recently were called **Kernels** – are Jupyter Notebooks in the browser that can run free of charge. This means you can execute your experiments from any device with an internet connection, although something bigger than a mobile phone is probably a good idea. The technical specification of the environment (as of the time of this writing) is quoted below from the Kaggle website; the most recent version can be verified at https://www.kaggle.com/docs/notebooks:

- 12 hours execution time for CPU/GPU, 9 hours for TPU
- 20 gigabytes of auto-saved disk space (/kaggle/working)
- Additional scratchpad disk space (outside /kaggle/working) that will not be saved outside of the current session

CPU specifications:

- 4 CPU cores
- 16 gigabytes of RAM

GPU specifications:

- 2 CPU cores
- 13 gigabytes of RAM

TPU specifications:

- 4 CPU cores
- 16 gigabytes of RAM

In this chapter, we will cover the following topics:

- Setting up a Notebook
- Running your Notebook
- Saving Notebooks to GitHub
- Getting the most out of Notebooks
- Kaggle Learn courses

Without further ado, let us jump into it. The first thing we need to do is figure out how to set up a Notebook.

Setting up a Notebook

There are two primary methods of creating a Notebook: from the front page or from a Dataset.

To proceed with the first method, go to the **Code** section of the menu on the left-hand side of the landing page at `https://www.kaggle.com/` and click the **+ New Notebook** button. This is the preferred method if you are planning an experiment that involves uploading your own dataset:

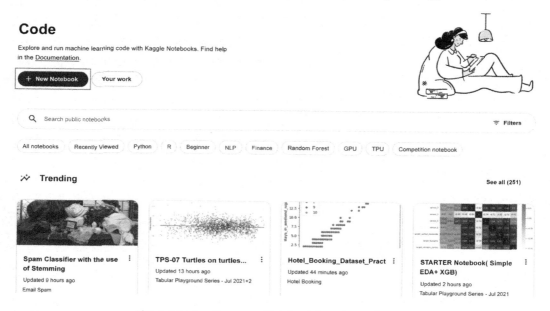

Figure 3.1: Creating a new Notebook from the Code page

Alternatively, you can go to the page of the Dataset you are interested in and click the **New Notebook** button there, as we saw in the previous chapter:

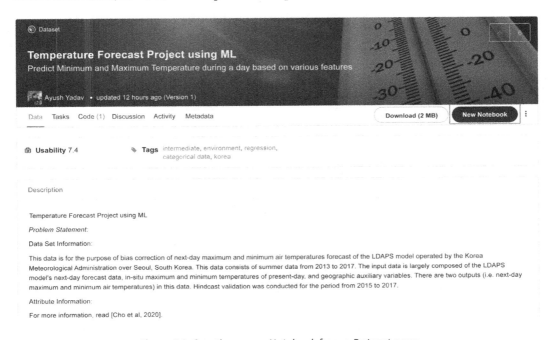

Figure 3.2: Creating a new Notebook from a Dataset page

Whichever method you choose, after clicking **New Notebook**, you will be taken to your **Notebook** page:

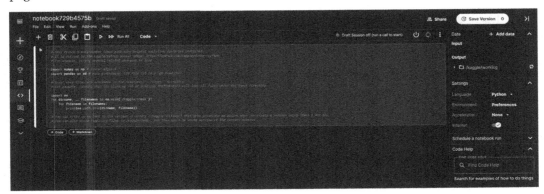

Figure 3.3: The Notebook page

On the right-hand side of the new **Notebook** page shown above, we have a number of settings that can be adjusted:

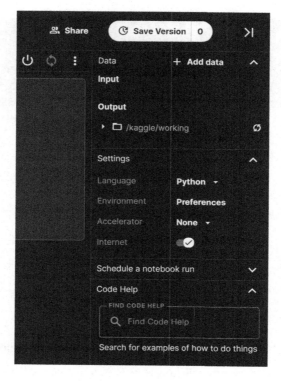

Figure 3.4: Notebook options

We will discuss the settings briefly. First, there is the coding **Language**. As of the time of this writing, the Kaggle environment only allows Python and R as available options for coding your Notebooks. By default, a new Notebook is initialized with the language set to Python – if you want to use R instead, click on the dropdown and select **R**.

Next comes **Environment**: this toggle allows you to decide whether to always use the latest Docker environment (the risky option; fast to get updates but dependencies might break with future updates) or pin the Notebook to the original version of the environment provided by Kaggle (the safe choice). The latter option is the default one, and unless you are conducting very active development work, there is no real reason to tinker with it.

Accelerator allows a user to choose how to run the code: on CPU (no acceleration), GPU (necessary for pretty much any serious application involving deep learning), or TPU. Keep in mind that moving from CPU to (a single) GPU requires only minimal changes to the code and can be handled via system device detection.

Migrating your code to TPU requires more elaborate rewriting, starting with data processing. An important point to keep in mind is that you can switch between CPU/GPU/TPU when you are working on your Notebook, but each time you do, the environment is restarted and you will need to run all your code from the beginning.

Finally, we have the **Internet** toggle which enables or disables online access. If you are connected and need to, for example, install an extra package, the download and installation of dependencies will take place automatically in the background. The most common situation in which you need to explicitly disable internet access is for submission to a competition that explicitly prohibits online access at submission time.

An important aspect of using Notebooks is that you can always take an existing one (created by yourself or another Kaggler) and clone it to modify and adjust to your needs. This can be achieved by clicking the **Copy and Edit** button at the top right of the Notebook page. In Kaggle parlance, the process is referred to as **forking**:

Figure 3.5: Forking an existing Notebook

A note on etiquette: If you have participated in a Kaggle competition before, you will probably have noticed that the leaderboard is flooded with forks of forks of well-scoring Notebooks. There is nothing wrong with building on somebody else's work – but if you do, remember to upvote the original author and give explicit credit to the creator of the reference work.

A Notebook you create is private (only visible to you) by default. If you want to make it available to others, you can choose between adding collaborators, so that only the users explicitly added to the list will be able to view or edit the content, or making the Notebook public, in which case everybody can see it.

Running your Notebook

All the coding is finished, the Notebook seems to be working fine, and you are ready to execute. To do that, go to the upper-right corner of your Notebook page and click **Save Version**.

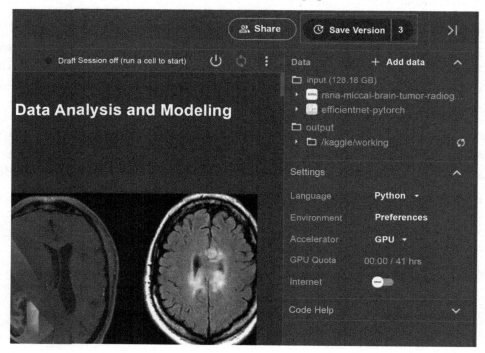

Figure 3.6: Saving your script

Save & Run All is usually used to execute the script, but there is also a **Quick Save** option, which can be used to save an intermediate version of the script before it is ready for submission:

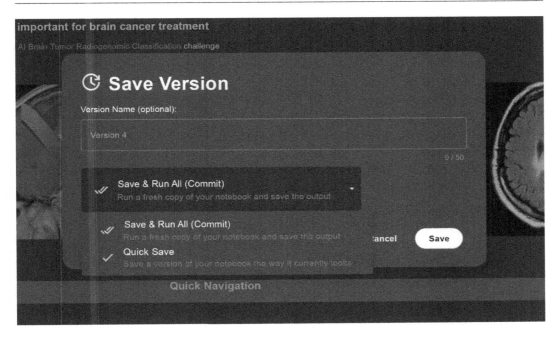

Figure 3.7: Different options for Save Version

Once you have launched your script(s), you can head to the lower-left corner and click on **Active Events**:

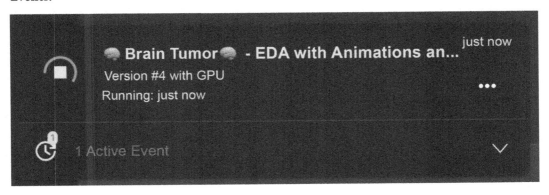

Figure 3.8: Monitoring active events

In this manner, you can monitor the behavior of your Notebooks. Normal execution is associated with the message **Running**; otherwise, it is displayed as **Failed**. Should you decide that you want to kill a running session for whatever reason (for instance, you realize that you forgot to use the most recent data), you can do it by clicking on the three dots on the right-hand side of your script entry under **Active Events** and you will receive a pop-up like the one shown in the figure below:

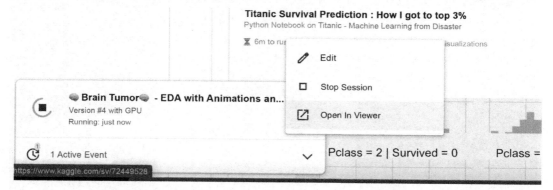

Figure 3.9: Canceling Notebook execution

Saving Notebooks to GitHub

A recently introduced feature (see https://www.kaggle.com/product-feedback/295170) allows you to store your code or your Notebook to the version control repository GitHub (https://github.com/). You can store your work both to public and private repositories, and this will happen automatically as you save a version of your code. Such a feature could prove quite useful for sharing your work with your Kaggle teammates, as well as for showcasing your work to the wider public.

In order to enable this feature, you need to open your Notebook; in the **File** menu, choose the **Link to GitHub** option.

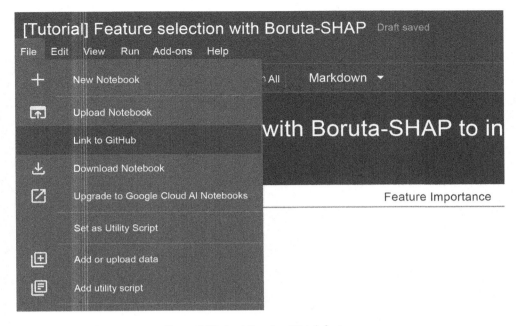

Figure 3.10: Enabling the GitHub feature

After choosing the option, you will have to link your GitHub account to the Notebook. You will explicitly be asked for linking permissions the first time you choose to link. For any subsequent links to new Notebooks, the operation will be carried out automatically.

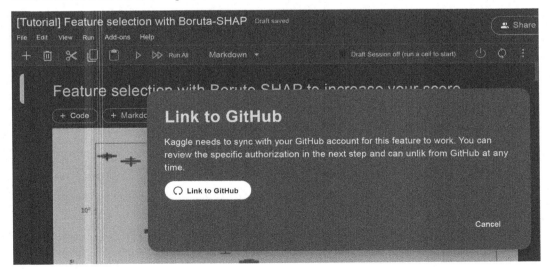

Figure 3.11: Linking to GitHub

Only after linking your Notebook will you be allowed to sync your work to a repository of your choice when you save it:

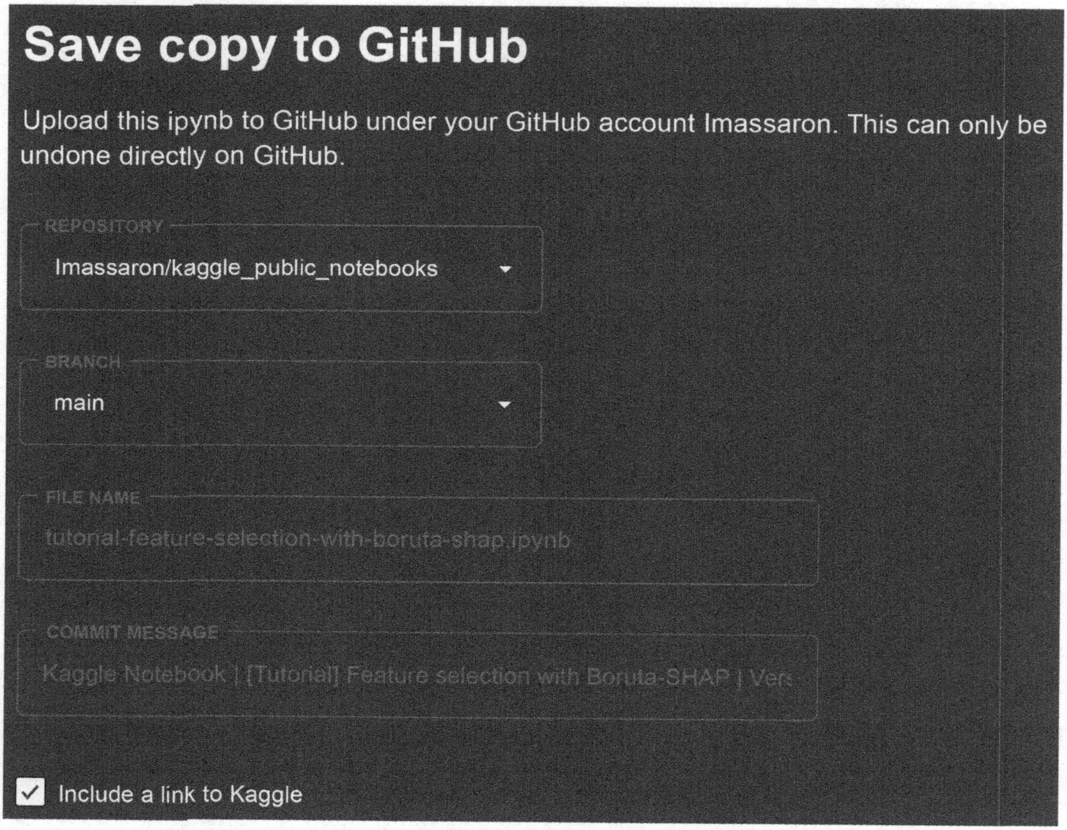

Save copy to GitHub

Upload this ipynb to GitHub under your GitHub account Imassaron. This can only be undone directly on GitHub.

REPOSITORY

Imassaron/kaggle_public_notebooks   ▾

BRANCH

main   ▾

FILE NAME

tutorial-feature-selection-with-boruta-shap.ipynb

COMMIT MESSAGE

Kaggle Notebook | [Tutorial] Feature selection with Boruta-SHAP | Vers

☑ Include a link to Kaggle

Figure 3.12: Committing your work to GitHub

After deciding on a repository and a branch (thus allowing you to store different development stages of your work), you can change the name of the file you are going to push to the repository and modify the commit message.

If you decide you no longer want to sync a particular Notebook on GitHub, all you have to do is to go back to the **File** menu and select **Unlink from GitHub**. Finally, if you want Kaggle to stop connecting with your GitHub repository, you can unlink your accounts from either your Kaggle account page under **My linked accounts** or from GitHub's settings pages (`https://github.com/settings/applications`).

Getting the most out of Notebooks

Kaggle provides a certain amount of resources for free, with the quotas resetting weekly. You get a certain number of hours to use with both GPU and TPU; it is 30 hours for TPU, but for GPU the numbers can vary from week to week (you can find the official statement describing the "floating" quotas policy here: `https://www.kaggle.com/product-feedback/173129`). You can always monitor your usage in your own profile:

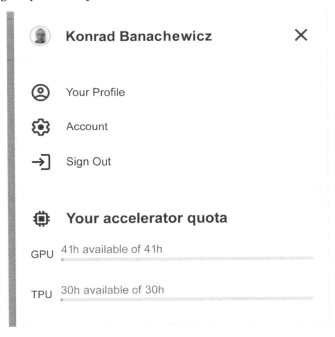

Figure 3.13: Current status for accelerator quotas

While the amounts might seem large at first glance, this initial impression can be deceptive; it is actually fairly easy to use your quota very quickly. Some practical suggestions that can help you control the usage of the resources:

- The counter for the quota (measuring how long you have been using your chosen accelerator, GPU or TPU) starts running the moment you **initialize** your Notebook.
- This means that you should always start by checking that GPU is disabled under settings (see *Figure 3.6* above). Write the boilerplate first, check your syntax, and enable/disable GPU for when you add the parts of the code that actually depend on GPU initialization. A reminder: the Notebook will restart when you change the accelerator.

- It is usually a good idea to run the code end-to-end on a small subset of data to get a feel for the execution time. This way, you minimize the risk that your code will crash due to exceeding this limit.

Sometimes the resources provided freely by Kaggle are not sufficient for the task at hand, and you need to move to a beefier machine. A good example is a recent tumor classification competition: `https://www.kaggle.com/c/rsna-miccai-brain-tumor-radiogenomic-classification/data`.

If your raw data is over 100GB, you need to either resize/downsample your images (which is likely to have an adverse impact on your model performance) or train a model in an environment capable of handling high-resolution images. You can set up the whole environment yourself (an example of this setup is the section *Using Kaggle Datasets in Google Colab* in *Chapter 2*), or you can stay within the framework of Notebooks but swap the underlying machine. This is where Google Cloud AI Notebooks come in.

Upgrading to Google Cloud Platform (GCP)

The obvious benefit to upgrading to GCP is getting access to more powerful hardware: a Tesla P100 GPU (provided free by Kaggle) is decent for many applications, but not top of the line in terms of performance, and 16GB RAM can also be quite limiting, especially in resource-intensive applications like large NLP models or high-resolution image processing. While the improvement in execution time is obvious, leading to faster iteration through the development cycle, it comes at a cost: you need to decide how much you are prepared to spend. For a powerful machine crunching the numbers, time is quite literally money.

In order to migrate your Notebook to the GCP environment, go to the sideline menu on the right-hand side and click on **Upgrade to Google Cloud AI Notebooks**:

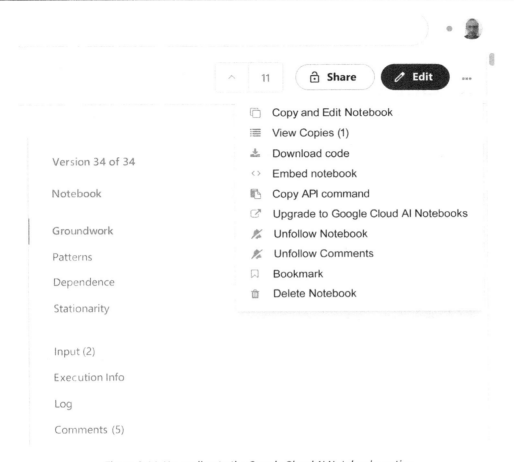

Figure 3.14: Upgrading to the Google Cloud AI Notebooks option

You will be greeted by the following prompt:

Upgrade to Google Cloud AI Platform Notebooks

Access more compute power by exporting your notebook and its dependencies to Google Cloud AI Platform Notebooks where you can customize a virtual machine without quotas or runtime limits.

This process is three steps:

1. Setup a billing-enabled Google Cloud Project
2. Setup your notebook instance and optionally customize your machine
3. Run your code without limits

Figure 3.15: Upgrade to Google Cloud AI Platform Notebooks prompt

When you click **Continue**, you will be redirected to the Google Cloud Platform console, where you need to configure your billing options. A reminder: **GCP is not free**. If it is your first time, you will need to complete a tutorial guiding you through the necessary steps.

One step beyond

As mentioned earlier in this chapter, Kaggle Notebooks are a fantastic tool for education and participating in competitions; but they also serve another extremely useful purpose, namely as a component of a portfolio you can use to demonstrate your data science skills.

There are many potential criteria to consider when building your data science portfolio (branding, audience reach, enabling a pitch to your potential employer, and so on) but none of them matter if nobody can find it. Because Kaggle is part of Google, the Notebooks are indexed by the most popular search engine in the world; so if someone is looking for a topic related to your code, it will show up in their search results.

Below, I show a personal example: a few years ago, I wrote a Notebook for a competition. The problem I wanted to tackle was adversarial validation (for those unfamiliar with the topic: a fairly easy way to see if your training and test sets have a similar distribution is to build a binary classifier trained to tell them apart; the concept is covered in more detail in *Chapter 6, Designing Good Validation*). When writing this chapter, I tried to search for the Notebook and, lo and behold, it shows up high up in the search results (notice the fact that I did not mention Kaggle or any personal details like my name in my query):

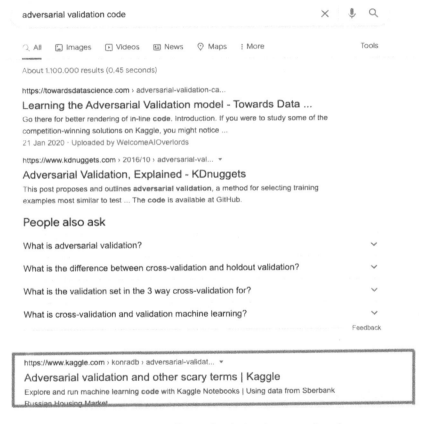

Figure 3.16: Konrad's Notebook showing up on Google

Moving on to other benefits of using Notebooks to demonstrate your skillset: just like **Competitions, Datasets,** and **Discussions, Notebooks** can be awarded votes/medals and thus position you in the progression system and ranking. You can stay away from the competitions track and become an Expert, Master, or Grandmaster purely by focusing on high-quality code the community appreciates.

The most up-to-date version of the progression requirements can be found at `https://www.kaggle.com/progression`; below we give a snapshot relevant to the Expert and Master tiers:

Expert

You've completed a significant body of work on Kaggle in one or more categories of expertise. Once you've reached the expert tier for a category, you will be entered into the site wide Kaggle Ranking for that category.

Competitions	Datasets	Notebooks	Discussions
☑ 🔵 2 bronze medals	☑ 🔵 3 bronze medals	☑ 🔵 5 bronze medals	☑ 🔵 50 bronze medals

Master

You've demonstrated excellence in one or more categories of expertise on Kaggle to reach this prestigious tier. Masters in the Competitions category are eligible for exclusive Master-Only competitions.

Competitions	Datasets	Notebooks	Discussions
☑ 🔵 1 gold medal	☐ 🔵 1 gold medal	☑ 🔵 10 silver medals	☑ 🔵 50 silver medals
☑ 🔵 2 silver medals	☐ 🔵 4 silver medals		☑ 200 medals in total

Figure 3.17: Tier progression requirements

Progressing in the Notebooks category can be a challenging experience; while easier than Competitions, it is definitely harder than Discussions. The most popular Notebooks are those linked to a specific competition: exploratory data analysis, end-to-end proof of concept solutions, as well as leaderboard chasing; it is an unfortunately common practice that people clone the highest-scoring public Notebook, tweak some parameters to boost the score, and release it to wide acclaim (if upvotes can be considered a measure of sentiment). This is not meant to discourage the reader from publishing quality work on Kaggle – a majority of Kagglers do appreciate novel work and quality does prevail in the long term – but a realistic adjustment of expectations is in order.

Your Kaggle profile comes with followers and gives you the possibility of linking other professional networks like LinkedIn or GitHub, so you can leverage the connections you gain inside the community:

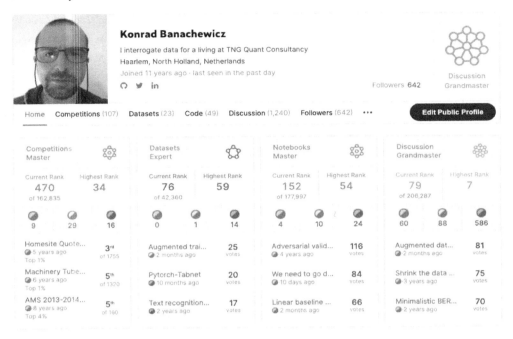

Figure 3.18: Konrad's Kaggle profile

In this day and age, it is easy to be skeptical about claims of "community building", but in the case of Kaggle, it happens to actually be true. Their brand recognition in the data science universe is second to none, both among practitioners and among recruiters who actually do their homework. In practice, this means that a (decent enough) Kaggle profile can get you through the door already; which, as we all know, is frequently the hardest step.

Martin Henze

https://www.kaggle.com/headsortails

We had the pleasure of speaking to Martin Henze, aka Heads or Tails, a Kaggle Grandmaster in Notebooks and Discussion and a Data Scientist at Edison Software. Martin is also the author of *Notebooks of the Week: Hidden Gems*, a weekly collection of the very best Notebooks that have escaped public notice. You can get notifications about new Hidden Gems posts by following his Kaggle profile or his accounts on Twitter and LinkedIn.

What's your favourite kind of competition and why? In terms of techniques, solving approaches, what is your specialty on Kaggle?

For a long time, my focus was on EDA (exploratory data analysis) notebooks rather than leaderboard predictions themselves. Most of my experience prior to Kaggle had been with tabular data, and the majority of my EDA notebooks deal with extracting intricate insights from newly launched tabular challenges. I still consider this my specialty on Kaggle, and I have spent a significant amount of time crafting the structure, data visualizations, and storytelling of my notebooks.

How do you approach a Kaggle competition? How different is this approach to what you do in your day-to-day work?

Even as Kaggle has shifted away from tabular competitions, I strongly believe that the data themselves are the most important aspect of any challenge. It is easy to focus too early on model architectures and hyperparameter tuning. But in many competitions, the key to success remains a data-centric approach that is built on detailed knowledge of the dataset and its quirks and peculiarities. This is true for image data, NLP, time series, and any other data structures you can think of. Therefore, I always start with an extensive EDA before building a simple baseline model, a CV framework, and then slowly iterating the complexity of this pipeline.

The main difference compared to my data science day job is probably that the kind of baseline models that most experienced people can build within the first week of a new challenge would be considered sufficient to put into production. In many cases, after those first few days we're more than 80% on the way to the ultimate winner's solution, in terms of scoring metric. Of course, the fun and the challenge of Kaggle are to find creative ways to get those last few percent of, say, accuracy. But in an industry job, your time is often more efficiently spent in tackling a new project instead.

Has Kaggle helped you in your career? If so, how?

Kaggle has shaped and supported my career tremendously. The great experience in the Kaggle community motivated me to transition from academia to industry. Today, I'm working as a data scientist in a tech startup and I'm continuously growing and honing my skills through Kaggle challenges.

In my case, my focus on constructing extensive Kaggle Notebooks helped me a lot, since I could easily use those as my portfolio. I don't know how often a hiring manager would actually look at those resources, but I frequently got the impression that my Grandmaster title might have opened more doors than my PhD did. Or maybe it was a combination of the two. In any case, I can much recommend having a portfolio of public Notebooks. Moreover, during my job search, I used the strategies I learned on Kaggle for various take-home assignments and they served me well.

In your experience, what do inexperienced Kagglers often overlook? What do you know now that you wish you'd known when you first started?

I think that we are all constantly growing in experience. And we're all wiser now than we were ten years, five years, or even one year ago. With that out of the way, one crucial aspect that is often overlooked is that you want to have a plan for what you're doing, and to execute and document that plan. And that's an entirely understandable mistake to make for new Kagglers, since everything is novel and complex and at least somewhat confusing. I know that Kaggle was confusing for me when I first joined. So many things you can do: forums, datasets, challenges, courses. And the competitions can be downright intimidating: Neuronal Cell Instance Segmentation; Stock Market Volatility Prediction. What even are those things? But the competitions are also the best place to start.

Because when a competition launches, nobody really has a clue about it. Yeah, maybe there is a person who has done their PhD on almost the same topic. But those are rare. Everyone else, we're all pretty much starting from zero. Digging into the data, playing with loss functions, running some simple starter models. When you join a competition at the beginning, you go through all that learning curve in an accelerated way, as a member of a community. And you learn alongside others who will provide you with tons of ideas. But you still need a plan.

And that plan is important, because it's easy to just blindly run some experiments and see all that GPU RAM being used and feel good about it. But then you forget which version of your model was doing best, and is there a correlation between local validation and leaderboard? Did I already test this combination of parameters? So write down what you are going to do and then log the results. There are more and more tools that do the logging for you, but this is also easily done through a custom script.

Machine learning is still mostly an experimental science, and the key to efficient experiments is to plan them well and to write down all of the results so you can compare and analyse them.

What mistakes have you made in competitions in the past?

I have made lots of mistakes and I hope that I managed to learn from them. Not having a robust cross-validation framework was one of them. Not accounting for differences between train and test. Doing too much EDA and neglecting the model building – that one was probably my signature mistake in my first few competitions. Doing not enough EDA and missing something important – yep, done that too. Not selecting my final two submissions. (Ended up making not much of a difference, but I still won't forget it again.)

The point about mistakes, though, is similar to my earlier point about experiments and having a plan. Mistakes are fine if you learn from them and if they help you grow and evolve. You still want to avoid making easy mistakes that could be avoided by foresight. But in machine learning (and science!) failure is pretty much part of the process. Not everything will always work. And that's fine. But you don't want to keep making the same mistakes over and over again. So the only real mistake is not to learn from your mistakes. This is true for Kaggle competitions and in life.

Are there any particular tools or libraries that you would recommend using for data analysis or machine learning?

I know that we increasingly live in a Python world, but when it comes to tabular wrangling and data visualization I still prefer R and its tidyverse: dplyr, ggplot2, lubridate, etc. The new tidymodels framework is a serious contender to sklearn. Even if you're a die-hard Python aficionado, it pays off to have a look beyond pandas and friends every once in a while. Different tools often lead to different viewpoints and more creativity. In terms of deep learning, I find PyTorch most intuitive alongside its FastAI interface. And, of course, everyone loves huggingface nowadays; and for very good reasons.

What's the most important thing someone should keep in mind or do when they're entering a competition?

The most important thing is to remember to have fun and to learn something. So much valuable insight and wisdom is being shared both during and after a competition that it would be a shame not to take it in and grow from it. Even if the only thing you care for is winning, you can only accomplish that by learning and experimenting and standing on the shoulders of this community. But there is so much more to Kaggle than the leaderboards, and once you start contributing and giving back to the community you will grow in a much more holistic way. I guarantee it.

Kaggle Learn courses

A great many things about Kaggle are about acquiring knowledge. Whether it be the things you learn in a competition, datasets you manage to find in the ever-growing repository, or demonstration of a hitherto unknown model class, there is always something new to find out. The newest addition to that collection is the courses gathered under the **Kaggle Learn** label: `https://www.kaggle.com/learn`. These are micro-courses marketed by Kaggle as "the single fastest way to gain the skills you'll need to do independent data science projects," the core unifying theme being a crash course introduction across a variety of topics. Each course is divided into small chapters, followed by coding practice questions. The courses are delivered using Notebooks, where portions of the necessary theory and exposition are intermingled with the bits you are expected to code and implement yourself.

Below, we provide a short overview of the most useful ones:

- **Intro to ML/Intermediate ML**: `https://www.kaggle.com/learn/intro-to-machine-learning` and `https://www.kaggle.com/learn/intermediate-machine-learning`

  These two courses are best viewed as a two-parter: the first one introduces different classes of models used in machine learning, followed by a discussion of topics common to different models like under/overfitting or model validation. The second one goes deeper into feature engineering, dealing with missing values and handling categorical variables. *Useful for people beginning their ML journey.*

- **pandas**: `https://www.kaggle.com/learn/pandas`

  This course provides a crash-course introduction to one of the most fundamental tools used in modern data science. You first learn how to create, read, and write data, and then move on to data cleaning (indexing, selecting, combining, grouping, and so on). *Useful for both beginners (pandas functionality can be overwhelming at times) and practitioners (as a refresher/reference) alike.*

- **Game AI**: `https://www.kaggle.com/learn/intro-to-game-ai-and-reinforcement-learning`

  This course is a great wrap-up of the tech-focused part of the curriculum introduced by Kaggle in the learning modules. You will write a game-playing agent, tinker with its performance, and use the minimax algorithm. *This one is probably best viewed as a practice-oriented introduction to reinforcement learning.*

- **Machine Learning Explainability**: `https://www.kaggle.com/learn/machine-learning-explainability`

  Building models is fun, but in the real world not everybody is a data scientist, so you might find yourself in a position where you need to explain what you have done to others. This is where this mini-course on model explainability comes in: you will learn to assess how relevant your features are with three different methods: permutation importance, SHAP, and partial dependence plots. *Extremely useful to anybody working with ML in a commercial setting, where projects live or die on how well the message is conveyed.*

- **AI Ethics**: `https://www.kaggle.com/learn/intro-to-ai-ethics`

  This last course is a very interesting addition to the proposition: it discusses the practical tools to guide the moral design of AI systems. You will learn how to identify the bias in AI models, examine the concept of AI fairness, and find out how to increase transparency by communicating ML model information. *Very useful for practitioners, as "responsible AI" is a phrase we will be hearing more and more of.*

Apart from the original content created by Kaggle, there are other learning opportunities available on the platform through user-created Notebooks; the reader is encouraged to explore them on their own.

Andrada Olteanu

`https://www.kaggle.com/andradaolteanu`

Andrada Olteanu is one Kaggle Notebooks Grandmaster who very much encourages learning from Notebooks. Andrada is a Z by HP Global Data Science Ambassador, Data Scientist at Endava, and Dev Expert at Weights & Biases. We caught up with Andrada about Notebook competitions, her career, and more.

What's your favourite kind of competition and why? In terms of techniques and solving approaches, what is your specialty on Kaggle?

I would say my specialty on Kaggle leans more towards Data Visualization, as it enables me to combine art and creativity with data.

I would not say I have a favorite type of competition, but I would rather say I like to switch it up occasionally and choose whatever I feel is interesting.

The beauty of Kaggle is that one can learn multiple areas of Data Science (computer vision, NLP, exploratory data analysis and statistics, time series, and so on) while also becoming familiar and comfortable with many topics (like sports, the medical field, finance and cryptocurrencies, worldwide events, etc.)

Another great thing is that, for example, if one wants to become more proficient in working with text data, there is almost always a Kaggle Competition that requires NLP. Or, if one wants to learn how to preprocess and model audio files, there are competitions that enable that skill as well.

Tell us about a particularly challenging competition you entered, and what insights you used to tackle the task.

The most challenging "competition" I have ever entered was the "Kaggle Data Science and Machine Learning Annual Survey". I know this is not a "real" competition – with a leaderboard and heavy-duty machine learning involved – however for me it was one of the competitions I have "sweated" during and learned the most.

This is a Notebook competition, where the users have to become creative in order to win one of the 5 prizes Kaggle puts on the table. I have participated in it 2 years in a row. In the first year (2020), it challenged my more "basic" visualization skills and forced me to think outside the box (I took 3rd place); in the second year (2021), I prepared for it for around 4 months by learning D3, in an attempt to get to a whole other level on my Data Visualization skills (still in review; so far, I have won the "Early Notebook Award" prize). The best insights I can give here are:

- *First, do not get lost within the data and try to create graphs that are as accurate as possible; if necessary, build double verification methods to be sure that what you are representing is clear and concise. Nothing is worse than a beautiful graph that showcases inaccurate insights.*

- *Try to find inspiration around you: from nature, from movies, from your work. You can draw on amazing themes and interesting ways to spruce up your visualization.*

Has Kaggle helped you in your career? If so, how?

Yes. Tremendously. I believe I owe a big part of where I am now in my career to Kaggle, and for this I am forever grateful. Through Kaggle I have became a Z by HP Ambassador; I have also discovered Weights & Biases, which is an amazing machine learning experiment platform and now I am a proud Dev Expert for them. Last but not least, through this platform I connected with my now Lead Data Scientist at Endava, who recruited me, and I have been working with him since. In short, my position at Endava and the connection I have with 2 huge companies (HP and Weights & Biases) are a direct result of my activity on the Kaggle platform.

I believe the most overlooked aspect of Kaggle is the community. Kaggle has the biggest pool of people, all gathered in one convenient place, from which one could connect, interact, and learn from.

The best way to leverage this is to take, for example, the first 100 people from each Kaggle section (Competitions, Datasets, Notebooks – and if you want, Discussions), and follow on Twitter/LinkedIn everybody that has this information shared on their profile. This way, you can start interacting on a regular basis with these amazing people, who are so rich in insights and knowledge.

What mistakes have you made in competitions in the past?

The biggest mistake I have made in competitions in the past is to not participate in them. I believe this is the biggest, most fundamental mistake beginners make when they enter onto the platform.

Out of fear (and I am talking from personal experience), they believe they are not ready, or they just don't know how to start. Fortunately, if you follow a simple system, it will become very easy to enter any competition:

- *Enter any competition you like or sounds interesting.*
- *Explore the description page and the data.*
- *If you have no idea how to start, no worries! Just enter the "Code" section and look around for Notebooks that have a lot of upvotes, or are made by experienced people, like Grandmasters. Start doing a "code along" Notebook, where you look at what others have done and "copy" it, researching and trying to improve it yourself. This is, in my opinion, the best way to learn – you never get stuck, and you learn by doing in a specific project.*

What's the most important thing someone should keep in mind or do when they're entering a competition?

They should keep in mind that it is OK to fail, as usually it is the best way to learn.

What they should also keep in mind is to always learn from the Competition Grandmasters, because they are usually the ones who share and explain machine learning techniques that one may never think of. The best way of learning something is to look at others that "have already made it," so your road to success will not be as bumpy, but rather much more painless, smooth, and quick. Take 2-3 Grandmasters that you really admire and make them your teachers; study their Notebooks, code along, and learn as much as possible.

Do you use other competition platforms? How do they compare to Kaggle?

I have never used any other competition platform – simply because I feel like Kaggle has it all.

Summary

In this chapter, we have discussed Kaggle Notebooks, multi-purpose, open coding environments that can be used for education and experimentation, as well as for promoting your data science project portfolio. You are now in a position to create your own Notebook, efficiently utilize the available resources, and use the results for competitions or your individual projects.

In the next chapter, we will introduce discussion forums, the primary form of exchanging ideas and opinions on Kaggle.

Join our book's Discord space

Join the book's Discord workspace for a monthly *Ask me Anything* session with the authors:

```
https://packt.link/KaggleDiscord
```

Leveraging Discussion Forums

Discussion forums are the primary means of information exchange on Kaggle. Whether it's discussing an ongoing competition, engaging in a conversation about a Dataset, or a Notebook presenting a novel approach, Kagglers talk about things all the time.

In this chapter, we present the discussion forums: how they are organized, and the code of conduct governing the wealth of information therein that can be used. We cover the following topics:

- How forums work
- Discussion approaches for example competitions
- Netiquette

How forums work

You can enter the discussion forum in several ways. The most direct way is by clicking on **Discussions** in the left-hand side panel:

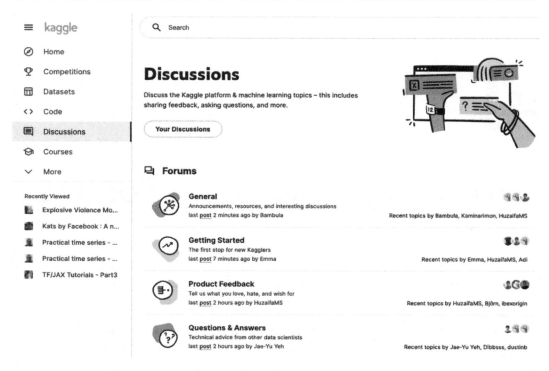

Figure 4.1: Entering the Discussions page from the main menu

The top section contains **Forums**, which are aggregations of general topics. Perusing those is useful whether you are participating in your first competition, have a suggestion to make, or just have a general question because you feel lost.

Below the forums, you can find the combined view of discussions across Kaggle: mostly conversations related to competitions (which form the bulk of activity on Kaggle), but also Notebooks or notable datasets. By default, they are sorted by **Hotness**; in other words, those with the highest participation and most activity are shown closer to the top. This section is where you can find content more relevant to the dynamic nature of the field: a collection of discussions from different subsets of Kaggle, with the ability to filter on specific criteria:

Figure 4.2: Discussions from across Kaggle

Depending on your interest, you can start personalizing the content by using the filters. Based on your preferences, you can filter by:

- **RECENCY**: Allows you to control the range of information you are catching up on
- **MY ACTIVITY**: If you need an overview of your comments/publications/views across all forums; useful if you are involved in multiple discussions simultaneously
- **ADMIN**: Provides a quick overview of announcements from Kaggle admins
- **TYPES**: Discussions can take place in the general forums, in specific competitions, or around datasets

- **TAGS**: While not present everywhere, several discussions are tagged, and this functionality allows a user to make use of that fact:

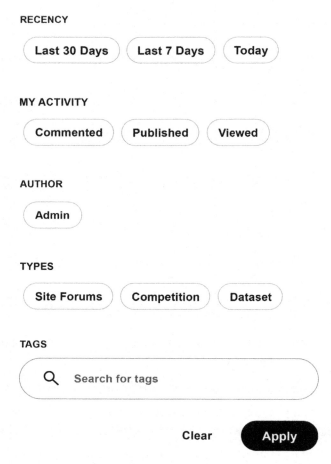

Figure 4.3: Available filters for discussions

The next figure shows a sample output of filtering on discussions on the **Beginner** tag:

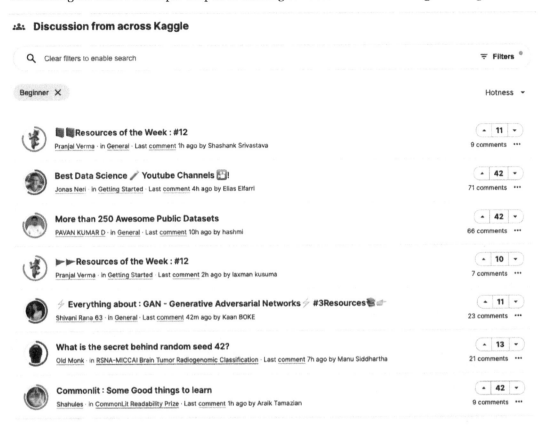

Figure 4.4: Filtering discussions to those tagged "Beginner"

As an alternative, you can also focus on a specific topic; since topics like computer vision attract a lot of interest, it is probably useful to sort the topics. You can sort by **Hotness, Recent Comments, Recently Posted, Most Votes,** and **Most Comments:**

Figure 4.5: The Computer Vision topics subset of the general discussion forum

People come to Kaggle for diverse reasons but, despite the growth in popularity of Notebooks, competitions remain the primary attraction. Each Kaggle competition has its own dedicated discussion forum, which you can enter by going into the competition page and selecting **Discussion**:

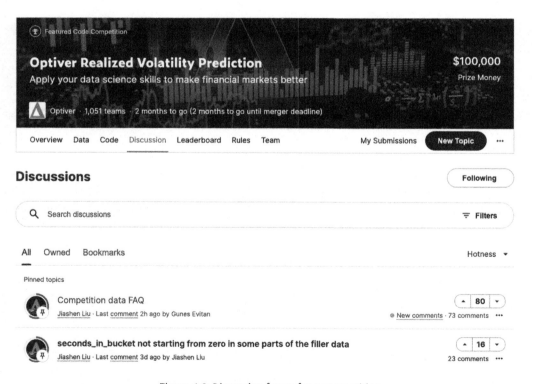

Figure 4.6: Discussion forum for a competition

It was not always the case, but these days virtually all competitions have an FAQ topic pinned at the top of their dedicated discussion forum. Starting there is a good idea for two main reasons:

- It saves you time; the most popular queries are probably addressed there.
- You avoid asking redundant or duplicate questions in the remainder of the forum, making everyone's experience better.

Like Notebooks, discussion forums have an option for you to bookmark particularly relevant topics for later reference:

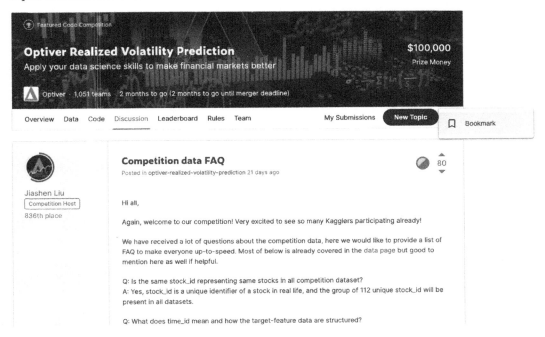

Figure 4.7: Bookmarking a topic in a discussion forum

An overview of all your bookmarked topics can be found on your profile page:

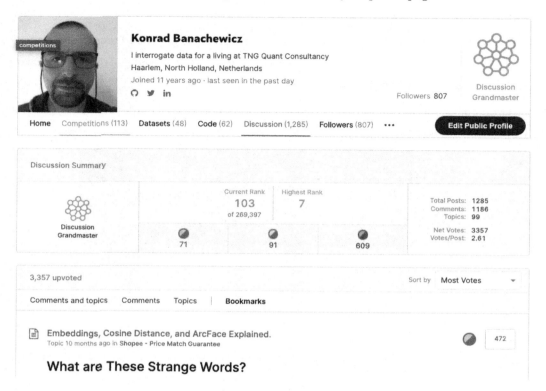

Figure 4.8: Bookmarking a topic in a discussion forum

Example discussion approaches

It is a completely normal thing to feel lost in a competition at some point: you came in, tried a few ideas, got some traction on the leaderboard, and then you hit the Kaggle version of a runner's wall. This is the moment when discussion forums are the place to consult.

As an example, we will look at the *Optiver Realized Volatility Prediction* competition (https://www.kaggle.com/c/optiver-realized-volatility-prediction), characterized by the organizers like this:

> *In the first three months of this competition, you'll build models that predict short-term volatility for hundreds of stocks across different sectors. You will have hundreds of millions of rows of highly granular financial data at your fingertips, with which you'll design your model forecasting volatility over 10-minute periods. Your models will be evaluated against real market data collected in the three-month evaluation period after training.*

There is quite a lot to unpack here, so we will walk over the main components of this challenge and show how they can be approached via the discussion forums. First, participation in this competition requires some level of financial knowledge; not quite experienced trader level maybe, but understanding the different manners of calculating volatility is certainly not trivial for a layman (which most Kagglers are in this specific matter). Luckily for the participants, the organizers were very active during the competition and provided guidance on resources intended to help newcomers to the field: `https://www.kaggle.com/c/optiver-realized-volatility-prediction/discussion/273923`.

If the entry knowledge still proves insufficient to get started, do not hesitate to figure things out in public and ask for help, like here: `https://www.kaggle.com/c/optiver-realized-volatility-prediction/discussion/263039`.

Or here: `https://www.kaggle.com/c/optiver-realized-volatility-prediction/discussion/250612`.

As the competition went on, people started developing increasingly sophisticated models to handle the problem. There is a balance to strike here: on the one hand, you might want to give something back if you have learned from veterans sharing their findings before; on the other hand, you do not want to give away your (potential) advantage by publishing all your great code as a Notebook. A reasonable compromise is discussing, for example, your feature ideas in a post in the forum competition, along the lines of this one: `https://www.kaggle.com/c/optiver-realized-volatility-prediction/discussion/273915`.

In recent years, more competitions are moving away from the fixed test dataset format and introduce some sort of variation: sometimes they enforce the usage of the Kaggle API (these competitions require submission from a Notebook), others introduce a special timetable split into a training phase and evaluation against live data. This was the case with Optiver:

> *Starting after the final submission deadline there will be periodic updates to the leaderboard to reflect market data updates that will be run against selected notebooks. Updates will take place roughly every two weeks, with an adjustment to avoid the winter holidays.*

While straightforward to formulate, this setup generated a few challenges for re-training and updating the models. Should you encounter this kind of situation, feel free to inquire, as participants did in this competition: https://www.kaggle.com/c/optiver-realized-volatility-prediction/discussion/249752.

A **validation scheme** for your trained model is always an important topic in a Kaggle competition, usually coupled with the perennial "CV vs LB" (cross-validation versus leaderboard) discussion. The Optiver competition was no exception to that rule: https://www.kaggle.com/c/optiver-realized-volatility-prediction/discussion/250650.

Unless the thread is already present – and it's always a good idea to check, so that redundancy can be minimized – you might want to consider a related type of thread: single-model performance. Sooner or later, everybody starts using ensembles of models, but they are not very efficient without good single-model components. The collaborative quest for knowledge does not stop there: if you think you have found a better way of approaching the problem, it is probably a good idea to share it. Either you will have done something useful for others, or you will find out why you were wrong (saving you time and effort); either way, a win, as shown, for instance, in this discussion: https://www.kaggle.com/c/optiver-realized-volatility-prediction/discussion/260694.

Apart from the obvious personal benefit (you get a peek into how other competitors are doing), such threads allow for information exchange in the community, facilitating the collaborative element and being helpful for beginners. An example of such a discussion can be found at https://www.kaggle.com/c/optiver-realized-volatility-prediction/discussion/250695.

If you have gone through the topics such as the ones listed above, there is a possibility you still find yourself wondering: *am I missing anything important?* Kaggle is the kind of place where it is perfectly fine to ask: `https://www.kaggle.com/c/optiver-realized-volatility-prediction/discussion/262203`.

Let's broaden our focus out to other competitions to wrap up this section. We mentioned validation above, which always links – at least for a Kaggler – to the topic of information leakage and overfitting. Leaks are discussed extensively in *Chapter 6*, which is dedicated to designing validation schemes. Here, we touch briefly on how they are approached via discussions. With Kaggle being a community of inquisitive people, if there is suspicion of leakage, somebody is likely to raise the topic.

For example, names of the files or IDs of records may contain timestamps, which means they can be reverse engineered to effectively peek into the future and produce an unrealistically low error metric value. Such a situation took place in the *Two Sigma Connect* competition (`https://www.kaggle.com/c/two-sigma-connect-rental-listing-inquiries/`). You can read up on the details in Kazanova's post: `https://www.kaggle.com/c/two-sigma-connect-rental-listing-inquiries/discussion/31870#176513`.

Another example is the *Airbus Ship Detection Challenge* (`https://www.kaggle.com/c/airbus-ship-detection`), in which the participants were tasked with locating ships in satellite images. It turned out that a significant proportion of test images were (random) crops of the images in the training images and matching the two was relatively straightforward: `https://www.kaggle.com/c/airbus-ship-detection/discussion/64355#377037`.

A rather infamous series of competitions were the ones sponsored by Santander. Of the three instances when the company organized a Kaggle contest, two involved data leakage: `https://www.kaggle.com/c/santander-value-prediction-challenge/discussion/61172`.

What happens next varies per competition: there have been instances when Kaggle decided to reset the competition with new or cleaned up data, but also when they allowed it to continue (because they perceived the impact as minimal). An example of handling such a situation can be found in the *Predicting Red Hat Business Value* competition: `https://www.kaggle.com/c/predicting-red-hat-business-value/discussion/23788`.

Although leaks in data can disturb a competition severely, the good news is that over the last 2-3 years, leakage has all but disappeared from Kaggle – so with any luck, this section will be read once but not become a staple of your experience on the platform.

The topic of experience on the platform is an excellent segue into a Grandmaster interview.

Yifan Xie

`https://www.kaggle.com/yifanxie`

Yifan Xie is a Discussions and Competitions Master, as well as the co-founder of Arion.ai. Here's what he had to say about competing in competitions and working with other Kagglers.

What's your favorite kind of competition and why? In terms of techniques and solving approaches, what is your specialty on Kaggle?

I don't really have a favorite type; I like tackling problems of all kinds. In terms of techniques, I have built up a solid pipeline of machine learning modules that allow me to quickly apply typical techniques and algorithms on most data problems. I would say this is a kind of competitive advantage for me: a focus on standardizing, both in terms of work routine and technical artifacts over time. This allows for quicker iteration and in turn helps improve efficiency when conducting data experiments, which is a core component of Kaggle.

How do you approach a Kaggle competition? How different is this approach to what you do in your day-to-day work?

Over time, I have developed a specific way of managing and gathering information for most of my major data endeavors. This is applicable to work, Kaggle competitions, and other side projects. Typically, I capture useful information such as bookmarks, data dictionaries, to-do lists, useful commands, and experiment results in a standardized format dedicated to each competition, and when competing in a team, I will share this info with my teammates.

Tell us about a particularly challenging competition you entered, and what insights you used to tackle the task?

For me, it has always been useful to understand the wider context of the competition; for instance, what are the social/engineering/financial processes that underpin and bring about the data we are working on? For competitions in which one can meaningfully observe individual data points, such as the Deepfake Detection Challenge, *I would build a specific dashboard (usually using Streamlit) that allows me to check individual data points (in this case, it was pair of true and fake videos), as well as building simple stat gathering into the dashboard to allow me a better feel of the data.*

Has Kaggle helped you in your career? If so, how?

I would say Kaggle is the platform that contributed the most to my current career path as a co-owner of a data science consultancy firm. It allowed me to build over several years the skillset and methodology to tackle data problems in different domains. I have both customers and colleagues who I got to know from forming teams on Kaggle competitions, and it has always served me very well as a source of knowledge, even though I am less active on it these days.

In your experience, what do inexperienced Kagglers often overlook? What do you know now that you wish you'd known when you first started?

For newcomers on Kaggle, the one error I can see is overlooking critical non-technical matters: rules on teaming, data usage, sharing of private information, usage of multiple accounts for innocuous reasons, etc. These are the types of error that could completely invalidate one's often multi-month competition efforts.

The one thing I wish I knew at the beginning would be not to worry about the day-to-day position on the public leaderboard – it brings unnecessary pressure on oneself, and causes overfitting.

Are there any particular tools or libraries that you would recommend using for data analysis or machine learning?

The usual: Scikit-learn, XGB/LGB, PyTorch, etc. The one tool I would recommend that people learn to master beyond basic usage would be NumPy, especially for more advanced ways to sort and subset information; stuff that a lazy approach via pandas makes easy, but for which a more elaborate equivalent version in NumPy would bring much better efficiency.

What's the most important thing someone should keep in mind or do when they're entering a competition?

There are four reasons to do any data science-related stuff, in my book: for profit, for knowledge, for fun, and for good. Kaggle for me is always a great source of knowledge and very often a great memory to draw upon, so my recommendation would always be to remind oneself that ranking is temporary, but knowledge/memory are permanent :)

Do you use other competition platforms? How do they compare to Kaggle?

I am a very active participant on Numerai. For me, based on my four reasons to do data science, it is more for profit, as they provide a payout via their cryptocurrency. It is more of a solitary effort, as there is not really an advantage to teaming; they don't encourage or forbid it, but it is just that more human resources don't always equate to better profit on a trading competition platform like Numerai.

Numerai for me is a more sustainable activity than Kaggle during busy periods of my working calendar, because the training data is usually unchanged at each round, and I can productionize to a high degree to automate the prediction and submission once the initial models are built.

The continuity feature of Numerai also makes it better suited for people who want to build dedicated machine learning pipelines for tabular datasets.

Netiquette

Anybody who has been online for longer than 15 minutes knows this: during a discussion, no matter how innocent the topic, there is always a possibility that people will become emotional, and a conversation will leave the civilized parts of the spectrum. Kaggle is no exception to the rule, so the community has guidelines for appropriate conduct: https://www.kaggle.com/community-guidelines.

Those apply not just to discussions, but also to Notebooks and other forms of communication. The main points you should keep in mind when interacting on Kaggle are:

- Don't slip into what Scott Adams calls the **mind-reading illusion**: Kaggle is an extremely diverse community of people from all over the world (for many of them, English is not their first language), so maintaining nuance is a massive challenge. Don't make assumptions and try to clarify whenever possible.

- Do not make things personal; Godwin's law is there for a reason. In particular, references to protected immutable characteristics are an absolute no-go area.

- Your mileage might vary, but the fact remains: this is not the Internet Wild West of the 1990s, when telling somebody online to RTFM was completely normal; putdowns tend to alienate people.

- Do not attempt to manipulate the progression system (the basis for awarding Kaggle medals): this aspect covers an entire spectrum of platform abuse, from explicitly asking for upvotes, to collusion, to outright cheating.

In short, do toward others as you would have them do to you, and things should work out fine.

Summary

In this chapter, we have talked about discussion forums, the primary manner of communication on the Kaggle platform. We demonstrated the forum mechanics, showed you examples of how discussions can be leveraged in more advanced competitions, and briefly summarized discussion netiquette.

This concludes the first, introductory part of this book. The next chapter marks the start of a more in-depth exploration of how to maximize what you get out of Kaggle, and looks at getting to grips with the huge variety of different tasks and metrics you must wrestle with in competitions.

Join our book's Discord space

Join the book's Discord workspace for a monthly *Ask me Anything* session with the authors:

```
https://packt.link/KaggleDiscord
```

Part II

Sharpening Your Skills for Competitions

5
Competition Tasks and Metrics

In a competition, you start by examining the target metric. Understanding how your model's errors are evaluated is key for scoring highly in every competition. When your predictions are submitted to the Kaggle platform, they are compared to a ground truth based on the target metric.

For instance, in the *Titanic* competition (https://www.kaggle.com/c/titanic/), all your submissions are evaluated based on *accuracy*, the percentage of surviving passengers you correctly predict. The organizers decided upon this metric because the aim of the competition is to find a model that estimates the probability of survival of a passenger under similar circumstances. In another knowledge competition, *House Prices - Advanced Regression Techniques* (https://www.kaggle.com/c/house-prices-advanced-regression-techniques), your work will be evaluated based on an *average difference* between your prediction and the ground truth. This involves computing the logarithm, squaring, and taking the square root, because the model is expected to be able to quantify as correctly as possible the order of the price of a house on sale.

In real-world data science, target metrics are also key for the success of your project, though there are certainly differences between the real world and a Kaggle competition. We could easily summarize by saying that there are more complexities in the real world. In real-world projects, you will often have not just one but multiple metrics that your model will be evaluated against. Frequently, some of the evaluation metrics won't even be related to how your predictions perform against the ground truth you are using for testing. For instance, the domain of knowledge you are working in, the scope of the project, the number of features considered by your model, the overall memory usage, any requirement for special hardware (such as a GPU, for instance), the latency of the prediction process, the complexity of the predicting model, and many other aspects may end up counting more than the mere predictive performance.

Real-world problems are indeed dominated by business and tech infrastructure concerns much more than you may imagine before being involved in any of them.

Yet you cannot escape the fact that the basic principle at the core of both real-world projects and Kaggle competitions is the same. Your work will be evaluated according to some criteria, and understanding the details of such criteria, optimizing the fit of your model in a smart way, or selecting its parameters according to the criteria will bring you success. If you can learn more about how model evaluation occurs in Kaggle, your real-world data science job will also benefit from it.

In this chapter, we are going to detail how evaluation metrics for certain kinds of problems strongly influence the way you can operate when building your model solution in a data science competition. We also address the variety of metrics available in Kaggle competitions to give you an idea of what matters most and, in the margins, we discuss the different effects of metrics on predictive performance and how to correctly translate them into your projects. We will cover the following topics:

- Evaluation metrics and objective functions
- Basic types of tasks: regression, classification, and ordinal
- The Meta Kaggle dataset
- Handling never-before-seen metrics
- Metrics for regression (standard and ordinal)
- Metrics for binary classification (label prediction and probability)
- Metrics for multi-class classification
- Metrics for object detection problems
- Metrics for multi-label classification and recommendation problems
- Optimizing evaluation metrics

Evaluation metrics and objective functions

In a Kaggle competition, you can find the evaluation metric in the left menu on the **Overview** page of the competition. By selecting the **Evaluation** tab, you will get details about the evaluation metric. Sometimes you will find the metric formula, the code to reproduce it, and some discussion of the metric. On the same page, you will also get an explanation about the submission file format, providing you with the header of the file and a few example rows.

The association between the evaluation metric and the submission file is important, because you have to consider that the metric works essentially after you have trained your model and produced some predictions. Consequently, as a first step, you will have to think about the difference between an **evaluation metric** and an **objective function**.

Boiling everything down to the basics, an objective function serves your model during training because it is involved in the process of error minimization (or score maximization, depending on the problem). In contrast, an evaluation metric serves your model *after* it has been trained by providing a score. Therefore, it cannot influence how the model fits the data, but does influence it in an indirect way: by helping you to select the most well-performing hyperparameter settings within a model, and the best models among competing ones. Before proceeding with the rest of the chapter, which will show you how this can affect a Kaggle competition and why the analysis of the Kaggle evaluation metric should be your first act in a competition, let's first discuss some terminology that you may encounter in the discussion forums.

You will often hear talk about objective functions, cost functions, and loss functions, sometimes interchangeably. They are not exactly the same thing, however, and we explain the distinction here:

- A **loss function** is a function that is defined on a single data point, and, considering the prediction of the model and the ground truth for the data point, computes a penalty.

- A **cost function** takes into account the whole dataset used for training (or a batch from it), computing a sum or average over the loss penalties of its data points. It can comprise further constraints, such as the L1 or L2 penalties, for instance. The cost function directly affects how the training happens.

- An **objective function** is the most general (and safe-to-use) term related to the scope of optimization during machine learning training: it comprises cost functions, but it is not limited to them. An objective function, in fact, can also take into account goals that are not related to the target: for instance, requiring sparse coefficients of the estimated model or a minimization of the coefficients' values, such as in L1 and L2 regularizations. Moreover, whereas loss and cost functions imply an optimization based on minimization, an objective function is neutral and can imply either a maximization or a minimization activity performed by the learning algorithm.

Likewise, when it comes to evaluation metrics, you'll hear about scoring functions and error functions. Distinguishing between them is easy: a **scoring function** suggests better prediction results if scores from the function are higher, implying a maximization process.

An **error function** instead suggests better predictions if smaller error quantities are reported by the function, implying a minimization process.

Basic types of tasks

Not all objective functions are suitable for all problems. From a general point of view, you'll find two kinds of problems in Kaggle competitions: **regression** tasks and **classification** tasks. Recently, there have also been **reinforcement learning** (RL) tasks, but RL doesn't use metrics for evaluation; instead, it relies on a ranking derived from direct match-ups against other competitors whose solutions are assumed to be as well-performing as yours (performing better in this match-up than your peers will raise your ranking, performing worse will lower it). Since RL doesn't use metrics, we will keep on referring to the regression-classification dichotomy, though **ordinal** tasks, where you predict ordered labels represented by integer numbers, may elude such categorization and can be dealt with successfully either using a regression or classification approach.

Regression

Regression requires you to build a model that can predict a real number; often a positive number, but there have been examples of negative number prediction too. A classic example of a regression problem is *House Prices - Advanced Regression Techniques*, because you have to guess the value of a house. The evaluation of a regression task involves computing a distance between your predictions and the values of the ground truth. This difference can be evaluated in different ways, for instance by squaring it in order to punish larger errors, or by applying a log to it in order to penalize predictions of the wrong scale.

Classification

When facing a **classification** task on Kaggle, there are more nuances to take into account. The classification, in fact, could be **binary**, **multi-class**, or **multi-label**.

In **binary** problems, you have to guess if an example should be classified or not into a specific class (usually called the *positive* class and compared to the *negative* one). Here, the evaluation could involve the straightforward prediction of the class ownership itself, or an estimation of the probability of such ownership. A typical example is the *Titanic* competition, where you have to guess a binary outcome: survival or not-survival. In this case, the requirement of the competition is just the prediction, but in many cases, it is necessary to provide a probability because in certain fields, especially for medical applications, it is necessary to rank positive predictions across different options and situations in order to make the best decision.

Though counting the exact number of correct matches in a binary classification may seem a valid approach, this won't actually work well when there is an imbalance, that is, a different number of examples, between the positive and the negative class. Classification based on an imbalanced distribution of classes requires evaluation metrics that take the imbalance into account, if you want to correctly track improvements on your model.

When you have more than two classes, you have a **multi-class** prediction problem. This also requires the use of suitable functions for evaluation, since it is necessary to keep track of the overall performance of the model, but also to ensure that the performance across the classes is comparable (for instance, your model could underperform with respect to certain classes). Here, each case can be in one class exclusively, and not in any others. A good example is *Leaf Classification* (`https://www.kaggle.com/c/leaf-classification`), where each image of a leaf specimen has to be associated with the correct plant species.

Finally, when your class predictions are not exclusive and you can predict multiple class ownership for each example, you have a **multi-label** problem that requires further evaluations in order to control whether your model is predicting the correct classes, as well as the correct number and mix of classes. For instance, in *Greek Media Monitoring Multilabel Classification (WISE 2014)* (`https://www.kaggle.com/c/wise-2014`), you had to associate each article with all the topics it deals with.

Ordinal

In a problem involving a prediction on an ordinal scale, you have to guess integer numeric labels, which are naturally ordered. As an example, the magnitude of an earthquake is on an ordinal scale. In addition, data from marketing research questionnaires is often recorded on ordinal scales (for instance, consumers' preferences or opinion agreement). Since an ordinal scale is made of ordered values, ordinal tasks can be considered somewhat halfway between regression and classification, and you can solve them in both ways.

The most common way is to treat your ordinal task as a **multi-class** problem. In this case, you will get a prediction of an integer value (the class label) but the prediction will not take into account that the classes have a certain order. You can get a feeling that there is something wrong with approaching the problem as a multi-class problem if you look at the prediction probability for the classes. Often, probabilities will be distributed across the entire range of possible values, depicting a multi-modal and often asymmetric distribution (whereas you should expect a Gaussian distribution around the maximum probability class).

The other way to solve the ordinal prediction problem is to treat it as a **regression** problem and then post-process your result. In this way, the order among classes will be taken into consideration, though the prediction output won't be immediately useful for scoring on the evaluation metric. In fact, in a regression you get a float number as an output, not an integer representing an ordinal class; moreover, the result will include the full range of values between the integers of your ordinal distribution and possibly also values outside of it. Cropping the output values and casting them into integers by unit rounding may do the trick, but this might lead to inaccuracies requiring some more sophisticated post-processing (we'll discuss more on this later in the chapter).

Now, you may be wondering what kind of evaluation you should master in order to succeed in Kaggle. Clearly, you always have to master the evaluation metric of the competition you have taken on. However, some metrics are more common than others, which is information you can use to your advantage. What are the most common metrics? How can we figure out where to look for insights in competitions that have used similar evaluation metrics? The answer is to consult the Meta Kaggle dataset.

The Meta Kaggle dataset

The Meta Kaggle dataset (`https://www.kaggle.com/kaggle/meta-kaggle`) is a collection of rich data about Kaggle's community and activity, published by Kaggle itself as a public dataset. It contains CSV tables filled with public activity from Competitions, Datasets, Notebooks, and Discussions. All you have to do is to start a Kaggle Notebook (as you saw in *Chapters 2* and *3*), add to it the Meta Kaggle dataset, and start analyzing the data. The CSV tables are updated daily, so you'll have to refresh your analysis often, but that's worth it given the insights you can extract.

We will sometimes refer to the Meta Kaggle dataset in this book, both as inspiration for many interesting examples of the dynamics in a competition and as a way to pick up useful examples for your learning and competition strategies. Here, we are going to use it in order to figure out what evaluation metrics have been used most frequently for competitions in the last seven years. By looking at the most common ones in this chapter, you'll be able to start any competition from solid ground and then refine your knowledge of the metric, picking up competition-specific nuances using the discussion you find in the forums.

Below, we introduce the code necessary to produce a data table of metrics and their counts per year. It is designed to run directly on the Kaggle platform:

```
import numpy as np
import pandas as pd
comps = pd.read_csv("/kaggle/input/meta-kaggle/Competitions.csv")
evaluation = ['EvaluationAlgorithmAbbreviation',
              'EvaluationAlgorithmName',
              'EvaluationAlgorithmDescription',]

compt = ['Title', 'EnabledDate', 'HostSegmentTitle']

df = comps[compt + evaluation].copy()
df['year'] = pd.to_datetime(df.EnabledDate).dt.year.values
df['comps'] = 1
time_select = df.year >= 2015
competition_type_select = df.HostSegmentTitle.isin(
                                    ['Featured', 'Research'])

pd.pivot_table(df[time_select&competition_type_select],
               values='comps',
               index=['EvaluationAlgorithmAbbreviation'],
               columns=['year'],
               fill_value=0.0,
               aggfunc=np.sum,
               margins=True
              ).sort_values(
                by=('All'), ascending=False).iloc[1:,:].head(20)
```

In this code, we read in the CSV table containing the data relating to the competitions. We focus on the columns representing the evaluation and the columns informing us about the competition name, start date, and type. We limit the rows to those competitions held since 2015 and that are of the Featured or Research type (which are the most common ones). We complete the analysis by creating a pandas pivot table, combining the evaluation algorithm with the year, and counting the number of competitions using it. We just display the top 20 algorithms.

Here is the resulting table (at the time of writing):

year Evaluation Algorithm	2015	2016	2017	2018	2019	2020	2021	Tot
AUC	4	4	1	3	3	2	0	17
LogLoss	2	2	5	2	3	2	0	16
MAP@{K}	1	3	0	4	1	0	1	10
CategorizationAccuracy	1	0	4	0	1	2	0	8
MulticlassLoss	2	3	2	0	1	0	0	8
RMSLE	2	1	3	1	1	0	0	8
QuadraticWeightedKappa	3	0	0	1	2	1	0	7
MeanFScoreBeta	1	0	1	2	1	2	0	7
MeanBestErrorAtK	0	0	2	2	1	1	0	6
MCRMSLE	0	0	1	0	0	5	0	6
MCAUC	1	0	1	0	0	3	0	5
RMSE	1	1	0	3	0	0	0	5
Dice	0	1	1	0	2	1	0	5
GoogleGlobalAP	0	0	1	2	1	1	0	5
MacroFScore	0	0	0	1	0	2	1	4
Score	0	0	3	0	0	0	0	3
CRPS	2	0	0	0	1	0	0	3
OpenImagesObjectDetectionAP	0	0	0	1	1	1	0	3
MeanFScore	0	0	1	0	0	0	2	3
RSNAObjectDetectionAP	0	0	0	1	0	1	0	2

Using the same variables we just instantiated in order to generate the table, you can also check the data to find the competitions where the metric of your choice has been adopted:

```
metric = 'AUC'
metric_select = df['EvaluationAlgorithmAbbreviation']==metric
print(df[time_select&competition_type_select&metric_select]
        [['Title', 'year']])
```

In the above snippet, we decided to represent the competitions that have been using the AUC metric. You just have to change the string representing the chosen metric and the resulting list will be updated accordingly.

Coming back to the table generated, we can examine the most popular evaluation metrics used in competitions hosted on Kaggle:

- The two top metrics are closely related to each other and to binary probability classification problems. The **AUC** metric helps to measure if your model's predicted probabilities tend to predict positive cases with high probabilities, and the **Log Loss** helps to measure how far your predicted probabilities are from the ground truth (and as you optimize for Log Loss, you also optimize for the AUC metric).

- In 3rd position, we find **MAP@{K}**, which is a common metric in recommender systems and search engines. In Kaggle competitions, this metric has been used mostly for information retrieval evaluations, such as in the *Humpback Whale Identification* competition (`https://www.kaggle.com/c/humpback-whale-identification`), where you have to precisely identify a whale and you have five possible guesses. Another example of MAP@{K} usage is in the *Quick, Draw! Doodle Recognition Challenge* (`https://www.kaggle.com/c/quickdraw-doodle-recognition/`), where your goal is to guess the content of a drawn sketch and you are allowed three attempts. In essence, when MAP@{K} is the evaluation metric, you can score not just if you can guess correctly, but also if your correct guess is among a certain number (the "K" in the name of the function) of other incorrect predictions.

- Only in 6th position can we find a regression metric, the **RMSLE**, or **Root Mean Squared Logarithmic Error**, and in 7th place the **Quadratic Weighted Kappa**, a metric particularly useful for estimating model performance on problems that involve guessing a progressive integer number (an ordinal scale problem).

As you skim through the list of top metrics, you will keep on finding metrics that are commonly discussed in machine learning textbooks. In the next few sections, after first discussing what to do when you meet a never-before-seen metric (something that happens in Kaggle competitions more frequently than you may expect), we will revise some of the most common metrics found in regression and classification competitions.

Handling never-before-seen metrics

Before proceeding, we have to consider that the top 20 table doesn't cover all the metrics used in competitions. We should be aware that there are metrics that have only been used once in recent years.

Let's keep on using the results from the previous code to find out what they are:

```
counts = (df[time_select&competition_type_select]
          .groupby('EvaluationAlgorithmAbbreviation'))
total_comps_per_year = (df[time_select&competition_type_select]
                        .groupby('year').sum())
single_metrics_per_year = (counts.sum()[counts.sum().comps==1]
                           .groupby('year').sum())
single_metrics_per_year
table = (total_comps_per_year.rename(columns={'comps': 'n_comps'})
         .join(single_metrics_per_year / total_comps_per_year)
         .rename(columns={'comps': 'pct_comps'}))
print(table)
```

As a result, we get the following table showing, for each year, how many competitions used a metric that has never been used afterward (n_comps), and the proportion of these competitions per year (pct_comps):

year	n_comps	pct_comps
2015	28	0.179
2016	19	0.158
2017	34	0.177
2018	35	0.229
2019	36	0.278
2020	43	0.302
2021	8	0.250

Observing the relative share of competitions with a never-to-be-seen-afterward metric, we immediately notice how it is growing year by year and that it reached the 25%-30% level in recent years, implying that typically one competition out of every three or four requires you to study and understand a metric from scratch.

You can get the list of such metrics that have occurred in the past with a simple code snippet:

```
print(counts.sum()[counts.sum().comps==1].index.values)
```

By executing the code, you will get a list similar to this one:

```
['AHD@{Type}' 'CVPRAutoDrivingAveragePrecision' 'CernWeightedAuc'
'FScore_1' 'GroupMeanLogMAE' 'ImageNetObjectLocalization'
'IndoorLocalization'  'IntersectionOverUnionObjectSegmentationBeta'
'IntersectionOverUnionObjectSegmentationWithClassification'
'IntersectionOverUnionObjectSegmentationWithF1' 'Jaccard'
'JaccardDSTLParallel' 'JigsawBiasAUC' 'LaplaceLogLikelihood'
'LevenshteinMean' 'Lyft3DObjectDetectionAP' 'M5_WRMSSE' 'MASpearmanR'
'MCRMSE' 'MCSpearmanR' 'MWCRMSE' 'MeanColumnwiseLogLoss'
'MulticlassLossOld' 'NDCG@{K}' 'NQMicroF1' 'NWRMSLE' 'PKUAutoDrivingAP'
'R2Score' 'RValue' 'RootMeanSquarePercentageError' 'SIIMDice' 'SMAPE'
'SantaResident' 'SantaRideShare' 'SantaWorkshopSchedule2019' 'TrackML'
'TravelingSanta2' 'TwoSigmaNews' 'WeightedAUC' 'WeightedMulticlassLoss'
'WeightedPinballLoss' 'WeightedRowwisePinballLoss' 'YT8M_
MeanAveragePrecisionAtK' 'ZillowMAE' 'football' 'halite' 'mab']
```

By close inspection, you can find many metrics relating to deep learning and reinforcement learning competitions.

What do you do when you meet a metric that has never been used before? Of course, you can rely on the discussions in the Kaggle discussion forums, where you can always find good inspiration and many Kagglers who will help you. However, if you want to build up your own knowledge about the metric, aside from Googling it, we advise that you try to experiment with it by coding the evaluation function by yourself, even in an imperfect way, and trying to simulate how the metric reacts to different types of error produced by the model. You could also directly test how it functions on a sample from the competition training data or synthetic data that you have prepared.

We can quote a few examples of this approach as used by Kagglers:

- *Carlo Lepelaars* with Spearman's Rho: `https://www.kaggle.com/carlolepelaars/understanding-the-metric-spearman-s-rho`

- Carlo Lepelaars with Quadratic Weighted Kappa: `https://www.kaggle.com/carlolepelaars/understanding-the-metric-quadratic-weighted-kappa`

- *Rohan Rao* with Laplace Log Likelihood: `https://www.kaggle.com/rohanrao/osic-understanding-laplace-log-likelihood`

This can give you increased insight into the evaluation and an advantage over other competitors relying only on answers from Googling and Kaggle forums.

Rohan Rao

https://www.kaggle.com/rohanrao

Before we start exploring different metrics, let's catch up with Rohan Rao (aka Vopani) himself, Quadruple Grandmaster and Senior Data Scientist at H2O.ai, about his successes on Kaggle and the wisdom he has to share with us.

What's your favourite kind of competition and why? In terms of techniques and solving approaches, what is your speciality on Kaggle?

I like to dabble with different types of competitions, but my favorite would certainly be time series ones. I don't quite like the typical approaches to and concepts of time series in the industry, so I tend to innovate and think out of the box by building solutions in an unorthodox way, which has ended up being very successful for me.

How do you approach a Kaggle competition? How different is this approach to what you do in your day-to-day work?

For any Kaggle competition, my typical workflow would look like this:

- *Understand the problem statement and read all the information related to rules, format, timelines, datasets, metrics, and deliverables.*

- *Dive deep into the data. Slice and dice it in every way possible and explore/visualize it to be able to answer any question about it.*

- *Build a simple pipeline with a baseline model and make a submission to confirm the process works.*

- *Engineer features, tune hyperparameters, and experiment with multiple models to get a sense of what's generally working and what's not.*

- *Constantly go back to analyzing the data, reading discussions on the forum, and tweaking the features and models to the fullest. Maybe team up at some point.*

- *Ensemble multiple models and decide which submissions to make as final.*

In my day-to-day work in data science, most of this happens too. But there are two crucial elements that are additionally required:

- *Curating and preparing datasets for the problem statement.*

- *Deploying the final model or solution into production.*

The majority of my time has been spent in these two activities for most of the projects I've worked on in the past.

Has Kaggle helped you in your career? If so, how?

The vast majority of everything I've learned in machine learning has come from Kaggle. The community, the platform, and the content are pure gold and there is an incredible amount of stuff you can learn.

What has benefitted me the most is the experience of competing in Kaggle competitions; it has given me immense confidence in understanding, structuring, and solving problems across domains, which I have been able to apply successfully in many of the companies and projects I worked on outside Kaggle.

Many recruiters have contacted me for opportunities looking at my Kaggle achievements, primarily in Competitions. It gives a fairly good indication of a candidate's ability in solving data science problems and hence it is a great platform to showcase your skills and build a portfolio.

What mistakes have you made in competitions in the past?

I've made some mistake in every competition! That's how you learn and improve. Sometimes it's a coding bug, sometimes a flawed validation setup, sometimes an incorrect submission selection!

What's important is to learn from these and ensure you don't repeat them. Iterating over this process automatically helps to improve your overall performance on Kaggle.

Are there any particular tools or libraries that you would recommend using for data analysis/machine learning?

I strongly believe in never marrying a technology. Use whatever works best, whatever is most comfortable and effective, but constantly be open to learning new tools and libraries.

Metrics for regression (standard and ordinal)

When working with regression problems, that is, problems that involve estimating a continuous value (that could range from minus infinity to infinity), the most commonly used error measures are **RMSE (root mean squared error)** and **MAE (mean absolute error)**, but you can also find slightly different error measures useful, such as RMSLE or MCRMSLE.

Mean squared error (MSE) and R squared

The root mean squared error is the root of the **mean squared error (MSE)**, which is nothing else but the mean of the good old **sum of squared errors (SSE)** that you learned about when you studied how a regression works.

Here is the formula for the MSE:

$$MSE = \frac{1}{n}SSE = \frac{1}{n}\sum_{i=1}^{n}(\hat{y}_i - y_i)^2$$

Let's start by explaining how the formula works. First of all, n indicates the number of cases, y_i is the ground truth, and $\hat{y}_i$ the prediction. You first get the difference between your predictions and your real values. You square the differences (so they become positive or simply zero), then you sum them all, resulting in your SSE. Then you just have to divide this measure by the number of predictions to obtain the average value, the MSE. Usually, all regression models minimize the SSE, so you won't have great problems trying to minimize MSE or its direct derivatives such as **R squared** (also called the **coefficient of determination**), which is given by:

$$R^2 = \frac{SSE}{SST} = \sum_{i=1}^{n}\frac{(\hat{y}_i - y_i)^2}{(y_i - \bar{y})^2}$$

Here, SSE (the sum of squared errors) is compared to the **sum of squares total (SST)**, which is just the variance of the response. In statistics, in fact, SST is defined as the squared difference between your target values and their mean:

$$SST = \sum_{i=1}^{n}(y_i - \bar{y})^2$$

To put it another way, R squared compares the squared errors of the model against the squared errors from the simplest model possible, the average of the response. Since both SSE and SST have the same scale, R squared can help you to determine whether transforming your target is helping to obtain better predictions.

Please remember that linear transformations, such as minmax (https://scikit-learn.org/stable/modules/generated/sklearn.preprocessing.MinMaxScaler.html) or standardization (https://scikit-learn.org/stable/modules/generated/sklearn.preprocessing.StandardScaler.html), do not change the performance of any regressor, since they are linear transformations of the target. **Non-linear** transformations, such as the square root, the cubic root, the logarithm, the exponentiation, and their combinations, should instead definitely modify the performance of your regression model on the evaluation metric (hopefully for the better, if you decide on the right transformation).

MSE is a great instrument for comparing regression models applied to the same problem. The bad news is that the MSE is seldom used in Kaggle competitions, since RMSE is preferred. In fact, by taking the root of MSE, its value will resemble the original scale of your target and it will be easier at a glance to figure out if your model is doing a good job or not. In addition, if you are considering the same regression model across different data problems (for instance, across various datasets or data competitions), R squared is better because it is perfectly correlated with MSE and its values range between 0 and 1, making all comparisons easier.

Root mean squared error (RMSE)

RMSE is just the square root of MSE, but this implies some subtle change. Here is its formula:

$$RMSE = \sqrt{\sum_{i=1}^{n} \frac{(\hat{y}_i - y_i)^2}{n}}$$

In the above formula, n indicates the number of cases, y_i is the ground truth, and $\hat{y}_i$ the prediction. In MSE, large prediction errors are greatly penalized because of the squaring activity. In RMSE, this dominance is lessened because of the root effect (however, you should always pay attention to outliers; they can affect your model performance a lot, no matter whether you are evaluating based on MSE or RMSE).

Consequently, depending on the problem, you can get a better fit with an algorithm using MSE as an objective function by first applying the square root to your target (if possible, because it requires positive values), then squaring the results. Functions such as the `TransformedTargetRegressor` in Scikit-learn help you to appropriately transform your regression target in order to get better-fitting results with respect to your evaluation metric.

Recent competitions where RMSE has been used include:

- *Avito Demand Prediction Challenge*: https://www.kaggle.com/c/avito-demand-prediction
- *Google Analytics Customer Revenue Prediction*: https://www.kaggle.com/c/ga-customer-revenue-prediction
- *Elo Merchant Category Recommendation* https://www.kaggle.com/c/elo-merchant-category-recommendation

Root mean squared log error (RMSLE)

Another common transformation of MSE is **root mean squared log error** (**RMSLE**). MCRMSLE is just a variant made popular by the COVID-19 forecasting competitions, and it is the column-wise average of the RMSLE values of each single target when there are multiple ones. Here is the formula for RMSLE:

$$RMSLE = \sqrt{\frac{1}{n}\sum_{i=1}^{n}(\log(\hat{y}_i + 1) - \log(y_i + 1))^2}$$

In the formula, n indicates the number of cases, y_i is the ground truth, and $\hat{y}_i$ the prediction. Since you are applying a logarithmic transformation to your predictions and your ground truth before all the other squaring, averaging, and rooting operations, you don't penalize huge differences between the predicted and the actual values, especially when both are large numbers. In other words, what you care the most about when using RMSLE is *the scale of your predictions with respect to the scale of the ground truth*. As with RMSE, machine learning algorithms for regression can better optimize for RMSLE if you apply a logarithmic transformation to the target before fitting it (and then reverse the effect using the exponential function).

Recent competitions using RMSLE as an evaluation metric are:

- *ASHRAE - Great Energy Predictor III*: https://www.kaggle.com/c/ashrae-energy-prediction

- *Santander Value Prediction Challenge*: https://www.kaggle.com/c/santander-value-prediction-challenge

- *Mercari Price Suggestion Challenge*: https://www.kaggle.com/c/mercari-price-suggestion-challenge

- *Sberbank Russian Housing Market*: https://www.kaggle.com/olgabelitskaya/sberbank-russian-housing-market

- *Recruit Restaurant Visitor Forecasting*: https://www.kaggle.com/c/recruit-restaurant-visitor-forecasting

By far, at the moment, RMSLE is the most used evaluation metric for regression in Kaggle competitions.

Mean absolute error (MAE)

The **MAE** (**mean absolute error**) evaluation metric is the absolute value of the difference between the predictions and the targets. Here is the formulation of MAE:

$$MAE = \frac{1}{n}\sum_{i=1}^{n}|\hat{y}_i - y_i|$$

In the formula, n stands for the number of cases, y_i is the ground truth, and $\hat{y}_i$ the prediction. MAE is not particularly sensitive to outliers (unlike MSE, where errors are squared), hence you may find it is an evaluation metric in many competitions whose datasets present outliers. Moreover, you can easily work with it since many algorithms can directly use it as an objective function; otherwise, you can optimize for it indirectly by just training on the square root of your target and then squaring the predictions.

In terms of downside, using MAE as an objective function results in much slower convergence, since you are actually optimizing for predicting the median of the target (also called the L1 norm), instead of the mean (also called the L2 norm), as occurs by MSE minimization. This results in more complex computations for the optimizer, so the training time can even grow exponentially based on your number of training cases (see, for instance, this Stack Overflow question: `https://stackoverflow.com/questions/57243267/why-is-training-a-random-forest-regressor-with-mae-criterion-so-slow-compared-to`).

Notable recent competitions that used MAE as an evaluation metric are:

- *LANL Earthquake Prediction*: `https://www.kaggle.com/c/LANL-Earthquake-Prediction`
- *How Much Did It Rain? II*: `https://www.kaggle.com/c/how-much-did-it-rain-ii`

Having mentioned the ASHRAE competition earlier, we should also mention that regression evaluation measures are quite relevant to forecasting competitions. For instance, the M5 forecasting competition was held recently (`https://mofc.unic.ac.cy/m5-competition/`) and data from all the other M competitions is available too. If you are interested in forecasting competitions, of which there are a few on Kaggle, please see `https://robjhyndman.com/hyndsight/forecasting-competitions/` for an overview about M competitions and how valuable Kaggle is for obtaining better practical and theoretical results from such competitions.

Essentially, forecasting competitions do not require a very different evaluation to regression competitions. When dealing with forecasting tasks, it is true that you can get some unusual evaluation metrics such as the **Weighted Root Mean Squared Scaled Error** (https://www.kaggle.com/c/m5-forecasting-accuracy/overview/evaluation) or the **symmetric mean absolute percentage error**, better known as **sMAPE** (https://www.kaggle.com/c/demand-forecasting-kernels-only/overview/evaluation). However, in the end they are just variations of the usual RMSE or MAE that you can handle using the right target transformations.

Metrics for classification (label prediction and probability)

Having discussed the metrics for regression problems, we are going now to illustrate the metrics for classification problems, starting from the binary classification problems (when you have to predict between two classes), moving to the multi-class (when you have more than two classes), and then to the multi-label (when the classes overlap).

Accuracy

When analyzing the performance of a binary classifier, the most common and accessible metric that is used is **accuracy**. A misclassification error is when your model predicts the wrong class for an example. The accuracy is just the complement of the misclassification error and it can be calculated as the ratio between the number of correct numbers divided by the number of answers:

$$Accuracy = \frac{correct\ answers}{total\ answers}$$

This metric has been used, for instance, in *Cassava Leaf Disease Classification* (https://www.kaggle.com/c/cassava-leaf-disease-classification) and *Text Normalization Challenge - English Language* (https://www.kaggle.com/c/text-normalization-challenge-english-language), where you scored a correct prediction only if your predicted text matched the actual string.

As a metric, the accuracy is focused strongly on the effective performance of the model in a real setting: it tells you if the model works as expected. However, if your purpose is to evaluate and compare and have a clear picture of how effective your approach really is, you have to be cautious when using the accuracy because it can lead to wrong conclusions when the classes are imbalanced (when they have different frequencies). For instance, if a certain class makes up just 10% of the data, a predictor that predicts nothing but the majority class will be 90% accurate, proving itself quite useless in spite of the high accuracy.

How can you spot such a problem? You can do this easily by using a **confusion matrix**. In a confusion matrix, you create a two-way table comparing the actual classes on the rows against the predicted classes on the columns. You can create a straightforward one using the Scikit-learn confusion_matrix function:

```
sklearn.metrics.confusion_matrix(
    y_true, y_pred, *, labels=None, sample_weight=None,
    normalize=None
)
```

Providing the y_true and y_pred vectors will suffice to return you a meaningful table, but you can also provide row/column labels and sample weights for the examples in consideration, and normalize (set the marginals to sum to 1) over the true examples (the rows), the predicted examples (the columns), or all the examples. A perfect classifier will have all the cases on the principal diagonal of the matrix. Serious problems with the validity of the predictor are highlighted if there are few or no cases on one of the cells of the diagonal.

In order to give you a better idea of how it works, you can try the graphical example offered by Scikit-learn at https://scikit-learn.org/stable/auto_examples/model_selection/ plot_confusion_matrix.html#sphx-glr-auto-examples-model-selection-plot-confusion-matrix-py:

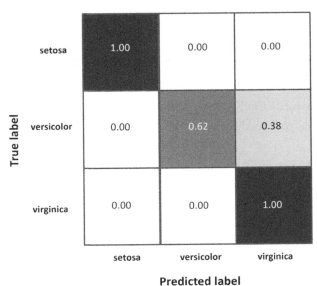

Figure 5.1: Confusion matrix, with each cell normalized to 1.00, to represent the share of matches

You can attempt to improve the usability of the accuracy by considering the accuracy relative to each of the classes and averaging them, but you will find it more useful to rely on other metrics such as **precision**, **recall**, and the **F1-score**.

Precision and recall

To obtain the precision and recall metrics, we again start from the confusion matrix. First, we have to name each of the cells:

		Predicted	
		Negative	Positive
Actual	**Negative**	True Negative	False Positive
	Positive	False Negative	True Positive

Table 5.1: Confusion matrix with cell names

Here is how we define the cells:

- **TP (true positives)**: These are located in the upper-left cell, containing examples that have correctly been predicted as positive ones.

- **FP (false positives)**: These are located in the upper-right cell, containing examples that have been predicted as positive but are actually negative.

- **FN (false negatives)**: These are located in the lower-left cell, containing examples that have been predicted as negative but are actually positive.

- **TN (true negatives)**: These are located in the lower-right cell, containing examples that have been correctly predicted as negative ones.

Using these cells, you can actually get more precise information about how your classifier works and how you can tune your model better. First, we can easily revise the accuracy formula:

$$Accuracy = \frac{(TP + TN)}{(TP + TN + FP + FN)}$$

Then, the first informative metric is called **precision** (or **specificity**) and it is actually the accuracy of the positive cases:

$$Precision = \frac{TP}{TP + FP}$$

In the computation, only the number of true positives and the number of false positives are involved. In essence, the metric tells you how often you are correct when you predict a positive.

Clearly, your model could get high scores by predicting positives for only the examples it has high confidence in. That is actually the purpose of the measure: to force models to predict a positive class only when they are sure and it is safe to do so.

However, if it is in your interest also to predict as many positives as possible, then you'll also need to watch over the **recall** (or **coverage** or **sensitivity** or even **true positive rate**) metric:

$$Recall = \frac{TP}{TP + FN}$$

Here, you will also need to know about false negatives. The interesting thing about these two metrics is that, since they are based on examples classification, and a classification is actually based on probability (which is usually set between the positive and negative class at the 0.5 threshold), you can change the threshold and have one of the two metrics improved at the expense of the other.

For instance, if you increase the threshold, you will get more precision (the classifier is more confident of the prediction) but less recall. If you decrease the threshold, you get less precision but more recall. This is also called the **precision/recall trade-off**.

The Scikit-learn website offers a simple and practical overview of this trade-off (`https://scikit-learn.org/stable/auto_examples/model_selection/plot_precision_recall.html`), helping you to trace a **precision/recall curve** and thus understand how these two measures can be exchanged to obtain a result that better fits your needs:

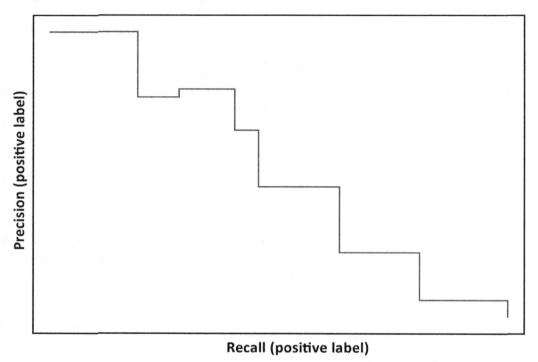

Figure 5.2: A two-class precision-recall curve with its characteristic steps

One metric associated with the precision/recall trade-off is the **average precision**. Average precision computes the mean precision for recall values from 0 to 1 (basically, as you vary the threshold from 1 to 0). Average precision is very popular for tasks related to object detection, which we will discuss a bit later on, but it is also very useful for classification in tabular data. In practice, it proves valuable when you want to monitor model performance on a very rare class (when the data is extremely imbalanced) in a more precise and exact way, which is often the case with fraud detection problems.

For more specific insights on this, read *Gael Varoquaux's* discussion: `http://gael-varoquaux.info/interpreting_ml_tuto/content/01_how_well/01_metrics.html#average-precision`.

The F1 score

At this point, you have probably already figured out that using precision or recall as an evaluation metric is not an ideal choice because you can only optimize one at the expense of the other. For this reason, there are no Kaggle competitions that use only one of the two metrics. You should combine them (as in the average precision). A single metric, the **F1 score**, which is the harmonic mean of precision and recall, is commonly considered to be the best solution:

$$F1 = 2 * \frac{precision * recall}{precision + recall}$$

If you get a high *F*1 score, it is because your model has improved in precision or recall or in both. You can find a fine example of the usage of this metric in the *Quora Insincere Questions Classification* competition (https://www.kaggle.com/c/quora-insincere-questions-classification).

In some competitions, you also get the **F-beta** score. This is simply the weighted harmonic mean between precision and recall, and beta decides the weight of the recall in the combined score:

$$F_\beta = \frac{(1 + \beta^2) * (precision * recall)}{(\beta^2 * precision + recall)}$$

Since we have already introduced the concept of threshold and classification probability, we can now discuss the log loss and ROC-AUC, both quite common classification metrics.

Log loss and ROC-AUC

Let's start with the **log loss**, which is also known as **cross-entropy** in deep learning models. The log loss is the difference between the predicted probability and the ground truth probability:

$$LogLoss = -\frac{1}{n}\sum_{i=1}^{n}[y_i \log(\hat{y_i}) + (1 - y_i)\log(1 - \hat{y_i})]$$

In the above formula, *n* stands for the number of examples, y_i is the ground truth for the ith case, and $\hat{y_i}$ the prediction.

If a competition uses the log loss, it is implied that the objective is to estimate as correctly as possible the probability of an example being of a positive class. You can actually find the log loss in quite a lot of competitions.

We suggest you have a look, for instance, at the recent *Deepfake Detection Challenge* (https://www.kaggle.com/c/deepfake-detection-challenge) or at the older *Quora Question Pairs* (https://www.kaggle.com/c/quora-question-pairs).

The **ROC curve**, or **receiver operating characteristic curve**, is a graphical chart used to evaluate the performance of a binary classifier and to compare multiple classifiers. It is the building block of the ROC-AUC metric, because the metric is simply the area delimited under the ROC curve. The ROC curve consists of the true positive rate (the recall) plotted against the false positive rate (the ratio of negative instances that are incorrectly classified as positive ones). It is equivalent to one minus the true negative rate (the ratio of negative examples that are correctly classified). Here are a few examples:

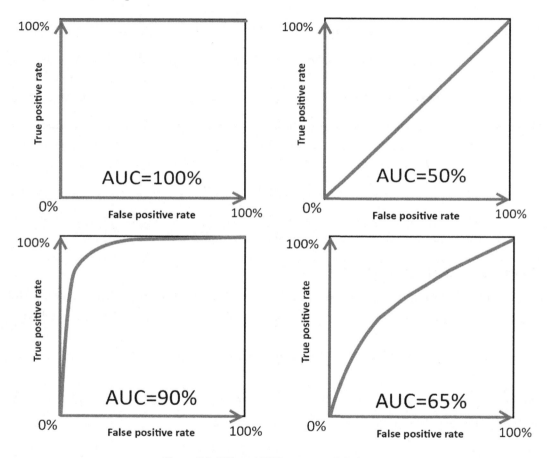

Figure 5.3: Different ROC curves and their AUCs

Ideally, a ROC curve of a well-performing classifier should quickly climb up the true positive rate (recall) at low values of the false positive rate. A ROC-AUC between 0.9 to 1.0 is considered very good.

A bad classifier can be spotted by the ROC curve appearing very similar, if not identical, to the diagonal of the chart, which represents the performance of a purely random classifier, as in the top left of the figure above; ROC-AUC scores near 0.5 are considered to be almost random results. If you are comparing different classifiers, and you are using the **area under the curve (AUC)**, the classifier with the higher area is the more performant one.

If the classes are balanced, or not too imbalanced, increases in the AUC are proportional to the effectiveness of the trained model and they can be intuitively thought of as the ability of the model to output higher probabilities for true positives. We also think of it as the ability to order the examples more properly from positive to negative. However, when the positive class is rare, the AUC starts high and its increments may mean very little in terms of predicting the rare class better. As we mentioned before, in such a case, average precision is a more helpful metric.

AUC has recently been used for quite a lot of different competitions. We suggest you have a look at these three:

- *IEEE-CIS Fraud Detection*: `https://www.kaggle.com/c/ieee-fraud-detection`
- *Riiid Answer Correctness Prediction*: `https://www.kaggle.com/c/riiid-test-answer-prediction`
- *Jigsaw Multilingual Toxic Comment Classification*: `https://www.kaggle.com/c/jigsaw-multilingual-toxic-comment-classification/`

You can read a detailed treatise in the following paper: Su, W., Yuan, Y., and Zhu, M. *A relationship between the average precision and the area under the ROC curve.* Proceedings of the 2015 International Conference on The Theory of Information Retrieval. 2015.

Matthews correlation coefficient (MCC)

We complete our overview of binary classification metrics with the **Matthews correlation coefficient (MCC)**, which made its appearance in *VSB Power Line Fault Detection* (`https://www.kaggle.com/c/vsb-power-line-fault-detection`) and *Bosch Production Line Performance* (`https://www.kaggle.com/c/bosch-production-line-performance`).

The formula for the MCC is:

$$MCC = \frac{(TP * TN) - (FP * FN)}{\sqrt{(TP + FP) * (TP + FN) * (TN + FP) * (TN + FN)}}$$

In the above formula, *TP* stands for true positives, *TN* for true negatives, *FP* for false positives, and *FN* for false negatives. It is the same nomenclature as we met when discussing precision and recall.

Behaving as a correlation coefficient, in other words, ranging from +1 (perfect prediction) to -1 (inverse prediction), this metric can be considered a measure of the quality of the classification even when the classes are quite imbalanced.

In spite of its complexity, the formula can be reformulated and simplified, as demonstrated by Neuron Engineer (`https://www.kaggle.com/ratthachat`) in his Notebook: `www.kaggle.com/ratthachat/demythifying-matthew-correlation-coefficients-mcc`.

The work done by Neuron Engineer in understanding the ratio of the evaluation metric is indeed exemplary. In fact, his reformulated MCC becomes:

$$MCC = \left(Pos_{precision} + Neg_{precision} - 1\right) * PosNegRatio$$

Where each element of the formula is:

$$Pos_{precision} = \frac{TP}{TP + FP}$$

$$Neg_{precision} = \frac{TN}{TN + FN}$$

$$PosNegRatio = \sqrt{\frac{PosPredictionCount * NegPredictionCount}{PosLabelCount * NegLabelCount}}$$

$$PosPredictionCount = TP + FP$$

$$NegPredictionCount = TN + FN$$

The reformulation helps to clarify, in a more intelligible form than the original, that you can get higher performance from improving both positive and negative class precision, but that's not enough: you also have to have positive and negative predictions in proportion to the ground truth, or your submission will be greatly penalized.

Metrics for multi-class classification

When moving to multi-class classification, you simply use the binary classification metrics that we have just seen, applied to each class, and then you summarize them using some of the averaging strategies that are commonly used for multi-class situations.

For instance, if you want to evaluate your solution based on the *F1* score, you have three possible averaging choices:

- **Macro averaging**: Simply calculate the *F1* score for each class and then average all the results. In this way, each class will count as much the others, no matter how frequent its positive cases are or how important they are for your problem, resulting therefore in equal penalizations when the model doesn't perform well with any class:

$$macro = \frac{F1_{class1} + F1_{class2} + \cdots + F1_{classN}}{N}$$

- **Micro averaging**: This approach will sum all the contributions from each class to compute an aggregated *F1* score. It results in no particular favor to or penalization of any class, since all the computations are made regardless of each class, so it can more accurately account for class imbalances:

$$micro = F1_{class1 + class2 + \cdots classN}$$

- **Weighting**: As with macro averaging, you first calculate the *F1* score for each class, but then you make a weighted average mean of all of them using a weight that depends on the number of true labels of each class. By using such a set of weights, you can take into account the frequency of positive cases from each class or the relevance of that class for your problem. This approach clearly favors the majority classes, which will be weighted more in the computations:

$$weighted = F1_{class1} * W_1 + F1_{class2} * W_2 + \cdots + F1_{classN} * W_n$$

$$W_1 + W_2 + \cdots + W_N = 1.0$$

Common multi-class metrics that you may encounter in Kaggle competitions are:

- **Multiclass accuracy (weighted)**: *Bengali.AI Handwritten Grapheme Classification* (`https://www.kaggle.com/c/bengaliai-cv19`)

- **Multiclass log loss (MeanColumnwiseLogLoss)**: *Mechanisms of Action (MoA) Prediction* (`https://www.kaggle.com/c/lish-moa/`)

- **Macro-F1** and **Micro-F1 (NQMicroF1)**: *University of Liverpool - Ion Switching* (`https://www.kaggle.com/c/liverpool-ion-switching`), *Human Protein Atlas Image Classification* (`https://www.kaggle.com/c/human-protein-atlas-image-classification/`), *TensorFlow 2.0 Question Answering* (`https://www.kaggle.com/c/tensorflow2-question-answering`)

- **Mean-F1**: *Shopee - Price Match Guarantee* (https://www.kaggle.com/c/shopee-product-matching/). Here, the *F1* score is calculated for every predicted row, then averaged, whereas the Macro-F1 score is defined as the mean of class-wise/label-wise *F1* scores.

Then there is also **Quadratic Weighted Kappa**, which we will explore later on as a smart evaluation metric for ordinal prediction problems. In its simplest form, the **Cohen Kappa** score, it just measures the agreement between your predictions and the ground truth. The metric was actually created for measuring **inter-annotation agreement**, but it is really versatile and has found even better uses.

What is inter-annotation agreement? Let's imagine that you have a labeling task: classifying some photos based on whether they contain an image of a cat, a dog, or neither. If you ask a set of people to do the task for you, you may incur some erroneous labels because someone (called the *judge* in this kind of task) may misinterpret a dog as a cat or vice versa. The smart way to do this job correctly is to divide the work among multiple judges labeling the same photos, and then measure their level of agreement based on the Cohen Kappa score.

Therefore, the Cohen Kappa is devised as a score expressing the level of agreement between two annotators on a labeling (classification) problem:

$$k = (p_0 - p_e)/(1 - p_e)$$

In the formula, p_0 is the relative observed agreement among raters, and p_e is the hypothetical probability of chance agreement. Using the confusion matrix nomenclature, this can be rewritten as:

$$k = \frac{2 * (TP * TN - FN * FP)}{(TP + FP) * (FP + TN) + (TP + FN) * (FN + TN)}$$

The interesting aspect of this formula is that the score takes into account the empirical probability that the agreement has happened just by chance, so the measure has a correction for all the most probable classifications. The metric ranges from 1, meaning complete agreement, to -1, meaning the judges completely oppose each other (total disagreement).

Values around 0 signify that agreement and disagreement among the judges is happening by mere chance. This helps you figure out if the model is really performing better than chance in most situations.

Andrey Lukyanenko

https://www.kaggle.com/artgor

Our second interview of the chapter is with Andrey Lukyanenko, a Notebooks and Discussions Grandmaster and Competitions Master. In his day job, he is a Machine Learning Engineer and TechLead at MTS Group. He had many interesting things to say about his Kaggle experiences!

What's your favourite kind of competition and why? In terms of techniques, solving approaches, what is your specialty on Kaggle?

I prefer competitions where solutions can be general enough to be transferable to other datasets/domains. I'm interested in trying various neural net architectures, state-of-the-art approaches, and post-processing tricks. I don't favor those competitions that require reverse engineering or creating some "golden features," as these approaches won't be applicable in other datasets.

While you were competing on Kaggle, you also became a Grandmaster in Notebooks (and ranked number one) and Discussions. Have you invested in these two objectives?

I have invested a lot of time and effort into writing Notebooks, but the Discussion Grandmaster rank happened kind of on its own.

Let's start with the Notebook ranking.

There was a special competition in 2018 called DonorsChoose.org Application Screening. DonorsChoose is a fund that empowers public school teachers from across the country to request much-needed materials and experiences for their students. It organized a competition, where the winning solutions were based not on the score on the leaderboard, but on the number of the upvotes on the Notebook. This looked interesting and I wrote a Notebook for the competition. Many participants advertised their analysis on social media and I did the same. As a result, I reached second place and won a Pixelbook (I'm still using it!).

I was very motivated by this success and continued writing Notebooks. At first, I simply wanted to share my analysis and get feedback, because I wanted to try to compare my analytics and visualization skills with other people to see what I could do and what people thought of it. People started liking my kernels and I wanted to improve my skills even further. Another motivation was a desire to improve my skill at making a quick MVP (minimum viable product). When a new competition starts, many people begin writing Notebooks, and if you want to be one of the first, you have to be able to do it fast without sacrificing quality. This is challenging, but fun and rewarding.

I was able to get the Notebook Grandmaster rank in the February of 2019; after some time, I reached first place and held it for more than a year. Now I write Notebooks less frequently, but I still enjoy doing it.

As for discussions, I think it kind of happened on its own. I answered the comments on my Notebooks, and shared and discussed ideas about competitions in which I took part, and my discussion ranking steadily increased.

Tell us about a particularly challenging competition you entered, and what insights you used to tackle the task.

It was the Predicting Molecular Properties *competition. I have written a blog post about it in more detail here (*`https://towardsdatascience.com/a-story-of-my-first-gold-medal-in-one-kaggle-competition-things-done-and-lessons-learned-c269d9c233d1`*). It was a domain-specific competition aimed at predicting interactions between atoms in molecules. Nuclear Magnetic Resonance (NMR) is a technology that uses principles similar to MRI to understand the structure and dynamics of proteins and molecules. Researchers around the world conduct NMR experiments to further understand the structure and dynamics of molecules, across areas like environmental science, pharmaceutical science, and materials science. In this competition, we tried to predict the magnetic interaction between two atoms in a molecule (the scalar coupling constant). State-of-the-art methods from quantum mechanics can calculate these coupling constants given only a 3D molecular structure as input. But these calculations are very resource-intensive, so can't be always used. If machine learning approaches could predict these values, it would really help medicinal chemists to gain structural insights faster and more cheaply.*

I usually write EDA kernels for new Kaggle competitions, and this one was no exception. A common approach for tabular data in Kaggle competitions is extensive feature engineering and using gradient boosting models. I used LGBM too in my early attempts, but knew that there should be better ways to work with graphs. I realized that domain expertise would provide a serious advantage, so I hunted for every piece of such information. Of course, I noticed that there were several active experts, who wrote on the forum and created kernels, so I read everything from them. And one day I received an e-mail from an expert in this domain who thought that our skills could complement each other. Usually, I prefer to work on competitions by myself for some time, but in this case, combining forces seemed to be a good idea to me. And this decision turned out to be a great one! With time we were able to gather an amazing team.

After some time, we noticed a potential for neural nets in the competition: a well-known Kaggler, Heng, posted an example of an MPNN (Message Passing Neural Network) model. After some time, I was even able to run it, but the results were worse compared to our models. Nevertheless, our team knew that we would need to work with these Neural Nets if we wanted to aim high. It was amazing to see how Christof was able to build new neural nets extremely fast. Soon, we focused only on developing those models.

After that, my role switched to a support one. I did a lot of experiments with our neural nets: trying various hyperparameters, different architectures, various little tweaks to training schedules, and so on. Sometimes I did EDA on our predictions to find our interesting or wrong cases, and later we used this information to improve our models even further.

We got the 8th place and I learned a lot during this competition.

Has Kaggle helped you in your career? If so, how?

Kaggle definitely helped me a lot, especially with my skills and my personal brand. Writing and publishing Kaggle Notebooks taught me not only EDA and ML skills, but it forced me to become adaptable, to be able to understand new topics and tasks quickly, to iterate more efficiently between approaches. At the same time, it provided a measure of visibility for me, because people appreciated my work.

My first portfolio (`https://erlemar.github.io/`) had a lot of different Notebooks, and half of them were based on old Kaggle competitions. It was definitely helpful in getting my first jobs. My Kaggle achievements also helped me attract recruiters from good companies, sometimes even to skip steps of the interview process, and even led me to several consulting gigs.

In your experience, what do inexperienced Kagglers often overlook? What do you know now that you wish you'd known when you first started?

I think we need to separate inexperienced Kagglers into two groups: those who are inexperienced in data science in general and those who are inexperienced on Kaggle.

Those who are inexperienced in general make a number of different mistakes (and it is okay, everyone started somewhere):

- *One of the most serious problems: lack of critical thinking and not knowing how to do their own research;*
- *Not knowing when and what tools/approaches to use;*
- *Blindly taking public Notebooks and using them without understanding how they work;*
- *Fixating on a certain idea and spending too much time pursuing it, even when it doesn't work;*
- *Despairing and losing motivation when their experiments fail.*

As for those people who have experience in data science but don't have experience with Kaggle, I'd say that the most serious thing they overlook is that they underestimate Kaggle's difficulty. They don't expect Kaggle to be very competitive, that you need to try many different things to succeed, that there are a lot of tricks that work only in competitions, that there are people who professionally participate in competitions.

Also, people often overestimate domain expertise. I admit that there were a number of competitions when the teams with domain experts in them won gold medals and prizes, but in most cases experienced Kagglers triumph.

Also, I have seen the following situation many times: some person proclaims that winning Kaggle is easy, and that he (or his group of people) will get a gold medal or many gold medals in the recent future. In most cases, they silently fail.

What mistakes have you made in competitions in the past?

- *Not enough looking in the data. Sometimes I wasn't able to generate better features or apply better postprocessing due to this. And reserve engineering and "golden features" is a whole additional topic.*
- *Spending too much time on a single idea because I hoped it would work. This is called sunk-cost fallacy.*
- *Not enough experiments. The effort pays off – if you don't spend enough time and resources on the competition, you won't get a high place on a leaderboard.*
- *Entering "wrong" competitions. There were competitions with leaks, reverse engineering, etc. There were competitions with an unreasonable split between public and private test data and a shake-up ensured. There were competitions that weren't interesting enough for me and I shouldn't have started participating in them.*
- *Teaming up with the wrong people. There were cases when my teammates weren't as active as I expected and it led to a worse team score.*

What's the most important thing someone should keep in mind or do when they're entering a competition?

I think it is important to remember your goal, know what are you ready to invest into this competition, and think about the possible outcomes. There are many possible goals that people have while entering a competition:

- *Winning money or getting a medal;*
- *Getting new skills or improving existing ones;*
- *Working with a new task/domain;*
- *Networking;*
- *PR;*
- *etc;*

Of course, it is possible to have multiple motivations.

As for what are you ready to invest, it is usually about the amount of time and effort you are ready to spend as well as the hardware that you have.

When I speak about the outcomes, I mean what will happen when the competition ends. It is possible that you will invest a lot in this competition and win, but you could also lose. Are you ready for this reality? Is winning a particular competition critical to you? Maybe you need to be prepared to invest more effort; on the other hand, maybe you have long-term goals and one failed competition won't hurt much.

Metrics for object detection problems

In recent years, deep learning competitions have become more and more common on Kaggle. Most of these competitions, focused on image recognition or on natural language processing tasks, have not required the use of evaluation metrics much different from the ones we have explored up to now. However, a couple of specific problems have required some special metric to be evaluated correctly: those relating to **object detection** and **segmentation**.

Classification + localization (cat)   Object detection (dog, cat)

Figure 5.4: Computer vision tasks. (Source: https://cocodataset.org/#explore?id=38282, https://cocodataset.org/#explore?id=68717)

In **object detection**, you don't have to classify an image, but instead find relevant portions of a picture and label them accordingly. For instance, in *Figure 5.4*, an object detection classifier has been entrusted to locate within a photo the portions of the picture where either dogs or cats are present and classify each of them with a proper label. The example on the left shows the localization of a cat using a rectangular box (called a **bounding box**). The example on the right presents how multiple cats and dogs are detected in the picture by bounding boxes and then correctly classified (the blue bounding boxes are for dogs, the red ones for cats).

In order to describe the spatial location of an object, in object detection we use **bounding boxes**, which define a rectangular area in which the object lies. A bounding box is usually specified using two (x, y) coordinates: the upper-left and lower-right corners. In terms of a machine learning algorithm, finding the coordinates of bounding boxes corresponds to applying a regression problem to multiple targets. However, you probably won't frame the problem from scratch but rely on pre-built and often pre-trained models such as Mask R-CNN (`https://arxiv.org/abs/1703.06870`), RetinaNet (`https://arxiv.org/abs/2106.05624v1`), FPN (`https://arxiv.org/abs/1612.03144v2`), YOLO (`https://arxiv.org/abs/1506.02640v1`), Faster R-CNN (`https://arxiv.org/abs/1506.01497v1`), or SDD (`https://arxiv.org/abs/1512.02325`).

In **segmentation**, you instead have a classification at the *pixel* level, so if you have a 320x200 image, you actually have to make 64,000 pixel classifications. Depending on the task, you can have a **semantic segmentation** where you have to classify every pixel in a photo, or an **instance segmentation** where you only have to classify the pixels representing objects of a certain type of interest (for instance, a cat as in our example in *Figure 5.5* below):

Semantic segmentation (**cat**, sofa)   Instance segmentation (cat)

Figure 5.5: Semantic segmentation and instance segmentation on the same image. (Source: https://cocodataset.org/#explore?id=338091)

Let's start with an overview of the specific metrics for these tasks, metrics that can work well for both problems, since, in both cases, you are predicting entire areas (rectangular ones in object detection, polygonal ones in segmentation) of a picture and you have to compare your predictions against a ground truth, which is, again, expressed as areas. On the side of segmentation, the easiest metric is the **pixel accuracy**, which, as the name suggests, is the accuracy on the pixel classification.

It is not a great metric because, as happens with accuracy on binary and multi-class problems, your score may look great if the relevant pixels do not take up very much of the image (you just predict the majority claim, thus you don't segment).

Therefore, there are two metrics that are used much more, especially in competitions: the **intersection over union** and the **dice coefficient**.

Intersection over union (IoU)

The **intersection over union** (IoU) is also known as the **Jaccard index**. When used in segmentation problems, using IoU implies that you have two images to compare: one is your prediction and the other is the mask revealing the ground truth, which is usually a binary matrix where the value 1 stands for the ground truth and 0 otherwise. In the case of multiple objects, you have multiple masks, each one labeled with the class of the object.

When used in object detection problems, you have the boundaries of two rectangular areas (those of the prediction and the ground truth), expressed by the coordinates of their vertices. For each classified class, you compute the area of overlap between your prediction and the ground truth mask, and then you divide this by the area of the union between your prediction and the ground truth, a sum that takes into account any overlap. In this way, you are proportionally penalized both if you predict a larger area than what it should be (the denominator will be larger) or a smaller one (the numerator will be smaller):

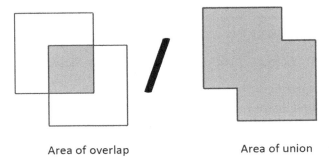

Area of overlap   Area of union

Figure 5.6: Visual representation of the IoU calculation

In *Figure 5.6* you can see a visual representation of the areas involved in the computation. By imagining the squares overlapping more, you can figure out how the metric efficiently penalizes your solution when your prediction, even if covering the ground truth, exceeds it (the area of union becomes larger).

Here are some examples of competitions where IoU has been used:

- *TGS Salt Identification Challenge* (`https://www.kaggle.com/c/tgs-salt-identification-challenge/`) with Intersection Over Union Object Segmentation

- *iMaterialist (Fashion) 2019 at FGVC6* (`https://www.kaggle.com/c/imaterialist-fashion-2019-FGVC6`) with Intersection Over Union Object Segmentation With Classification

- *Airbus Ship Detection Challenge* (`https://www.kaggle.com/c/airbus-ship-detection`) with Intersection Over Union Object Segmentation Beta

Dice

The other useful metric is the **Dice coefficient**, which is the area of overlap between the prediction and ground truth doubled and then divided by the sum of the prediction and ground truth areas:

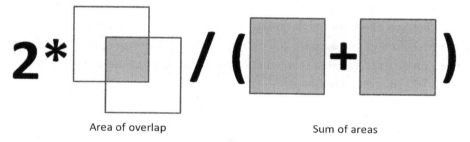

Area of overlap   Sum of areas

Figure 5.7: Visual representation of the Dice calculation

In this case, with respect to the Jaccard index, you do not take into account the overlap of the prediction with the ground truth in the denominator. Here, the expectation is that, as you maximize the area of overlap, you predict the correct area size. Again, you are penalized if you predict areas larger than you should be predicting. In fact, the two metrics are positively correlated and they produce almost the same results for a single classification problem.

The differences actually arise when you are working with multiple classes. In fact, both with IoU and the Dice coefficient, when you have multiple classes you average the result of all of them. However, in doing so, the IoU metric tends to penalize the overall average more if a single class prediction is wrong, whereas the Dice coefficient is more lenient and tends to represent the average performance.

Examples of Kaggle competitions using the Dice coefficient (it is often encountered in competitions with medical purposes, but not necessarily only there, because it can also be used for clouds and cars):

- *HuBMAP - Hacking the Kidney*: `https://www.kaggle.com/c/hubmap-kidney-segmentation`
- *Ultrasound Nerve Segmentation*: `https://www.kaggle.com/c/ultrasound-nerve-segmentation`
- *Understanding Clouds from Satellite Images*: `https://www.kaggle.com/c/understanding_cloud_organization`
- *Carvana Image Masking Challenge*: `https://www.kaggle.com/c/carvana-image-masking-challenge`

IoU and Dice constitute the basis for all the more complex metrics in segmentation and object detection. By choosing an appropriate threshold level for IoU or Dice (usually 0.5), you can decide whether or not to confirm a detection, therefore a classification. At this point, you can use previously discussed metrics for classification, such as precision, recall, and *F1*, such as is done in popular object detection and segmentation challenges such as Pascal VOC (`http://host.robots.ox.ac.uk/pascal/VOC/voc2012`) or COCO (`https://cocodataset.org`).

Metrics for multi-label classification and recommendation problems

Recommender systems are one of the most popular applications of data analysis and machine learning, and there are quite a few competitions on Kaggle that have used the recommendation approach. For instance, the *Quick, Draw! Doodle Recognition Challenge* was a prediction evaluated as a recommender system. Some other competitions on Kaggle, however, truly strived to build effective recommender systems (such as *Expedia Hotel Recommendations*: `https://www.kaggle.com/c/expedia-hotel-recommendations`) and RecSYS, the conference on recommender systems (`https://recsys.acm.org/`), even hosted one of its yearly contests on Kaggle (*RecSYS 2013*: `https://www.kaggle.com/c/yelp-recsys-2013`).

Mean Average Precision at K (MAP@{K}) is typically the metric of choice for evaluating the performance of recommender systems, and it is the most common metric you will encounter on Kaggle in all the competitions that try to build or approach a problem as a recommender system.

There are also some other metrics, such as the **precision at k**, or **P@K**, and the **average precision at k**, or **AP@K**, which are loss functions, in other words, computed at the level of each single prediction. Understanding how they work can help you better understand the MAP@K and how it can perform both in recommendations and in multi-label classification.

In fact, analogous to recommender systems, multi-label classifications imply that your model outputs a series of class predictions. Such results could be evaluated using some average of some binary classification metrics (such as in *Greek Media Monitoring Multilabel Classification (WISE 2014)*, which used the mean *F1* score: https://www.kaggle.com/c/wise-2014) as well as metrics that are more typical of recommender systems, such as MAP@K. In the end, you can deal with both recommendations and multi-label predictions as *ranking tasks*, which translates into a set of ranked suggestions in a recommender system and into a set of labels (without a precise order) in multi-label classification.

MAP@{K}

MAP@K is a complex metric and it derives from many computations. In order to understand the MAP@K metric fully, let's start with its simplest component, the **precision at** k **(P@K)**. In this case, since the prediction for an example is a ranked sequence of predictions (from the most probable to the least), the function takes into account only the top k predictions, then it computes how many matches it got with respect to the ground truth and divides that number by k. In a few words, it is quite similar to an accuracy measure averaged over k predictions.

A bit more complex in terms of computation, but conceptually simple, the **average precision at** k **(AP@K)** is the average of P@K computed over all the values ranging from *1* to k. In this way, the metric evaluates how well the prediction works overall, using the top prediction, then the top two predictions, and so on until the top k predictions.

Finally, **MAP@K** is the mean of the AP@K for the entire predicted sample, and it is a metric because it comprises all the predictions in its evaluation. Here is the MAP@5 formulation you can find in the *Expedia Hotel Recommendations* competition (https://www.kaggle.com/c/expedia-hotel-recommendations):

$$MAP@5 = \frac{1}{|U|} \sum_{u=1}^{|U|} \sum_{k=1}^{\min(5,n)} P(k)$$

In the formula, $|U|$ is the number of user recommendations, $P(k)$ is the precision at cutoff k, and n is the number of predicted hotel clusters (you could predict up to 5 hotels for each recommendation).

It is clearly a bit more daunting than our explanation, but the formula just expresses that the MAP@K is the mean of all the AP@K evaluations over all the predictions.

Having completed this overview of specific metrics for different regression and classification metrics, let's discuss how to deal with evaluation metrics in a Kaggle competition.

Optimizing evaluation metrics

Summing up what we have discussed so far, an objective function is a function inside your learning algorithm that measures how well the algorithm's internal model is fitting the provided data. The objective function also provides feedback to the algorithm in order for it to improve its fit across successive iterations. Clearly, since the entire algorithm's efforts are recruited to perform well based on the objective function, if the Kaggle evaluation metric perfectly matches the objective function of your algorithm, you will get the best results.

Unfortunately, this is not frequently the case. Often, the evaluation metric provided can only be approximated by existing objective functions. Getting a good approximation, or striving to get your predictions performing better with respect to the evaluation criteria, is the secret to performing well in Kaggle competitions. When your objective function does not match your evaluation metric, you have a few alternatives:

1. Modify your learning algorithm and have it incorporate an objective function that matches your evaluation metric, though this is not possible for all algorithms (for instance, algorithms such as LightGBM and XGBoost allow you to set custom objective functions, but most Scikit-learn models don't allow this).

2. Tune your model's hyperparameters, choosing the ones that make the result shine the most when using the evaluation metric.

3. Post-process your results so they match the evaluation criteria more closely. For instance, you could code an optimizer that performs transformations on your predictions (probability calibration algorithms are an example, and we will discuss them at the end of the chapter).

Having the competition metric incorporated into your machine learning algorithm is really the most effective method to achieve better predictions, though only a few algorithms can be hacked into using the competition metric as your objective function. The second approach is therefore the more common one, and many competitions end up in a struggle to get the best hyperparameters for your models to perform on the evaluation metric.

If you already have your evaluation function coded, then doing the right cross-validation or choosing the appropriate test set plays the lion share. If you don't have the coded function at hand, you have to first code it in a suitable way, following the formulas provided by Kaggle.

Invariably, doing the following will make the difference:

- Looking for all the relevant information about the evaluation metric and its coded function on a search engine
- Browsing through the most common packages (such as Scikit-learn: `https://scikit-learn.org/stable/modules/model_evaluation.html#model-evaluation` or TensorFlow: `https://www.tensorflow.org/api_docs/python/tf/keras/losses`)
- Browsing GitHub projects (for instance, *Ben Hammer's* Metrics project: `https://github.com/benhamner/Metrics`)
- Asking or looking around in the forums and available Kaggle Notebooks (both for the current competition and for similar competitions)
- In addition, as we mentioned before, querying the Meta Kaggle dataset (`https://www.kaggle.com/kaggle/meta-kaggle`) and looking in the **Competitions** table will help you find out which other Kaggle competitions used that same evaluation metric, and immediately provides you with useful code and ideas to try out

Let's discuss in greater detail the alternatives you have when your evaluation metric doesn't match your algorithm's objective function. We'll start by exploring custom metrics.

Custom metrics and custom objective functions

As a first option when your objective function does not match your evaluation metric, we learned above that you can solve this by creating your own custom objective function, but that only a few algorithms can easily be modified to incorporate a specific objective function.

The good news is that the few algorithms that allow this are among the most effective ones in Kaggle competitions and data science projects. Of course, creating your own custom objective function may sound a little bit tricky, but it is an incredibly rewarding approach to increasing your score in a competition. For instance, there are options to do this when using gradient boosting algorithms such as XGBoost, CatBoost, and LightGBM, as well as with all deep learning models based on TensorFlow or PyTorch.

You can find great tutorials for custom metrics and objective functions in TensorFlow and PyTorch here:

- `https://towardsdatascience.com/custom-metrics-in-keras-and-how-simple-they-are-to-use-in-tensorflow2-2-6d079c2ca279`

- `https://petamind.com/advanced-keras-custom-loss-functions/`

- `https://kevinmusgrave.github.io/pytorch-metric-learning/extend/losses/`

These will provide you with the basic function templates and some useful suggestions about how to code a custom objective or evaluation function.

> If you want just to get straight to the custom objective function you need, you can try this Notebook by RNA (`https://www.kaggle.com/bigironsphere`): `https://www.kaggle.com/bigironsphere/loss-function-library-keras-pytorch/notebook`. It contains a large range of custom loss functions for both TensorFlow and PyTorch that have appeared in different competitions.

If you need to create a custom loss in LightGBM, XGBoost, or CatBoost, as indicated in their respective documentation, you have to code a function that takes as inputs the prediction and the ground truth, and that returns as outputs the gradient and the hessian.

> You can consult this post on Stack Overflow for a better understanding of what a gradient and a hessian are: `https://stats.stackexchange.com/questions/231220/how-to-compute-the-gradient-and-hessian-of-logarithmic-loss-question-is-based`.

From a code implementation perspective, all you have to do is to create a function, using closures if you need to pass more parameters beyond just the vector of predicted labels and true labels. Here is a simple example of a **focal loss** (a loss that aims to heavily weight the minority class in the loss computations as described in Lin, T-Y. et al. *Focal loss for dense object detection*: `https://arxiv.org/abs/1708.02002`) function that you can use as a model for your own custom functions:

```
from scipy.misc import derivative
import xgboost as xgb

def focal_loss(alpha, gamma):
    def loss_func(y_pred, y_true):
        a, g = alpha, gamma
        def get_loss(y_pred, y_true):
            p = 1 / (1 + np.exp(-y_pred))
```

```
                    loss = (-(a * y_true + (1 - a)*(1 - y_true)) *
                            ((1 - (y_true * p + (1 - y_true) *
                             (1 - p)))**g) * (y_true * np.log(p) +
                            (1 - y_true) * np.log(1 - p)))
                    return loss
                partial_focal = lambda y_pred: get_loss(y_pred, y_true)
                grad = derivative(partial_focal, y_pred, n=1, dx=1e-6)
                hess = derivative(partial_focal, y_pred, n=2, dx=1e-6)
                return grad, hess
            return loss_func

    xgb = xgb.XGBClassifier(objective=focal_loss(alpha=0.25, gamma=1))
```

In the above code snippet, we have defined a new cost function, focal_loss, which is then fed into an XGBoost instance's object parameters. The example is worth showing because the focal loss requires the specification of some parameters in order to work properly on your problem (alpha and gamma). The more simplistic solution of having their values directly coded into the function is not ideal, since you may have to change them systematically as you are tuning your model. Instead, in the proposed function, when you input the parameters into the focal_loss function, they reside in memory and they are referenced by the loss_func function that is returned to XGBoost. The returned cost function, therefore, will work, referring to the alpha and gamma values that you have initially instantiated.

Another interesting aspect of the example is that it really makes it easy to compute the gradient and the hessian of the cost function by means of the derivative function from SciPy. If your cost function is differentiable, you don't have to worry about doing any calculations by hand. However, creating a custom objective function requires some mathematical knowledge and quite a lot of effort to make sure it works properly for your purposes. You can read about the difficulties that *Max Halford* experienced while implementing a focal loss for the LightGBM algorithm, and how he overcame them, here: https://maxhalford.github.io/blog/lightgbm-focal-loss/. Despite the difficulty, being able to conjure up a custom loss can really determine your success in a Kaggle competition where you have to extract the maximum possible result from your model.

If building your own objective function isn't working out, you can simply lower your ambitions, give up building your function as an objective function used by the optimizer, and instead code it as a custom *evaluation metric*. Though your model won't be directly optimized to perform against this function, you can still improve its predictive performance with hyperparameter optimization based on it. This is the second option we talked about in the previous section.

Just remember, if you are writing a metric from scratch, sometimes you may need to abide by certain code conventions for your function to work properly. For instance, if you use Scikit-learn, you have to convert your functions using the make_scorer function. The make_scorer function is actually a wrapper that makes your evaluation function suitable for working with the Scikit-learn API. It will wrap your function while considering some meta-information, such as whether to use probability estimates or predictions, whether you need to specify a threshold for prediction, and, last but not least, the directionality of the optimization, that is, whether you want to maximize or minimize the score it returns:

```
from sklearn.metrics import make_scorer
from sklearn.metrics import average_precision_score
scorer = make_scorer(average_precision_score,
average='weighted', greater_is_better=True, needs_proba=False)
```

In the above example, you prepare a scorer based on the average precision metric, specifying that it should use a weighted computation when dealing with multi-class classification problems.

 If you are optimizing for your evaluation metric, you can apply grid search, random search, or some more sophisticated optimization such as Bayesian optimization and find the set of parameters that makes your algorithm perform optimally for your evaluation metric, even if it works with a different cost function. We will explore how to best arrange parameter optimization and obtain the best results on Kaggle competitions after having discussed model validation, specifically in the chapter dealing with tabular data problems.

Post-processing your predictions

Post-processing tuning implies that your predictions are transformed, by means of a function, into something else in order to present a better evaluation. After building your custom loss or optimizing for your evaluation metric, you can also improve your results by leveraging the characteristics of your evaluation metric using a specific function applied to your predictions. Let's take the Quadratic Weighted Kappa, for instance. We mentioned previously that this metric is useful when you have to deal with the prediction of an ordinal value. To recap, the original Kappa coefficient is a chance-adjusted index of agreement between the algorithm and the ground truth. It is a kind of accuracy measurement corrected by the probability that the match between the prediction and the ground truth is due to a fortunate chance.

Here is the original version of the Kappa coefficient, as seen before:

$$k = (p_0 - p_e)/(1 - p_e)$$

In the formula, p_0 is the relative observed agreement among raters, and p_e is the hypothetical probability of chance agreement. Here, you need just two matrices, the one with the observed scores and the one with the expected scores based on chance agreement. When the Kappa coefficient is weighted, you also consider a weight matrix and the formula turns into this:

$$k = (p_0 - p_e)/(1 - p_p)$$

The matrix p_p contains the penalizations to weight errors differently, which is very useful for ordinal predictions since this matrix can penalize much more when the predictions deviate further from the ground truths. Using the quadratic form, that is, squaring the resulting k, makes the penalization even more severe. However, optimizing for such a metric is really not easy, since it is very difficult to implement it as a cost function. Post-processing can help you.

An example can be found in the *PetFinder.my Adoption Prediction* competition (`https://www.kaggle.com/c/petfinder-adoption-prediction`). In this competition, given that the results could have 5 possible ratings (0, 1, 2, 3, or 4), you could deal with them either using a classification or a regression. If you used a regression, a post-processing transformation of the regression output could improve the model's performance against the Quadratic Weighted Kappa metric, outperforming the results you could get from a classification directly outputting discrete predictions.

In the case of the PetFinder competition, the post-processing consisted of an optimization process that started by transforming the regression results into integers, first using the boundaries [0.5, 1.5, 2.5, 3.5] as thresholds and, by an iterative fine-tuning, finding a better set of boundaries that maximized the performance. The fine-tuning of the boundaries required the computations of an optimizer such as SciPy's `optimize.minimize`, which is based on the Nelder-Mead algorithm. The boundaries found by the optimizer were validated by a cross-validation scheme. You can read more details about this post-processing directly from the post made by *Abhishek Thakur* during the competition: `https://www.kaggle.com/c/petfinder-adoption-prediction/discussion/76107`.

Aside from the PetFinder competition, many other competitions have demonstrated that smart post-processing can lead to improved results and rankings. We'll point out a few examples here:

- https://www.kaggle.com/khoongweihao/post-processing-technique-c-f-1st-place-jigsaw
- https://www.kaggle.com/tomooinubushi/postprocessing-based-on-leakage
- https://www.kaggle.com/saitodevel01/indoor-post-processing-by-cost-minimization

Unfortunately, post-processing is often very dependent on the metric you are using (understanding the metric is imperative for devising any good post-processing) and often also data-specific, for instance, in the case of time series data and leakages. Hence, it is very difficult to generalize any procedure for figuring out the right post-processing for any competition. Nevertheless, always be aware of this possibility and be on the lookout in a competition for any hint that post-processing results is favorable. You can always get hints about post-processing from previous competitions that have been similar, and by forum discussion – eventually, someone will raise the topic.

Predicted probability and its adjustment

To complete the above discussion on metrics optimization (post-processing of predictions), we will discuss situations where it is paramount to predict correct probabilities, but you are not sure if the algorithm you are using is doing a good job. As we detailed previously, classification probabilities concern both binary and multiclass classification problems, and they are commonly evaluated using the logarithmic loss (aka log loss or logistic loss or cross-entropy loss) in its binary or multi-class version (for more details, see the previous sections on *Metrics for classification (label prediction and probability)* and *Metrics for multi-class classification*).

However, evaluating or optimizing for the log loss may not prove enough. The main problems to be on the lookout for when striving to achieve correct probabilistic predictions with your model are:

- Models that do not return a truly probabilistic estimate
- Unbalanced distribution of classes in your problem
- Different class distribution between your training data and your test data (on both public and private leaderboards)

The first point alone provides reason to check and verify the quality of classification predictions in terms of modeled uncertainty. In fact, even if many algorithms are provided in the Scikit-learn package together with a `predict_proba` method, this is a very weak assurance that they will return a true probability.

Let's take, for instance, decision trees, which are the basis of many effective methods to model tabular data. The probability outputted by a classification decision tree (`https://scikit-learn.org/stable/modules/generated/sklearn.tree.DecisionTreeClassifier.html`) is based on terminal leaves; that is, it depends on the distribution of classes on the leaf that contains the case to be predicted. If the tree is fully grown, it is highly likely that the case is in a small leaf with very few other cases, so the predicted probability will be very high. If you change parameters such as `max_depth`, `max_leaf_nodes`, or `min_samples_leaf`, the resulting probability will drastically change from higher values to lower ones depending on the growth of the tree.

Decision trees are the most common base model for ensembles such as bagging models and random forests, as well as boosted models such as gradient boosting (with its high-performing implementations XGBoost, LightGBM, and CatBoost). But, for the same reasons – probability estimates that are not truly based on solid probabilistic estimations – the problem affects many other commonly used models, such as support-vector machines and k-nearest neighbors. Such aspects were mostly unknown to Kagglers until the *Otto Group Product Classification Challenge* (`https://www.kaggle.com/c/otto-group-product-classification-challenge/overview/`), when it was raised by *Christophe Bourguignat* and others during the competition (see `https://www.kaggle.com/cbourguignat/why-calibration-works`), and easily solved at the time using the calibration functions that had recently been added to Scikit-learn.

Aside from the model you will be using, the presence of imbalance between classes in your problem may also result in models that are not at all reliable. Hence, a good approach in the case of unbalanced classification problems is to rebalance the classes using undersampling or oversampling strategies, or different custom weights for each class to be applied when the loss is computed by the algorithm. All these strategies may render your model more performant; however, they will surely distort the probability estimates and you may have to adjust them in order to obtain an even better model score on the leaderboard.

Finally, a third point of concern is related to how the test set is distributed. This kind of information is usually concealed, but there are often ways to estimate it and figure it out (for instance, by trial and error based on the public leaderboard results, as we mentioned in *Chapter 1, Introducing Kaggle and Other Data Science Competitions*).

For instance, this happened in the *iMaterialist Furniture Challenge* (`https://www.kaggle.com/c/imaterialist-challenge-furniture-2018/`) and the more popular *Quora Question Pairs* (`https://www.kaggle.com/c/quora-question-pairs`). Both competitions gave rise to various discussions on how to post-process in order to adjust probabilities to test expectations (see `https://swarbrickjones.wordpress.com/2017/03/28/cross-entropy-and-training-test-class-imbalance/` and `https://www.kaggle.com/dowakin/probability-calibration-0-005-to-1b` for more details on the method used). From a general point of view, assuming that you do not have an idea of the test distribution of classes to be predicted, it is still very beneficial to correctly predict probability based on the priors you get from the training data (and until you get evidence to the contrary, that is the probability distribution that your model should mimic). In fact, it will be much easier to correct your predicted probabilities if your predicted probability distribution matches those in the training set.

The solution, when your predicted probabilities are misaligned with the training distribution of the target, is to use the **calibration function** provided by Scikit-learn, `CalibratedClassifierCV`:

```
sklearn.calibration.CalibratedClassifierCV(base_estimator=None, *,
    method='sigmoid', cv=None, n_jobs=None, ensemble=True)
```

The purpose of the calibration function is to apply a post-processing function to your predicted probabilities in order to make them adhere more closely to the empirical probabilities seen in the ground truth. Provided that your model is a Scikit-learn model or behaves similarly to one, the function will act as a wrapper for your model and directly pipe its predictions into a post-processing function. You have the choice between using two methods for post-processing. The first is the **sigmoid** method (also called Plat's scaling), which is nothing more than a logistic regression. The second is the **isotonic regression**, which is a non-parametric regression; beware that it tends to overfit if there are few examples.

You also have to choose how to fit this calibrator. Remember that it is a model that is applied to the results of your model, so you have to avoid overfitting by systematically reworking predictions. You could use a **cross-validation** (more on this in the following chapter on *Designing Good Validation*) and then produce a number of models that, once averaged, will provide your predictions (`ensemble=True`). Otherwise, and this is our usual choice, resort to an **out-of-fold prediction** (more on this in the following chapters) and calibrate on that using all the data available (`ensemble=False`).

Even if `CalibratedClassifierCV` can handle most situations, you can also figure out some empirical way to fix probability estimates for the best performance at test time. You can use any transformation function, from a handmade one to a sophisticated one derived by genetic algorithms, for instance. Your only limit is simply that you should cross-validate it and possibly have a good final result from the public leaderboard (but not necessarily, because you should trust your local cross-validation score more, as we are going to discuss in the next chapter). A good example of such a strategy is provided by Silogram (`https://www.kaggle.com/psilogram`), who, in the *Microsoft Malware Classification Challenge*, found out a way to tune the unreliable probabilistic outputs of random forests into probabilistic ones simply by raising the output to a power determined by grid search (see `https://www.kaggle.com/c/malware-classification/discussion/13509`).

Sudalai Rajkumar

`https://www.kaggle.com/sudalairajkumar`

In our final interview of the chapter, we speak to Sudalai Rajkumar, SRK, a Grandmaster in Competitions, Datasets, and Notebooks, and a Discussion Master. He is ranked #1 in the Analytics Vidhya data science platform, and works as an AI/ML advisor for start-ups.

What's your favourite kind of competition and why? In terms of techniques and solving approaches, what is your specialty on Kaggle?

My favorite kinds of competition are ones that involve a good amount of feature engineering. I think that is my strength as well. I am generally interested in data exploration to get a deep understanding of the data (which you can infer from my series of simple exploration Notebooks (`https://www.kaggle.com/sudalairajkumar/code`)) and then creating features based on it.

How do you approach a Kaggle competition? How different is this approach to what you do in your day-to-day work?

The framework for a competition involves data exploration, finding the right validation method, feature engineering, model building, and ensembling/stacking. All these are involved in my day job as well. But in addition to this, there is a good amount of stakeholder discussion, data collection, data tagging, model deployment, model monitoring, and data storytelling that is involved in my daily job.

Tell us about a particularly challenging competition you entered, and what insights you used to tackle the task.

Santander Product Recommendation *is a memorable competition that we entered. Rohan & I did a lot of feature engineering and built multiple models. When we did final ensembling, we used different weights for different products and some of them did not add up to 1. From the data exploration and understanding, we hand-picked these weights, which helped us. This made us realise the domain/data importance in solving problems and how data science is an art as much as science.*

Has Kaggle helped you in your career? If so, how?

Kaggle played a very important role in my career. I was able to secure my last two jobs mainly because of Kaggle. Also, the success from Kaggle helps to connect with other stalwarts in the data science field easily and learn from them. It also helps a lot in my current role as AI / ML advisor for start-ups, as it gives credibility.

In your experience, what do inexperienced Kagglers often overlook? What do you know now that you wish you'd known when you first started?

Understanding the data in depth. Often this is overlooked, and people get into model-building right away. Exploring the data plays a very important role in the success of any Kaggle competition. This helps to create proper cross validation and to create better features and to extract more value from the data.

What mistakes have you made in competitions in the past?

It is a very big list, and I would say that they are learning opportunities. In every competition, out of 20-30 ideas that I try, only 1 may work. These mistakes/failures give much more learning than the actual success or things that worked. For example, I learnt about overfitting the very hard way by falling from top deciles to bottom deciles in one of my very first competitions. But that learning stayed with me forever thereafter.

Are there any particular tools or libraries that you would recommend using for data analysis/machine learning?

I primarily use XGBoost/LightGBM in the case of tabular data. I also use open source AutoML libraries and Driverless AI to get early benchmarks these days. I use Keras, Transformers, and PyTorch for deep learning models.

What's the most important thing someone should keep in mind or do when they're entering a competition?

Consistency is the key. Each competition will have its own ups and downs. There will be multiple days without any progress, but we should not give up and keep trying. I think this is applicable for anything and not just Kaggle competitions.

Do you use other competition platforms? How do they compare to Kaggle?

I have also taken part on other platforms like the Analytics Vidhya DataHack platform, Driven Data, CrowdAnalytix etc. They are good too, but Kaggle is more widely adopted and global in nature, so the amount of competition on Kaggle is much higher compared to other platforms.

Summary

In this chapter, we have discussed evaluation metrics in Kaggle competitions. First, we explained how an evaluation metric can differ from an objective function. We also remarked on the differences between regression and classification problems. For each type of problem, we analyzed the most common metrics that you can find in a Kaggle competition.

After that, we discussed the metrics that have never previously been seen in a competition and that you won't likely see again. Finally, we explored and studied different common metrics, giving examples of where they have been used in previous Kaggle competitions. We then proposed a few strategies for optimizing an evaluation metric. In particular, we recommended trying to code your own custom cost functions and provided suggestions on possible useful post-processing steps.

You should now have grasped the role of an evaluation metric in a Kaggle competition. You should also have a strategy to deal with every common or uncommon metric, by retracing past competitions and by gaining a full understanding of the way a metric works. In the next chapter, we are going to discuss how to use evaluation metrics and properly estimate the performance of your Kaggle solution by means of a validation strategy.

Join our book's Discord space

Join the book's Discord workspace for a monthly *Ask me Anything* session with the authors:

`https://packt.link/KaggleDiscord`

6

Designing Good Validation

In a Kaggle competition, in the heat of modeling and submitting results, it may seem enough to take at face value the results you get back from the leaderboard. In the end, you may think that what counts in a competition is your ranking. This is a common error that is made repeatedly in competitions. In actual fact, you won't know what the actual leaderboard (the private one) looks like until after the competition has closed, and trusting the public part of it is not advisable because it is quite often misleading.

In this chapter, we will introduce you to the importance of **validation** in data competitions. You will learn about:

- What overfitting is and how a public leaderboard can be misleading
- The dreadful shake-ups
- The different kinds of validation strategies
- Adversarial validation
- How to spot and leverage leakages
- What your strategies should be when choosing your final submissions

Monitoring your performances when modeling and distinguishing when overfitting happens is a key competency not only in data science competitions but in all data science projects. Validating your models properly is one of the most important skills that you can learn from a Kaggle competition and that you can resell in the professional world.

Snooping on the leaderboard

As we previously described, in each competition, Kaggle divides the test set into a **public part**, which is visualized on the ongoing leaderboard, and a **private part**, which will be used to calculate the final scores. These test parts are usually randomly determined (although in time series competitions, they are determined based on time) and the entire test set is released without any distinction made between public and private.

> Recently, in order to avoid the scrutinizing of test data in certain competitions, Kaggle has even held back the test data, providing only some examples of it and replacing them with the real test set when the submission is made. These are called **Code** competitions because you are not actually providing the predictions themselves, but a Notebook containing the code to generate them.

Therefore, a submission derived from a model will cover the entire test set, but only the public part will immediately be scored, leaving the scoring of the private part until after the competition has closed.

Given this, three considerations arise:

- In order for a competition to work properly, training data and test data should be from **the same distribution**. Moreover, the private and public parts of the test data should resemble each other in terms of distribution.

- Even if the training and test data are apparently from the same distribution, the **lack of sufficient examples** in either set could make it difficult to obtain aligned results between the training data and the public and private test data.

- The public test data should be regarded as a holdout test in a data science project: to be used only for final validation. Hence, it should not be queried much in order to avoid what is called **adaptive overfitting**, which implies a model that works well on a specific test set but underperforms on others.

Keeping in mind these three considerations is paramount to understanding the dynamics of a competition. In most competitions, there are always quite a few questions in the discussion forums about how the training, public, and private test data relate to each other, and it is quite common to see submissions of hundreds of solutions that have only been evaluated based on their efficacy on the public leaderboard.

It is also common to hear discussions about **shake-ups** that revolutionize the rankings. They are, in fact, a rearranging of the final rankings that can disappoint many who previously held better positions on the public leaderboard. Anecdotally, shake-ups are commonly attributed to differences between the training and test set or between the private and public parts of the test data. They are measured *ex ante* based on how competitors have seen their expected local scores correlate with the leaderboard feedback and *ex post* by a series of analyses based on two figures:

- A general shake-up figure based on `mean(abs(private_rank-public_rank)/number_of_teams)`

- A top leaderboard shake-up figure, taking into account only the top 10% of public ranks

These *ex post* figures were first devised by *Steve Donoho* (`https://www.kaggle.com/breakfastpirate`) who compiled a ranking of the worst Kaggle shake-ups (see `https://www.kaggle.com/c/recruit-restaurant-visitor-forecasting/discussion/49106#278831`). They are nowadays easily available, recreated by many Notebooks based on the Meta Kaggle dataset we discussed in *Chapter 5, Competition Tasks and Metrics* (see `https://www.kaggle.com/jtrotman/meta-kaggle-competition-shake-up`). For instance, by consulting these figures, you may find out how dreadful the *RSNA Intracranial Hemorrhage Detection* competition was for many because of its shake-ups, especially in the top positions.

However, aside from an *ex post* evaluation, there are quite a few lessons that we can get from previous shake-ups that can help you in your Kaggle competitions. A few researchers from UC Berkeley think so too. In their paper presented at NIPS 2019, Roelofs, Fridovich-Keil et al. study in detail a few thousand Kaggle competitions to gain insight into the public-private leaderboard dynamics in Kaggle competitions. Although they focus on a limited subset of competitions (120, above a certain number of participants, focused on binary classification), they obtained some interesting findings:

- There is little adaptive overfitting; in other words, public standings usually do hold in the unveiled private leaderboard.

- Most shake-ups are due to random fluctuations and overcrowded rankings where competitors are too near to each other, and any slight change in the performance in the private test sets causes major changes in the rankings.

- Shake-ups happen when the training set is very small or the training data is not **independent and identically distributed (i.i.d.)**.

 The full paper, Roelofs, R., Fridovich-Keil, S. et al. *A meta-analysis of overfitting in machine learning*. Proceedings of the 33rd International Conference on Neural Information Processing Systems. 2019, can be found at this link: `https://papers.nips.cc/paper/2019/file/ee39e503b6bedf0c98c388b7e8589aca-Paper.pdf`.

In our long experience of Kaggle competitions, however, we have seen quite a lot of problems with adaptive overfitting since the beginning. For instance, you can read *Greg Park*'s analysis of one of the first competitions we ever took part in: `http://gregpark.io/blog/Kaggle-Psychopathy-Postmortem/`. Since this is quite a common and persistent problem for many Kagglers, we suggest a strategy that is a bit more sophisticated than simply following what happens on the public leaderboard:

- Always build reliable cross-validation systems for local scoring.

- Always try to control non-i.i.d distributions using the best validation scheme dictated by the situation. Unless clearly stated in the description of the competition, it is not an easy task to spot non-i.i.d. distributions, but you can get hints from discussion or by experimenting using stratified validation schemes (when stratifying according to a certain feature, the results improve decisively, for instance).

- Correlate local scoring with the public leaderboard in order to figure out whether or not they go in the same direction.

- Test using adversarial validation, revealing whether or not the test distribution is similar to the training data.

- Make your solutions more robust using ensembling, especially if you are working with small datasets.

In the following sections, we are going to explore each of these ideas (except for ensembling, which is the topic of a future chapter) and provide you with all the best tools and strategies to obtain the best results, especially on the private dataset.

The importance of validation in competitions

If you think about a competition carefully, you can imagine it as a huge system of experiments. Whoever can create the most systematic and efficient way to run these experiments wins.

In fact, in spite of all your theoretical knowledge, you will be in competition with the hundreds or thousands of data professionals who have more or less the same competencies as you.

In addition, they will be using exactly the same data as you and roughly the same tools for learning from the data (TensorFlow, PyTorch, Scikit-learn, and so on). Some will surely have better access to computational resources, although the availability of Kaggle Notebooks and generally decreasing cloud computing prices mean the gap is no longer so wide. Consequently, if you look at differences in knowledge, data, models, and available computers, you won't find many discriminating factors between you and the other competitors that could explain huge performance differences in a competition. Yet, some participants consistently outperform others, implying there is some underlying success factor.

In interviews and meet-ups, some Kagglers describe this success factor as "grit," some others as "trying everything," some others again as a "willingness to put everything you have into a competition." These may sound a bit obscure and magic. Instead, we call it **systematic experimentation**. In our opinion, the key to successful participation resides in the number of experiments you conduct and the way you run all of them. The more experiments you undertake, the more chances you will have to crack the problem better than other participants. This number certainly depends on a few factors, such as the time you have available, your computing resources (the faster the better, but as we previously mentioned, this is not such a strong differentiator *per se*), your team size, and their involvement in the task. This aligns with the commonly reported grit and engagement as keys for success.

However, these are not the only factors affecting the result. You have to take into account that the way you run your experiments also has an impact. *Fail fast and learn from it* is an important factor in a competition. Of course, you need to reflect carefully both when you fail and when you succeed in order to learn something from your experiences, or your competition will just turn into a random sequence of attempts in the hope of picking the right solution.

Therefore, *ceteris paribus*, having a proper **validation strategy** is the great discriminator between successful Kaggle competitors and those who just overfit the leaderboard and end up in lower-than-expected rankings after a competition.

Validation is the method you use to correctly evaluate the errors that your model produces and to measure how its performance improves or decreases based on your experiments.

Generally, the impact of choosing proper validation is too often overlooked in favor of more quantitative factors, such as having the latest, most powerful GPU or a larger team producing submissions.

Nevertheless, if you count only on the firepower of experiments and their results on the leaderboard, it will be like "throwing mud at the wall and hoping something will stick" (see http:// gregpark.io/blog/Kaggle-Psychopathy-Postmortem/). Sometimes such a strategy will work, but most often it won't, because you will miss important opportunities to experiment in the right direction, and you won't even be able to see the shining gem you managed to produce in the middle of all that mud. For instance, if you concentrate too much on trying your luck on the public leaderboard using a random, unsystematic strategy, even if you produce great solutions, you may end up not choosing your final submission correctly and missing the best scoring one on the private leaderboard.

Having a proper validation strategy can help you decide which of your models should be submitted for ranking on the private test set. Though the temptation to submit your top public leaderboard models may be high, *always consider your own validation scores*. For your final submissions, depending on the situation and whether or not you trust the leaderboard, choose your best model based on the leaderboard and your best based on your local validation results. If you don't trust the leaderboard (especially when the training sample is small or the examples are non-i.i.d.), submit models that have two of the best validation scores, picking two very different models or ensembles. In this way, you will reduce the risk of choosing solutions that won't perform on the private test set.

Having pointed out the importance of having a method of experimenting, what is left is all a matter of the practicalities of validation. In fact, when you model a solution, you take a series of interrelated decisions:

1. How to process your data
2. What model to apply
3. How to change the model's architecture (especially true for deep learning models)
4. How to set the model's hyperparameters
5. How to post-process the predictions

Even if the public leaderboard is perfectly correlated with the private one, the limited number of daily submissions (a limitation present in all competitions) prevents you from even scratching the surface of possible tests that you could do in all the aforementioned areas. Having a proper validation system tells you beforehand if what you are doing could work on the leaderboard.

Dmitry Larko

https://www.kaggle.com/dmitrylarko

Dmitry Larko is a Kaggle Competition Grandmaster and the chief data scientist at H2O.ai. He has over a decade of experience in ML and data science. He discovered Kaggle in December 2012 and participated in his first competition a few months later. He is a strong advocate of validation in Kaggle competitions, as he told us in his interview.

What's your favorite kind of competition and why? In terms of techniques and solving approaches, what is your specialty on Kaggle?

I have mostly participated in competitions for tabular datasets but also enjoy competitions for computer vision.

How do you approach a Kaggle competition? How different is this approach to what you do in your day-to-day work?

I always try to start simple and build a submission pipeline for smaller/simpler models first. A major step here is to create a proper validation scheme so you can validate your ideas in a robust way. Also, it is always a good idea to spend as much time as you can looking at the data and analyzing it.

In my day-to-day work, I am building an AutoML platform, so a lot of things I try on Kaggle end up being implemented as a part of this platform.

Tell us about a particularly challenging competition you entered, and what insights you used to tackle the task.

Nothing comes to my mind, and it doesn't matter, because what is technically challenging for me could be a piece of cake for somebody else. Technical challenges are not that important; what's important is to remember that a competition is somewhat like a marathon, not a sprint. Or you can see it as a marathon of sprints if you like. So, it is important not to get exhausted, sleep well, exercise, and take a walk in a park to regenerate your brain for new ideas. To win a Kaggle competition, you will need all your creativity and expertise and sometimes even a bit of luck.

Has Kaggle helped you in your career? If so, how?

I got my current job thanks to the fact I was a Kaggle Competition Grandmaster. For my current employer, this fact was evidence enough of my expertise in the field.

In your experience, what do inexperienced Kagglers often overlook? What do you know now that you wish you'd known when you first started?

Mostly they overlook the right validation scheme and follow the feedback from the public leaderboard. That ends badly in most cases, leading to something known as a "shake-up" on Kaggle.

Also, they rush to skip exploratory data analysis and build models right away, which leads to simplistic solutions and mediocre leaderboard scores.

What mistakes have you made in competitions in the past?

My main mistake is really the same that an inexperienced person will make – following the leaderboard score and not my internal validation. Every time I decided to do so, it cost me several places on the leaderboard.

Are there any particular tools or libraries that you would recommend using for data analysis or machine learning?

That would be the usual suspects. For tabular data: LightGBM, XGBoost, CatBoost; for deep learning: PyTorch, PyTorch-Lightning, timm; and Scikit-learn for everyone.

What's the most important thing someone should keep in mind or do when they're entering a competition?

Start simple, always validate; believe in your validation score and not the leaderboard score.

Bias and variance

A good validation system helps you with metrics that are more reliable than the error measures you get from your training set. In fact, metrics obtained on the training set are affected by the capacity and complexity of each model. You can think of the **capacity** of a model as its memory that it can use to learn from data.

Each model has a set of internal parameters that help the model to record the patterns taken from the data. Every model has its own skills for acquiring patterns, and some models will spot certain rules or associations whereas others will spot others. As a model extracts patterns from data, it records them in its "memory."

You also hear about the capacity or expressiveness of a model as a matter of **bias and variance**. In this case, the bias and variance of a model refer to the predictions, but the underlying principle is strictly related to the expressiveness of a model. Models can be reduced to mathematical functions that map an input (the observed data) to a result (the predictions). Some mathematical functions are more complex than others, in the number of internal parameters they have and in the ways they use them:

- If the mathematical function of a model is not complex or expressive enough to capture the complexity of the problem you are trying to solve, we talk of **bias**, because your predictions will be limited ("biased") by the limits of the model itself.
- If the mathematical function at the core of a model is too complex for the problem at hand, we have a **variance** problem, because the model will record more details and noise in the training data than needed and its predictions will be deeply influenced by them and become erratic.

Nowadays, given the advances in machine learning and the available computation resources, the problem is always due to variance, since deep neural networks and gradient boosting, the most commonly used solutions, often have a mathematical expressiveness that exceeds what most of the problems you will face need in order to be solved.

When all the useful patterns that a certain model can extract have been captured, if the model has not exhausted its capacity, it will then start memorizing data characteristics and signals that are unrelated to the prediction (usually referred to as **noise**). While the initially extracted patterns will help the model to generalize to a test dataset and predict more correctly, not everything that it learns specifically about the training set will help; instead, it may damage its performance. The process of learning elements of the training set that have no generalization value is commonly called **overfitting**.

The core purpose of validation is to explicitly define a score or loss value that separates the generalizable part of that value from that due to overfitting the training set characteristics.

This is the **validation loss**. You can see the situation visualized in the following figure of learning curves:

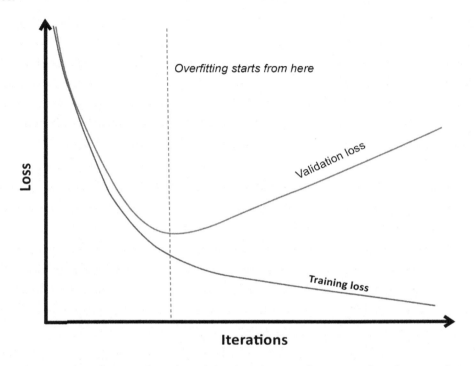

Figure 6.1: Learning more from the training data does not always mean learning to predict

If you graph the loss measure on the y-axis against some measure of learning effort of the model (this could be epochs for neural networks, or rounds for gradient boosting) on the x-axis, you will notice that learning always seems to happen on the training dataset, but this is not always true on other data.

The same thing happens even if you change the hyperparameters, process the data, or decide on a different model altogether. The curves will change shape, but you'll always have a sweet point where overfitting starts. That point can be different across models and between the various choices that you make in your modeling efforts. If you have properly computed the point when overfitting starts thanks to a correct validation strategy, your model's performance will surely correlate with the leaderboard results (both public and private), and your validation metrics will provide you with a proxy to evaluate your work without making any submissions.

You can hear about overfitting at various levels:

- At the level of the training data, when you use a model that is too complex for the problem
- At the level of the validation set itself, when you tune your model too much with respect to a specific validation set
- At the level of the public leaderboard, when your results are far from what you would expect from your training
- At the level of the private leaderboard, when in spite of the good results on the public leaderboard, your private scores will be disappointing

Though slightly different in meaning, they all equally imply that your model is not generalizable, as we have described in this section.

Trying different splitting strategies

As previously discussed, the validation loss is based on a data sample that is not part of the training set. It is an empirical measure that tells you how good your model is at predicting, and a more correct one than the score you get from your training, which will tell you mostly how much your model has memorized the training data patterns. Correctly choosing the data sample you use for validation constitutes your validation strategy.

To summarize the strategies for validating your model and measuring its performance correctly, you have a couple of choices:

- The first choice is to **work with a holdout system**, incurring the risk of not properly choosing a representative sample of the data or overfitting to your validation holdout.
- The second option is to **use a probabilistic approach** and rely on a series of samples to draw your conclusions on your models. Among the probabilistic approaches, you have cross-validation, **leave-one-out** (**LOO**), and bootstrap. Among the cross-validation strategies, there are different nuances depending on the sampling strategies you take based on the characteristic of your data (simple random sampling, stratified sampling, sampling by groups, time sampling).

What all these strategies have in common is that they are **sampling strategies**. It means that they help you to infer a general measure (the performance of your model) based on a small part of your data, randomly selected. Sampling is at the root of statistics and it is not an exact procedure because, based on your sampling method, your available data, and the randomness of picking up certain cases as part of your sample, you will experience a certain degree of error.

For instance, if you rely on a biased sample, your evaluation metric may be estimated incorrectly (over- or under-estimated). However, if properly designed and implemented, sampling strategies generally provide you with a good estimate of your general measure.

The other aspect that all these strategies have in common is that they are **partitions**, which divide cases in an exclusive way as either part of the training or part of the validation. In fact, as we discussed, since most models have a certain memorization capability, using the same cases in both training and validation leads to inflated estimates because it allows the model to demonstrate its memorization abilities; instead, we want it to be evaluated on its ability to derive patterns and functions that work on *unseen* examples.

The basic train-test split

The first strategy that we will analyze is the **train-test split**. In this strategy, you sample a portion of your training set (also known as the **holdout**) and you use it as a test set for all the models that you train using the remaining part of the data.

The great advantage of this strategy is that it is very simple: you pick up a part of your data and you check your work on that part. You usually split the data 80/20 in favor of the training partition. In Scikit-learn, it is implemented in the `train_test_split` function. We'll draw your attention to a couple of aspects of the method:

- When you have large amounts of data, you can expect that the test data you extract is similar to (representative of) the original distribution on the entire dataset. However, since the extraction process is based on randomness, you always have the chance of extracting a non-representative sample. In particular, the chance increases if the training sample you start from is small. Comparing the extracted holdout partition using **adversarial validation** (more about this in a few sections) can help you to make sure you are evaluating your efforts in a correct way.

- In addition, to ensure that your test sampling is representative, especially with regard to how the training data relates to the target variable, you can use **stratification**, which ensures that the proportions of certain features are respected in the sampled data. You can use the `stratify` parameter in the `train_test_split` function and provide an array containing the class distribution to preserve.

We have to remark that, even if you have a representative holdout available, sometimes a simple train-test split is not enough for ensuring a correct tracking of your efforts in a competition.

In fact, as you keep checking on this test set, you may drive your choices to some kind of adaptation overfitting (in other words, erroneously picking up the noise of the training set as signals), as happens when you frequently evaluate on the public leaderboard. For this reason, a probabilistic evaluation, though more computationally expensive, is more suited for a competition.

Probabilistic evaluation methods

Probabilistic evaluation of the performance of a machine learning model is based on the statistical properties of a sample from a distribution. By sampling, you create a smaller set of your original data that is expected to have the same characteristics. In addition, what is left untouched from the sampling constitutes a sample in itself, and it is also expected to have the same characteristics as the original data. By training and testing your model on this sampled data and repeating this procedure a large number of times, you are basically creating a statistical estimator measuring the performance of your model. Every sample may have some "error" in it; that is, it may not be fully representative of the true distribution of the original data. However, as you sample more, the mean of your estimators on these multiple samples will converge to the true mean of the measure you are estimating (this is an observed outcome that, in probability, is explained by a theorem called the *Law of Large Numbers*).

Probabilistic estimators naturally require more computations than a simple train-test split, but they offer more confidence that you are correctly estimating the right measure: the general performance of your model.

k-fold cross-validation

The most used probabilistic validation method is **k-fold cross-validation**, which is recognized as having the ability to correctly estimate the performance of your model on unseen test data drawn from the same distribution.

 This is clearly explained in the paper Bates, S., Hastie, T., and Tibshirani, R.; *Cross-validation: what does it estimate and how well does it do it?* arXiv preprint arXiv:2104.00673, 2021 (https://arxiv.org/pdf/2104.00673.pdf).

k-fold cross-validation can be successfully used to compare predictive models, as well as when selecting the hyperparameters for your model that will perform the best on the test set.

There are quite a few different variations of k-fold cross-validation, but the simplest one, which is implemented in the KFold function in Scikit-learn, is based on the splitting of your available training data into k partitions. After that, for k iterations, one of the k partitions is taken as a test set while the others are used for the training of the model.

The k validation scores are then averaged and that averaged score value is the k-fold validation score, which will tell you the estimated average model performance on any unseen data. The standard deviation of the scores will inform you about the uncertainty of the estimate. *Figure 6.2* demonstrates how 5-fold cross-validation is structured:

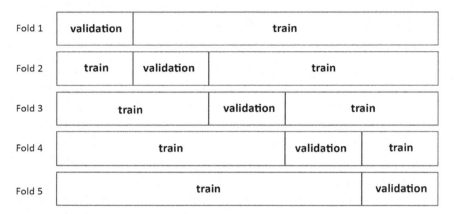

Figure 6.2: How a 5-fold validation scheme is structured

One important aspect of the k-fold cross-validation score you have to keep in mind is that it estimates the average score of a model trained on the same quantity of data as k - *1* folds. If, afterward, you train your model on all your data, the previous validation estimate no longer holds. As k approaches the number n of examples, you have an increasingly correct estimate of the model derived on the full training set, yet, due to the growing correlation between the estimates you obtain from each fold, you will lose all the probabilistic estimates of the validation. In this case, you'll end up having a number showing you the performance of your model on your training data (which is still a useful estimate for comparison reasons, but it won't help you in correctly estimating the generalization power of your model).

When you reach $k = n$, you have the LOO validation method, which is useful when you have a few cases available. The method is mostly an unbiased fitting measure since it uses almost all the available data for training and just one example for testing. Yet it is not a good estimate of the expected performance on unseen data. Its repeated tests over the whole dataset are highly correlated with each other and the resulting LOO metric represents more the performance of the model on the dataset itself than the performance the model would have on unknown data.

The correct k number of partitions to choose is decided based on a few aspects relative to the data you have available:

- The smaller the k (the minimum is 2), the smaller each fold will be, and consequently, the more bias in learning there will be for a model trained on k - *1* folds: your model validated on a smaller k will be less well-performing with respect to a model trained on a larger k.

- The higher the k, the more the data, yet the more correlated your validation estimates: you will lose the interesting properties of k-fold cross-validation in estimating the performance on unseen data.

Commonly, k is set to 5, 7, or 10, more seldom to 20 folds. We usually regard k = 5 or k = 10 as a good choice for a competition, with the latter using more data for each training (90% of the available data), and hence being more suitable for figuring out the performance of your model when you retrain on the full dataset.

When deciding upon what k to choose for a specific dataset in a competition, we find it useful to reflect on two perspectives.

Firstly, the choice of the number of folds should reflect your goals:

- If your purpose is performance estimation, you need models with low bias estimates (which means no systematic distortion of estimates). You can achieve this by using a higher number of folds, usually between 10 and 20.

- If your aim is parameter tuning, you need a mix of bias and variance, so it is advisable to use a medium number of folds, usually between 5 and 7.

- Finally, if your purpose is just to apply variable selection and simplify your dataset, you need models with low variance estimates (or you will have disagreement). Hence, a lower number of folds will suffice, usually between 3 and 5.

When the size of the available data is quite large, you can safely stay on the lower side of the suggested bands.

Secondly, if you are just aiming for performance estimation, consider that the more folds you use, the fewer cases you will have in your validation set, so the more the estimates of each fold will be correlated. Beyond a certain point, increasing k renders your cross-validation estimates less predictive of unseen test sets and more representative of an estimate of how well-performing your model is on your training set. This also means that, with more folds, you can get the perfect out-of-fold prediction for stacking purposes, as we will explain in detail in *Chapter 9, Ensembling with Blending and Stacking Solutions*.

In Kaggle competitions, *k*-fold cross-validation is often applied not only for validating your solution approach and figuring out the performance of your model, but to produce your prediction. When you cross-validate, you are subsampling, and averaging the results of multiple models built on subsamples of the data is an effective strategy for fighting against variance, and often more effective than training on all the data available (we will discuss this more in *Chapter 9*). Hence, many Kaggle competitors use the models built during cross-validation to provide a series of predictions on the test set that, averaged, will provide them with the solution.

k-fold variations

Since it is based on random sampling, *k*-fold can provide unsuitable splits when:

- You have to preserve the proportion of small classes, both at a target level and at the level of features. This is typical when your target is highly imbalanced. Typical examples are spam datasets (because spam is a small fraction of the normal email volume) or any credit risk dataset where you have to predict the not-so-frequent event of a defaulted loan.

- You have to preserve the distribution of a numeric variable, both at a target level and at the level of features. This is typical of regression problems where the distribution is quite skewed or you have heavy, long tails. A common example is house price prediction, where you have a consistent small portion of houses on sale that will cost much more than the average house.

- Your cases are non-i.i.d, in particular when dealing with time series forecasting.

In the first two scenarios, the solution is the **stratified *k*-fold**, where the sampling is done in a controlled way that preserves the distribution you want to preserve. If you need to preserve the distribution of a single class, you can use StratifiedKFold from Scikit-learn, using a stratification variable, usually your target variable but also any other feature whose distribution you need to preserve. The function will produce a set of indexes that will help you to partition your data accordingly. You can also obtain the same result with a numeric variable, after having discretized it, using pandas.cut or Scikit-learn's KBinsDiscretizer.

It is a bit more complicated when you have to stratify based on multiple variables or overlapping labels, such as in multi-label classification.

You can find a solution in the **Scikit-multilearn** package (http://scikit.ml/), in particular, the IterativeStratification command that helps you to control the order (the number of combined proportions of multiple variables) that you want to preserve (http://scikit.ml/api/skmultilearn.model_selection.iterative_stratification.html). It implements the algorithm explained by the following papers:

- Sechidis, K., Tsoumakas, G., and Vlahavas, I. (2011). *On the stratification of multi-label data. Machine Learning and Knowledge Discovery in Databases, 145-158.* http://lpis.csd.auth.gr/publications/sechidis-ecmlpkdd-2011.pdf

- Szymański, P. and Kajdanowicz, T.; *Proceedings of the First International Workshop on Learning with Imbalanced Domains: Theory and Applications,* PMLR 74:22-35, 2017. http://proceedings.mlr.press/v74/szyma%C5%84ski17a.html

You can actually make good use of stratification even when your problem is not a classification, but a regression. Using stratification in regression problems helps your regressor to fit during cross-validation on a similar distribution of the target (or of the predictors) to the one found in the entire sample. In these cases, in order to have StratifiedKFold working correctly, you have to use a discrete proxy for your target instead of your continuous target.

The first, simplest way of achieving this is to use the pandas cut function and divide your target into a large enough number of bins, such as 10 or 20:

```
import pandas as pd
y_proxy = pd.cut(y_train, bins=10, labels=False)
```

In order to determine the number of bins to be used, *Abhishek Thakur* prefers to use **Sturges' rule** based on the number of examples available, and provide that number to the pandas cut function (see https://www.kaggle.com/abhishek/step-1-create-folds):

```
import numpy as np
bins = int(np.floor(1 + np.log2(len(X_train))))
```

An alternative approach is to focus on the distributions of the features in the training set and aim to reproduce them. This requires the use of **cluster analysis** (an unsupervised approach) on the features of the training set, thus excluding the target variable and any identifiers, and then using the predicted clusters as strata. You can see an example in this Notebook (https://www.kaggle.com/lucamassaron/are-you-doing-cross-validation-the-best-way), where first a PCA (principal component analysis) is performed to remove correlations, and then a *k*-means cluster analysis is performed. You can decide on the number of clusters to use by running empirical tests.

Proceeding with our discussion of the cases where *k*-fold can provide unsuitable splits, things get tricky in the third scenario, when you have non-i.i.d. data, such as in the case of some grouping happening among examples. The problem with non-i.i.d. examples is that the features and target are correlated between the examples (hence it is easier to predict all the examples if you know just one example among them). In fact, if you happen to have the same group divided between training and testing, your model may learn to distinguish the groups and not the target itself, producing a good validation score but very bad results on the leaderboard. The solution here is to use GroupKFold: by providing a grouping variable, you will have the assurance that each group will be placed either in the training folds or in the validation ones, but never split between the two.

 Discovering groupings in the data that render your data non-i.i.d. is actually not an easy task to accomplish. Unless stated by the competition problem, you will have to rely on your ability to investigate the data (using unsupervised learning techniques, such as cluster analysis) and the domain of the problem. For instance, if your data is about mobile telephone usage, you may realize that some examples are from the same user by noticing sequences of similar values in the features.

Time series analysis presents the same problem, and since data is non-i.i.d., you cannot validate by random sampling because you will mix different time frames and later time frames could bear traces of the previous ones (a characteristic called **auto-correlation** in statistics). In the most basic approach to validation in time series, you can use a training and validation split based on time, as illustrated by *Figure 6.3*:

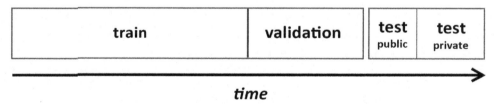

Figure 6.3: Training and validation splits are based on time

Your validation capabilities will be limited, however, since your validation will be anchored to a specific time. For a more complex approach, you can use time split validation, TimeSeriesSplit, as provided by the Scikit-learn package (sklearn.model_selection.TimeSeriesSplit). TimeSeriesSplit can help you set the timeframe of your training and testing portions of the time series.

In the case of the training timeframe, the `TimeSeriesSplit` function can help you to set your training data so it involves all the past data before the test timeframe, or limit it to a fixed period lookback (for instance, always using the data from three months before the test timeframe for training).

In *Figure 6.4*, you can see the structure of a time-based validation strategy involving a growing training set and a moving validation set:

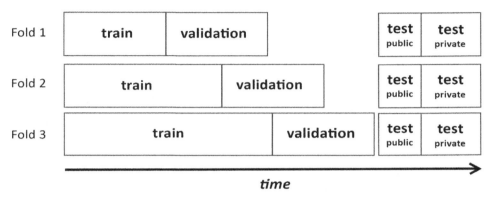

Figure 6.4: The training set is growing over time

In *Figure 6.5*, you can instead see how the strategy changes if you stipulate that the training set has a fixed lookback:

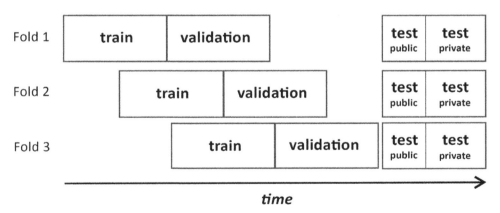

Figure 6.5: Training and validation splits are moving over time

In our experience, going by a fixed lookback helps to provide a fairer evaluation of time series models since you are always counting on the same training set size.

By instead using a growing training set size over time, you confuse the effects of your model performance across time slices with the decreasing bias in your model (since more examples mean less bias).

Finally, remember that `TimeSeriesSplit` can be set to keep a pre-defined gap between your training and test time. This is extremely useful when you are told that the test set is a certain amount of time in the future (for instance, a month after the training data) and you want to test if your model is robust enough to predict that far into the future.

Nested cross-validation

At this point, it is important to introduce **nested cross-validation**. Up to now, we have only discussed testing models with respect to their final performance, but often you also need to test their intermediate performance when tuning their hyperparameters. In fact, you cannot test how certain model parameters work on your test set and then use the same data in order to evaluate the final performance. Since you have specifically found the best parameters that work on the test set, your evaluation measure on the same test set will be too optimistic; on a different test set, you will probably not obtain the exact same result. In this case, you have to distinguish between a **validation set**, which is used to evaluate the performance of various models and hyperparameters, and a **test set**, which will help you to estimate the final performance of the model.

If you are using a test-train split, this is achieved by splitting the test part into two new parts. The usual split is 70/20/10 for training, validation, and testing, respectively (but you can decide differently). If you are using cross-validation, you need nested cross-validation; that is, you do cross-validation based on the split of another cross-validation. Essentially, you run your usual cross-validation, but when you have to evaluate different models or different parameters, you run cross-validation based on the fold split.

The example in *Figure 6.6* demonstrates this internal and external cross-validation structure. Within the external part, you determine the portion of the data used to test your evaluation metric. Within the internal part, which is fed by the training data from the external part, you arrange training/validation splits in order to evaluate and optimize specific model choices, such as deciding which model or hyperparameter values to pick:

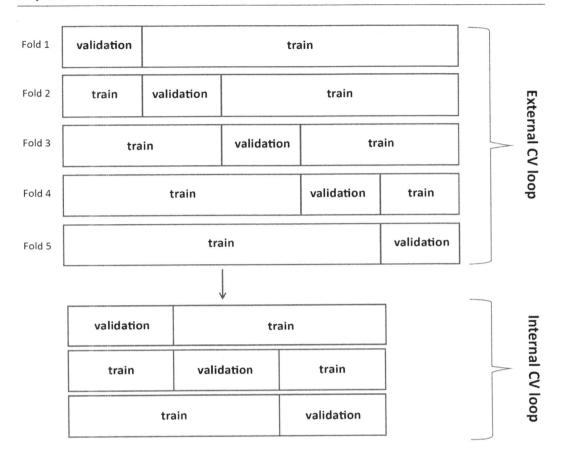

Figure 6.6: How nested cross-validation is structured in an external and an internal loop

This approach has the advantage of making your test and parameter search fully reliable, but in doing so you incur a couple of problems:

- A reduced training set, since you first split by cross-validation, and then you split again
- More importantly, it requires a huge amount of model building: if you run two nested 10-fold cross-validations, you'll need to run 100 models

Especially for this last reason, some Kagglers tend to ignore nested cross-validation and risk some adaptive fitting by using the same cross-validation for both model/parameter search and performance evaluation, or using a fixed test sample for the final evaluation. In our experience, this approach can work as well, though it may result in overestimating model performance and overfitting if you are generating out-of-fold predictions to be used for successive modeling (something we are going to discuss in the next section). We always suggest you try the most suitable methodology for testing your models. If your aim is to correctly estimate your model's performance and reuse its predictions in other models, remember that using nested cross-validation, whenever possible, can provide you with a less overfitting solution and could make the difference in certain competitions.

Producing out-of-fold predictions (OOF)

An interesting application of cross-validation, besides estimating your evaluation metric performance, is producing test predictions and out-of-fold predictions. In fact, as you train on portions of your training data and predict on the remaining ones, you can:

- **Predict on the test set**: The average of all the predictions is often more effective than re-training the same model on all the data: this is an ensembling technique related to blending, which will be dealt with in *Chapter 9, Ensembling with Blending and Stacking Solutions*.
- **Predict on the validation set**: In the end, you will have predictions for the entire training set and can re-order them in the same order as the original training data. These predictions are commonly referred to as **out-of-fold** (**OOF**) **predictions** and they can be extremely useful.

The first use of OOF predictions is to estimate your performance since you can compute your evaluation metric directly on the OOF predictions. The performance obtained is different from the cross-validated estimates (based on sampling); it doesn't have the same probabilistic characteristics, so it is not a valid way to measure generalization performance, but it can inform you about the performance of your model on the specific set you are training on.

A second use is to produce a plot and visualize the predictions against the ground truth values or against other predictions obtained from different models. This will help you in understanding how each model works and if their predictions are correlated.

The last use is to create meta-features or meta-predictors. This will also be fully explored in *Chapter 9*, but it is important to remark on now, as OOF predictions are a byproduct of cross-validation and they work because, during cross-validation, your model is always predicting on examples that it has not seen during training time.

Since every prediction in your OOF predictions has been generated by a model trained on different data, these predictions are unbiased and you can use them without any fear of overfitting (though there are some caveats that will be discussed in the next chapter).

Generating OOF predictions can be done in two ways:

- By coding a procedure that stores the validation predictions into a prediction vector, taking care to arrange them in the same index position as the examples in the training data
- By using the Scikit-learn function `cross_val_predict`, which will automatically generate the OOF predictions for you

We will be seeing this second technique in action when we look at adversarial validation later in this chapter.

Subsampling

There are other validation strategies aside from k-fold cross-validation, but they do not have the same generalization properties. We have already discussed LOO, which is the case when $k = n$ (where n is the number of examples). Another choice is **subsampling**. Subsampling is similar to k-fold, but you do not have fixed folds; you use as many as you think are necessary (in other words, take an educated guess). You repetitively subsample your data, each time using the data that you sampled as training data and the data that has been left unsampled for your validation. By averaging the evaluation metrics of all the subsamples, you will get a validation estimate of the performances of your model.

Since you are systematically testing all your examples, as in k-fold, you actually need quite a lot of trials to have a good chance of testing all of them. For the same reason, some cases may be tested more than others if you do not apply enough subsamples. You can run this sort of validation using `ShuffleSplit` from Scikit-learn.

The bootstrap

Finally, another option is to try the **bootstrap**, which has been devised in statistics to conclude the error distribution of an estimate; for the same reasons, it can be used for performance estimation. The bootstrap requires you to draw a sample, *with replacement*, that is the same size as the available data.

At this point, you can use the bootstrap in two different ways:

- As in statistics, you can bootstrap multiple times, train your model on the samples, and compute your evaluation metric on the training data itself. The average of the bootstraps will provide your final evaluation.
- Otherwise, as in subsampling, you can use the bootstrapped sample for your training and what is left not sampled from the data as your test set.

In our experience, the first method of calculating the evaluation metric on the bootstrapped training data, often used in statistics for linear models in order to estimate the value of the model's coefficients and their error distributions, is much less useful in machine learning. This is because many machine learning algorithms tend to overfit the training data, hence you can never have a valid metric evaluation on your training data, even if you bootstrap it. For this reason, Efron and Tibshirani (see *Efron, B. and Tibshirani, R. Improvements on cross-validation: the 632+ bootstrap method.* Journal of the American Statistical Association 92.438 (1997): 548-560.) proposed **the 632+ estimator** as a final validation metric.

At first, they proposed a simple version, called the 632 bootstrap:

$$Err_{.632} = 0.368 * err_{fit} + 0.632 * err_{bootstrap}$$

In this formula, given your evaluation metric *err*, err_{fit} is your metric computed on the training data and $err_{bootstrap}$ is the metric computed on the bootstrapped data. However, in the case of an overfitted training model, err_{fit} would tend to zero, rendering the estimator not very useful. Therefore, they developed a second version of the 632+ bootstrap:

$$Err_{.632} + (1 - w) * err_{fit} + w * err_{bootstrap}$$

Where *w* is:

$$w = \frac{0.632}{1 - 0.632R}$$

$$R = \frac{err_{bootstrap} - err_{fit}}{\gamma - err_{fit}}$$

Here you have a new parameter, γ, which is the **no-information error rate**, estimated by evaluating the prediction model on all possible combinations of targets and predictors. Calculating γ is indeed intractable, as discussed by the developers of Scikit-learn (`https://github.com/scikit-learn/scikit-learn/issues/9153`).

Given the limits and intractability of using the bootstrap as in classical statistics for machine learning applications, you can instead use the second method, getting your evaluation from the examples left not sampled by the bootstrap.

In this form, the bootstrap is an alternative to cross-validation, but as with subsampling, it requires building many more models and testing them than for cross-validation. However, it makes sense to know about such alternatives in case your cross-validation is showing too high a variance in the evaluation metric and you need more intensive checking through testing and re-testing.

Previously, this method has been implemented in Scikit-learn (`https://github.com/scikit-learn/scikit-learn/blob/0.16.X/sklearn/cross_validation.py#L613`) but was then removed. Since you cannot find the bootstrap anymore on Scikit-learn and it bootstrapped even the test data, you can use our own implementation. Here is our example:

```
import random
def Bootstrap(n, n_iter=3, random_state=None):
    """

    Random sampling with replacement cross-validation generator.
    For each iter a sample bootstrap of the indexes [0, n) is
    generated and the function returns the obtained sample
    and a list of all the excluded indexes.
    """

    if random_state:
        random.seed(random_state)
    for j in range(n_iter):
        bs = [random.randint(0, n-1) for i in range(n)]
        out_bs = list({i for i in range(n)} - set(bs))
        yield bs, out_bs
```

In conclusion, the bootstrap is indeed an alternative to cross-validation. It is certainly more widely used in statistics and finance. In machine learning, the golden rule is to use the k-fold cross-validation approach. However, we suggest not forgetting about the bootstrap in all those situations where, due to outliers or a few examples that are too heterogeneous, you have a large standard error of the evaluation metric in cross-validation. In these cases, the bootstrap will prove much more useful in validating your models.

Ryan Chesler

https://www.kaggle.com/ryches

Our second interview of the chapter is with Ryan Chesler, a Discussions Grandmaster and Notebooks and Competitions Master. He is a Data Scientist at H2O.ai and one of the organizers of the San Diego Machine Learning group on Meetup (https://www.meetup.com/San-Diego-Machine-Learning/). The importance of validation came up in a few of his answers.

What's your favourite kind of competition and why? In terms of techniques and solving approaches, what is your specialty on Kaggle?

I tend to dabble in all kinds of competitions. It is more interesting to sample varied problems than specialize in a specific niche like computer vision or natural language processing. The ones I find most interesting are the ones where there are deep insights that can be derived from the data and error of predictions. For me, error analysis is one of the most illuminating processes; understanding where the model is failing and trying to find some way to improve the model or input data representation to address the weakness.

How do you approach a Kaggle competition? How different is this approach to what you do in your day-to-day work?

My approach is similar in both cases. Many people seem to favor exploratory data analysis before any modeling efforts, but I find that the process of preparing the data for modeling is usually sufficient. My typical approach is to manually view the data and make some preliminary decisions about how I think I can best model the data and different options to explore. After this, I build the model and evaluate performance, and then focus on analysing errors and reason about the next modeling steps based on where I see the model making errors.

Has Kaggle helped you in your career? If so, how?

Yes, it helped me get my current job. I work at H2O and they greatly value Kaggle achievements. My previous job also liked that I performed well in competitions.

You are also the organizer of a meetup in San Diego with over two thousand participants. Is this related to your experience with Kaggle?

Yes, it is absolutely related. I started from very little knowledge and tried out a Kaggle competition without much success at first. I went to a local meetup and found people to team up with and learn from. At the time, I got to work with people of a much higher skill level than me and we did really well in a competition, 3rd/4500+ teams.

After this, the group stopped being as consistent and I wanted to keep the community going, so I made my own group and started organizing my own events. I've been doing that for almost 4 years and I get to be on the opposite side of the table teaching people and helping them get started. We originally just focused on Kaggle competitions and trying to form teams, but have slowly started branching off to doing book clubs and lectures on various topics of interest. I attribute a lot of my success to having this dedicated weekly time to study and think about machine learning.

In your experience, what do inexperienced Kagglers often overlook? What do you know now that you wish you'd known when you first started?

In my experience, a lot of people overstate the importance of bias-variance trade-off and overfitting. This is something I have seen people consistently worry about too much. The focus should not be making training and validation performance close, but make validation performance as good as possible.

What mistakes have you made in competitions in the past?

My consistent mistake is not exploring enough. Sometimes I have ideas that I discount too early and turn out to be important for improving performance. Very often I can get close to competitive performance on the first try, but iterating and continuing to improve as I try new things takes a slightly different skill that I am still working on mastering.

Are there any particular tools or libraries that you would recommend using for data analysis or machine learning?

I use a lot of the standard tools: XGBoost, LightGBM, Pytorch, TensorFlow, Scikit-learn. I don't have any strong affinity for a specific tool or library, just whatever is relevant to the problem.

What's the most important thing someone should keep in mind or do when they're entering a competition?

I think the most important thing people have to keep in mind is good validation. Very often I see people fooling themselves thinking their performance is improving but then submitting to the leaderboard and realizing it didn't actually go how they expected. It is an important skill to understand how to match assumptions with your new unseen data and build a model that is robust to new conditions.

Tuning your model validation system

At this point, you should have a complete overview of all possible validation strategies. When you approach a competition, you devise your validation strategy and you implement it. Then, you test if the strategy you have chosen is correct.

As a golden rule, be guided in devising your validation strategy by the idea that you have to replicate the same approach used by the organizers of the competition to split the data into training, private, and public test sets. Ask yourself how the organizers have arranged those splits. Did they draw a random sample? Did they try to preserve some specific distribution in the data? Are the test sets actually drawn from the same distribution as the training data?

These are not the questions you would ask yourself in a real-world project. Contrary to a real-world project where you have to generalize at all costs, a competition has a much narrower focus on having a model that performs on the given test set (especially the private one). If you focus on this idea from the beginning, you will have more of a chance of finding out the best validation strategy, which will help you rank more highly in the competition.

Since this is a trial-and-error process, as you try to find the best validation strategy for the competition, you can systematically apply the following two consistency checks in order to figure out if you are on the right path:

1. First, you have to check if your local tests are consistent, that is, that the single cross-validation fold errors are not so different from each other or, when you opt for a simple train-test split, that the same results are reproducible using different train-test splits.

2. Then, you have to check if your local validation error is consistent with the results on the public leaderboard.

If you're failing the first check, you have a few options depending on the following possible origins of the problem:

*   You don't have much training data
*   The data is too diverse and every training partition is very different from every other (for instance, if you have too many **high cardinality** features, that is, features with too many levels – like zip codes – or if you have multivariate outliers)

In both cases, the point is that you lack data with respect to the model you want to implement. Even when the problem just appears to be that the data is too diverse, plotting learning curves will make it evident to you that your model needs more data.

In this case, unless you find out that moving to a simpler algorithm works on the evaluation metric (in which case trading variance for bias may worsen your model's performance, but not always), your best choice is to use an extensive validation approach. This can be implemented by:

- Using larger k values (thus approaching LOO where $k = n$). Your validation results will be less about the capability of your model to perform on unseen data, but by using larger training portions, you will have the advantage of more stable evaluations.
- Averaging the results of multiple k-fold validations (based on different data partitions picked by different random seed initializations).
- Using repetitive bootstrapping.

Keep in mind that when you find unstable local validation results, you won't be the only one to suffer from the problem. Usually, this is a common problem due to the data's origin and characteristics. By keeping tuned in to the discussion forums, you may get hints at possible solutions. For instance, a good solution for high cardinality features is target encoding; stratification can help with outliers; and so on.

The situation is different when you've passed the first check but failed the second; your local cross-validation is consistent but you find that it doesn't hold on the leaderboard. In order to realize this problem exists, you have to keep diligent note of all your experiments, validation test types, random seeds used, and leaderboard results if you submitted the resulting predictions. In this way, you can draw a simple scatterplot and try fitting a linear regression or, even simpler, compute a correlation between your local results and the associated public leaderboard scores. It costs some time and patience to annotate and analyze all of these, but it is the most important meta-analysis of your competition performances that you can keep track of.

When the mismatch is because your validation score is systematically lower or higher than the leaderboard score, you actually have a strong signal that something is missing from your validation strategy, but this problem does not prevent you from improving your model. In fact, you can keep on working on your model and expect improvements to be reflected on the leaderboard, though not in a proportional way. However, systematic differences are always a red flag, implying something is different between what you are doing and what the organizers have arranged for testing the model.

An even worse scenario occurs when your local cross-validation scores do not correlate at all with the leaderboard feedback. This is really a red flag. When you realize this is the case, you should immediately run a series of tests and investigations in order to figure out why, because, regardless of whether it is a common problem or not, the situation poses a serious threat to your final rankings. There are a few possibilities in such a scenario:

- You figure out that the test set is drawn from a different distribution to the training set. The adversarial validation test (that we will discuss in the next section) is the method that can enlighten you in such a situation.

- The data is non-i.i.d. but this is not explicit. For instance, in *The Nature Conservancy Fisheries Monitoring* competition (`https://www.kaggle.com/c/the-nature-conservancy-fisheries-monitoring`), images in the training set were taken from similar situations (fishing boats). You had to figure out by yourself how to arrange them in order to avoid the model learning to identify the target rather than the context of the images (see, for instance, this work by *Anokas*: `https://www.kaggle.com/anokas/finding-boatids`).

- The multivariate distribution of the features is the same, but some groups are distributed differently in the test set. If you can figure out the differences, you can set your training set and your validation accordingly and gain an edge. You need to probe the public leaderboard to work this out.

- The test data is drifted or trended, which is usually the case in time series predictions. Again, you need to probe the public leaderboard to get some insight about some possible post-processing that could help your score, for instance, applying a multiplier to your predictions, thus mimicking a decreasing or increasing trend in the test data.

As we've discussed before, probing the leaderboard is the act of making specifically devised submissions in order to get insights about the composition of the public test set. It works particularly well if the private test set is similar to the public one. There are no general methods for probing, so you have to devise a probing methodology according to the type of competition and problem.

For instance, in the paper *Climbing the Kaggle Leaderboard by Exploiting the Log-Loss Oracle* (`https://export.arxiv.org/pdf/1707.01825`), Jacob explains how to get fourth position in a competition without even downloading the training data.

With regard to regression problems, in the recent *30 Days of ML* organized by Kaggle, *Hung Khoi* explained how probing the leaderboard helped him to understand the differences in the mean and standard deviation of the target column between the training dataset and the public test data (see: `https://www.kaggle.com/c/30-days-of-ml/discussion/269541`).

He used the following equation:

$$RMSE^2 = MSE = variance + (mean - guessed_{value})^2$$

Essentially, you need just two submissions to solve for the mean and variance of the test target, since there are two unknown terms – variance and mean.

You can also get some other ideas about leaderboard probing from *Chris Deotte* (`https://www.kaggle.com/cdeotte`) from this post, `https://www.kaggle.com/cdeotte/lb-probing-strategies-0-890-2nd-place`, relevant to the *Don't Overfit II competition* (`https://www.kaggle.com/c/dont-overfit-ii`).

 If you want to get a feeling about how probing information from the leaderboard is a double-edged sword, you can read about how *Zahar Chikishev* managed to probe information from the *LANL Earthquake Prediction* competition, ending up in 87th place in the private leaderboard after leading in the public one: `https://towardsdatascience.com/how-to-lb-probe-on-kaggle-c0aa21458bfe`

Using adversarial validation

As we have discussed, cross-validation allows you to test your model's ability to generalize to unseen datasets coming from the same distribution as your training data. Hopefully, since in a Kaggle competition you are asked to create a model that can predict on the public and private datasets, you should expect that such test data is from the same distribution as the training data. In reality, this is not always the case.

Even if you do not overfit to the test data because you have based your decision not only on the leaderboard results but also considered your cross-validation, you may still be surprised by the results. This could happen in the event that the test set is even slightly different from the training set on which you have based your model. In fact, the target probability and its distribution, as well as how the predictive variables relate to it, inform your model during training about certain expectations that cannot be satisfied if the test data is different from the training data.

Hence, it is not enough to avoid overfitting to the leaderboard as we have discussed up to now, but, in the first place, it is also advisable to find out if your test data is comparable to the training data. Then, if they differ, you have to figure out if there is any chance that you can mitigate the different distributions between training and test data and build a model that performs on that test set.

Adversarial validation has been developed just for this purpose. It is a technique allowing you to easily estimate the degree of difference between your training and test data. This technique was long rumored among Kaggle participants and transmitted from team to team until it emerged publicly thanks to a post by *Zygmunt Zając* (`https://www.kaggle.com/zygmunt`) on his FastML blog.

The idea is simple: take your training data, remove the target, assemble your training data together with your test data, and create a new binary classification target where the positive label is assigned to the test data. At this point, run a machine learning classifier and evaluate for the ROC-AUC evaluation metric (we discussed this metric in the previous chapter on *Detailing Competition Tasks and Metrics*).

If your ROC-AUC is around 0.5, it means that the training and test data are not easily distinguishable and are apparently from the same distribution. ROC-AUC values higher than 0.5 and nearing 1.0 signal that it is easy for the algorithm to figure out what is from the training set and what is from the test set: in such a case, don't expect to be able to easily generalize to the test set because it clearly comes from a different distribution.

> You can find an example Notebook written for the *Sberbank Russian Housing Market* competition (`https://www.kaggle.com/c/sberbank-russian-housing-market`) that demonstrates a practical example of adversarial validation and its usage in a competition here: `https://www.kaggle.com/konradb/adversarial-validation-and-other-scary-terms`.

Since your data may be of different types (numeric or string labels) and you may have missing cases, you'll need some data processing before being able to successfully run the classifier. Our suggestion is to use the random forest classifier because:

- It doesn't output true probabilities but its results are intended as simply ordinal, which is a perfect fit for an ROC-AUC score.

- The random forest is a flexible algorithm based on decision trees that can do feature selection by itself and operate on different types of features without any pre-processing, while rendering all the data numeric. It is also quite robust to overfitting and you don't have to think too much about fixing its hyperparameters.

- You don't need much data processing because of its tree-based nature. For missing data, you can simply replace the values with an improbable negative value such as -999, and you can deal with string variables by converting their strings into numbers (for instance, using the Scikit-learn label encoder, `sklearn.preprocessing.LabelEncoder`). As a solution, it performs less well than one-hot encoding, but it is very speedy and it will work properly for the problem.

Although building a classification model is the most direct way to adversarially validate your test set, you can also use other approaches. One approach is to map both training and test data into a lower-dimensional space, as in this post (`https://www.kaggle.com/nanomathias/distribution-of-test-vs-training-data`) by *NanoMathias* (`https://www.kaggle.com/nanomathias`). Although requiring more tuning work, such an approach based on t-SNE and PCA has the great advantage of being graphically representable in an appealing and understandable way.

Don't forget that our brains are more adept at spotting patterns in visual representations than numeric ones (for an articulate discussion about our visual abilities, see `https://onlinelibrary.wiley.com/doi/full/10.1002/qua.24480`).

PCA and t-SNE are not the only tools that can help you to reduce the dimensionality of your data and allow you to visualize it. UMAP (`https://github.com/lmcinnes/umap`) can often provide a faster low dimensionality solution with clear and distinct data clusters. Variational auto-encoders (discussed in *Chapter 7, Modeling for Tabular Competitions*) can instead deal with non-linear dimensionality reduction and offer a more useful representation than PCA; they are more complicated to set up and tune, however.

Example implementation

While you can find examples of adversarial validation in the original article by Zygmunt and the Notebook we linked, we have created a fresh example for you, based on the Playground competition *Tabular Playground Series – Jan 2021* (`https://www.kaggle.com/c/tabular-playground-series-jan-2021`).

You start by importing some Python packages and getting the training and test data from the competition:

```
import numpy as np
import pandas as pd
from sklearn.ensemble import RandomForestClassifier
```

```
from sklearn.model_selection import cross_val_predict
from sklearn.metrics import roc_auc_score


train = pd.read_csv("../input/tabular-playground-series-jan-2021/train.csv")
test = pd.read_csv("../input/tabular-playground-series-jan-2021/test.csv")
```

Data preparation is short and to the point. Since all features are numeric, you won't need any label encoding, but you do have to fill any missing values with a negative number (-1 usually works fine), and drop the target and also any identifiers; when the identifier is progressive, the adversarial validation may return a high ROC-AUC score:

```
train = train.fillna(-1).drop(["id", "target"], axis=1)
test = test.fillna(-1).drop(["id", axis=1])
X = train.append(test)
y = [0] * len(train) + [1] * len(test)
```

At this point, you just need to generate `RandomForestClassifier` predictions for your data using the `cross_val_predict` function, which automatically creates a cross-validation scheme and stores the predictions on the validation fold:

```
model = RandomForestClassifier()
cv_preds = cross_val_predict(model, X, y, cv=5, n_jobs=-1,
method='predict_proba')
```

As a result, you obtain predictions that are unbiased (they are not overfit as you did not predict on what you trained) and that can be used for error estimation. Please note that `cross_val_predict` won't fit your instantiated model, so you won't get any information from it, such as what the important features used by the model are. If you need such information, you just need to fit it first by calling `model.fit(X, y)`.

Finally, you can query the ROC-AUC score for your predictions:

```
print(roc_auc_score(y_true=y, y_score=cv_preds[:,1]))
```

You should obtain a value of around 0.49-0.50 (`cross_val_predict` won't be deterministic unless you use cross-validation with a fixed `random_seed`). This means that you cannot easily distinguish training from test data. Hence, they come from the same distribution.

Handling different distributions of training and test data

ROC-AUC scores of 0.8 or more would alert you that the test set is peculiar and quite distinguishable from the training data. In these cases, what can you do? You actually have a few strategies at hand:

- Suppression
- Training on cases most similar to the test set
- Validating by mimicking the test set

With **suppression,** you remove the variables that most influence the result in the adversarial test set until the distributions are the same again. To do so, you require an iterative approach. This time, you fit your model to all your data, and then you check the importance measures (provided, for instance, by the feature_importances_ method in the Scikit-learn RandomForest classifier) and the ROC-AUC fit score. At this point, you remove the most important variable for the model from your data and run everything again. You repeat this cycle where you train, measure the ROC-AUC fit, and drop the most important variable from your data until the fitted ROC-AUC score decreases to around 0.5.

The only problem with this method is that you may actually be forced to remove the majority of important variables from your data, and any model you then build on such variable censored data won't be able to predict sufficiently correctly due to the lack of informative features.

When you **train on the examples most similar to the test set,** you instead take a different approach, focusing not on the *variables* but on the *samples* you are using for training. In this case, you pick up from the training set only the samples that fit the test distribution. Any trained model then suits the testing distribution (but it won't be generalizable to anything else), which should allow you to test the best on the competition problem. The limitation of this approach is that you are cutting down the size of your dataset and, depending on the number of samples that fit the test distribution, you may suffer from a very biased resulting model due to the lack of training examples. In our previous example, picking up just the adversarial predictions on the training data that exceed a probability of 0.5 and summing them results in picking only 1,495 cases (the number is so small because the test set is not very different from the training set):

```
print(np.sum(cv_preds[:len(X), 1] > 0.5))
```

Finally, with the strategy of **validating by mimicking the test set,** you keep on training on all the data, but for validation purposes, you pick your examples only from the adversarial predictions on the training set that exceed a probability of 0.5 (or an even higher threshold such as 0.9).

Having a validation set tuned to the test set will allow you to pick all the possible hyperparameters and model choices that will favor a better result on the leaderboard.

In our example, we can figure out that feature_19 and feature_54 appear the most different between the training/test split from the output of the following code:

```
model.fit(X, y)
ranks = sorted(list(zip(X.columns, model.feature_importances_)),
               key=lambda x: x[1], reverse=True)
for feature, score in ranks:
    print(f"{feature:10} : {score:0.4f}")
```

To conclude, we have a few more remarks on adversarial validation. First, using it will generally help you to perform better in competitions, but not always. Kaggle's Code competitions, and other competitions where you cannot fully access the test set, cannot be inspected by adversarial validation. In addition, adversarial validation can inform you about the test data as a whole, but it cannot advise you on the split between the private and the public test data, which is the cause of the most common form of public leaderboard overfitting and consequent shake-up.

Finally, adversarial validation, though a very specific method devised for competitions, has quite a few practical use cases in the real world: how often have you picked the wrong test set to validate your models? The method we have presented here can enlighten you about whether you are using the test data, and any validation data, in your projects properly. Moreover, data changes and models in production may be affected by such changes and produce bad predictions if you don't retrain them. This is called **concept drift**, and by using adversarial validation, you can immediately understand if you have to retrain new models to put into production or if you can leave the previous ones in operation.

Giuliano Janson

https://www.kaggle.com/adjgiulio

Giuliano Janson is a Competitions Grandmaster and senior applied scientist for ML and NLP at Zillow Group. He spoke to us about his competition wins, the importance of cross-validation, and data leakages, the subject of the upcoming section.

What's your favorite kind of competition and why? In terms of techniques and solving approaches, what is your specialty on Kaggle?

My perfect competition is made up of a) an interesting problem to solve, b) a mid-size dataset that is small enough to fit in memory but not too small to become an overfitting headache, and c) an opportunity to be creative from a feature engineering perspective. The combination of those three dimensions is where I'm at my best in competitive ML because I feel I have the means to use rigor and creativity without having to worry about engineering constraints.

How do you approach a Kaggle competition? How different is this approach to what you do in your day-to-day work?

A Kaggle competition is a marathon. Going into a competition, I know I can get 90 to 95% of my best final score with a couple of days of work. The rest is a slow grind. The only success metric is your score; nothing else matters.

My daily work looks more like a series of sprints. Model performance is only a small portion of what I need to consider. A go-live date might be just as important, or other aspects such as interpretability, scalability, and maintainability could tip the scale in a totally different direction. After each sprint, priorities are reassessed and the end product might look totally different from what was originally envisioned. Also, modeling is a small part of my day. I spend far more time talking to people, managing priorities, building use cases, scrubbing data, and thinking about everything that it takes to make a prototype model a successful production solution.

Tell us about a particularly challenging competition you entered, and what insights you used to tackle the task.

One of the two competitions I won, the Genentech Cancer competition, was a Masters-only competition. The data provided was raw transactional data. There was no nice tabular dataset to start from. This is the type of work I love because feature engineering is actually one of my favorite parts of ML. Since I had worked in healthcare for a decade at the time of the competition, I had business and clinical insights on the data, but most of all, I had engineering insights on the complexity of correctly handling this type of data and about all the things that can go wrong when this type of transactional raw data is not handled carefully. That turned out to be key to winning, as one of the initial hypotheses regarding a possible source of leakage turned out to be true, and provided a "golden feature" that gave the final boost to our model. The insight from the competition is to always be extra careful when doing feature engineering or setting up validation approaches. Leakage can be very hard to detect and the usual train/validation/test approach to model validation will provide no help in identifying leakage in most cases, thus putting a model at risk of underperforming in production.

Has Kaggle helped you in your career? If so, how?

Kaggle has helped me in two ways. First, it provided a low barrier entry point to modern ML, a ton of exposure to cutting-edge modeling techniques, and forced me to truly understand the art and science of professional-grade model validation techniques. Second, Kaggle provided access to some of the brightest minds in applied ML. What I learned teaming up with some of the top Kaggle participants are lessons I cherish and try to share with my teammates every day.

How have you built up your portfolio thanks to Kaggle?

My professional career hasn't been directly impacted much by my Kaggle résumé. By that, I mean I haven't got job offers or interviews as a result of my Kaggle standings. I started Kaggle when I was already in a senior data science role, albeit with not much of an ML focus. Thanks to what I learned on Kaggle, I was able to better advocate a change in my career to move into an ML-focused job.

To this date, many folks I work with enjoy chatting about competitive ML and are curious about tips and tricks from my Kaggle experience, but it is also true that a large portion of the ML community might not even know what Kaggle is.

In your experience, what do inexperienced Kagglers often overlook? What do you know now that you wish you'd known when you first started?

The importance of proper cross-validation is easily overlooked by participants new to competitive ML. A solid cross-validation framework allows you to measure improvement reliably and objectively. And in a competition that might be as long as six months, the best models do not usually come from those who have the best initial ideas, but from those who are willing to iterate and adjust based on empirical feedback from the data. A great validation framework is at the foundation of it all.

What mistakes have you made in competitions in the past?

One of the lessons learned that I always share with people new to ML is to "never get over-enamored with overly complex ideas." When facing a new complex problem, it is easy to be tempted to build complex solutions. Complex solutions usually require time to develop. But the main issue is that complex solutions are often of marginal value, conditional on robust baselines. For example, imagine you want to model the outcome of an election and start thinking about a series of features to capture complex conditional relationships among observable and latent geographic, socio-economic, and temporal features. You could spend weeks developing these features, under the assumption that because they are so well thought out, they will be impactful.

The mistake is that while often those complex features could be very powerful on their own, conditional on a series of simple features and on a model that can already build highly optimized, data-driven deep interaction, all of a sudden, the complex features we built with time and effort may lead to little to no marginal improvement. My advice is to stick to Occam's razor and try easy things before being tempted by more complex approaches.

Are there any particular tools or libraries that you would recommend using for data analysis or machine learning?

I'm a pandas and Scikit-learn person. I love how pandas enables easy data manipulation and exploration and how I can quickly prototype models using Scikit-learn in a matter of minutes. Most of my prototype work is done using these two libraries. That said, my final models are often based on XGBoost. For deep learning, I love using Keras.

Handling leakage

A common issue in Kaggle competitions that can affect the outcome of the challenge is data leakage. **Data leakage**, often mentioned simply as **leakage** or with other fancy names (such as *golden features*), involves information in the training phase that won't be available at prediction time. The presence of such information (leakage) will make your model over-perform in training and testing, allowing you to rank highly in the competition, but will render unusable or at best suboptimal any solution based on it from the sponsor's point of view.

 We can define leakage as "when information concerning the ground truth is artificially and unintentionally introduced within the training feature data, or training metadata" as stated by *Michael Kim* (`https://www.kaggle.com/mikeskim`) in his presentation at *Kaggle Days San Francisco* in 2019.

Leakage is often found in Kaggle competitions, despite careful checking from both the sponsor and the Kaggle team. Such situations are due to the subtle and sneaky nature of leakage, which can unexpectedly appear due to the intense searching undertaken by Kagglers, who are always looking for any way to score better in a competition.

Don't confuse data leakage with a leaky validation strategy. In a leaky validation strategy, the problem is that you have arranged your validation strategy in a way that favors better validation scores because some information leaks from the training data. It has nothing to do with the competition itself, but it relates to how you are handling your validation. It occurs if you run any pre-processing modifying your data (normalization, dimensionality reduction, missing value imputation) before separating training and validation or test data.

In order to prevent leaky validation, if you are using Scikit-learn to manipulate and process your data, you absolutely have to exclude your validation data from any fitting operation. Fitting operations tend to create leakage if applied to any data you use for validation. The best way to avoid this is to use Scikit-learn pipelines (`https://scikit-learn.org/stable/modules/generated/sklearn.pipeline.Pipeline.html`), which will enclose both your data processing and model together, thereby avoiding any risk of inadvertently applying any leaking transformation to your data.

Data leakage instead is therefore something that is not strictly related to validation operations, though it affects them deeply. Even though this chapter is principally devoted to validation strategies, at this point we consider it necessary to discuss data leakage, since this issue can profoundly affect how you evaluate your models and their ability to generalize beyond the competition test sets.

Generally speaking, leakage can originate at a feature or example level. **Feature leakage** is by far the most common. It can be caused by the existence of a proxy for the target, or by a feature that is posterior to the target itself. A target proxy could be anything derived from processing the label itself or from the test split process; for instance, when defining identifiers, specific identifiers (a numeration arc, for instance) may be associated with certain target responses, making it easier for a model to guess if properly fed with the information processed in the right way. A more subtle way in which data processing can cause leakage is when the competition organizers have processed the training and test set together before splitting it. Historically, leakages in Kaggle competitions have been found in:

1. Mishandled data preparation from organizers, especially when they operate on a combination of training and test data (for example, in *Loan Default Prediction* (`https://www.kaggle.com/c/loan-default-prediction`), organizers initially used features with aggregated historical data that leaked future information).

2. Row order when it is connected to a time index or to specific data groups (for instance, in *Telstra Network Disruptions* (`https://www.kaggle.com/c/telstra-recruiting-network`), the order of records in a feature hinted at proxy information, the location, which was not present in the data and which was very predictive).

3. Column order when it is connected to a time index (you get hints by using the columns as rows).

4. Feature duplication in consecutive rows because it can hint at examples with correlated responses, such as in *Bosch Production Line Performance* (see the first-place solution by *Beluga* at `https://www.kaggle.com/c/bosch-production-line-performance/discussion/25434`).

5. Image metadata (as in *Two Sigma Connect: Rental Listing Inquiries* (`https://www.kaggle.com/c/two-sigma-connect-rental-listing-inquiries`)).

6. Hashes or other easily crackable anonymization practices of encodings and identifiers.

The trouble with posterior information originates from the way we deal with information when we do not consider the effects of time and of the sequence of cause and effect that spans across time. Since we are looking back at the past, we often forget that certain variables that make sense at the present moment do not have value in the past. For instance, if you have to calculate a credit score for a loan to a new company, knowing that payments of the borrowed money are often late is a great indicator of the lower reliability and higher risk represented by the debtor, but you cannot know this before you have lent out the money. This is also a problem that you will commonly find when analyzing company databases in your projects: your query data will represent present situations, not past ones. Reconstructing past information can also be a difficult task if you cannot specify that you wish to retrieve only the information that was present at a certain time. For this reason, great effort has to be spent on finding these leaking features and excluding or adjusting them before building any model.

Similar problems are also common in Kaggle competitions based on the same kind of data (banking or insurance, for instance), though, since much care is put into the preparation of the data for the competition, they appear in more subtle ways and forms. In general, it is easy to spot these leaking features since they strongly correlate with the target, and a domain expert can figure out why (for instance, knowing at what stage the data is recorded in the databases). Therefore, in competitions, you never find such obvious features, but derivatives of them, often transformed or processed features that have slipped away from the control of the sponsor. Since the features are often anonymized to preserve the sponsor's business, they end up lurking among the others. This has given rise to a series of hunts for the golden/magic features, a search to combine existing features in the dataset in order to have the leakage emerge.

You can read an enlightening post by *Corey Levison* here: `https://www.linkedin.com/pulse/winning-13th-place-kaggles-magic-competition-corey-levinson/`. It tells the story of how the *Santander Customer Transaction Prediction* competition turned into a hunt for magic features for his team.

Another good example is provided by *dune_dweller* here: `https://www.kaggle.com/c/telstra-recruiting-network/discussion/19239#109766`. By looking at how the data was ordered, dune_dweller found out that the data was likely in time order. Putting this information in a new feature increased the score.

The other way in which leakage can occur is by **training example leakage**. This happens especially with non-i.i.d. data. This means that some cases correlate between themselves because they are from the same period (or from contiguous ones) or the same group. If such cases are not all together either in the training or test data, but separated between them, there is a high chance that the machine learning algorithm will learn how to spot the cases (and derive the predictions) rather than using general rules. An often-cited example of such a situation involves the team of *Prof. Andrew Ng* (see `https://twitter.com/nizkroberts/status/931121395748270080`). In 2017, they wrote a paper using a dataset of 100,000 x-rays from 30,000 patients. They used a random split in order to separate training and test data, not realizing that the x-rays of the same patient could end up partly in the training set and partly in the test set. Practitioners such as Nick Roberts spotted this fact, pointing out a possible leakage that could have inflated the performances of the model and that led to a substantial revision of the paper itself.

What happens when there is a data leakage in a Kaggle competition? Kaggle has clear policies about it and will either:

- Let the competition continue as is (especially if the leakage only has a small impact)
- Remove the leakage from the set and relaunch the competition
- Generate a new test set that does not have the leakage present

In particular, Kaggle recommends making any leakage found public, though this is not compulsory or sanctioned if it doesn't happen. However, in our experience, if there is any leakage in a competition, it will soon become very apparent and the discussion forums will start lighting up with a discussion about magic stuff and the like. You will soon know, if you are attentive to what is being said in the forums and able to put together all the hints provided by different Kagglers.

However, please beware that some players may even use discussions about magic features to distract other competitors from serious modeling. For instance, in *Santander Customer Transaction Prediction*, there was a famous situation involving some Kagglers who fueled in other participants an interest in magic features that weren't actually so magic, directing their efforts in the wrong direction (see the discussion here: `https://www.kaggle.com/c/santander-customer-transaction-prediction/discussion/87057#502362`).

Our suggestion is to carefully read the discussions around leakage and magic features that arise in the competition's forum, and decide whether to pursue the research and use any leakage found based on your own interest and motivations for participating in the competition.

Not exploiting any leakage may really damage your final rankings, though it will surely spoil your learning experience (because leakage is a distortion and you cannot claim anything about the models using it). If you are not participating in a competition in order to gain a reputation or to later approach the sponsor for an opportunity to be hired, it is perfectly fine to use any leakage you come across. Otherwise, just ignore it and keep on working hard on your models (who knows; maybe Kaggle will reset or fix the competition by the end, rendering the leakage ineffective to the great disappointment of the many who used it).

Leakages are very different from competition to competition. If you want to get an idea of a few real leakages that have happened in Kaggle competitions, you can have a look at these three memorable ones:

- `https://www.kaggle.com/c/predicting-red-hat-business-value/discussion/22807` from *Predicting Red Hat Business Value* (`https://www.kaggle.com/c/predicting-red-hat-business-value`) where the problem arose because of an imperfect train/test split methodology of the competition.

- `https://www.kaggle.com/c/talkingdata-mobile-user-demographics/discussion/23403` from *TalkingData Mobile User Demographics* (`https://www.kaggle.com/c/talkingdata-mobile-user-demographics`) where a series of problems and non-i.i.d cases affected the correct train/test split of the competition.

- `https://www.kaggle.com/c/two-sigma-connect-rental-listing-inquiries/discussion/31870` from *Two Sigma Connect: Rental Listing Inquiries* (`https://www.kaggle.com/c/two-sigma-connect-rental-listing-inquiries`) where metadata (the creation time of each folder) did the trick.

Summary

Having arrived at the end of the chapter, we will summarize the advice we have discussed along the way so you can organize your validation strategy and reach the end of a competition with a few suitable models to submit.

In this chapter, we first analyzed the dynamics of the public leaderboard, exploring problems such as adaptive overfitting and shake-ups. We then discussed the importance of validation in a data science competition, building a reliable system, tuning it to the leaderboard, and then keeping track of your efforts.

Having discussed the various validation strategies, we also saw the best way of tuning your hyperparameters and checking your test data or validation partitions by using adversarial validation. We concluded by discussing some of the various leakages that have been experienced in Kaggle competitions and we provided advice about how to deal with them.

Here are our closing suggestions:

- Always spend the first part of the competition building a reliable validation scheme, favoring more a k-fold over a train-test split, given its probabilistic nature and ability to generalize to unseen data.

- If your validation scheme is unstable, use more folds or run it multiple times with different data partitions. Always check your test set using adversarial validation.

- Keep track of results based on both your validation scheme and the leaderboard. For the exploration of possible optimizations and breakthroughs (such as magic features or leakages), trust your validation score more.

- As we explained at the beginning of the chapter, use your validation scores when deciding your final submissions to the competition. For your final submissions, depending on the situation and whether or not you trust the leaderboard, choose among your best local cross-validated models and good-scoring submissions on the leaderboard, favoring the first over the second.

At this point of our journey, we are ready to discuss how to tackle competitions using tabular data, which is numeric or categorical data arranged in matrices (with rows representing the examples and columns the features). In the next chapter, we discuss the Tabular Playground Series, a monthly contest organized by Kaggle using tabular data (organized by *Inversion*: https://www.kaggle.com/inversion).

In addition, we will introduce you to some specific techniques to help you shine in these competitions, such as feature engineering, target encoding, denoising autoencoders, and some neural networks for tabular data, as an alternative to the recognized state-of-the-art learning algorithms in tabular data problems (the gradient boosting algorithms such as XGBoost, LightGBM, or CatBoost).

Join our book's Discord space

Join the book's Discord workspace for a monthly *Ask me Anything* session with the authors:

```
https://packt.link/KaggleDiscord
```

7

Modeling for Tabular Competitions

Until 2017, there was no need to distinguish too much between competition types and, since the vast majority of competitions were based on tabular data, you could not even find mention of "tabular competitions" on Kaggle forums. Suddenly, something changed. After a relative shortage of competitions (see `https://www.kaggle.com/general/49904`), deep learning competitions took the upper hand and tabular competitions became rarer, disappointing many. They became so rare that Kaggle recently had to launch a series of tabular competitions based on synthetic data. What happened?

By 2017-2018, data science had grown to full maturity and many companies had initiated their data journeys. Data science was still a hot topic, but no longer such an uncommon one. Solutions to problems similar to those that had populated Kaggle for years at the time had become standard practice in many companies. Under these circumstances, sponsors were less motivated to launch external tabular competitions, since they were already dealing with the same problems internally. By contrast, deep learning is still a much-undiscovered domain and will continue to be for a long time, so it makes sense to start competitions to challenge the state of the art and see if something new emerges.

In this chapter, we will discuss tabular competitions. We will touch on some famous historical ones and also focus on the more recent reality of the Tabular Playground Series, because tabular problems are standard practice for the majority of data scientists around and there really is a lot to learn from Kaggle. We will start by discussing **exploratory data analysis (EDA)** and **feature engineering**, two common activities in these competitions.

After presenting key strategies for feature engineering, we will expand to many related topics, such as categorical encoding, feature selection, target transformations, and pseudo-labeling. We will end by touching on deep learning methodologies for tabular data, presenting a few specialized deep neural networks such as TabNet and illustrating a denoising autoencoder. We will explain why autoencoders have become so relevant for recent Kaggle competitions while still being marginal in real-world applications.

We will cover:

- The Tabular Playground Series
- Setting a random state for reproducibility
- The importance of EDA
- Reducing the size of your data
- Applying feature engineering
- Pseudo-labeling
- Denoising with autoencoders
- Neural networks for tabular competitions

The chapter won't cover every topic related to tabular competitions, but you can easily find this in many other books since they are at the core of data science. What this chapter will do is present a range of special techniques and approaches that characterize tabular competitions on Kaggle and that you won't easily find elsewhere, except on Kaggle forums.

The Tabular Playground Series

Due to the large demand for tabular problems, Kaggle staff started an experiment in 2021, launching a monthly contest called the Tabular Playground Series. The contests were based on synthetic datasets that replicated public data or data from previous competitions. The synthetic data was created thanks to a deep learning generative network called **CTGAN**.

You can find the CTGAN code at `https://github.com/sdv-dev/CTGAN`. There's also a relevant paper explaining how it works by modeling the probability distribution of rows in tabular data and then generating realistic synthetic data (see `https://arxiv.org/pdf/1907.00503v2.pdf`).

Synthetic Data Vault (`https://sdv.dev/`), an MIT initiative, created the technology behind CTGAN and quite a number of tools around it. The result is a set of open-source software systems built to help enterprises generate synthetic data that mimics real data; it can help data scientists to create anonymous datasets based on real ones, as well as augment existing ones for modeling purposes.

Kaggle launched 13 fairly successful competitions in 2021, which have attracted many Kagglers despite not offering points, medals, or prizes (only some merchandise). Here is the 2021 list; you can use it to locate specific problems by type or metric and look for related resources such as focused discussions or Notebooks:

Month	Problem	Variables	Metric	Missing data
January 2021	Regression on an unspecified problem	Numeric	RMSE	No
February 2021	Regression predicting the value of an insurance claim	Numeric and categorical	RMSE	No
March 2021	Binary classification predicting an insurance claim	Numeric and categorical	AUC	No
April 2021	Binary classification on a replica very similar to the original Titanic dataset	Numeric and categorical	Accuracy	Yes

May 2021	Multiclass classification predicting the category on an e-commerce product given various attributes about the listing	Categorical	Multiclass LogLoss	No
June 2021	Multiclass classification predicting the category on an e-commerce product given various attributes about the listing	Numeric and categorical	Multiclass LogLoss	No
July 2021	Multiple regression predicting air pollution in a city via various input sensor values (for example, a time series)	Numeric, time	RMSLE	Yes
August 2021	Regression calculating the loss associated with a loan default	Numeric	RMSE	No
30 Days of ML	Regression on the value of an insurance claim	Numeric and categorical	RMSE	No

September 2021	Binary classification predicting whether a claim will be made on an insurance policy	Numeric	AUC	Yes
October 2021	Binary classification predicting the biological response of molecules given various chemical properties	Numeric and categorical	AUC	No
November 2021	Binary classification identifying spam emails via various features extracted from the email	Numeric	AUC	No
December 2021	Multiclass classification based on the original *Forest Cover Type Prediction* competition	Numeric and categorical	Multiclass classification accuracy	No

Table 7.1: Tabular Playground Series competitions in 2021

The Tabular Playground competitions continued in 2022, with even more sophisticated and challenging problems:

January 2022	Forecasting the sales of Kaggle merchandise from two fictitious independent store chains	Dates and categorical	Symmetric mean absolute percentage error (SMAPE)	No
February 2022	Classifying 10 different bacteria species using data from a genomic analysis technique that contains some data compression and data loss	Numeric	Categorization accuracy	No

Table 7.2: Tabular Playground Series competitions in 2022

Much of this chapter has been written by observing the code and discussion that emerged in these competitions, instead of analyzing more glorious competitions from the past. As we mentioned, we believe that tabular competitions are indeed gone for good given the changed professional landscape, and that you will find it more useful to read suggestions and hints relating to the present than the past.

As in other fully fledged competitions with Kaggle points and medals, in tabular competitions we recommend you follow a simple, yet very effective, pipeline that we have discussed elsewhere in the book:

- Explorative data analysis (EDA)
- Data preparation
- Modeling (using a cross-validation strategy for model validation)

- Post-processing
- Submission

As a rule, you also have to take care to maintain reproducibility and to save all the models (from every fold), the list of the parameters used, all the fold predictions, all the out-of-fold predictions, and all predictions from models trained on all the data.

You should save all this information in a way that makes it easy to recover and reconstruct, for instance using appropriate labeling, keeping track of MD5 hashing values (you can refer to this Stack Overflow answer for details: `https://stackoverflow.com/questions/16874598/how-do-i-calculate-the-md5-checksum-of-a-file-in-python`), and tracking the CV scores and leaderboard results from each experiment. Most Kagglers do this with simple tools such as `.txt` files or Excel spreadsheets, but there exist ways that are more sophisticated, such as using:

- **DVC** (`https://dvc.org/`)
- **Weights and Biases** (`https://wandb.ai/site`)
- **MLflow** (`https://mlflow.org/`)
- **Neptune** (`https://neptune.ai/experiment-tracking`)

In the end, what matters are the results, not the tool you use, so try your best to keep order in your experiments and models, even in the heat of a competition.

Before we proceed, consider also thinking about the technology that Kaggle used to generate the data for these competitions; if you can properly understand how the data has been generated, you get an important advantage. In addition, understanding how synthetic data works can really have an impact on the way you do data science in the real world, because it gives you a way to easily obtain more varied data for training.

For instance, let's take the *Google Brain – Ventilator Pressure Prediction* competition (`https://www.kaggle.com/c/ventilator-pressure-prediction`). In this competition, you had to develop machine learning for mechanical ventilation control. Although you could obtain good results by modeling the data provided with deep learning, given the synthetic origin of the data, you could also reverse engineer its generative process and obtain a top leaderboard result, as *Jun Koda* (`https://www.kaggle.com/junkoda`) did and explains in his post: `https://www.kaggle.com/c/ventilator-pressure-prediction/discussion/285278`.

Generating artificial data by yourself and understanding synthetic data has never been so easy, as you can verify from this Notebook (`https://www.kaggle.com/lucamassaron/how-to-use-ctgan-to-generate-more-data`), derived from a Notebook originally coded and tested by *Dariush Bahrami* (`https://www.kaggle.com/dariushbahrami`).

Setting a random state for reproducibility

Before we start discussing the steps and models you may use in a tabular competition, it will be useful to return to the theme of **reproducibility** we mentioned above.

In most of the commands in the code you see on Kaggle Notebooks, you will find a parameter declaring a number, a **seed**, as the random state. This setting is important for the reproducibility of your results. Since many algorithms are not deterministic but are based on randomness, by setting a seed you influence the behavior of the random generator, making it *predictable* in its randomness: the same random seed corresponds to the same sequence of random numbers. In other words, it allows you to obtain the same results after every run of the same code.

That is why you find a random seed setting parameter in all machine learning algorithms in Scikit-learn as well as in all Scikit-learn-compatible models (for instance, XGBoost, LightGBM, and CatBoost, to name the most popular ones).

Reproducibility of results is important in real-world projects as well as in Kaggle competitions. In the real world, having a reproducible model allows for better tracking of model development and consistency. In Kaggle competitions, reproducibility helps in testing hypotheses better because you are controlling any source of variation in your models. For instance, if you created a new feature, putting it into a reproducible pipeline will help you understand if the feature is advantageous or not. You will be sure that any improvement or deterioration in the model can be attributed only to the feature, and not to the effects of some random process that has changed since the last time you ran the model.

Again, reproducibility can be used to your advantage when dealing with public Notebooks. Most often, these Notebooks will have a fixed seed that could be 0, 1, or 42. The value 42 is quite popular because it is a reference to Douglas Adam's *The Hitchhiker's Guide to the Galaxy*, in which it is the "Answer to the Ultimate Question of Life, the Universe, and Everything," calculated by an enormous supercomputer named Deep Thought over a period of 7.5 million years. Now, if everyone in a competition is using the same random seed, it could have a double effect:

- The random seed might be working too well with the public leaderboard, which means overfitting

- A lot of Kagglers will produce similar results that will influence their standings in the private leaderboard in the same way

By changing the random seed, you are avoiding overfitting and also breaking rank; in other words, you are getting different results from everyone else, which could put you at an advantage in the end. In addition, if you end up winning a Kaggle competition, you need to demonstrate how your models produced the winning submission, so it is paramount that everything is completely reproducible if you want to obtain your prize quickly.

TensorFlow and PyTorch models don't explicitly use a random seed parameter, so it is more challenging to ensure their complete reproducibility. The following code snippet, when run, sets the same random seed for TensorFlow and PyTorch models:

```
def seed_everything(seed,
                    tensorflow_init=True,
                    pytorch_init=True):
    """
    Seeds basic parameters for reproducibility of results
    """
    random.seed(seed)
    os.environ["PYTHONHASHSEED"] = str(seed)
    np.random.seed(seed)
    if tensorflow_init is True:
        tf.random.set_seed(seed)
    if pytorch_init is True:
        torch.manual_seed(seed)
        torch.cuda.manual_seed(seed)
        torch.backends.cudnn.deterministic = True
        torch.backends.cudnn.benchmark = False
```

As for Scikit-learn, it is instead advisable to set the random seed directly – when it is allowed by the class or the function – using the random_state parameter.

The importance of EDA

The term **EDA** comes from the work of *John W. Tukey*, one of the most prominent exponents of modern statistical methodology. In his 1977 book *Exploratory Data Analysis* (hence the acronym EDA), Tukey thinks of EDA as a way to explore data, uncover evidence, and develop hypotheses that can later be confirmed by statistical tests.

His idea was that how we define statistical hypotheses could be based more on observation and reasoning than just sequential tests based on mathematical computations. This idea translates well to the world of machine learning because, as we will discuss in the next section, data can be improved and pre-digested so that learning algorithms can work better and more efficiently.

In an EDA for a Kaggle competition, you will be looking for:

- Missing values and, most importantly, missing value patterns correlated with the target.
- Skewed numeric variables and their possible transformations.
- Rare categories in categorical variables that can be grouped together.
- Potential outliers, both univariate and multivariate.
- Highly correlated (or even duplicated) features. For categorical variables, focus on categories that overlap.
- The most predictive features for the problem.

You achieve this by several descriptive analyses, graphs, and charts, first examining each distinct feature (**univariate analysis**, in statistical terms), then matching a couple of variables (**bivariate** analysis, such as in a scatterplot), and finally considering more features together at once (a **multivariate** approach).

If you are feeling lazy or unsure about how and where to start, relying on automated strategies initially can help you. For instance, you may find that **AutoViz** (https://github.com/AutoViML/AutoViz), a popular rapid EDA freeware tool, can save you a lot of time. You can install it on your Notebook by running the following command:

```
pip install git+git://github.com/AutoViML/AutoViz.git
```

You can obtain a clearer understanding of what AutoViz can do for you by reading this Medium article by *Dan Roth* at https://towardsdatascience.com/autoviz-a-new-tool-for-automated-visualization-ec9c1744a6ad or browsing a few interesting public Notebooks such as https://www.kaggle.com/gvyshnya/automating-eda-and-feature-importance-detection by *Georgii Vyshnia* (https://www.kaggle.com/gvyshnya).

In the latter link, you will also find references to another tool, **Sweetviz** (https://github.com/fbdesignpro/sweetviz). Sweetviz has an overview article and tutorial based on the Titanic dataset, at https://towardsdatascience.com/powerful-eda-exploratory-data-analysis-in-just-two-lines-of-code-using-sweetviz-6c943d32f34.

Another popular tool that you may find useful using is **Pandas Profiling** (`https://github.com/pandas-profiling/pandas-profiling`), which is more reliant on classical statistical descriptive statistics and visualization, as explained by this article: `https://medium.com/analytics-vidhya/pandas-profiling-5ecd0b977ecd`.

Waiting for other Kagglers to publish interesting EDA Notebooks could also be a solution, so always keep an eye on the Notebooks sections; sometimes, precious hints may appear. This should kick-start your modeling phase and help you understand the basic dos and don'ts of the competition. However, remember that EDA stops being a commodity and becomes an asset for the competition when it is *highly specific to the problem at hand*; this is something that you will never find from automated solutions and seldom in public Notebooks. You have to do your EDA by yourself and gather key, winning insights.

All things considered, our suggestion is to look into the automated tools a bit because they are really easy to learn and run. You will save a lot of time that you can instead spend looking at charts and reasoning about possible insights, and that will certainly help your competition performance. However, after doing that, you need to pick up Matplotlib and Seaborn and try something by yourself on not-so-standard plots that depend on the type of data provided and the problem.

 For example, if you are given a series of measurements performed over time, plotting the continuous function based on time is as useful as plotting the single recorded points in time, for instance showing different lags between one observation and another, a fact that may point to revealing insights for better predictions.

Dimensionality reduction with t-SNE and UMAP

There are many possible plots you can create when doing EDA and it is not our intention to list them all here, but there are a couple of dimensionality reduction plots that are worth spending a few words on because they can provide as much information as very specific and data-tailored charts. These are **t-SNE** (`https://lvdmaaten.github.io/tsne/`) and **UMAP** (`https://github.com/lmcinnes/umap`).

t-SNE and UMAP are two techniques, often used by data scientists, that allow you to project multivariate data into lower dimensions. They are often used to represent complex sets of data in two dimensions. 2-D UMAP and t-SNE plots can reveal the presence of outliers and relevant clusters for your data problem.

In fact, if you can plot the scatter graph of the resulting 2-D projection and color it by target value, the plot may give you hints about possible strategies for dealing with subgroups.

Although it is related to an image competition, a good example of how UMAP and t-SNE can help you understand your data better is *Chris Deotte*'s analysis for the *SIIM-ISIC Melanoma Classification* competition (see `https://www.kaggle.com/c/siim-isic-melanoma-classification/discussion/168028`). In this example, Chris has related training and test data on the same low-dimensionality projections, highlighting portions where only test examples were present.

> Though UMAP and t-SNE offer invaluable help in discovering patterns in data that are hard to find, you still can use them as features in your modeling efforts. An interesting example of this usage was demonstrated in the *Otto Group Product Classification Challenge*, where *Mike Kim* used t-SNE projections as training features for the competition (`https://www.kaggle.com/c/otto-group-product-classification-challenge/discussion/14295`).

As stated by the article *How to t-SNE Effectively* (`https://distill.pub/2016/misread-tsne/`), you have to use these techniques properly, because it is easy to spot clusters and patterns where there are none. The same warning is valid for UMAP, because it can also produce plots that can be misread. Guides such as `https://pair-code.github.io/understanding-umap/` offer sound advice on the performance of both UMAP and t-SNE on real-world data, providing suggestions and caveats.

Despite these dangers, in our experience, these approaches are certainly more revealing than the classical methods based on variance restructuring by linear combination such as PCA or SVD. Compared to these approaches, UMAP and t-SNE manage to reduce the dimensionality extremely, allowing visual charting of the results while maintaining the topography of the data. As a side effect, they are much slower to fit. However, NVIDIA has released its **RAPIDS** suite (`https://developer.nvidia.com/rapids`) based on CUDA, which, using a GPU-powered Notebook or script, returns the results of both UMAP and t-SNE in a very reasonable timeframe, allowing their effective use as an EDA tool.

> You can find a useful example of applying both UMAP and t-SNE with a RAPIDS implementation and a GPU for data exploration purposes for the *30 Days of ML* competition at the following link: `https://www.kaggle.com/lucamassaron/interesting-eda-tsne-umap/`.

In the figure below, which is the output of the example Notebook above, you can see how multiple clusters populate the dataset, but none of them could be deemed to reveal a particular relationship with the target:

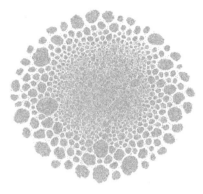

Figure 7.1: Multiple clusters appearing in a t-SNE plot

In another Notebook (`https://www.kaggle.com/lucamassaron/really-not-missing-at-random`), the same techniques are applied to the binary indicators for missing samples instead, revealing evocative figures that hint at specific and separate areas dominated by a certain type of response. Indeed, in that example, missing samples did not occur at random and they were quite predictive:

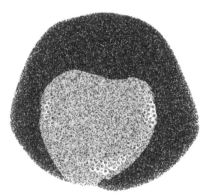

Figure 7.2: This t-SNE plot easily reveals areas where the positive target is predominant

Reducing the size of your data

If you are working directly on Kaggle Notebooks, you will find their limitations quite annoying and dealing with them a timesink. One of these limitations is the out-of-memory errors that will stop the execution and force you to restart the script from the beginning. This is quite common in many competitions. However, unlike deep learning competitions based on text or images where you can retrieve the data from disk in small batches and have them processed, most of the algorithms that work with tabular data require handling all the data in memory.

The most common situation is when you have uploaded the data from a CSV file using Pandas' read_csv, but the DataFrame is too large to be handled for feature engineering and machine learning in a Kaggle Notebook. The solution is to compress the size of the Pandas DataFrame you are using without losing any information (**lossless compression**). This can easily be achieved using the following script derived from the work by *Guillaume Martin* (you can find the original Notebook here: https://www.kaggle.com/gemartin/load-data-reduce-memory-usage).

```
def reduce_mem_usage(df, verbose=True):
    numerics = ['int16', 'int32', 'int64',
                'float16', 'float32', 'float64']
    start_mem = df.memory_usage().sum() / 1024**2
    for col in df.columns:
        col_type = df[col].dtypes
        if col_type in numerics:
            c_min = df[col].min()
            c_max = df[col].max()
            if str(col_type)[:3] == 'int':
                if c_min > np.iinfo(np.int8).min and c_max < np.iinfo(np.
int8).max:
                    df[col] = df[col].astype(np.int8)
                elif c_min > np.iinfo(np.int16).min and c_max < np.iinfo(np.
int16).max:
                    df[col] = df[col].astype(np.int16)
                elif c_min > np.iinfo(np.int32).min and c_max < np.iinfo(np.
int32).max:
                    df[col] = df[col].astype(np.int32)
                elif c_min > np.iinfo(np.int64).min and c_max < np.iinfo(np.
int64).max:
```

```
                    df[col] = df[col].astype(np.int64)
            else:
                if c_min > np.finfo(np.float32).min and c_max < np.finfo(np.
float32).max:
                    df[col] = df[col].astype(np.float32)
                else:
                    df[col] = df[col].astype(np.float64)
    end_mem = df.memory_usage().sum() / 1024**2
    if verbose: print('Mem. usage decreased to {:5.2f} Mb ({:.1f}%
reduction)'.format(end_mem, 100 * (start_mem - end_mem) / start_mem))
    return df
```

 Guillaume Martin was not the first to propose an idea like this on Kaggle. The very first Kaggler with this idea of compressing a Pandas DataFrame was *Arjan Groen*, who wrote a reducing function during the Zillow competition (https://www.kaggle. com/arjanso/reducing-dataframe-memory-size-by-65).

This script leverages the fact that all the numeric features in a dataset reside in a specific range of values. Since we have different types of integer and floating-point numeric variables in Python, based on the number of bytes they occupy in memory, the script compares the range of values found in each feature to the maximum and minimum value that each numeric type can accept. This is done in order to set the feature to the numeric type that works with its range of values and that requires the lowest memory.

The approach works like a breeze on Kaggle Notebooks, but with some caveats. Once you have set the best-fitting numeric type for each feature by compression, you cannot apply any feature engineering that may result in values exceeding the capacity of the set numeric types, because such an operation will produce erroneous results. Our suggestion is to apply it after feature engineering or before major transformations that do not rescale your existing data. Combining it with the garbage collection library gc and the gc.collect() method will improve the memory situation of your Kaggle Notebook.

Another way to reduce the size of your data (among other things) is to use feature engineering (in particular, feature selection and data compression).

Applying feature engineering

In real-world projects, what can make the difference between a successful machine learning model and a mediocre one is often the data, not the model. When we talk about data, the differentiator between bad, good, and excellent data is not just the lack of missing values and the reliability of the values (its "quality"), or the number of available examples (its "quantity"). In our experience, the real differentiator is the informational value of the content itself, which is represented by the type of features.

The features are the real clay to mold in a data science project, because they contain the information that models use to separate the classes or estimate the values. Every model has an expressiveness and an ability to transform features into predictions, but if you are lacking on the side of features, no model can bootstrap you and offer better predictions. *Models only make apparent the value in data. They are not magic in themselves.*

On Kaggle, apart from the rare competitions where you can look for further data to add, all participants have the same data available from the beginning. At that point, how you handle the data makes most of the difference. Overlooking the fact that you can improve the data you have is a common mistake made by many Kagglers. **Feature engineering**, a set of techniques for transforming data into more useful information for your models, is invariably the key to performing better in competitions. Even the more powerful models you can apply need you to process the data and render it into a more understandable form.

Feature engineering is also the way you embed any **prior knowledge** (usually specialist expertise on the problem) into the data: by summing, subtracting, or dividing the existing features, you obtain indicators or estimates that you know can better explain the problem you are dealing with. There are also other purposes of feature engineering, which are less valuable in a Kaggle competition but could prove important in a real-world project. The first is to reduce the size of the training data (this could also be useful in a Kaggle competition when working with Notebooks, which have limits in memory). The second is to make interpretation of the resulting model easier by using features understandable to humans.

Each domain may have encoded specific variable transformations that are not necessarily self-evident, but well known to experts of the fields. Just think of finance, where you have to separate signals from noise for different sets of features representing market and company data, by applying specific transformations like Kalman filters or wavelet transformations. Given the large number of possible fields and the complexity of many feature engineering procedures, in this section, we won't enter into specific domains of expertise and their particular ways of dealing with features.

Instead, we will present you with the most common and most general techniques that you can apply in any tabular competition.

Easily derived features

Deriving features with transformations is the simplest approach, but often the most effective. For instance, computing feature ratios (dividing one feature by another) can prove quite effective because many algorithms cannot mimic divisions (for example, gradient boosting) or can have a hard time trying to (for example, deep neural networks). Here are the most common transformations to try out:

- **Time feature processing**: Splitting a date into its elements (year, month, day); transforming it into week of the year and weekday; computing differences between dates; computing differences with key events (for instance, holidays).

  For dates, another common transformation is extracting time elements from a date or a time. Cyclic continuous transformations (based on sine and cosine transformations) are also useful for representing the continuity of time and creating periodic features:

  ```
  cycle = 7
  df['weekday_sin'] = np.sin(2 * np.pi * df['col1'].dt.dayofweek /
  cycle)
  df['weekday_cos'] = np.cos(2 * np.pi * df['col1'].dt.dayofweek /
  cycle)
  ```

- **Numeric feature transformations**: Scaling; normalization; logarithmic or exponential transformations; separating the integer and decimal parts; summing, subtracting, multiplying, or dividing two numeric features. Scaling obtained by standardization (the z-score method used in statistics) or by normalization (also called min-max scaling) of numeric features can make sense if you are using algorithms sensitive to the scale of features, such as any neural network.

- **Binning of numeric features**: This is used to transform continuous variables into discrete ones by distributing their values into a number of bins. Binning helps remove noise and errors in data and it allows easy modeling of non-linear relationships between the binned features and the target variable when paired with **one-hot encoding** (see the Scikit-learn implementation, for instance: `https://scikit-learn.org/stable/modules/generated/sklearn.preprocessing.KBinsDiscretizer.html`).

- **Categorical feature encoding**: One-hot encoding; a categorical data processing that merges two or three categorical features together; or the more sophisticated target encoding (more on this in the following sections).

- **Splitting and aggregating categorical features based on the levels**: For instance, in the *Titanic* competition (`https://www.kaggle.com/c/titanic`) you can split names and surnames, as well their initials, to create new features.

- **Polynomial features** are created by raising features to an exponent. See, for instance, this Scikit-learn function: `https://scikit-learn.org/stable/modules/generated/sklearn.preprocessing.PolynomialFeatures.html`.

While they are not proper feature engineering but more data cleaning techniques, missing data and outlier treatments involve making changes to the data that nevertheless transform your features, and they can help signals from the data emerge:

- **Missing values treatment**: Make binary features that point out missing values, because sometimes missingness is not random and a missing value could have some important reason behind it. Usually, missingness points out something about the way data is recorded, acting like a proxy variable for something else. It is just like in census surveys: if someone doesn't tell you their income, it means they are extremely poor or are extremely rich. If required by your learning algorithm, replace the missing values with the mean, median, or mode (it is seldom necessary to use methods that are more sophisticated).

 You can refer to this complete guide written by *Parul Pandey* (`https://www.kaggle.com/parulpandey`) as a reference: `https://www.kaggle.com/parulpandey/a-guide-to-handling-missing-values-in-python`.

Just keep in mind that some models can handle missing values by themselves and do so fairly better than many standard approaches, because the missing-values handling is part of their optimization procedure. The models that can handle missing values by themselves are all gradient boosting models:

- XGBoost: `https://xgboost.readthedocs.io/en/latest/faq.html`
- LightGBM: `https://lightgbm.readthedocs.io/en/latest/Advanced-Topics.html`
- CatBoost: `https://catboost.ai/docs/concepts/algorithm-missing-values-processing.html`

- **Outlier capping or removal**: Exclude, cap to a maximum or minimum value, or modify outlier values in your data. To do so, you can use sophisticated multivariate models, such as those present in Scikit-learn (`https://scikit-learn.org/stable/modules/outlier_detection.html`).

  Otherwise, you can simply locate the outlying samples in a univariate fashion, basing your judgment on how many standard deviations they are from the mean, or their distance from the boundaries of the **interquartile range (IQR)**. In this case, you might simply exclude any points that are above the value of `1.5 * IQR + Q3` (upper outliers) and any points that are below `Q1 - 1.5 * IQR` (lower outliers). Once you have found the outliers, you can also proceed by pointing them out with a binary variable.

All these data transformations can add predictive performance to your models, but they are seldom decisive in a competition. Though it is necessary, you cannot simply rely on basic feature engineering. In the following sections, we'll suggest more complex procedures for extracting value from your data.

Meta-features based on rows and columns

In order to perform competitively, you need trickier feature engineering. A good place to start is looking at features based on each **row**, considered separately:

- Compute the mean, median, sum, standard deviation, minimum, or maximum of the numeric values (or of a subset of them)
- Count the missing values
- Compute the frequencies of common values found in the rows (for instance, considering the binary features and counting the positive values)
- Assign each row to a cluster derived from a cluster analysis such as k-means

These **meta-features** (called thus because they are features that are representative of a set of single features) help to distinguish the different kinds of samples found in your data by pointing out specific groups of samples to your algorithm.

Meta-features can also be built based on **columns**. Aggregation and summarization operations on single features instead have the objective of providing further information about the value of numeric and categorical features; *is this characteristic common or rare?* This is information that the model cannot grasp because it cannot count categorical instances in a feature.

As meta-features, you can use any kind of column statistic (such as mode, mean, median, sum, standard deviation, min, max, and also skewness and kurtosis for numerical features). For column-wise meta-features, you can proceed in a few different ways:

- **Frequency encoding**: Simply count the frequency of the values in a categorical feature and then create a new feature where you replace those values with their frequency. You can also apply frequency encoding to numeric features when there are frequently recurring values.

- **Frequencies and column statistics computed with respect to a relevant group**: In this case, you can create new features from the values of both numeric and categorical features because you are considering distinct groups in the data. A group could be a cluster you compute by cluster analysis, or a group you can define using a feature (for instance, age may produce age groups, locality may provide areas, and so on). The meta-features describing each group are then applied to each sample based on its group. For instance, using a Pandas groupby function, you can create your meta-features, which are then merged with the original data based on the grouping variable. The trickiest part of this feature engineering technique is finding meaningful groups in data to compute the features on.

- Further column frequencies and statistics can be derived by combining more groups together.

The list is certainly not exhaustive, but it should give you an idea of how to look for new features at the feature level and at the row level using frequencies and statistics.

Let's see a simple example based on the *Amazon Employee Access Challenge* data. First, we will apply a frequency encoding on the ROLE_TITLE feature:

```
import pandas as pd
train = pd.read_csv("../input/amazon-employee-access-challenge/train.csv")

# Frequency count of a feature
feature_counts = train.groupby('ROLE_TITLE').size()
print(train['ROLE_TITLE'].apply(lambda x: feature_counts[x]))
```

The result will show that the feature classes have been replaced by their observed frequency.

We now proceed to encode the ROLE_TITLE feature based on the groupings of the ROLE_DEPTNAME, because we expect that different titles may be more common in certain departments and rarer in others.

The result is a new feature composed of both, which we use to count the frequency of its values:

```
feature_counts = train.groupby(['ROLE_DEPTNAME', 'ROLE_TITLE']).size()
print(train[['ROLE_DEPTNAME', 'ROLE_TITLE']].apply(lambda x: feature_
counts[x[0]][x[1]], axis=1))
```

 You can find all the working code and the results in this Kaggle Notebook: `https://www.kaggle.com/lucamassaron/meta-features-and-target-encoding/`.

Target encoding

Categorical features are usually not a challenge to deal with, thanks to simple functions offered by Scikit-learn such as:

- `LabelEncoder`
- `OneHotEncoder`
- `OrdinalEncoder`

These functions can transform categories into numeric features and then into binary features that are easily dealt with by machine learning algorithms. However, when the number of categories to deal with is too large, the dataset resulting from a one-hot encoding strategy becomes **sparse** (most values in it will be zero values) and cumbersome to handle for the memory and processor of your computer or Notebook. In these situations, we talk about a **high-cardinality feature**, which requires special handling.

 Since early Kaggle competitions, high-cardinality variables have in fact been processed using an encoding function that is computed according to Micci-Barreca, D. *A preprocessing scheme for high-cardinality categorical attributes in classification and prediction problems*. ACM SIGKDD Explorations Newsletter 3.1 (2001): 27-32.

The idea behind this approach is to transform the many categories of a categorical feature into their corresponding expected target value. In the case of a regression, this is the average expected value for that category; for a binary classification, it is the conditional probability given that category; for a multiclass classification, you have instead the conditional probability for each possible outcome.

For instance, in the *Titanic* GettingStarted competition (https://www.kaggle.com/competitions/titanic), where you have to figure out the survival probability of each passenger, target encoding a categorical feature, such as the gender feature, would mean replacing the gender value with its average probability of survival.

In this way, the categorical feature is transformed into a numeric one without having to convert the data into a larger and sparser dataset. In short, this is **target encoding** and it is indeed very effective in many situations because it resembles a stacked prediction based on the high-cardinality feature. Like stacked predictions, however, where you are essentially using a prediction from another model as a feature, target encoding brings about the risk of overfitting. In fact, when some categories are too rare, using target encoding is almost equivalent to providing the target label. There are ways to avoid this.

Before seeing the implementation you can directly import into your code, let's see an actual code example of target encoding. This code was used for one of the top-scoring submissions of the *PetFinder.my Adoption Prediction* competition:

```python
import numpy as np
import pandas as pd
from sklearn.base import BaseEstimator, TransformerMixin


class TargetEncode(BaseEstimator, TransformerMixin):

    def __init__(self, categories='auto', k=1, f=1,
                 noise_level=0, random_state=None):
        if type(categories)==str and categories!='auto':
            self.categories = [categories]
        else:
            self.categories = categories
        self.k = k
        self.f = f
        self.noise_level = noise_level
        self.encodings = dict()
        self.prior = None
        self.random_state = random_state

    def add_noise(self, series, noise_level):
        return series * (1 + noise_level *
```

```
                              np.random.randn(len(series)))

    def fit(self, X, y=None):
        if type(self.categories)=='auto':
            self.categories = np.where(X.dtypes == type(object()))[0]

        temp = X.loc[:, self.categories].copy()
        temp['target'] = y
        self.prior = np.mean(y)
        for variable in self.categories:
            avg = (temp.groupby(by=variable)['target']
                        .agg(['mean', 'count']))
            # Compute smoothing
            smoothing = (1 / (1 + np.exp(-(avg['count'] - self.k) /
                        self.f)))
            # The bigger the count the less full_avg is accounted
            self.encodings[variable] = dict(self.prior * (1 -
                            smoothing) + avg['mean'] * smoothing)

        return self

    def transform(self, X):
        Xt = X.copy()
        for variable in self.categories:
            Xt[variable].replace(self.encodings[variable],
                                inplace=True)
            unknown_value = {value:self.prior for value in
                            X[variable].unique()
                            if value not in
                            self.encodings[variable].keys()}
            if len(unknown_value) > 0:
                Xt[variable].replace(unknown_value, inplace=True)
            Xt[variable] = Xt[variable].astype(float)
            if self.noise_level > 0:
                if self.random_state is not None:
                    np.random.seed(self.random_state)
                Xt[variable] = self.add_noise(Xt[variable],
```

```
                                                        self.noise_level)
        return Xt


    def fit_transform(self, X, y=None):
        self.fit(X, y)
        return self.transform(X)
```

The input parameters of the function are:

- categories: The column names of the features you want to target-encode. You can leave 'auto' on and the class will pick the object strings.
- k (int): Minimum number of samples to take a category average into account.
- f (int): Smoothing effect to balance the category average versus the prior probability, or the mean value relative to all the training examples.
- noise_level: The amount of noise you want to add to the target encoding in order to avoid overfitting. Start with very small numbers.
- random_state: The reproducibility seed in order to replicate the same target encoding when noise_level > 0.

Notice the presence of the k and the f parameters. In fact, for a level i of a categorical feature, we are looking for an approximate value that can help us better predict the target using a single encoded variable. Replacing the level with the observed conditional probability could be the solution, but doesn't work well for levels with few observations. The solution is to blend the observed posterior probability on that level (the probability of the target given a certain value of the encoded feature) with the a priori probability (the probability of the target observed on the entire sample) using a lambda factor. This is called the **empirical Bayesian approach**.

In practical terms, we are using a function to determine if, for a given level of a categorical variable, we are going to use the conditional target value, the average target value, or a blend of the two. This is dictated by the lambda factor, which, for a fixed k parameter (usually it has a unit value, implying a minimum cell frequency of two samples) has different output values depending on the f value that we choose.

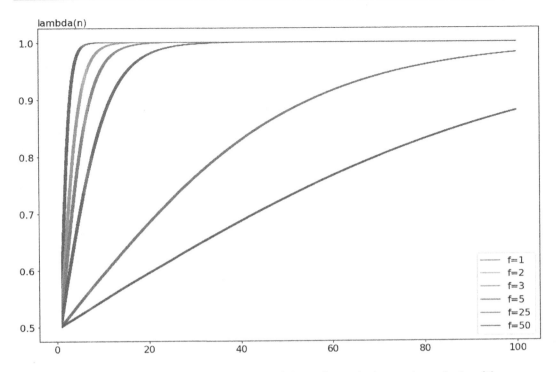

Figure 7.3: Plot of lambda values (on the y-axis) depending on f values and sample size of the categorical value (on the x-axis)

As shown by the chart, where the x-axis represents the number of cases for a given categorical level and the y-axis the weight of the conditional target value, smaller f values tend to switch abruptly from using the average target to using the conditional value. Higher values of f tend to blend the conditional value with the average unless we are dealing with a categorical level with a large sample size.

Therefore, for a fixed k, higher values of f dictate less trust in the observed empirical frequency and more reliance on the empirical probability for all cells. The right value for f is usually a matter of testing (supported by cross-validation), since you can consider the f parameter a hyperparameter in itself.

After all these explanations, the class is actually quite straightforward to use. Instantiate it with the name of the features you want to target-encode and the parameters you want to try and fit it on some training data. Then, you can transform any other piece of data, target-encoding only the fitted features:

```
te = TargetEncode(categories='ROLE_TITLE')
te.fit(train, train['ACTION'])
te.transform(train[['ROLE_TITLE']])
```

The example works on the same *Amazon Employee Access Challenge* data we used before and it target-encodes only the ROLE_TITLE feature.

 Instead of writing your own code, you can also use the package from https:// github.com/scikit-learn-contrib/category_encoders and its Target Encoder (http://contrib.scikit-learn.org/category_encoders/targetencoder. html). It is an out-of-the-box solution that works exactly like the code in this section.

Using feature importance to evaluate your work

Applying too much feature engineering can have side effects. If you create too many correlated features or features that are not important for the problem, models could take too long to complete their training and you may get worse results. This may seem like a paradox, but it is explained by the fact that every variable carries some noise (a random component due to measurement or recording errors) that may be picked by mistake by the model: the more variables you use, the higher the chance your model may pick up noise instead of signals. Therefore, you should try to keep only the relevant features in the dataset you use for training; consider feature selection as a part of your feature engineering process (the pruning phase).

Figuring out the features you need to keep is a hard problem because, as the number of available features grows, the number of possible combinations grows too. There are various ways to select features, but first it is important to think about the stage in your data preparation pipeline where the selection has to happen.

Based on our experiences, we suggest you consider placing feature selection at the *end* of your data preparation pipeline. Since features share a part of their variance with other features, you cannot evaluate their effectiveness by testing them one at a time; you have to consider them all at once in order to correctly figure out which you should use.

In addition, you should then test the effectiveness of your selected features using cross-validation. Therefore, after you have all the features prepared and you have a consistent pipeline and a working model (it doesn't need to be a fully optimized model, but it should work properly and return acceptable results for the competition), you are ready to test what features should be retained and what could be discarded. At this point, there are various ways to operate feature selection:

- Classical approaches used in statistics resort to forward addition or backward elimination by testing each feature entering or leaving the set of predictors. Such an approach can be quite time-consuming, though, because it relies on some measure of internal importance of variables or on their effect on the performance of the model with respect to a specific metric, which you have to recalculate for every feature at every step of the process.

- For regression models, using lasso selection can provide a hint about all the important yet correlated features (the procedure may, in fact, retain even highly correlated features), by using the **stability selection** procedure. In stability selection, you test multiple times (using a bagging procedure) what features should be retained – considering only the features whose coefficients are not zero at each test – and then you apply a voting system to keep the ones that are most frequently assigned non-zero coefficients.

 You can get more details about the procedure at this repository: `https://github.com/scikit-learn-contrib/stability-selection`.

- For tree-based models, such as random forests or gradient boosting, a decrease in impurity or a gain in the target metric based on splits are common ways to rank features. A threshold can cut away the least important ones.

- Always for tree-based models, but easily generalizable to other models, test-based randomization of features (or simple comparisons with random features) helps to distinguish features that do help the model to predict correctly from features that are just noise or redundant.

An example of how randomizing features helps in selecting important features is proposed in this example by *Chris Deotte* in the *Ventilator Pressure Prediction* competition: https://www.kaggle.com/cdeotte/lstm-feature-importance. This Notebook tests the role of features in an LSTM-based neural network. First, the model is built and the baseline performance is recorded. Then, one by one, features are shuffled and the model is required to predict again. If the resulting prediction worsens, it suggests that you shuffled an important feature that shouldn't be touched. Instead, if the prediction performance stays the same or even improves, the shuffled feature is not influential or even detrimental to the model.

There is also No Free Lunch in importance evaluation. Shuffling doesn't require any re-training, which is a great advantage when training a fresh model costs time. However, it can fail in certain situations. Shuffling can sometimes create unrealistic input combinations that make no sense to evaluate. In other cases, it can be fooled by the presence of highly correlated features (incorrectly determining that one is important and the other is not). In this case, proceeding by removing the feature (instead of shuffling it), retraining the model, and then evaluating its performance against the baseline is the best solution.

In another approach based on shuffled features, **Boruta** (https://github.com/scikit-learn-contrib/boruta_py) uses random features to test the validity of the model in an iterative fashion. An alternative version of the Boruta selection procedure, **BorutaShap** (https://github.com/Ekeany/Boruta-Shap), leverages SHAP values in order to combine feature selection and for explainability reasons. The resulting selection is usually more reliable than simple rounds of removal or randomization of features, because features are tested multiple times against random features until they can statistically prove their importance. Boruta or BorutaShap may take up to 100 iterations and it can only be performed using tree-based machine learning algorithms.

If you are selecting features for a linear model, Boruta may actually overshoot. This is because it will consider the features important both for their main effects and their interactions together with other features (but in a linear model, you care only about the main effects and a selected subset of interactions). You can still effectively use Boruta when selecting for a linear model by using a gradient boosting whose max depth is set to one tree, so you are considering only the main effects of the features and not their interactions.

You can have a look at how simple and quick it is to set up a BorutaShap feature selection by following this tutorial Notebook presented during the *30 Days of ML* competition: https://www.kaggle.com/lucamassaron/tutorial-feature-selection-with-boruta-shap.

Bojan Tunguz

https://www.kaggle.com/tunguz

Bojan Tunguz is one Kaggler who definitely understands the importance of feature engineering (and is also a great fan of XGBoost☺). We were keen to speak to him about his experiences as a Machine Learning Modeler at NVIDIA and, impressively, a Kaggle Quadruple Grandmaster.

What's your favorite kind of competition and why? In terms of techniques and solving approaches, what is your specialty on Kaggle?

I love any non-code competition. This has changed a lot over the years. I used to be really into the image competitions, but the sophistication of the engineering stack required to be competitive in these has increased tremendously over the years. For a while I was really into the NLP competitions, but those have always been rare on Kaggle. One constant over the years, though, has been my interest in tabular data problems. Those used to be the quintessential Kaggle competition problems but have unfortunately become extinct. I am still very interested in that area of ML and have moved into doing some basic research in this domain. Compared to the other areas of ML/DL, there has been very little progress on improving ML for tabular data, and I believe there is a lot of opportunity here.

How do you approach a Kaggle competition? How different is this approach to what you do in your day-to-day work?

I have always taken the game aspect of Kaggle seriously. What that means for me is I usually start new Kaggle competitions very playfully – submitting simple solutions, whimsical solutions, modified solutions from other players, blends, etc. These help me get a feel for the problem, what sorts of things work, how far can I get with a few simple tricks, etc. Some of this is also applicable to my day-to-day modeling, but there one important aspect is missing – and that's the support and feedback from the community and the leaderboard. When you are working on your own or with a small team, you never know if what you are building is the best that can be done, or if a better solution is possible.

Tell us about a particularly challenging competition you entered, and what insights you used to tackle the task.

The most challenging and the most important competition of my Kaggle career was the Home Credit Default Risk *competition. It is the second biggest Kaggle competition of all time, and it happened during a particularly challenging time in my life.*

Credit underwriting is a very challenging data science problem and requires a lot of intelligent feature engineering and a reliable validation scheme. My own personal insight was to use simple linear modeling for feature selection, and it helped our overall model. Our team won that competition, and to this day I consider this victory the highlight of my Kaggle career.

Has Kaggle helped you in your career? If so, how?

Kaggle has been the single biggest booster of my ML career. Out of four ML jobs that I have held, three have been a direct consequence of my Kaggle success. It is impossible to overstate how important a Kaggle credential can be in one's career.

In your experience, what do inexperienced Kagglers often overlook? What do you know now that you wish you'd known when you first started?

There are two aspects of all ML problems, and Kaggle competitions in particular, that I have either underappreciated or not bothered enough with for way too long: feature engineering and a robust validation strategy. I love ML libraries and algorithms and have a tendency to start building the ML algorithm as soon as I can. But the single biggest impact on your model's performance will come from very good features. Unfortunately, feature engineering is more of an art than a science and is usually very model- and dataset-dependent. Most of the more interesting feature engineering tricks and practices are rarely, if ever, taught in standard ML courses or resources. Many of them cannot be taught and are dependent on some special problem-specific insights. But the mindset of looking into feature engineering as default is something that can be cultivated. It will usually take many years of practice to get good at it.

Are there any tools or libraries that you would recommend using for Kaggling?

XGBoost is all you need!

Pseudo-labeling

In competitions where the number of examples used for training can make a difference, **pseudo-labeling** can boost your scores by providing further examples taken from the test set. The idea is to add examples from the test set whose predictions you are confident about to your training set.

First introduced in the *Santander Customer Transaction Prediction* competition by team Wizard-ry (read here: `https://www.kaggle.com/c/santander-customer-transaction-prediction/discussion/89003`), pseudo-labeling simply helps models to refine their coefficients thanks to more data available, but it won't always work. First of all, it is not necessary in some competitions. That is, adding pseudo-labels won't change the result; it may even worsen it if there is some added noise in the pseudo-labeled data.

Unfortunately, you cannot know for sure beforehand whether or not pseudo-labeling will work in a competition (you have to test it empirically), though plotting learning curves may provide you with a hint as to whether having more data could be useful (see this example provided by Scikit-learn: `https://scikit-learn.org/stable/auto_examples/model_selection/plot_learning_curve.html`).

Second, it is not easy to decide which parts of the test set predictions to add or how to tune the entire procedure for the best results. Generally, this is the procedure:

1. Train your model
2. Predict on the test set
3. Establish a confidence measure
4. Select the test set elements to add
5. Build a new model with the combined data
6. Predict using this model and submit

A good example of the complete procedure for obtaining pseudo-labeling is offered by Chris Deotte in the *Instant Gratification* competition: `https://www.kaggle.com/cdeotte/pseudo-labeling-qda-0-969`. You don't need to know more than a few tricks in order to apply it.

There are a few caveats you should consider when trying to apply pseudo-labeling:

- You should have a very good model that produces good predictions for them to be usable in training. Otherwise, you will just add more noise.
- Since it is impossible to have entirely perfect predictions in the test set, you need to distinguish the good ones from the ones you shouldn't use. If you are predicting using CV folds, check the standard deviation of your predictions (this works both with regression and classification problems) and pick only the test examples where the standard deviation is the lowest. If you are predicting probabilities, use only high-end or low-end predicted probabilities (the cases where the model is actually more confident).

- In the second stage, when you concatenate the training examples with the test ones, do not put in more than 50% test examples. Ideally, a share of 70% original training examples and 30% pseudo-labeled examples is the best. If you put in too many pseudo-labeled examples, your new model will risk learning little from the original data and more from the easier test examples, resulting in a distilled model that does not perform better than the original. In fact, as you are training, your model is also learning how to deal with noise in labels, but pseudo-labeled examples do not have this noise.

> Don't forget that you cannot completely trust your pseudo-labels, so keep in mind that you are also partially spoiling your data by using test predictions as training examples. The trick works when you get more benefits from doing so than negative effects.

- If you depend on validation for early stopping, fixing hyperparameters, or simply evaluating your model, do not use pseudo-labels in the validation. They could be highly misleading. Always use the original training cases for the same reasons we quoted above.
- If possible, use a different kind of model when training to estimate the pseudo-labels and when training your final model using both the original labels and the pseudo-labels. This will ensure you are not simply enforcing the same information your previous model used, but you are also extracting new information from the pseudo-labels.

Clearly, pseudo-labeling is more of an art than a science. It can make the difference in certain competitions but needs to be executed very well to generate results. Consider it a resource, and always try one submission based on pseudo-labels.

Denoising with autoencoders

Autoencoders, initially better known for non-linear data compression (a kind of non-linear PCA) and image denoising, started being recognized as an interesting tool for tabular competitions after *Michael Jahrer* (https://www.kaggle.com/mjahrer) successfully used them to win the *Porto Seguro's Safe Driver Prediction* competition (https://www.kaggle.com/c/porto-seguro-safe-driver-prediction). *Porto Seguro* was a popular, insurance-based risk analysis competition (more than 5,000 participants) characterized by particularly noisy features.

Michael Jahrer describes how he found a better representation of the numeric data for subsequent neural net supervised learning by using **denoising autoencoders (DAEs)**. A DAE can produce a new dataset with a huge number of features based on the activations of the hidden layers at the center of the network, as well as the activations of the middle layers encoding the information.

In his famous post (`https://www.kaggle.com/c/porto-seguro-safe-driver-prediction/discussion/44629`), Michael Jahrer describes how a DAE can not only remove noise but also automatically create new features, so the representation of the features is learned in a similar way to what happens in image competitions. In the post, he mentions the secret sauce for the DAE recipe, which is not simply the layers, but the **noise** you put into the data in order to augment it. He also made clear that the technique requires stacking together training and test data, implying that the technique would not have applications beyond winning a Kaggle competition. In fact, after this winning exploit, the technique disappeared from the forums and most competitions until its recent re-emergence during the Tabular Playground Series.

DAEs are technically composed of an **encoding** part and a **decoding** part. The encoding part takes the training data as input and is followed by a few dense layers. Ideally, you have a hidden middle layer, whose activations just encode all the training information. If the number of nodes in this middle layer is smaller than the original input shape, you have a **compression** and hopefully, in statistical terms, you are representing some latent dimensionality that is behind the generative process of the input data; otherwise, you are simply eliminating redundancies and separating noise from signal (which is not a bad result).

In the second part of the layer, the decoder part, you are enlarging the layers again until they regain the shape of the original input. The output is compared with the input to compute an error loss to backpropagate to the network.

From these solutions, you can deduce that there are two types of DAEs:

- In **bottleneck DAEs**, mimicking the approach used in image processing, you take as new features the activations from the middle layer, the one separating the encoding part from the decoding part. These architectures have an hourglass shape, first reducing the number of neurons layer by layer until the middle bottleneck layer, then enlarging it back in the second part. The number of hidden layers is always odd.

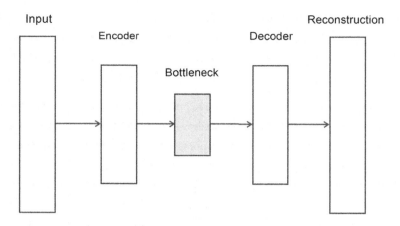

Figure 7.4: In a bottleneck DAE, you take only the bottleneck layer weights as features

- In **deep stack DAEs,** you take all the activations from the hidden layers, without distinguishing between the encoding, decoding, or middle layer. In these architectures, layers are the same size. The number of hidden layers can be even or odd.

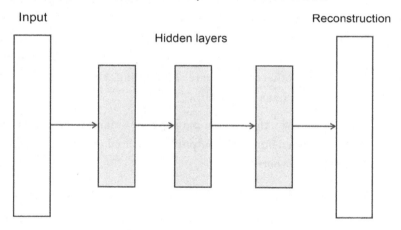

Figure 7.5: In a deep stack DAE, you take all the stacked hidden layer weights as features

As we mentioned, an important aspect often discussed is adding some **random noise** to your DAE. In order to help train any kind of DAE, you need to inject noise that helps to augment the training data and avoid the overparameterized neural network just memorizing inputs (in other words, overfitting). In the *Porto Seguro* competition, Michael Jahrer added noise by using a technique called **swap noise**, which he described as follows:

Here I sample from the feature itself with a certain probability "inputSwapNoise" in the table above. 0.15 means 15% of features replaced by values from another row.

What is described is basically an augmentation technique called **mixup** (which is also used in image augmentation: `https://arxiv.org/abs/1710.09412`). In mixup for tabular data, you decide a probability for mixing up. Based on that probability, you change some of the original values in a sample, replacing them with values from a more or less similar sample from the same training data.

In his walkthrough (`https://www.kaggle.com/springmanndaniel/1st-place-turn-your-data-into-daeta`), *Danzel* describes three approaches to this: column-wise, row-wise, and random:

- In **column-wise** noise swapping, you swap values in a certain number of columns. The proportion of columns whose values are to be swapped is decided based on your mixup probability.

- In **row-wise** noise swapping, you always swap a certain number of the values in each row. Essentially, every row contains the same proportion of swapped values, based on the mixup probability, but the features swapped change from row to row.

- In **random** noise swapping, you fix a number of values to be swapped, based on the mixup probability, and you randomly pick them up from the entire dataset (this is somewhat similar to row-wise swapping in effect).

Like pseudo-labeling, DAE is also more of an art than a science, which is another way to say that it is all trial and error. It won't always work and the details that make it work on one problem probably won't help for another. In order to obtain a good DAE for your competition, you need to keep an eye on a series of aspects that need to be tested and tuned:

- Architecture of the DAE (deep stack tends to work better, but you need to determine the number of units per layer and the number of layers)

- Learning rate and batch size

- Loss (also distinguishing between the loss of numeric and categorical features helps)

- Stopping point (the lowest loss is not always the best; use validation and early stopping if possible)

Depending on the problem, you should expect to face some difficulties in setting up the right architecture and adjusting it to work properly. Your efforts, however, could be rewarded by a top result on the final private leaderboard. In fact, in recent tabular competitions, DAE techniques appeared as part of the recipe of many winning submissions:

- Danzel (`https://www.kaggle.com/springmanndaniel`) reported in `https://www.kaggle.com/c/tabular-playground-series-jan-2021/discussion/216037` having used the hidden weights of three 1,500-neuron layers, expanding the original data from 14 columns to 4,500. This new, processed dataset was used as input in other neural networks and gradient boosting models.

- *Ren Zhang* (`https://www.kaggle.com/ryanzhang`) discussed his solution (`https://www.kaggle.com/c/tabular-playground-series-feb-2021/discussion/222745`) and shared his code (`https://github.com/ryancheunggit/Denoise-Transformer-AutoEncoder`), revealing that he used stacked transformer encoders rather than your typical linear and ReLU activated hidden layers (and that such an approach can mean it takes up to 20 hours to train a proper DAE). In his approach, he also suggested adding some random noise to the data (by using a noise mask) to be reconstructed and to compute the loss based not only on the error from reconstructing the original data, but also from the noise mask. Using this combined loss helps the network to converge better. Studying the code provided in the GitHub link and the graph in the Kaggle discussion post will help you to understand better and easily replicate this innovative approach.

- *JianTT* (`https://www.kaggle.com/jiangtt`) noticed how some techniques key to DAEs, in particular creating new observations by adding noise, can be useful for training better algorithms without the need of creating a complete DAE: `https://www.kaggle.com/c/tabular-playground-series-apr-2021/discussion/235739`.

If you don't want to spend too much time building your own DAE, but you would like to explore whether something like it could work for the competition you are taking on, you can test out a couple of pre-prepared solutions. First, you can refer to a Notebook for a PyTorch network from *Hung Khoi* (`https://www.kaggle.com/hungkhoi/train-denoise-transformer-autoencoder`) and re-adapt it to your needs, or you can use the Kaggler library from *Jeong-Yoon Lee* (`https://www.kaggle.com/jeongyoonlee`). In his Notebook, Jeong-Yoon Lee presents how it works on one of the Tabular Playground competitions: `https://www.kaggle.com/jeongyoonlee/dae-with-2-lines-of-code-with-kaggler`.

Neural networks for tabular competitions

Having discussed neural networks with DAEs, we have to complete this chapter by discussing how neural networks can help you in a tabular competition more generally. Gradient boosting solutions still clearly dominate tabular competitions (as well as real-world projects); however, sometimes neural networks can catch signals that gradient boosting models cannot get, and can be excellent single models or models that shine in an ensemble.

 As many Grandmasters of the present and the past often quote, mixing together diverse models (such as a neural network and a gradient boosting model) always produces better results than single models taken separately in a tabular data problem. *Owen Zhang*, previously number one on Kaggle, discusses at length in the following interview how neural networks and GBMs can be blended nicely for better results in a competition: `https://www.youtube.com/watch?v=LgLcfZjNF44`.

Building a neural network quickly for a tabular competition is no longer a daunting challenge. Libraries such as TensorFlow/Keras and PyTorch make things easy, and having some pre-made networks such as TabNet already packaged for you into libraries makes them even easier.

To quickly get started with building your own network, you can use various resources. We warmly suggest referring to the book we published, *Machine Learning Using TensorFlow Cookbook* (`https://www.packtpub.com/product/machine-learning-using-tensorflow-cookbook/9781800208865`), since there is an extensive chapter devoted to building DNNs with TensorFlow for tabular problems (*Chapter 7, Predicting with Tabular Data*). In the book, you can also find many other suggestions and recipes for using TensorFlow for Kaggle.

Otherwise, you can refer to a few online resources introducing you to the topic, as presented during the *30 Days of ML* competition:

- Watch this video that explains how to use TensorFlow for tabular data: `https://www.youtube.com/watch?v=nQgUt_uADSE`
- Use the code from the tutorial on GitHub: `https://github.com/lmassaron/deep_learning_for_tabular_data`
- Most importantly, find the tutorial Notebook applied to the competition here: `https://www.kaggle.com/lucamassaron/tutorial-tensorflow-2-x-for-tabular-data`

The key things to take into account when building these solutions are:

- Use activations such as GeLU, SeLU, or Mish instead of ReLU; they are quoted in quite a few papers as being more suitable for modeling tabular data and our own experience confirms that they tend to perform better.

- Experiment with batch size.

- Use augmentation with mixup (discussed in the section on autoencoders).

- Use quantile transformation on numeric features and force, as a result, uniform or Gaussian distributions.

- Leverage embedding layers, but also remember that embeddings do not model everything. In fact, they miss interactions between the embedded feature and all the others (so you have to force these interactions into the network with direct feature engineering).

In particular, remember that embedding layers are reusable. In fact, they consist only of a matrix multiplication that reduces the input (a sparse one-hot encoding of the high cardinality variable) to a dense one of lower dimensionality. By recording and storing away the embedding of a trained neural network, you can transform the same feature and use the resulting embeddings in many other different algorithms, from gradient boosting to linear models.

Refer to the diagram in *Figure 7.6* for a clearer understanding of the process involving a categorical variable with 24 levels. In the chart, we demonstrate how a value from a categorical feature is transformed from a textual or an integer value into a vector of values that a neural network can handle:

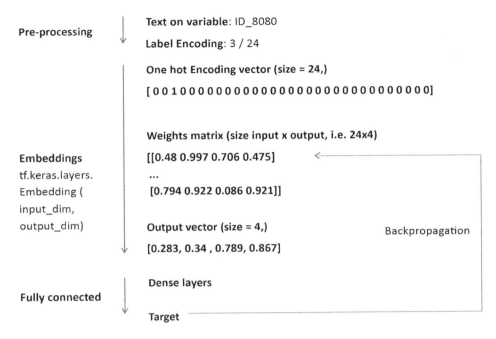

Figure 7.6: How an embedding layer works

Everything starts with knowing how many distinct values the feature has. This constitutes the dictionary size and it is an important piece of information. In this example, we considered a feature presenting 24 distinct values. This information allows us to create a one-hot-encoded vector of size 24 representing each of the possible feature values. The resulting vector is then multiplied by a matrix whose row size corresponds to the size of the one-hot-encoded vector and column size to the size of the output dimensions. In this way, with a vector-matrix multiplication, the input of the categorical variable will be transformed into a multidimensional numeric one. The effectiveness of the multiplication is ensured by the backpropagation algorithm of the neural network, which will update each value in the matrix so the most predictive result is obtained from the multiplication.

If you don't want to build your own deep neural network in TensorFlow or PyTorch, you can rely on a few out-of-the-box architectural solutions. All these solutions come out of the box because they are packaged or because other Kagglers have written them based on the original papers. Based on their success in tabular competitions, here are the main ones you can try when taking on a tabular competition yourself:

- **TabNet** is a network devised by Google researchers (Arık, S. O. and Pfister. T. *Tabnet: Attentive interpretable tabular learning.* arXiv 2020. `https://www.aaai.org/AAAI21Papers/AAAI-1063.ArikS.pdf`) that promises to help you select and process the relevant features and to deal with both categorical and numeric features in a smart way. It doesn't have many hyperparameters to tune, though the results may deeply differ between an untuned network and a tuned one (hence the necessity of spending some time to make it work at its best). Here you have a few implementations, such as the excellent `pytorch-tabnet` package (`https://github.com/dreamquark-ai/tabnet`) or the implementations coded by *Yirun Zhang* (`https://www.kaggle.com/gogo827jz`), found at `https://www.kaggle.com/ludovick/introduction-to-tabnet-kfold-10-training` and `https://www.kaggle.com/ludovick/introduction-to-tabnet-kfold-10-inference`. Both were devised for the *Mechanism of Action (MoA) Prediction* competition.

- **Neural Oblivious Decision Ensembles (NODE)** is an architecture that tries to mimic in a neural network how a decision tree works (Popov, S., Morozov, S., and Babenko, A. *Neural oblivious decision ensembles for deep learning on tabular data.* arXiv preprint arXiv:1909.06312, 2019. `https://arxiv.org/abs/1909.06312`). You can use the implementation offered by Yirun Zhang for TensorFlow at `https://www.kaggle.com/gogo827jz/moa-neural-oblivious-decision-ensembles-tf-keras` or for PyTorch at `https://www.kaggle.com/gogo827jz/moa-public-pytorch-node`.

- You can use a wide range of models, such as Wide & Deep, DeepFM, xDeepFM, AutoInt, and many others based on factorization machines and mostly devised for click-through rate estimation. You don't have to build all these neural architectures by yourself; you can rely on packages such as DeepCTR (`https://github.com/shenweichen/DeepCTR`) or DeepTables (`https://github.com/DataCanvasIO/deeptables`) as suggested by *Changhao Lee* (`https://www.kaggle.com/leechh`) and *Jian Yang* (`https://www.kaggle.com/jackguagua`), second and first place respectively in the *Categorical Feature Encoding Challenge II* competition.

In conclusion, you can build your own neural network for tabular data by mixing together embedding layers for categorical features and dense layers for numeric ones. However, if it doesn't pay off, you can always rely on quite a wide range of good solutions provided by well-written packages. Always be on the lookout for a new package appearing: it may help you to perform better both in Kaggle competitions and real-world projects. Also, as a piece of advice based on our experience, don't expect a neural network to be the best model in a tabular competition; this seldom happens. Instead, blend solutions from classical tabular data models, such as gradient boosting models and neural networks, because they tend to pick up different signals from the data that you can integrate together in an ensemble.

Jean-François Puget

`https://www.kaggle.com/cpmpml`

We spoke to Jean-François Puget, aka CPMP, about the importance of reproducibility, how to work with data, his best competition, and more. As a Kaggle Grandmaster in Competitions and Discussions, and a Distinguished Engineer at RAPIDS, NVIDIA, he had many good insights to share with us. The editor particularly likes what he has to say about the scientific method.

What's your favorite kind of competition and why? In terms of techniques and solving approaches, what is your specialty on Kaggle?

I like competitions with a scientific background, or a background I can relate to. I dislike anonymous data and synthetic data, unless the data is generated via a very precise physics simulation. More generally, I like Kaggle competitions on domains I don't know much about, as this is where I will learn the most. It is not the most effective way to get ranking points, but it is the one I entertain most.

How do you approach a Kaggle competition? How different is this approach to what you do in your day-to-day work?

I start by looking at data and understanding it as well as possible. I try to find patterns in it, especially predictive patterns. What I often do is plot samples using two features or derived features on the x and y axis, and a third feature for color coding samples. One of the three features can be the target. I use lots of visualization, as I believe that human vision is the best data analysis tool there is.

The second thing I spend time on is how to assess model or pipeline performance. Indeed, it is extremely important to be able to evaluate the performance of a model as accurately as possible. There is no surprise here; evaluation is often a variant of k-fold cross-validation. But the fold definition can be tailored to the competition type (time-based folds for forecasting competitions, group k-fold when samples are linked together for some reason, e.g., actions with the same user ID, etc.).

I then create an end-to-end baseline that goes from data to submission, and try it. If this is a code competition, then testing that you have gotten your pipeline right is key.

Then I try more complex models (if using deep learning models), or more features (if using XGBoost or other models from RAPIDS or sklearn). I submit these to see if there is a correlation between my local evaluation score and the public test score. If the correlation is good, then I submit less and less.

After a few weeks, I spend time doing hyperparameter tuning. But I do it only once, or maybe twice with a last tuning near the end of the competition. Indeed, hyperparameter tuning is one of the best ways to overfit, and I fear overfitting a lot.

Tell us about a particularly challenging competition you entered, and what insights you used to tackle the task.

One of the competitions I am the most proud of is the TalkingData AdTracking Fraud Detection Challenge *competition, where we had a very large volume of click history and we had to predict which clicks led to some app downloads. There were very few features and a large number of rows (like half a billion). At the time I only had a 64 GB machine, and I had to implement a very efficient way to create new features and evaluate them. I had a few insights in this competition. First, that the click that led to an app download was the last click on the app download page for a user. Therefore, the "time to next click from the same user on the same app" was the most important feature. A derived insight was this: there were quite a number of clicks from the same user and app with the same timestamp. I hypothesized that the one with a download, if any, was the last one. A third insight was to use a matrix factorization approach to approximate feature value co-occurrences. I implemented a libFM model in Keras at the time, and adding the latent vectors as features helped. The only other team doing this was the top team. With this, I got a solo 6th place among teams of GMs. I was not a Kaggle GM yet.*

Has Kaggle helped you in your career? If so, how?

Kaggle helped me twice. At IBM, Kaggle was a great source of knowledge on SOTA machine learning practices. I used that knowledge to inform and guide the development of IBM machine learning tooling (IBM Watson Studio and IBM Watson Machine Learning).

For instance, I managed to have IBM support Python packages in 2016 at a time when IBM was a Java/Scala powerhouse. Without me, IBM would have bet on Spark and Scala for machine learning, and would have missed the Python wave entirely. I also pushed for XGBoost very early, when IBM wanted to only support Spark ML or TensorFlow.

The second time Kaggle helped me was for getting my current job. NVIDIA was looking for Kaggle competition GMs with good social presence to help promote the NVIDIA stack, including the RAPIDS GPU accelerated ML package.

In your experience, what do inexperienced Kagglers often overlook? What do you know now that you wish you'd known when you first started?

The one thing that differentiates Kagglers from other data scientists is the evaluation of model performance. Kagglers need to master this, because if they don't, then they choose submissions that look great on the public leaderboard but perform poorly on the private leaderboard. Once a Kaggler knows how to build models that perform well on the private leaderboard, then they know how to build models that perform well on new data, i.e., models that do not overfit.

The other thing that inexperienced Kagglers do is to ask if method/model X can work in a given competition. My answer to this is always, "Try it and see if it works or not." People often miss that machine learning is an experimental science. In order to build good models, one must follow the scientific method:

- *Make a hypothesis (e.g., adding this feature, or adding this NN layer, will improve pipeline performance)*
- *Run an experiment to test the hypothesis (train the modified pipeline)*
- *Analyze experiment results (is CV score better than before? Where is it better? Where is it worse?)*

Each experiment should be done so that it can confirm or reject a hypothesis. For this, an experiment should change only one thing at a time. Often, inexperienced people change many things, then cannot conclude what worked or not.

Are there any particular tools or libraries that you would recommend using for data analysis and machine learning?

I use Matplotlib plots mostly for data exploration. I do data wrangling in Pandas if the dataset is small, or in cuDF (from RAPIDS) if the dataset is large. For machine learning, I use cuML from RAPIDS, XGBoost with GPU acceleration, and PyTorch. If possible, I will use pretrained models, for instance NLP models from Hugging Face, or image classification models from the timm package.

> **What's the most important thing someone should keep in mind or do when they're entering a competition?**
>
> *Make sure you can spend enough time on it.*

Summary

In this chapter, we have discussed tabular competitions on Kaggle. Since most of the knowledge applicable in a tabular competition overlaps with standard data science knowledge and practices, we have focused our attention on techniques more specific to Kaggle.

Starting from the recently introduced Tabular Playground Series, we touched on topics relating to reproducibility, EDA, feature engineering, feature selection, target encoding, pseudo-labeling, and neural networks applied to tabular datasets.

EDA is a crucial phase if you want to get insights on how to win a competition. It is also quite unstructured and heavily dependent on the kind of data you have. Aside from giving you general advice on EDA, we brought your attention to techniques such as t-SNE and UMAP that can summarize your entire dataset at a glance. The next phase, feature engineering, is also strongly dependent on the kind of data you are working on. We therefore provided a series of possible feature engineering ideas that you can try applying to your specific case. As for feature selection, after a brief overview, we drew your attention to techniques based on feature importance and randomization, which can be applied to almost any machine learning algorithm.

After explaining target encoding, which we wanted to point out cannot be dealt with in an automated way, we moved on to special techniques that you probably won't apply in your real-world projects but that can work very well in Kaggle competitions: pseudo-labeling and denoising autoencoders for tabular competitions. Finally, after discussing how categorical features can also be dealt with using embedding layers in neural networks, we gave you a quick overview of the pre-made neural architectures that could work for tabular data.

In the next chapter, we will complete our overview of all the techniques that you need to take on tabular competitions by discussing how best to perform hyperparameter optimization.

Join our book's Discord space

Join the book's Discord workspace for a monthly *Ask me Anything* session with the authors:

`https://packt.link/KaggleDiscord`

8

Hyperparameter Optimization

How a Kaggle solution performs is not simply determined by the type of learning algorithm you choose. Aside from the data and the features that you use, it is also strongly determined by the algorithm's **hyperparameters**, the parameters of the algorithm that have to be fixed *prior to* training, and cannot be learned during the training process. Choosing the right variables/data/ features is most effective in tabular data competitions; however, hyperparameter optimization is effective in *all* competitions, of any kind. In fact, given fixed data and an algorithm, hyperparameter optimization is the only sure way to enhance the predictive performance of the algorithm and climb the leaderboard. It also helps in ensembling, because an ensemble of tuned models always performs better than an ensemble of untuned ones.

You may hear that tuning hyperparameters manually is possible if you know and understand the effects of your choices on the algorithm. Many Kaggle Grandmasters and Masters have declared that they often rely on directly tuning their models in competitions. They operate selectively on the most important hyperparameters in a bisection operation style, exploring smaller and smaller intervals of a parameter's values until they find the value that produces the best result. Then, they move on to another parameter. This works perfectly well if there is a single minimum for each parameter and if the parameters are independent from each other. In this case, the search is mostly driven by experience and knowledge of learning algorithms. In our experience, however, that is not the case with most tasks you will encounter on Kaggle. The sophistication of the problems and the algorithms used requires a systematic approach that only a search algorithm can provide. Hence, we decided to write this chapter.

In this chapter, we will explore how to extend your cross-validation approach to find the best hyperparameters that can generalize to your test set. The idea is to deal with the pressure and scarcity of time and resources that you experience in competitions. For this reason, we will concentrate on **Bayesian optimization methods**, which are a proven way to optimize for complex models and data problems based on the resources you have available. We won't limit ourselves to searching for the best values for pre-defined hyperparameters; we will also delve into the problem of neural network architecture.

We will cover the following topics:

- Basic optimization techniques
- Key parameters and how to use them
- Bayesian optimization

Let's start!

Basic optimization techniques

The core algorithms for hyperparameter optimization, found in the Scikit-learn package, are **grid search** and **random search**. Recently, the Scikit-learn contributors have also added the **halving algorithm** to improve the performances of both grid search and random search strategies.

In this section, we will discuss all these basic techniques. By mastering them, not only will you have effective optimization tools for some specific problems (for instance, SVMs are usually optimized by grid search) but you will also be familiar with the basics of how hyperparameter optimization works.

To start with, it is crucial to figure out what the necessary ingredients are:

- A model whose hyperparameters have to be optimized
- A search space containing the boundaries of the values to search between for each hyperparameter
- A cross-validation scheme
- An evaluation metric and its score function

All these elements come together in the search method to determine the solution you are looking for. Let's see how it works.

Grid search

Grid search is a method that searches through the hyperparameters exhaustively, and is not feasible in high-dimensional space. For every parameter, you pick a set of values you want to test. You then test all the possible combinations in this set. That is why it is exhaustive: you try everything. It is a very simple algorithm and it suffers from the curse of dimensionality, but, on the positive side, it's *embarrassingly parallel* (see `https://www.cs.iusb.edu/~danav/teach/b424/b424_23_embpar.html` for a definition of this computer science term). This means you can obtain an optimal tuning very quickly, if you have enough processors to run the search on.

As an example, let's take a classification problem and **support-vector machine classification (SVC)**. **Support-vector machines (SVMs)** for both classification and regression problems are probably the machine learning algorithm that you will use grid search for the most. Using the `make_classification` function from Scikit-learn, we can generate a classification dataset quickly:

```
from sklearn.datasets import make_classification
from sklearn.model_selection import train_test_split

X, y = make_classification(n_samples=300, n_features=50,
                           n_informative=10,
                           n_redundant=25, n_repeated=15,
                           n_clusters_per_class=5,
                           flip_y=0.05, class_sep=0.5,
                           random_state=0)
```

For our next step, we define a basic SVC algorithm and set the search space. Since the **kernel function** of the SVC (the internal function that transforms the input data in an SVM) determines the different hyperparameters to set, we provide a list containing two dictionaries of distinct search spaces for parameters to be used depending on the type of kernel chosen. We also set the evaluation metric (we use accuracy in this case, since the target is perfectly balanced):

```
from sklearn import svm
svc = svm.SVC()
svc = svm.SVC(probability=True, random_state=1)

from sklearn import model_selection
search_grid = [
```

```
                    {'C': [1, 10, 100, 1000], 'kernel': ['linear']},
                    {'C': [1, 10, 100, 1000], 'gamma': [0.001, 0.0001],
                    'kernel': ['rbf']}
                    ]

scorer = 'accuracy'
```

In our example, a linear kernel doesn't require the tuning of the gamma parameter, though it is very important for a radial basis function kernel. Therefore, we provide two dictionaries: the first containing the parameters for the linear kernel, the second containing parameters for a radial basis function kernel. Each dictionary only contains a reference to the kernel it is relevant to and only the range of parameters that are relevant for that kernel.

It is important to note that the evaluation metric can be different from the cost function optimized by the algorithm. In fact, as discussed in *Chapter 5, Competition Tasks and Metrics*, you may encounter scenarios in which the evaluation metric for the competition is different, but you cannot modify the cost function of your algorithm. Under these circumstances, tuning the hyperparameters according to your evaluation metric can still help in obtaining a well-performing model. Though built around the algorithm's cost function, the optimal set of hyperparameters found will be the one returning the best evaluation metric under such constraints. It probably won't be the theoretically best result that you could obtain for the problem, but it may often not be far from it.

All the ingredients (model, search space, evaluation metric, cross-validation scheme) are combined into the GridSearchCV instance, and then the model is fit to the data:

```
search_func = model_selection.GridSearchCV(estimator=svc,
                                           param_grid=search_grid,
                                           scoring=scorer,
                                           n_jobs=-1,
                                           cv=5)
search_func.fit(X, y)

print (search_func.best_params_)
print (search_func.best_score_)
```

After a while, depending on the machine you are running the optimization on, you will obtain the best combination based on cross-validated results.

In conclusion, grid search is a very simple optimization algorithm that can leverage the availability of multi-core computers. It can work fine with machine learning algorithms that do not require many tunings (such as SVM and the ridge and lasso regressions) but, in all other cases, its applicability is quite narrow. First, it is limited to optimizing hyperparameters by discrete choice (you need a limited set of values to cycle through). In addition, you cannot expect it to work effectively on algorithms requiring *multiple* hyperparameters to be tuned. This is because of the exploding complexity of the search space, and because most of the computational inefficiency is due to the fact that the search is trying parameter values blindly, most of which do not work for the problem.

Random search

Random search, which simply samples the search space randomly, is feasible in high-dimensional spaces and is widely used in practice. The downside of random search, however, is that it doesn't use information from prior experiments to select the next setting (a problem shared by grid search, we should note). In addition, to find the best solution as fast as possible, you cannot do anything except hope to be lucky you catch the right hyperparameters.

Random search works incredibly well and it is simple to understand. Despite the fact it relies on randomness, it isn't just based on blind luck, though it may initially appear to be. In fact, it works like random sampling in statistics: the main point of the technique is that if you do enough random tests, you have a good possibility of finding the right parameters without wasting energy on testing slightly different combinations of similarly performing combinations.

Many AutoML systems rely on random search when there are too many parameters to set (see Golovin, D. et al. *Google Vizier: A Service for Black-Box Optimization*, 2017). As a rule of thumb, consider looking at random search when the dimensionality of your hyperparameter optimization problem is sufficiently high (for example, over 16).

Below, we run the previous example using random search:

```
import scipy.stats as stats
from sklearn.utils.fixes import loguniform

search_dict = {'kernel': ['linear', 'rbf'],
               'C': loguniform(1, 1000),
               'gamma': loguniform(0.0001, 0.1)
               }
```

```
scorer = 'accuracy'

search_func = model_selection.RandomizedSearchCV
              (estimator=svc,param_distributions=search_dict, n_iter=6,
              scoring=scorer, n_jobs=-1, cv=5)

search_func.fit(X, y)

print (search_func.best_params_)
print (search_func.best_score_)
```

Notice that, now, we don't care about running the search on separate spaces for the different kernels. Contrary to grid search, where each parameter, even the ineffective ones, is systematically tested, which requires computational time, here the efficiency of the search is not affected by the set of hyperparameters tested. The search doesn't depend on irrelevant parameters, but is guided by chance; any trial is useful, even if you are testing only one valid parameter among many for the chosen kernel.

Halving search

As we mentioned, both grid search and random search work in an uninformed way: if some tests find out that certain hyperparameters do not impact the result or that certain value intervals are ineffective, the information is not propagated to the following searches.

For this reason, Scikit-learn has recently introduced the `HalvingGridSearchCV` and `HalvingRandomSearchCV` estimators, which can be used to search a parameter space using **successive halving** applied to the grid search and random search tuning strategies.

In halving, a large number of hyperparameter combinations are evaluated in an initial round of tests but using a small amount of computational resources. This is achieved by running the tests on a subsample of a few cases from your training data. A smaller training set needs fewer computations to be tested, so fewer resources (namely time) are used at the cost of more imprecise performance estimations. This initial round allows the selection of a subset of candidate hyperparameter values, which have performed better on the problem, to be used for the second round, when the training set size is increased.

The following rounds proceed in a similar way, allocating larger and larger subsets of the training set to be searched as the range of tested values is restricted (testing now requires more time to execute, but returns a more precise performance estimation), while the number of candidates continues to be halved.

Here is an example applied to the previous problem:

```
from sklearn.experimental import enable_halving_search_cv
from sklearn.model_selection import HalvingRandomSearchCV

search_func = HalvingRandomSearchCV(estimator=svc,
                                    param_distributions=search_dict,
                                    resource='n_samples',
                                    max_resources=100,
                                    aggressive_elimination=True,
                                    scoring=scorer,
                                    n_jobs=-1,
                                    cv=5,
                                    random_state=0)

search_func.fit(X, y)

print (search_func.best_params_)
print (search_func.best_score_)
```

In this way, halving provides information to the successive optimization steps via the selection of the candidates. In the next sections, we will discuss even smarter ways to achieve a more precise and efficient search through the space of hyperparameters.

Kazuki Onodera

https://www.kaggle.com/onodera

Let's pause for an interview with another Kaggler. Kazuki Onodera is a Competitions Grandmaster and Discussions Master who has around 7 years of competition experience. He's also a Senior Deep Learning Data Scientist at NVIDIA and a member of the NVIDIA KGMON (Kaggle Grandmasters of NVIDIA) team.

What's your favorite kind of competition and why? In terms of techniques and solving approaches, what is your specialty on Kaggle?

Instacart Market Basket Analysis. *This competition proved quite challenging for the Kaggle community because of its use of anonymized data related to customer orders over time in order to predict which previously purchased products will be in a user's next order. The reason why I like it is that I love feature engineering and I could come up with a bunch of good and interesting features everyone else couldn't, which allowed me to get second place in the competition.*

How do you approach a Kaggle competition? How different is this approach to what you do in your day-to-day work?

I try to imagine how a model works, and delve into false negatives and false positives. Same as in my daily work.

Tell us about a particularly challenging competition you entered, and what insights you used to tackle the task.

Human Protein Atlas - Single Cell Classification. *This competition was a kind of instance segmentation competition, but no masks were provided. So, it turned into being a weakly supervised multi-label classification problem. I created a two-stage pipeline for removing label noise.*

Has Kaggle helped you in your career? If so, how?

Yes. I'm now working in the NVIDIA KGMON (Kaggle Grandmasters of NVIDIA) team. Kaggle launches many different machine learning competitions, different with regards to data type, tabular, image, natural language, and signal, as well as with regards to sector and domain: industry, finance, astronomy, pathology, sports, retail, and so on. I bet nobody can access and have experience with all these kinds of data except Kagglers.

In your experience, what do inexperienced Kagglers often overlook? What do you know now that you wish you'd known when you first started?

Target analysis. Also, seed averaging is quite overlooked: always simple but powerful.

What mistakes have you made in competitions in the past?

Target analysis. Top teams always analyze the target better than others, so if I couldn't get a better place in a competition, I go and read about the top solutions, because they always describe to me the knowledge about the data that I missed during the competition.

Are there any particular tools or libraries that you would recommend using for data analysis or machine learning?

Just Python and Jupyter Notebooks.

What's the most important thing someone should keep in mind or do when they're entering a competition?

If you can learn from a defeat, you haven't really lost.

Do you use other competition platforms? How do they compare to Kaggle?

KDD Cup and RecSys. Both meet the minimum requirements for being interesting and challenging.

Key parameters and how to use them

The next problem is using the right set of hyperparameters for each kind of model you use. In particular, in order to be efficient in your optimization, you need to know the values of each hyperparameter that it actually makes sense to test for each distinct algorithm.

In this section, we will examine the most common models used in Kaggle competitions, especially the tabular ones, and discuss the hyperparameters you need to tune in order to obtain the best results. We will distinguish between classical machine learning models and gradient boosting models (which are much more demanding in terms of their space of parameters) for generic tabular data problems.

As for neural networks, we can give you an idea about specific parameters to tune when we present the standard models (for instance, the TabNet neural model has some specific parameters to set so that it works properly). However, most of the optimization on deep neural networks in Kaggle competitions is not performed on standard models, but on *custom* ones. Consequently, apart from basic learning parameters such as the learning rate and the batch size, optimization in neural networks is based on the specific characteristics of the neural architecture of your model. You have to deal with the problem in an ad hoc way. Near the end of the chapter, we will discuss an example of **neural architecture search (NAS)** using KerasTuner (`https://keras.io/keras_tuner/`).

Linear models

The linear models that need to be tuned are usually linear regressions or logistic regressions with regularization:

- C: The range you should search is np.logspace(-4, 4, 10); smaller values specify stronger regularization.

- alpha: You should search the range np.logspace(-2, 2, 10); smaller values specify stronger regularization, larger values specify stronger regularization. Also take note that higher values take more time to process when using lasso.

- l1_ratio: You should pick from the list [.1, .5, .7, .9, .95, .99, 1]; it applies only to elastic net.

In Scikit-learn, depending on the algorithm, you find either the hyperparameter C (logistic regression) or alpha (lasso, ridge, elastic net).

Support-vector machines

SVMs are a family of powerful and advanced supervised learning techniques for classification and regression that can automatically fit linear and non-linear models. Scikit-learn offers an implementation based on LIBSVM, a complete library of SVM classification and regression implementations, and LIBLINEAR, a scalable library for linear classification ideal for large datasets, especially sparse text-based ones. In their optimization, SVMs strive to separate target classes in classification problems using a decision boundary characterized by the largest possible margin between classes.

Though SVMs work fine with default parameters, they are often not optimal, and you need to test various value combinations using cross-validation to find the best ones. Listed according to their importance, you have to set the following parameters:

- C: The penalty value. Decreasing it makes the margin between classes larger, thus ignoring more noise but also making the model more generalizable. A best value can normally be found in the range np.logspace(-3, 3, 7).

- kernel: This parameter will determine how non-linearity will be implemented in an SVM and it can be set to 'linear', 'poly', 'rbf', 'sigmoid', or a custom kernel. The most commonly used value is certainly rbf.

- degree: Works with kernel='poly', signaling the dimensionality of the polynomial expansion. It is ignored by other kernels. Usually, setting its values to between 2 and 5 works the best.

- gamma: A coefficient for `'rbf'`, `'poly'`, and `'sigmoid'`. High values tend to fit data in a better way, but can lead to some overfitting. Intuitively, we can imagine gamma as the influence that a single example exercises over the model. Low values make the influence of each example reach further. Since many points have to be considered, the SVM curve will tend to take a shape less influenced by local points and the result will be a smoother decision contour curve. High values of gamma, instead, mean the curve takes into account how points are arranged locally more and, as a result, you get a more irregular and wiggly decision curve. The suggested grid search range for this hyperparameter is `np.logspace(-3, 3, 7)`.

- nu: For regression and classification with nuSVR and nuSVC, this parameter sets a tolerance for the training points that are near to the margin and are not classified correctly. It helps in ignoring misclassified points just near or on the margin, hence it can render the classification decision curve smoother. It should be in the range $[0,1]$ since it is a proportion relative to your training set. Ultimately, it acts like C, with high proportions enlarging the margin.

- epsilon: This parameter specifies how much error SVR will accept, by defining an epsilon large range where no penalty is associated with an incorrect prediction of the example during the training of the algorithm. The suggested search range is `np.logspace(-4, 2, 7)`.

- penalty, loss, and dual: For LinearSVC, these parameters accept the (`'l1'`, `'squared_hinge'`, False), (`'l2'`, `'hinge'`, True), (`'l2'`, `'squared_hinge'`, True), and (`'l2'`, `'squared_hinge'`, False) combinations. The (`'l2'`, `'hinge'`, True) combination is analogous to the SVC(kernel=`'linear'`) learner.

It may appear that an SVM has many hyperparameters to set, but many settings are specific only to implementations or to kernels, so you only have to select the relevant parameters.

Random forests and extremely randomized trees

Leo Breiman and *Adele Cutler* originally devised the idea at the core of the random forest algorithm, and the name of the algorithm remains a trademark of theirs today (though the algorithm is open source). Random forests are implemented in Scikit-learn as RandomForestClassifier or RandomForestRegressor.

A random forest works in a similar way to bagging, also devised by Leo Breiman, but operates only using binary split decision trees, which are left to grow to their extremes. Moreover, it samples the cases to be used in each of its models using **bootstrapping**. As the tree is grown, at each split of a branch, the set of variables considered for the split is drawn randomly, too.

This is the secret at the heart of the algorithm: it ensembles trees that, due to different samples and variables considered at the splits, are very different from each other. As they are different, they are also uncorrelated. This is beneficial because when the results are ensembled, much variance is ruled out, as the extreme values on both sides of a distribution tend to balance out. In other words, bagging algorithms guarantee a certain level of diversity in the predictions, allowing them to develop rules that a single learner (such as a decision tree) might not come across. All this diversity is useful because it helps in building a distribution whose average is a better predictor than any of the individual trees in the ensemble.

Extra Trees (also known as **extremely randomized trees**), represented in Scikit-learn by the `ExtraTreesClassifier`/`ExtraTreesRegressor` classes, are a more randomized kind of random forest that produces a lower variance in the estimates at the cost of greater bias of the estimators. However, when it comes to CPU efficiency, Extra Trees can deliver a considerable speed-up compared to random forests, so they can be ideal when you are working with large datasets in terms of both examples and features. The reason for the resulting higher bias but better speed is the way splits are built in an Extra Tree. Random forests, after drawing a random set of features to be considered for splitting a branch of a tree, carefully search among them for the best values to assign to each branch. By contrast, in Extra Trees, both the set of candidate features for the split and the actual split value are decided completely randomly. So, there's no need for much computation, though the randomly chosen split may not be the most effective one (hence the bias).

For both algorithms, the key hyperparameters that should be set are as follows:

- `max_features`: This is the number of sampled features that are present at every split, which can determine the performance of the algorithm. The lower the number, the speedier, but with higher bias.
- `min_samples_leaf`: This allows you to determine the depth of the trees. Large numbers diminish the variance and increase the bias.
- `bootstrap`: This is a Boolean that allows bootstrapping.
- `n_estimators`: This is the number of trees. Remember that the more trees the better, though there is a threshold beyond which we get diminishing returns depending on the data problem. Also, this comes at a computational cost that you have to take into account based on the resources you have available.

Extra Trees are a good alternative to random forests, especially when the data you have is particularly noisy. Since they trade some variance reduction for more bias given their random choice of splits, they tend to overfit less on important yet noisy features that would otherwise dominate the splits in a random forest.

Gradient tree boosting

Gradient tree boosting or **gradient boosting decision trees** (**GBDT**) is an improved version of boosting (boosting works by fitting a sequence of weak learners on reweighted versions of the data). Like AdaBoost, GBDT is based on a gradient descent function. The algorithm has proven to be one of the most proficient ones from the family of models that are based on ensembles, though it is characterized by an increased variance of estimates, more sensitivity to noise in data (both problems can be mitigated by using subsampling), and significant computational costs due to non-parallel operations.

Apart from deep learning, gradient boosting is the most developed machine learning algorithm. Since AdaBoost and the initial gradient boosting implementation, as developed by *Jerome Friedman*, various other implementations of the algorithms appeared, the most recent ones being XGBoost, LightGBM, and CatBoost.

LightGBM

The high-performance LightGBM algorithm (`https://github.com/Microsoft/LightGBM`) is capable of being distributed on multiple computers and handling large amounts of data quickly. It was developed by a team at Microsoft as an open-source project on GitHub (there is also an academic paper: `https://papers.nips.cc/paper/2017/hash/6449f44a102fde848669bdd9eb 6b76fa-Abstract.html`).

LightGBM is based on decision trees, like XGBoost, but it follows a different strategy. While XG-Boost uses decision trees to split on a variable and explore different tree splits at that variable (the **level-wise** tree growth strategy), LightGBM concentrates on one split and goes on splitting from there in order to achieve a better fit (the **leaf-wise** tree growth strategy). This allows LightGBM to quickly reach a good fit of the data, and to generate alternative solutions compared to XGBoost (which is good, if you expect to blend the two solutions together in order to reduce the variance of the estimates). Algorithmically speaking, if we think of the structure of splits operated by a decision tree as a graph, XGBoost pursues a *breadth-first* search (BFS) and LightGBM a *depth-first* search (DFS).

Tuning LightGBM may appear daunting; it has more than a hundred parameters to tune that you can explore at this page: `https://github.com/Microsoft/LightGBM/blob/master/docs/ Parameters.rst` (also here: `https://lightgbm.readthedocs.io/en/latest/Parameters.html`).

As a rule of thumb, you should focus on the following hyperparameters, which usually have the most impact on the results:

- n_estimators: An integer between 10 and 10,000 that sets the number of iterations.
- learning_rate: A real number between 0.01 and 1.0, usually sampled from a log-uniform distribution. It represents the step size of the gradient descent procedure that computes the weights for the summed ensemble of all the iterations of the algorithm up to this point.
- max_depth: An integer between 1 and 16, representing the maximum number of splits on features. Setting it to a number below 0 allows the maximum possible number of splits, usually risking overfitting to data.
- num_leaves: An integer between 2 and 2^max_depth, representing the number of final leaves each tree will have at most.
- min_data_in_leaf: An integer between 0 and 300 that determines the minimum number of data points in one leaf.
- min_gain_to_split: A float between 0 and 15; it sets the minimum gain of the algorithm for tree partitioning. By setting this parameter, you can avoid unnecessary tree splits and thus reduce overfitting (it corresponds to the gamma parameter in XGBoost).
- max_bin: An integer between 32 and 512 that sets the maximum number of bins that feature values will be bucketed into. Having this parameter larger than the default value of 255 implies more risk of producing overfitting results.
- subsample: A real number between 0.01, and 1.0, representing the portion of the sample to be used in training.
- subsample_freq: An integer between 0 and 10 specifying the frequency, in terms of iterations, at which the algorithm will subsample the examples.

 Note that, if set to zero, the algorithm will ignore any value given to the subsample parameter. In addition, it is set to zero by default, therefore just setting the subsample parameter won't work.

- feature_fraction: A real number between 0.1 and 1.0 allowing you to specify the portion of features to be subsampled. Subsampling the features is another way to allow more randomization to play a role in the training, fighting noise and multicollinearity present in the features.
- subsample_for_bin: An integer between 30 and the number of examples. This sets the number of examples that are sampled for the construction of histogram bins.

- `reg_lambda`: A real number between 0 and 100.0 that sets the L2 regularization. Since it is more sensitive to the scale than to the exact number of the parameter, it is usually sampled from a log-uniform distribution.

- `reg_alpha`: A real number between 0 and 100.0, usually sampled from a log-uniform distribution, which sets the L1 regularization.

- `scale_pos_weight`: A real number between 1e-6 and 500, better sampled from the log-uniform distribution. The parameter weights the positive cases (thus effectively upsampling or downsampling) against the negative cases, which are kept to the value of 1.

Although the number of hyperparameters to tune when using LightGBM may appear daunting, in reality only a few of them matter a lot. Given a fixed number of iterations and learning rate, just a few are the most impactful (`feature_fraction`, `num_leaves`, `subsample`, `reg_lambda`, `reg_alpha`, `min_data_in_leaf`), as explained in this blog article by *Kohei Ozaki*, a Kaggle Grandmaster: `https://medium.com/optuna/lightgbm-tuner-new-optuna-integration-for-hyperparameter-optimization-8b7095e99258`. Kohei Ozaki leverages this fact in order to create a fast-tuning procedure for Optuna (you'll find more on the Optuna optimizer at the end of this chapter).

XGBoost

XGBoost (`https://github.com/dmlc/XGBoost`) stands for **eXtreme Gradient Boosting**. It is an open-source project that is not part of Scikit-learn, though it has recently been expanded by a Scikit-learn wrapper interface that makes it easier to incorporate XGBoost into a Scikit-learn-style data pipeline.

The XGBoost algorithm gained momentum and popularity in 2015 data science competitions, such as those on Kaggle and the KDD Cup 2015. As the creators (*Tianqui Chen*, *Tong He*, and *Carlos Guestrin*) report in papers they wrote on the algorithm, out of 29 challenges held on Kaggle during 2015, 17 winning solutions used XGBoost as a standalone solution or as part of an ensemble of multiple different models. Since then, the algorithm has always retained a strong appeal among the community of data scientists, though it struggled to keep pace with the innovation brought about by other GBM implementations such as LightGBM and CatBoost.

Aside from good performance both in terms of accuracy and computational efficiency, XGBoost is also a *scalable* solution, using at best multi-core processors as well as distributed machines.

XGBoost represents a new generation of GBM algorithms thanks to important tweaks to the initial tree boost GBM algorithm:

- Sparsity-awareness; it can leverage sparse matrices, saving both memory (no need for dense matrices) and computation time (zero values are handled in a special way).

- Approximate tree learning (weighted quantile sketch), which produces similar results but in much less time compared to the classical complete explorations of possible branch cuts.

- Parallel computing on a single machine (using multi-threading during the search for the best split) and, similarly, distributed computations on multiple machines.

- Out-of-core computations on a single machine, leveraging a data storage solution called **column block**. This arranges data on a disk by columns, thus saving time by pulling data from the disk in the way the optimization algorithm (which works on column vectors) expects it.

XGBoost can also deal with missing data in an effective way. Other tree ensembles based on standard decision trees require missing data first to be imputed using an off-scale value, such as a negative number, in order to develop an appropriate branching of the tree to deal with missing values.

As for XGBoost's parameters (`https://xgboost.readthedocs.io/en/latest/parameter.html`), we have decided to highlight a few key ones you will find across competitions and projects:

- `n_estimators`: Usually an integer ranging from 10 to 5,000.

- `learning_rate`: A real number ranging from 0.01 to 1.0, better sampled from the log-uniform distribution.

- `min_child_weight`: Usually an integer between 1 and 10.

- `max_depth`: Usually an integer between 1 and 50.

- `max_delta_step`: Usually an integer sampled between 0 and 20, representing the maximum delta step we allow for each leaf output.

- `subsample`: A real number from 0.1 to 1.0 indicating the proportion of examples to be subsampled.

- `colsample_bytree`: A real number from 0.1 to 1.0 indicating the subsample ratio of columns by tree.

- `colsample_bylevel`: A real number from 0.1 to 1.0 indicating the subsample ratio by level in trees.

- **reg_lambda**: A real number between 1e-9 and 100.0, preferably sampled from the log-uniform distribution. This parameter controls the L2 regularization.

- **reg_alpha**: A real number between 1e-9 and 100.0, preferably sampled from the log-uniform distribution. This parameter controls the L1 regularization.

- **gamma**: Specifying the minimum loss reduction for tree partitioning, this parameter requires a real number between 1e-9 and 0.5, preferably sampled from the log-uniform distribution.

- **scale_pos_weight**: A real number between 1e-6 and 500.0, preferably sampled from the log-uniform distribution, which represents a weight for the positive class.

Like LightGBM, XGBoost also has many similar hyperparameters to tune, hence all of the considerations previously made for LightGBM are also valid for XGBoost.

CatBoost

In July 2017, Yandex, the Russian search engine, made another interesting GBM algorithm public, CatBoost (https://catboost.ai/), whose name comes from putting together the two words "Category" and "Boosting." In fact, its strong point is its ability to handle categorical variables, which make up most of the information in most relational databases, by adopting a mixed strategy of one-hot encoding and target encoding. Target encoding is a way to express categorical levels by assigning them an appropriate numeric value for the problem at hand; more on this can be found in *Chapter 7, Modeling for Tabular Competitions*.

The idea used by CatBoost to encode categorical variables is not new, but it is a kind of feature engineering that has been used before, mostly in data science competitions. Target encoding, also known as likelihood encoding, impact coding, or mean encoding, is simply a way to transform your labels into a number based on their association with the target variable. If you have a regression, you could transform labels based on the mean target value typical of that level; if it is a classification, it is simply the probability of classification of your target given that label (the probability of your target conditional on each category value). It may appear a simple and smart feature engineering trick but it has side effects, mostly in terms of overfitting, because you are taking information from the target into your predictors.

CatBoost has quite a few parameters (see https://catboost.ai/en/docs/references/training-parameters/). We have limited our discussion to the eight most important ones:

- **iterations**: Usually an integer between 10 and 1,000, but it can increase based on the problem.

- `depth`: An integer between 1 and 8; usually higher values require longer fitting times and do not produce better results.

- `learning_rate`: A real value between 0.01 and 1.0, better sampled from the log-uniform distribution.

- `random_strength`: A real number log-linearly sampled from the range 1e-9 to 10.0, which specifies the randomness level for scoring splits.

- `bagging_temperature`: A real value between 0.0 and 1.0 that sets the Bayesian bootstrap.

- `border_count`: An integer between 1 and 255 indicating the splits for numerical features.

- `l2_leaf_reg`: An integer between 2 and 30; the value for L2 regularization.

- `scale_pos_weight`: A real number between 0.01 and 10.0 representing the weight for the positive class.

Even if CatBoost may appear to be just another GBM implementation, it has quite a few differences (highlighted also by the different parameters being used) that may provide great help in a competition, both as a single-model solution and as a model integrated into a larger ensemble.

HistGradientBoosting

Recently, Scikit-learn has introduced a new version of gradient boosting inspired by LightGBM's binned data and histograms (see this presentation at EuroPython by *Olivier Grisel*: https://www.youtube.com/watch?v=urVUlKbQfQ4). Either as a classifier (HistGradientBoostingClassifier) or a regressor (HistGradientBoostingRegressor), it can be used for enriching ensembles with different models and it presents a much shorter and essential range of hyperparameters to be tuned:

- `learning_rate`: A real number between 0.01 and 1.0, usually sampled from a log-uniform distribution.

- `max_iter`: An integer that can range from 10 to 10,000.

- `max_leaf_nodes`: An integer from 2 to 500. It interacts with max_depth; it is advisable to set only one of the two and leave the other set to None.

- `max_depth`: An integer between 2 and 12.

- `min_samples_leaf`: An integer between 2 and 300.

- `l2_regularization`: A float between 0.0 and 100.0.

- `max_bins`: An integer between 32 and 512.

Even if Scikit-learn's `HistGradientBoosting` is nothing too different from LightGBM or XG-Boost, it does provide a different way to implement GBMs in a competition, and models built by `HistGradientBoosting` may provide a contribution when ensembling multiple predictions, such as in blending and stacking.

Having reached the end of this section, you should be more familiar with the most common machine learning algorithms (only deep learning solutions have not been discussed) and their most important hyperparameters to tune, which will help you in building an outstanding solution in a Kaggle competition. Knowing the basic optimization strategies, usable algorithms, and their key hyperparameters is just a starting point. In the next section, we will begin an in-depth discussion about how to tune them more optimally using Bayesian optimization.

Alberto Danese

https://www.kaggle.com/albedan

Our second interview of the chapter is with Alberto Danese, Head of Data Science at Nexi, an Italian credit card and digital payments company. A Competitions Grandmaster who joined the platform in 2015, he obtained most of his gold medals as a solo competitor.

What's your favorite kind of competition and why? In terms of techniques and solving approaches, what is your specialty on Kaggle?

I've always worked in the Financial Services industry, dealing mostly with structured data, and I do prefer competitions that belong to this category. I enjoy being able to have a practical grasp of what the data is all about and doing some smart feature engineering in order to squeeze every bit of information out of the data.

Technically speaking, I've got good experience with classical ML libraries and especially with Gradient Boosting Decision Trees: the most common libraries (XGBoost, LightGBM, CatBoost) are always my first choice.

How do you approach a Kaggle competition? How different is this approach to what you do in your day-to-day work?

I always spend a lot of time just exploring the data and trying to figure out what the problem that the sponsor is actually trying to solve with machine learning is. Different from what newbies usually think about Kaggle, I don't spend so much time on all the "tweaking" of the specific ML algorithm — and apparently this approach has paid off!

In my daily job, understanding the data is also extremely important, but there are some additional phases that are completely missing in a Kaggle competition. I've got to:

- *Define a business problem to be solved with ML (together with colleagues in the business departments)*
- *Find the data, sometimes also from external data providers*
- *And when the ML part is done, understand how to put it in production and manage the evolutions*

Tell us about a particularly challenging competition you entered, and what insights you used to tackle the task.

I enjoyed the TalkingData AdTracking Fraud Detection Challenge, *with which I became a Grandmaster. Besides being on an extremely interesting topic (fighting fraud from click-farms), it really pushed me to do efficient feature engineering, as the volumes were huge (more than 100M labeled rows) and cutting on computation times was key in order to test different approaches. It also forced me to understand how to exploit lag/lead features (and other window functions) in the best way, in order to create a sort of time series in an otherwise classical ML problem.*

Has Kaggle helped you in your career? If so, how?

Definitely! Being able to achieve great objective and verifiable results is no doubt something that makes a resume stand out. When I was hired by Cerved (a marketing intelligence service company) in 2016, the hiring manager was perfectly aware of what Kaggle was – and having some real-world projects to talk about during an interview is something extremely valuable. For sure Kaggle had an important role in the evolution of my career.

In your experience, what do inexperienced Kagglers often overlook? What do you know now that you wish you'd known when you first started?

I think that everyone just starts coding, maybe forking a public kernel and just changing a few lines or parameters. This is perfectly fine at the beginning! But you do have to spend a decent amount of time not coding, but studying the data and understanding the problem.

What mistakes have you made in competitions in the past?

Not sure if it counts as a mistake, but I have often preferred to compete solo: on one hand it's great as it forces you to handle every single aspect of a competition, and you're able to manage your time as you wish. But I've really enjoyed collaborating with teammates on a couple of competitions as well: I probably should consider teaming up more often, as you can learn a lot from collaborating.

> ## Are there any particular tools or libraries that you would recommend using for data analysis or machine learning?
> *Besides the usual ones, I've always been a great fan of* `data.table` *(starting from the R version): I think it's not getting the credit it deserves! It's really a great package when you want to deal with huge data on a local machine.*
>
> ## What's the most important thing someone should keep in mind or do when they're entering a competition?
> *Understand the problem and the data first: don't start coding right away!*

Bayesian optimization

Leaving behind grid search (feasible only when the space of experiments is limited), the usual choice for the practitioner is to apply random search optimization or try a **Bayesian optimization (BO)** technique, which requires a more complex setup.

Originally introduced in the paper *Practical Bayesian optimization of machine learning algorithms* by Snoek, J., Larochelle, H., and Adams, R. P. (http://export.arxiv.org/pdf/1206.2944), the key idea behind Bayesian optimization is that we optimize a **proxy function** (also called a **surrogate function**) rather than the true objective function (which grid search and random search both do). We do this if there are no gradients, if testing the true objective function is costly (if it is not, then we simply go for random search), and if the search space is noisy and complex enough.

Bayesian search balances *exploration* with *exploitation*. At the start, it explores randomly, thus training the surrogate function as it goes. Based on that surrogate function, the search exploits its initial approximate knowledge of how the predictor works in order to sample more useful examples and minimize the cost function. As the *Bayesian* part of the name suggests, we are using priors in order to make smarter decisions about sampling during optimization. This way, we reach a minimization more quickly by limiting the number of evaluations we need to make.

Bayesian optimization uses an **acquisition function** to tell us how promising an observation will be. In fact, to manage the tradeoff between exploration and exploitation, the algorithm defines an acquisition function that provides a single measure of how useful it would be to try any given point.

Usually, Bayesian optimization is powered by Gaussian processes. Gaussian processes perform better when the search space has a smooth and predictable response. An alternative when the search space is more complex is using tree algorithms (for instance, random forests), or a completely different approach called **Tree Parzen Estimators** or **Tree-structured Parzen Estimators (TPEs)**.

Instead of directly building a model that estimates the success of a set of parameters, thus acting like an oracle, TPEs estimate the parameters of a multivariate distribution that define the best-performing values of the parameters, based on successive approximations provided by the experimentations. In this way, TPEs derive the best set of parameters by sampling them from a probabilistic distribution, and not directly from a machine learning model like Gaussian processes does.

We will discuss each of these approaches, first by examining Scikit-optimize and KerasTuner, both based on Gaussian processes (Scikit-optimize can also use random forests and KerasTuner can use multi-armed bandits), and then Optuna, which is principally based on TPE (though it also offers different strategies: `https://optuna.readthedocs.io/en/stable/reference/samplers.html`).

Though Bayesian optimization is considered the state of the art for hyperparameter tuning, always keep in mind that for more complex parameter spaces, using Bayesian optimization provides no advantage in terms of time and computation spent over a solution simply found by random search. For instance, in Google Cloud Machine Learning Engine services, the usage of Bayesian optimization is limited to problems involving at most sixteen parameters. For larger numbers of parameters, it resorts to random sampling.

Using Scikit-optimize

Scikit-optimize (`skopt`) has been developed using the same API as Scikit-learn, as well as making extensive use of NumPy and SciPy functions. In addition, it was created by some of the contributors to the Scikit-learn project, such as *Gilles Louppe*.

Based on Gaussian process algorithms, the package is well maintained, though sometimes it has to catch up because of improvements on the Scikit-learn, NumPy, or SciPy sides. For instance, at the time of writing, in order to run it properly on Kaggle Notebooks you have to roll back to older versions of these packages, as explained in a GitHub issue (`https://github.com/scikit-optimize/scikit-optimize/issues/981`).

The package has an intuitive API and it is quite easy to hack it and use its functions in custom optimization strategies. Scikit-optimize is also renowned for its useful graphical representations. In fact, by visualizing the results of an optimization process (using Scikit-optimize's `plot_objective` function), you can figure out whether you can re-define the search space for the problem and formulate an explanation of how optimization works for a problem.

In our worked example, we will refer to the work that can be found in the following Kaggle
Notebooks:

- https://www.kaggle.com/lucamassaron/tutorial-bayesian-optimization-with-lightgbm
- https://www.kaggle.com/lucamassaron/scikit-optimize-for-lightgbm

Our purpose here is to show you how to quickly handle an optimization problem for a competition
such as *30 Days of ML*, a recent competition that involved many Kagglers in learning new skills
and applying them in a competition lasting 30 days. The goal of this competition is to predict
the value of an insurance claim, so it is a regression problem. You can find out more about this
initiative and download the data necessary for the example we are going to present (materials
are always available to the public), by visiting https://www.kaggle.com/thirty-days-of-ml.

 If you cannot access the data because you have not taken part in the competition previously, you can use this Kaggle Dataset: https://www.kaggle.com/
lucamassaron/30-days-of-ml.

The following code will present how to load the data for this problem and then set up a Bayesian
optimization process that will improve the performance of a LightGBM model.

We start by loading the packages:

```
# Importing core libraries
import numpy as np
import pandas as pd
from time import time
import pprint
import joblib
from functools import partial

# Suppressing warnings because of skopt verbosity
import warnings
warnings.filterwarnings("ignore")

# Classifiers
import lightgbm as lgb

# Model selection
```

```
from sklearn.model_selection import KFold

# Metrics
from sklearn.metrics import mean_squared_error
from sklearn.metrics import make_scorer

# Skopt functions
from skopt import BayesSearchCV
from skopt.callbacks import DeadlineStopper, DeltaYStopper
from skopt.space import Real, Categorical, Integer
```

As a next step, we load the data. The data doesn't need much processing, aside from turning some categorical features with alphabetical letters as levels into ordered numeric ones:

```
# Loading data
X = pd.read_csv("../input/30-days-of-ml/train.csv")
X_test = pd.read_csv("../input/30-days-of-ml/test.csv")

# Preparing data as a tabular matrix
y = X.target
X = X.set_index('id').drop('target', axis='columns')
X_test = X_test.set_index('id')

# Dealing with categorical data
categoricals = [item for item in X.columns if 'cat' in item]
cat_values = np.unique(X[categoricals].values)
cat_dict = dict(zip(cat_values, range(len(cat_values))))
X[categoricals] = X[categoricals].replace(cat_dict).astype('category')
X_test[categoricals] = X_test[categoricals].replace(cat_dict).
astype('category')
```

After making the data available, we define a reporting function that can be used by Scikit-optimize for various optimization tasks. The function takes the data and the optimizer as inputs. It can also handle **callback functions**, which are functions that perform actions such as reporting, early stopping based on having reached a certain threshold of time spent searching or performance not improving (for instance, not seeing improvements for a certain number of iterations), or saving the state of the processing after each optimization iteration:

```python
# Reporting util for different optimizers
def report_perf(optimizer, X, y, title="model", callbacks=None):
    """
    A wrapper for measuring time and performance of optimizers

    optimizer = a sklearn or a skopt optimizer
    X = the training set
    y = our target
    title = a string label for the experiment
    """
    start = time()

    if callbacks is not None:
        optimizer.fit(X, y, callback=callbacks)
    else:
        optimizer.fit(X, y)

    d=pd.DataFrame(optimizer.cv_results_)
    best_score = optimizer.best_score_
    best_score_std = d.iloc[optimizer.best_index_].std_test_score
    best_params = optimizer.best_params_

    print((title + " took %.2f seconds, candidates checked: %d, best CV
           score: %.3f" + u" \u00B1"+" %.3f") %
                        (time() - start,
                         len(optimizer.cv_results_['params']),
                         best_score,
                         best_score_std))
    print('Best parameters:')
    pprint.pprint(best_params)
    print()
    return best_params
```

We now have to prepare the scoring function (upon which the evaluation is based), the validation strategy (based on cross-validation), the model, and the search space. For the scoring function, which should be a root mean squared error metric, we refer to the practices in Scikit-learn where you always minimize a function (if you have to maximize, you minimize its negative).

The `make_scorer` wrapper can easily replicate such practices:

```
# Setting the scoring function
scoring = make_scorer(partial(mean_squared_error, squared=False),
                      greater_is_better=False)


# Setting the validation strategy
kf = KFold(n_splits=5, shuffle=True, random_state=0)


# Setting the basic regressor
reg = lgb.LGBMRegressor(boosting_type='gbdt',
                        metric='rmse',
                        objective='regression',
                        n_jobs=1,
                        verbose=-1,
                        random_state=0)
```

Setting the search space requires the use of different functions from Scikit-optimize, such as `Real`, `Integer`, or `Choice`, each one sampling from a different kind of distribution that you define as a parameter (usually the uniform distribution, but the log-uniform is also used when you are more interested in the scale effect of a parameter than its exact value):

```
# Setting the search space
search_spaces = {

    # Boosting learning rate
    'learning_rate': Real(0.01, 1.0, 'log-uniform'),

    # Number of boosted trees to fit
    'n_estimators': Integer(30, 5000),

    # Maximum tree leaves for base learners
    'num_leaves': Integer(2, 512),

    # Maximum tree depth for base learners
    'max_depth': Integer(-1, 256),

    # Minimal number of data in one leaf
    'min_child_samples': Integer(1, 256),
```

```
    # Max number of bins buckets
    'max_bin': Integer(100, 1000),           .

    # Subsample ratio of the training instance
    'subsample': Real(0.01, 1.0, 'uniform'),

    # Frequency of subsample
    'subsample_freq': Integer(0, 10),

    # Subsample ratio of columns
    'colsample_bytree': Real(0.01, 1.0, 'uniform'),

    # Minimum sum of instance weight
    'min_child_weight': Real(0.01, 10.0, 'uniform'),

    # L2 regularization
    'reg_lambda': Real(1e-9, 100.0, 'log-uniform'),

    # L1 regularization
    'reg_alpha': Real(1e-9, 100.0, 'log-uniform'),
}
```

Once you have defined:

- Your cross-validation strategy
- Your evaluation metric
- Your base model
- Your hyperparameter search space

All that is left is just to feed them into your optimization function, BayesSearchCV. Based on the CV scheme provided, this function will look for the minimum of your scoring function based on values within the search space. You can set a maximum number of iterations performed, the kind of surrogate function (Gaussian processes (GP) works on most occasions), and the random seed for reproducibility:

```
# Wrapping everything up into the Bayesian optimizer
opt = BayesSearchCV(estimator=reg,
                    search_spaces=search_spaces,
```

```
                        scoring=scoring,
                        cv=kf,
                        n_iter=60,              # max number of trials
                        n_jobs=-1,              # number of jobs
                        iid=False,
                        # if not iid it optimizes on the cv score
                        return_train_score=False,
                        refit=False,
                        # Gaussian Processes (GP)
                        optimizer_kwargs={'base_estimator': 'GP'},
                        # random state for replicability
                        random_state=0)
```

At this point, you can start the search using the reporting function we defined previously. After a while, the function will return the best parameters for the problem.

```
# Running the optimizer
overdone_control = DeltaYStopper(delta=0.0001)
# We stop if the gain of the optimization becomes too small
time_limit_control = DeadlineStopper(total_time=60 * 60 * 6)
# We impose a time limit (6 hours)

best_params = report_perf(opt, X, y,'LightGBM_regression',
                        callbacks=[overdone_control, time_limit_
control])
```

In the example, we set a limit on operations by specifying a maximum time allowed (6 hours) before stopping and reporting the best results. Since the Bayesian optimization approach blends together exploration and exploitation of different combinations of hyperparameters, stopping at any time will always return the best solution found so far (but not necessarily the best one possible). This is because the acquisition function will always give priority of exploration to the most promising parts of the search space, based on the estimated performances returned by the surrogate function and their uncertainty intervals.

Customizing a Bayesian optimization search

The BayesSearchCV function offered by Scikit-optimize is certainly convenient, because it wraps and arranges all the elements of a hyperparameter search by itself, but it also has limitations. For instance, you may find it useful in a competition to:

- Have more control over each search iteration, for instance mixing random search and Bayesian search

- Be able to apply early stopping on algorithms

- Customize your validation strategy more

- Stop experiments that do not work early (for instance, immediately evaluating the performance of the single cross-validation folds when it is available, instead of waiting to have all folds averaged at the end)

- Create clusters of hyperparameter sets that perform in a similar way (for instance, in order to create multiple models differing only in the hyperparameters used, to be used for a blending ensemble)

Each of these tasks would not be too complex if you could modify the BayesSearchCV internal procedure. Luckily, Scikit-optimize lets you do just this. In fact, behind BayesSearchCV, as well as behind other wrappers from the package, there are specific minimizing functions that you can use as standalone parts of your own search function:

- gp_minimize: Bayesian optimization using Gaussian processes

- forest_minimize: Bayesian optimization using random forests or extremely randomized trees

- gbrt_minimize: Bayesian optimization using gradient boosting

- dummy_minimize: Just random search

In the following example, we are going to modify the previous search using our own custom search function. The new custom function will accept early stopping during training and it will prune experiments if one of the fold validation results is not a top-performing one.

 You can find the next example working in a Kaggle Notebook at https://www.kaggle.com/lucamassaron/hacking-bayesian-optimization.

As in the previous example, we start by importing the necessary packages.

```
# Importing core libraries
import numpy as np
import pandas as pd
from time import time
import pprint
```

```
import joblib
from functools import partial

# Suppressing warnings because of skopt verbosity
import warnings
warnings.filterwarnings("ignore")

# Classifier/Regressor
from xgboost import XGBRegressor

# Model selection
from sklearn.model_selection import KFold, StratifiedKFold
from sklearn.model_selection import cross_val_score
from sklearn.model_selection import train_test_split

# Metrics
from sklearn.metrics import mean_squared_error
from sklearn.metrics import make_scorer

# Skopt functions
from skopt import BayesSearchCV
from skopt.callbacks import DeadlineStopper, DeltaYStopper
from skopt.space import Real, Categorical, Integer
from skopt import gp_minimize, forest_minimize
from skopt import gbrt_minimize, dummy_minimize

# Decorator to convert a list of parameters to named arguments
from skopt.utils import use_named_args

# Data processing
from sklearn.preprocessing import OrdinalEncoder
```

In the same way as before, we upload the data from the *30 Days of ML* competition:

```
# Loading data
X_train = pd.read_csv("../input/30-days-of-ml/train.csv")
X_test = pd.read_csv("../input/30-days-of-ml/test.csv")
```

```python
# Preparing data as a tabular matrix
y_train = X_train.target
X_train = X_train.set_index('id').drop('target', axis='columns')
X_test = X_test.set_index('id')

# Pointing out categorical features
categoricals = [item for item in X_train.columns if 'cat' in item]

# Dealing with categorical data using OrdinalEncoder
ordinal_encoder = OrdinalEncoder()
X_train[categoricals] = ordinal_encoder.fit_transform(X_train[categoricals])
X_test[categoricals] = ordinal_encoder.transform(X_test[categoricals])
```

Now we set all the necessary elements for a hyperparameter search, that is, the scoring function, the validation strategy, the search space, and the machine learning model to be optimized. The scoring function and the validation strategy will later become the core elements constituting the objective function, the function the Bayesian optimization will strive to minimize.

```python
# Setting the scoring function
scoring = partial(mean_squared_error, squared=False)
# Setting the cv strategy
kf = KFold(n_splits=5, shuffle=True, random_state=0)
# Setting the search space
space = [Real(0.01, 1.0, 'uniform', name='learning_rate'),
         Integer(1, 8, name='max_depth'),
         Real(0.1, 1.0, 'uniform', name='subsample'),
         # Subsample ratio of columns by tree
         Real(0.1, 1.0, 'uniform', name='colsample_bytree'),
         # L2 regularization
         Real(0, 100., 'uniform', name='reg_lambda'),
         # L1 regularization
         Real(0, 100., 'uniform', name='reg_alpha'),
         # minimum sum of instance weight (hessian)
         Real(1, 30, 'uniform', name='min_child_weight')
         ]
model = XGBRegressor(n_estimators=10_000,
                     booster='gbtree', random_state=0)
```

Notice this time that we have not included the number of estimators (the n_estimators parameter) in the search space. Instead, we set it when instantiating the model and we enter a high value, since we expect to stop the model early based on a validation set.

As a next step, you now need to create the objective function. The objective function should just accept as input the parameters to be optimized and return the resulting score. However, the objective function also needs to accept the elements necessary for the search you have just prepared. Naturally, you could refer to them from inside the function. However, it is a good practice to take them into the function itself, in its internal memory space. This has its advantages; for instance, you will make the elements immutable and they will be carried along with the objective function (by pickling or if you distribute the search task on a multi-processor level). You can obtain this second result by creating a make function that takes in the elements, with the modified objective function being returned by the make function. With this simple structure, your objective function will incorporate all the elements such as the data and the model, and you will only need to pass in the parameters to be tested.

Let's start coding the function. We will stop along the way to discuss some relevant aspects:

```python
# The objective function to be minimized
def make_objective(model, X, y, space, cv, scoring, validation=0.2):
    # This decorator converts your objective function
    # with named arguments into one that accepts a list as argument,
    # while doing the conversion automatically.
    @use_named_args(space)
    def objective(**params):
        model.set_params(**params)
        print("\nTesting: ", params)
        validation_scores = list()
        for k, (train_index, test_index) in enumerate(kf.split(X, y)):
            val_index = list()
            train_examples = int(train_examples * (1 - validation))
            train_index, val_index = (train_index[:train_examples],
                                      train_index[train_examples:])

            start_time = time()
            model.fit(X.iloc[train_index,:], y[train_index],
```

```
                    early_stopping_rounds=50,
                    eval_set=[(X.iloc[val_index,:], y[val_index])],
                    verbose=0
                )
            end_time = time()

            rounds = model.best_iteration

            test_preds = model.predict(X.iloc[test_index,:])
            test_score = scoring(y[test_index], test_preds)
            print(f"CV Fold {k+1} rmse:{test_score:0.5f}-{rounds}
                    rounds - it took {end_time-start_time:0.0f} secs")
            validation_scores.append(test_score)
```

In this first part of the function, you simply create an objective function, doing cross-validation and fitting the data using early stopping. We have used an aggressive early stopping strategy to save time, but you could raise the number of patient rounds if you believe that it might work better for your problem. Notice that the validation examples are sequentially taken out from the examples in the training folds (see how train_index and val_index are defined in the code), leaving the out-of-fold examples (test_index derived from the kf cross-validation splitting) untouched for the final validation. This is important if you do not want to incur adaptive overfitting on the data you use for early stopping.

In the next part, before moving on to the cross-validation loop and proceeding to the remaining cross-validation folds to be trained and tested, you analyze the result obtained by the fold on the out-of-fold set:

```
            if len(history[k]) >= 10:
                threshold = np.percentile(history[k], q=25)
                if test_score > threshold:
                    print(f"Early stopping for under-performing fold:
                            threshold is {threshold:0.5f}")
                    return np.mean(validation_scores)

            history[k].append(test_score)
        return np.mean(validation_scores)

    return objective
```

Notice that we are keeping a global dictionary, history, containing the results obtained from each fold up to now. We can compare the results across multiple experiments and cross-validations; the cross-validation is reproducible due to the random seed, so the results of the same fold are perfectly comparable. If the result of the present fold is sub-par compared to the previously obtained folds in other iterations (using the bottom quartile as a reference), the idea is to stop and return the average of the folds tested so far. The rationale for this is that if one fold doesn't present acceptable results, then the whole cross-validation probably won't either. You can therefore just quit and move on to another set of more promising parameters. It is a kind of early stopping on cross-validation that should speed up your search and allow you to cover more experiments in less time.

Next, using our make_objective function, we put together all the elements (model, data, search space, validation strategy, and scoring function) into a single function, the objective function. As a result, we now have a function that only takes in the parameters to be optimized and returns a score, based on which the minimization engine of the optimization will decide the next experiments:

```
objective = make_objective(model,
                            X_train, y_train,
                            space=space,
                            cv=kf,
                            scoring=scoring)
```

Since we want to control each step of the optimization and save it for later use, we also prepare a callback function that will save a list of the experiments executed and their results, at every iteration of the minimization process. Simply by using these two pieces of information, the minimization engine can be halted at any time, and it can thereafter resume the optimization from the checkpoint:

```
def onstep(res):
    global counter
    x0 = res.x_iters    # List of input points
    y0 = res.func_vals # Evaluation of input points
    print('Last eval: ', x0[-1],
            ' - Score ', y0[-1])
    print('Current iter: ', counter,
            ' - Best Score ', res.fun,
            ' - Best Args: ', res.x)
```

```
    # Saving a checkpoint to disk
    joblib.dump((x0, y0), 'checkpoint.pkl')
    counter += 1
```

At this point, we are ready to start. Bayesian optimization needs some starting points to work properly. We create a number of experiments with random search (using the dummy_minimize function) and save their results:

```
counter = 0
history = {i:list() for i in range(5)}
used_time = 0
gp_round = dummy_minimize(func=objective,
                          dimensions=space,
                          n_calls=30,
                          callback=[onstep],
                          random_state=0)
```

We can then retrieve the saved experiments and print the sequence of sets of hyperparameters that the Bayesian optimization has tested, along with their results. In fact, we can find the set of parameters and their results contained in the x0 and y0 lists:

```
x0, y0 = joblib.load('checkpoint.pkl')
print(len(x0))
```

At this point, we can even resume the Bayesian optimization with some changes in the search space, the acquisition function, the number of calls, or the callbacks:

```
x0, y0 = joblib.load('checkpoint.pkl')

gp_round = gp_minimize(func=objective,
                       x0=x0,         # already examined values for x
                       y0=y0,         # observed values for x0
                       dimensions=space,
                       acq_func='gp_hedge',
                       n_calls=30,
                       n_initial_points=0,
                       callback=[onstep],
                       random_state=0)
```

Once we are satisfied that we don't need to continue calling the optimization function, we can print both the best score obtained (based on our inputs and validation scheme) and the set of best hyperparameters:

```
x0, y0 = joblib.load('checkpoint.pkl')
print(f"Best score: {gp_round.fun:0.5f}")
print("Best hyperparameters:")
for sp, x in zip(gp_round.space, gp_round.x):
    print(f"{sp.name:25} : {x}")
```

Based on the best result, we can re-train our model for use in the competition.

Now we have the set of parameters and their results (the x0 and y0 lists), we could also explore the different results and cluster together the ones that are similar in output but different in the set of parameters used. This will help us to train a more diverse set of models with similar performances but different optimization strategies. This is the ideal situation for **blending**, which is the averaging of multiple models in order to lower the variance of the estimates and obtain a better public and private leaderboard score.

 Refer to *Chapter 9, Ensembling with Blending and Stacking Solutions*, for a discussion on blending.

Extending Bayesian optimization to neural architecture search

Moving on to deep learning, neural networks also seem to have quite a few hyperparameters to fix:

- Batch size
- Learning rate
- The kind of optimizer and its internal parameters

All these parameters influence how the network learns and they can make a big impact; just a slight difference in batch size or learning rate can determine whether a network can reduce its error beyond a certain threshold or not.

That being said, these learning parameters are not the only ones that you can optimize when working with **deep neural networks** (**DNNs**). How the network is organized in layers and the details of its architecture can make even more of a difference.

In fact, technically speaking, an **architecture** implies the representational capacity of the deep neural network, which means that, depending on the layers you use, the network will either be able to read and process all the information available in the data, or it will not. While you had a large but limited set of choices with other machine learning algorithms, with DNNs your choices seem unlimited, because the only apparent limit is your knowledge and experience in handling parts of neural networks and putting them together.

Common best practices for great deep learning practitioners when assembling well-performing DNNs depend mainly on:

- Relying on pre-trained models (so you have to be very knowledgeable about the solutions available, such as those found on Hugging Face (`https://huggingface.co/models`) or on GitHub)
- Reading cutting-edge papers
- Copying top Kaggle Notebooks from the same competition or previous ones
- Trial and error
- Ingenuity and luck

In a famous lesson given by *Professor Geoffrey Hinton*, he states that you can achieve similar and often better results using automated methods such as Bayesian optimization. Bayesian optimization will also avoid you getting stuck because you cannot figure out the best combinations of hyperparameters among the many possible ones.

For a recording of Prof. Geoffrey Hinton's lesson, see `https://www.youtube.com/watch?v=i0cKa0di_lo`.

For the slides, see `https://www.cs.toronto.edu/~hinton/coursera/lecture16/lec16.pdf`.

As we mentioned before, even in most sophisticated AutoML systems, when you have too many hyperparameters, relying on random optimization may produce better results or the same results in the same amount of time as Bayesian optimization. In addition, in this case, you also have to fight against an optimization landscape with sharp turns and surfaces; in DNN optimization, many of your parameters won't be continuous but Boolean instead, and just one change could unexpectedly transform the performance of your network for the better or for the worse.

Our experience tells us that random optimization may not be suitable for a Kaggle competition because:

- You have limited time and resources
- You can leverage your previous optimization results in order to find better solutions

Bayesian optimization in this scenario is ideal: you can set it to work based on the time and computational resources that you have and do it by stages, refining your settings through multiple sessions. Moreover, it is unlikely that you will easily be able to leverage parallelism for tuning DNNs, since they use GPUs, unless you have multiple very powerful machines at hand. By working sequentially, Bayesian optimization just needs one good machine to perform the task. Finally, even if it is hard to find optimal architectures by a search, due to the optimization landscape you leverage information from previous experiments, especially at the beginning, totally avoiding combinations of parameters that won't work. With random optimization, unless you change the search space along the way, all combinations are always liable to be tested.

There are also drawbacks, however. Bayesian optimization models the hyperparameter space using a surrogate function built from previous trials, which is not an error-free process. It is not a remote possibility that the process ends up concentrating only on a part of the search space while ignoring other parts (which may instead contain the minimum you are looking for). The solution to this is to run a large number of experiments to be safe, or to alternate between random search and Bayesian optimization, challenging the Bayesian model with random trials that can force it to reshape its search model in a more optimal way.

For our example, we use again the data from the *30 Days of ML* initiative by Kaggle, a regression task. Our example is based on TensorFlow, but with small modifications it can run on other deep learning frameworks such as PyTorch or MXNet.

 As before, you can find the example on Kaggle here: `https://www.kaggle.com/` `lucamassaron/hacking-bayesian-optimization-for-dnns`.

Let's begin:

```
import tensorflow as tf
```

After importing the TensorFlow package, we leverage its `Dataset` function to create an iterable capable of feeding our neural network with batches of data:

```
def df_to_dataset(dataframe, shuffle=True, batch_size=32):
    dataframe = dataframe.copy()
    labels = dataframe.pop('target')
    ds = tf.data.Dataset.from_tensor_slices((dict(dataframe),
                                             labels))
    if shuffle:
        ds = ds.shuffle(buffer_size=len(dataframe))
    ds = ds.batch(batch_size)
    return ds


tf.keras.utils.get_custom_objects().update({'leaky-relu': tf.keras.layers.
Activation(tf.keras.layers.LeakyReLU(alpha=0.2))})
```

We have also made leaky ReLU activation a custom object for our model; it can be called by a string, and there is no need to directly use the function.

We proceed to code a function that creates our deep neural network model based on a set of hyperparameters:

```
def create_model(cat0_dim, cat1_dim, cat2_dim,
                 cat3_dim, cat4_dim, cat5_dim,
                 cat6_dim, cat7_dim, cat8_dim, cat9_dim,
                 layers, layer_1, layer_2, layer_3, layer_4, layer_5,
                 activation, dropout, batch_normalization, learning_rate,
                 **others):

    dims = {'cat0': cat0_dim, 'cat1': cat1_dim, 'cat2': cat2_dim,
            'cat3': cat3_dim, 'cat4': cat4_dim, 'cat5': cat5_dim,
            'cat6': cat6_dim, 'cat7': cat7_dim, 'cat8': cat8_dim,
            'cat9': cat9_dim}

    vocab = {h:X_train['cat4'].unique().astype(int)
             for h in ['cat0', 'cat1', 'cat2', 'cat3',
                       'cat4', 'cat5', 'cat6', 'cat7',
                       'cat8', 'cat9']}

    layers = [layer_1, layer_2, layer_3, layer_4, layer_5][:layers]

    feature_columns = list()
```

```python
for header in ['cont1', 'cont2', 'cont3', 'cont4', 'cont5',
               'cont6','cont7', 'cont8', 'cont9', 'cont10',
               'cont11', 'cont12', 'cont13']:

    feature_columns.append(tf.feature_column.numeric_column(header))

for header in ['cat0', 'cat1', 'cat2', 'cat3', 'cat4', 'cat5',
               'cat6', 'cat7', 'cat8', 'cat9']:
    feature_columns.append(
        tf.feature_column.embedding_column(
        tf.feature_column.categorical_column_with_vocabulary_list(
        header, vocabulary_list=vocab[header]),
        dimension=dims[header]))

feature_layer = tf.keras.layers.DenseFeatures(feature_columns)

network_struct = [feature_layer]

for nodes in layers:
    network_struct.append(
            tf.keras.layers.Dense(nodes, activation=activation))
    if batch_normalization is True:
            network_struct.append(
            tf.keras.layers.BatchNormalization())
    if dropout > 0:
        network_struct.append(tf.keras.layers.Dropout(dropout))

model = tf.keras.Sequential(network_struct +
                            [tf.keras.layers.Dense(1)])

model.compile(optimizer=tf.keras.optimizers.Adam(
                    learning_rate=learning_rate),
            loss= tf.keras.losses.MeanSquaredError(),
            metrics=['mean_squared_error'])

return model
```

Internally, the code in the `create_model` function customizes the neural network architecture based on the inputs provided. For instance, as parameters for the function you can provide the dimensions of the embeddings for each categorical variable, or define the structure and number of dense layers present in the network. All these parameters are related to the parameter space you want to be explored by Bayesian optimization, hence every input parameter of the function creating the model should be related to a **sampling function** defined in the search space. All you have to do is to place the sampling functions in a list, in the same order as expected by the `create_model` function:

```
# Setting the search space

space = [Integer(1, 2, name='cat0_dim'),
         Integer(1, 2, name='cat1_dim'),
         Integer(1, 2, name='cat2_dim'),
         Integer(1, 3, name='cat3_dim'),
         Integer(1, 3, name='cat4_dim'),
         Integer(1, 3, name='cat5_dim'),
         Integer(1, 4, name='cat6_dim'),
         Integer(1, 4, name='cat7_dim'),
         Integer(1, 6, name='cat8_dim'),
         Integer(1, 8, name='cat9_dim'),
         Integer(1, 5, name='layers'),
         Integer(2, 256, name='layer_1'),
         Integer(2, 256, name='layer_2'),
         Integer(2, 256, name='layer_3'),
         Integer(2, 256, name='layer_4'),
         Integer(2, 256, name='layer_5'),
         Categorical(['relu', 'leaky-relu'], name='activation'),
         Real(0.0, 0.5, 'uniform', name='dropout'),
         Categorical([True, False], name='batch_normalization'),
         Categorical([0.01, 0.005, 0.002, 0.001], name='learning_rate'),
         Integer(256, 1024, name='batch_size')
         ]
```

As previously illustrated, you now combine all the elements related to the search into an objective function to be created by a function incorporating your basic search elements, such as the data and the cross-validation strategy:

```python
def make_objective(model_fn, X, space, cv, scoring, validation=0.2):
    # This decorator converts your objective function with named arguments
    # into one that accepts a list as argument, while doing the conversion
    # automatically.
    @use_named_args(space)
    def objective(**params):

        print("\nTesting: ", params)
        validation_scores = list()

        for k, (train_index, test_index) in enumerate(kf.split(X)):
            val_index = list()
            train_examples = len(train_index)
            train_examples = int(train_examples * (1 - validation))
            train_index, val_index = (train_index[:train_examples],
                                      train_index[train_examples:])

            start_time = time()

            model = model_fn(**params)
            measure_to_monitor = 'val_mean_squared_error'
            modality='min'

            early_stopping = tf.keras.callbacks.EarlyStopping(
                            monitor=measure_to_monitor,
                            mode=modality,
                            patience=5,
                            verbose=0)

            model_checkpoint = tf.keras.callbacks.ModelCheckpoint(
                            'best.model',
                            monitor=measure_to_monitor,
                            mode=modality,
```

```
                                    save_best_only=True,
                                    verbose=0)

        run = model.fit(df_to_dataset(
                            X_train.iloc[train_index, :],
                            batch_size=params['batch_size']),
                        validation_data=df_to_dataset(
                            X_train.iloc[val_index, :],
                            batch_size=1024),
                        epochs=1_000,
                        callbacks=[model_checkpoint,
                                    early_stopping],
                        verbose=0)

        end_time = time()

        rounds = np.argmin(
                run.history['val_mean_squared_error']) + 1

        model = tf.keras.models.load_model('best.model')
        shutil.rmtree('best.model')

        test_preds = model.predict(df_to_dataset(
                            X.iloc[test_index, :], shuffle=False,
                            batch_size=1024)).flatten()
                            test_score = scoring(
                            X.iloc[test_index, :]['target'],
                            test_preds)
        print(f"CV Fold {k+1} rmse:{test_score:0.5f} - {rounds}
            rounds - it took {end_time-start_time:0.0f} secs")
        validation_scores.append(test_score)

        if len(history[k]) >= 10:
            threshold = np.percentile(history[k], q=25)
            if test_score > threshold:
                print(f"Early stopping for under-performing fold:
                        threshold is {threshold:0.5f}")
```

```
            return np.mean(validation_scores)


        history[k].append(test_score)
    return np.mean(validation_scores)


    return objective
```

The next step is to provide a sequence of random search runs (as a way to start building some feedback from the search space) and gather the results as a starting point. Then, we can feed them into a Bayesian optimization and proceed by using forest_minimize as a surrogate function:

```
counter = 0
history = {i:list() for i in range(5)}
used_time = 0
gp_round = dummy_minimize(func=objective,
                          dimensions=space,
                          n_calls=10,
                          callback=[onstep],
                          random_state=0)


gc.collect()


x0, y0 = joblib.load('checkpoint.pkl')


gp_round = gp_minimize(func=objective,
                       x0=x0,   # already examined values for x
                       y0=y0,   # observed values for x0
                       dimensions=space,
                       n_calls=30,
                       n_initial_points=0,
                       callback=[onstep],
                       random_state=0)


gc.collect()
```

Notice that after the first ten rounds of random search, we proceed with our search using a random forest algorithm as a surrogate function. That will ensure better and faster results than using a Gaussian process.

As before, in this process we have to strive to make the optimization feasible within the time and resources we have (for instance, by setting a low number of n_calls). Hence, we can proceed with batches of search iterations by saving the state of the optimization, checking the results obtained, and deciding thereafter to proceed or conclude the optimization process and not invest more time and energy into looking for a better solution.

Creating lighter and faster models with KerasTuner

If the previous section has puzzled you because of its complexity, KerasTuner can offer you a fast solution for setting up an optimization without much hassle. Though it uses Bayesian optimization and Gaussian processes by default, the new idea behind KerasTuner is **hyperband optimization**. Hyperband optimization uses the bandit approach to figure out the best parameters (see http://web.eecs.umich.edu/~mosharaf/Readings/HyperBand.pdf). This works quite well with neural networks, whose optimization landscape is quite irregular and discontinuous, and thus not always suitable for Gaussian processes.

 Keep in mind that you cannot avoid building the function that builds a custom network using input hyperparameters; KerasTuner just makes it much easier to handle.

Let's start from the beginning. KerasTuner (https://keras.io/keras_tuner/) was announced as a "flexible and efficient hyperparameter tuning for Keras models" by *François Chollet*, the creator of Keras.

The recipe proposed by Chollet for running KerasTuner is made up of simple steps, starting from your existing Keras model:

1. Wrap your model in a function with hp as the first parameter.
2. Define hyperparameters at the beginning of the function.
3. Replace DNN static values with hyperparameters.
4. Write the code that models a complex neural network from the given hyperparameters.
5. If necessary, dynamically define hyperparameters as you build the network.

We'll now explore how all these steps can work for you in a Kaggle competition by using an example. At the moment, KerasTuner is part of the stack offered by any Kaggle Notebook, hence you don't need to install it. In addition, the TensorFlow add-ons are part of the Notebook's pre-installed packages.

If you are not using a Kaggle Notebook and you need to try KerasTuner, you can easily install both using the following commands:

```
!pip install -U keras-tuner
!pip install -U tensorflow-addons
```

 You can find this example already set up on a Kaggle Notebook here: `https://www.kaggle.com/lucamassaron/kerastuner-for-imdb/`.

Our first step is to import the necessary packages (creating shortcuts for some commands, such as for pad_sequences) and to upload the data we will be using directly from Keras:

```
import numpy as np
import pandas as pd
import tensorflow as tf
from tensorflow import keras
import tensorflow_addons as tfa
from sklearn.model_selection import train_test_split

from tensorflow.keras.models import Sequential
from tensorflow.keras.layers import LeakyReLU
from tensorflow.keras.layers import Activation
from tensorflow.keras.optimizers import SGD, Adam
from tensorflow.keras.wrappers.scikit_learn import KerasClassifier
from tensorflow.keras.callbacks import EarlyStopping, ModelCheckpoint

pad_sequences = keras.preprocessing.sequence.pad_sequences

imdb = keras.datasets.imdb(train_data, train_labels),
(test_data, test_labels) = imdb.load_data(num_words=10000)

train_data, val_data, train_labels, val_labels = train_test_split(train_
data, train_labels, test_size=0.30,
                shuffle=True, random_state=0)
```

This time, we are using the IMDb dataset, which is available in the Keras package (`https://keras.io/api/datasets/imdb/`). The dataset has some interesting characteristics:

- It is a dataset of 25,000 movie reviews from IMDb
- The reviews are labeled by sentiment (positive/negative)
- The target classes are balanced (hence accuracy works as a scoring measure)
- Each review is encoded as a list of word indexes (integers)
- For convenience, words are indexed by overall frequency

In addition, it has been successfully used in a popular Kaggle competition on word embeddings (`https://www.kaggle.com/c/word2vec-nlp-tutorial/overview`).

This example involves natural language processing. This type of problem is often solved by using **recurrent neural networks (RNNs)** based on LSTM or GRU layers. BERT, RoBERTa, and the other transformer-based models often achieve better results – being pre-trained models relying on large language corpora – but this is not necessarily true in all problems, and RNNs can prove a strong baseline to beat or a good addition to an ensemble of neural models. In our example, all words are already numerically indexed. We just add to the existing indices the numeric codes that denote padding (so we can easily normalize all the text to the phrase length), the start of the sentence, an unknown word, and an unused word:

```
# A dictionary mapping words to an integer index
word_index = imdb.get_word_index()

# The first indices are reserved
word_index = {k:(v+3) for k,v in word_index.items()}
word_index["<PAD>"] = 0
word_index["<START>"] = 1
word_index["<UNK>"] = 2  # unknown
word_index["<UNUSED>"] = 3

reverse_word_index = dict([(value, key) for (key, value) in word_index.items()])

def decode_review(text):
    return ' '.join([reverse_word_index.get(i, '?') for i in text])
```

The next step involves creating a custom layer for **attention**. Attention is the foundation of transformer models and it is one of the most innovative ideas in neural NLP of recent times.

 For all the details of how these kinds of layers work, see the seminal paper on attention: Vaswani, A. et al. *Attention is all you need.* Advances in neural information processing systems. 2017 (https://proceedings.neurips.cc/paper/2017/fil e/3f5ee243547dee91fbd053c1c4a845aa-Paper.pdf).

The idea of attention can be easily conveyed. LSTM and GRU layers output processed sequences, but not all the elements in these output sequences are necessarily important for your predictions. Instead of averaging all the output sequences using a pool layer across the stratified sequences, you can actually take a *weighted average* of them (and during the training phase learn the correct weights to be used). This weighting process (**attention**) definitely improves the results you are going to pass on further. Of course, you can make this approach even more sophisticated using multiple attention layers (we call this **multi-head attention**), but in our example a single layer will suffice because we want to demonstrate that using attention is more effective in this problem than simply averaging or just concatenating all the results together:

```python
from tensorflow.keras.layers import Dense, Dropout
from tensorflow.keras.layers import Flatten, RepeatVector, dot, multiply,
Permute, Lambda
K = keras.backend

def attention(layer):
    # --- Attention is all you need --- #
    _,_,units = layer.shape.as_list()
    attention = Dense(1, activation='tanh')(layer)
    attention = Flatten()(attention)
    attention = Activation('softmax')(attention)
    attention = RepeatVector(units)(attention)
    attention = Permute([2, 1])(attention)
    representation = multiply([layer, attention])
    representation = Lambda(lambda x: K.sum(x, axis=-2),
                           output_shape=(units,))(representation)
    # --------------------------------- #
    return representation
```

As a further variation in our experiments on the architecture of the DNNs for this problem, we also want to test the effectiveness of using different kinds of optimizers such as **Rectified Adam** (an adaptive learning Adam optimizer; read this post to learn more: https://lessw.medium.com/ new-state-of-the-art-ai-optimizer-rectified-adam-radam-5d854730807b) or **Stochastic Weighted Averaging (SWA)**. SWA is a way to average the weights traversed during the optimization based on a modified learning rate schedule: if your model tends to overfit or overshoot, SWA helps in getting near to an optimal solution and it is proven to work especially in NLP problems.

```python
def get_optimizer(option=0, learning_rate=0.001):
    if option==0:
        return tf.keras.optimizers.Adam(learning_rate)
    elif option==1:
        return tf.keras.optimizers.SGD(learning_rate,
                                momentum=0.9, nesterov=True)
    elif option==2:
        return tfa.optimizers.RectifiedAdam(learning_rate)
    elif option==3:
        return tfa.optimizers.Lookahead(
                    tf.optimizers.Adam(learning_rate), sync_period=3)
    elif option==4:
        return tfa.optimizers.SWA(tf.optimizers.Adam(learning_rate))
    elif option==5:
        return tfa.optimizers.SWA(
                    tf.keras.optimizers.SGD(learning_rate,
                                    momentum=0.9, nesterov=True))
    else:
        return tf.keras.optimizers.Adam(learning_rate)
```

Having defined two key functions, we now face the most important function to code: the one that will provide different neural architectures given the parameters. We don't encode all the various parameters we want to connect to the different architectural choices; we only provide the hp parameter, which should contain all the possible parameters we want to use, and that will be run by KerasTuner. Aside from hp in the function input, we fix the size of the vocabulary and the length to be padded (adding dummy values if the effective length is shorter or cutting the phrase if the length is longer):

```python
layers = keras.layers
models = keras.models
```

```
def create_tunable_model(hp, vocab_size=10000, pad_length=256):

    # Instantiate model params
    embedding_size = hp.Int('embedding_size', min_value=8,
                            max_value=512, step=8)
    spatial_dropout = hp.Float('spatial_dropout', min_value=0,
                            max_value=0.5, step=0.05)
    conv_layers = hp.Int('conv_layers', min_value=1,
                            max_value=5, step=1)
    rnn_layers = hp.Int('rnn_layers', min_value=1,
                            max_value=5, step=1)
    dense_layers = hp.Int('dense_layers', min_value=1,
                            max_value=3, step=1)
    conv_filters = hp.Int('conv_filters', min_value=32,
                            max_value=512, step=32)
    conv_kernel = hp.Int('conv_kernel', min_value=1,
                            max_value=8, step=1)
    concat_dropout = hp.Float('concat_dropout', min_value=0,
                            max_value=0.5, step=0.05)
    dense_dropout = hp.Float('dense_dropout', min_value=0,
                            max_value=0.5, step=0.05)
```

In the first part of the function, we simply recover all the settings from the hp parameter. We also make explicit the range of the search space for each of them. Contrary to the solutions we've seen so far, this part of the work is done *inside* the model function, not outside.

The function continues by defining the different layers using the parameters extracted from hp. In some cases, a parameter will switch on or off a part of the network performing certain data processing. For instance, in the code we inserted a branch of the graph (conv_filters and conv_kernel) that processes the sequence of words using convolutional layers, which, in their 1D form, can also prove useful for NLP problems, since they can catch local sequences of words and meanings that LSTMs may find harder to grasp.

Now we can define the actual model:

```
inputs = layers.Input(name='inputs',shape=[pad_length])
layer  = layers.Embedding(vocab_size, embedding_size,
                            input_length=pad_length)(inputs)
```

```
layer  = layers.SpatialDropout1D(spatial_dropout)(layer)


for l in range(conv_layers):
    if l==0:
        conv = layers.Conv1D(filters=conv_filters,
                    kernel_size=conv_kernel, padding='valid',
                    kernel_initializer='he_uniform')(layer)
    else:
        conv = layers.Conv1D(filters=conv_filters,
                    kernel_size=conv_kernel, padding='valid',
                    kernel_initializer='he_uniform')(conv)


avg_pool_conv = layers.GlobalAveragePooling1D()(conv)
max_pool_conv = layers.GlobalMaxPooling1D()(conv)


representations = list()
for l in range(rnn_layers):

    use_bidirectional = hp.Choice(f'use_bidirectional_{l}',
                                values=[0, 1])
    use_lstm = hp.Choice(f'use_lstm_{l}', values=[0, 1])
    units = hp.Int(f'units_{l}', min_value=8, max_value=512, step=8)

    if use_lstm == 1:
        rnl = layers.LSTM
    else:
        rnl = layers.GRU

    if use_bidirectional==1:
        layer = layers.Bidirectional(rnl(units,
                        return_sequences=True))(layer)
    else:
        layer = rnl(units, return_sequences=True)(layer)

    representations.append(attention(layer))
```

```
    layer = layers.concatenate(representations + [avg_pool_conv,
                                                  max_pool_conv])
    layer = layers.Dropout(concat_dropout)(layer)

    for l in range(dense_layers):
        dense_units = hp.Int(f'dense_units_{l}', min_value=8,
                             max_value=512, step=8)
        layer = layers.Dense(dense_units)(layer)
        layer = layers.LeakyReLU()(layer)
        layer = layers.Dropout(dense_dropout)(layer)

    layer = layers.Dense(1, name='out_layer')(layer)
    outputs = layers.Activation('sigmoid')(layer)

    model = models.Model(inputs=inputs, outputs=outputs)
```

We start by defining the input layer and transform it with a subsequent embedding layer that will encode the sequence values into dense layers. Some dropout regularization is applied to the process using `SpatialDropout1D`, a function that will randomly drop entire columns of the output matrix (standard dropout drops random single elements in the matrix instead). After these initial phases, we split the network into one pipeline based on convolutions (`Conv1D`) and another based on recurrent layers (GRU or LSTM). It is after the recurrent layers that we apply the attention layer. Finally, the outputs of these two pipelines are concatenated and, after a few more dense layers, they arrive at the final output node, a sigmoid since we have to represent a probability bounded in the range 0 to 1.

After the model definition, we set the learning parameters and compile the model before returning it:

```
    hp_learning_rate = hp.Choice('learning_rate',
                                 values=[0.002, 0.001, 0.0005])
    optimizer_type = hp.Choice('optimizer', values=list(range(6)))
    optimizer = get_optimizer(option=optimizer_type,
                              learning_rate=hp_learning_rate)

    model.compile(optimizer=optimizer,
                  loss='binary_crossentropy',
                  metrics=['acc'])
```

```
    return model
```

Note that we have built the model using the functional API of Keras, not the sequential one. We would advise you to avoid the sequential one, in fact; it is easier to set up, but severely restricts your potential architectures.

At this point, most of the work is already done. As a suggestion, having worked out many optimizations using KerasTuner ourselves, we prefer to first build a *non-parametric* model, using all the possible architectural features that we want to test, with the mutually exclusive parts of the network set to the most complex solutions. After we have set up the generative function and our model seems to be working properly, we can, for instance, represent its graph and have it successfully fit some examples as a test. After that, we start inserting the parametric variables into the architecture and setting up the hp parameter definitions.

 In our experience, starting with a parametric function immediately will take more time and debugging effort. The idea behind KerasTuner is to let you think of your DNNs as a set of modular circuits and to help you optimize how the data flows inside them.

Now, we import KerasTuner. First, we set the tuner itself, and then we start the search:

```
import keras_tuner as kt

tuner = kt.BayesianOptimization(hypermodel=create_tunable_model,
                                objective='val_acc',
                                max_trials=100,
                                num_initial_points=3,
                                directory='storage',
                                project_name='imdb',
                                seed=42)

tuner.search(train_data, train_labels,
             epochs=30,
             batch_size=64,
             validation_data=(val_data, val_labels),
             shuffle=True,
             verbose=2,
```

```
        callbacks = [EarlyStopping('val_acc',
                                    patience=3,
                                    restore_best_weights=True)]
    )
```

As a tuner, we opt for the Bayesian optimization one, but you can also try the Hyperband tuner (`https://keras.io/api/keras_tuner/tuners/hyperband/`) and check if it works better for your problem. We provide our model function to the `hypermodel` parameter. Then, we set the objective using a string or a function, the maximum number of trials (KerasTuner will stop earlier if there is nothing more to be done), and the initial number of random trials – the more the better – in order to inform the Bayesian process. Early stopping is a standard and well-performing practice in modeling DNNs that you absolutely cannot ignore. Finally, but importantly, we set the directory where we want to save our search and a seed number for reproducibility of the optimization steps.

The search phase is run like a standard fit of a Keras model and – this is quite important – it accepts callbacks. Therefore, you can easily add early stopping to your model. In this case, the given epoch number should therefore be considered the maximum number of epochs. You may also want to optimize the batch size, which we haven't done in our example. This still requires some extra work, but you can get an idea of how to achieve it by reading this GitHub closed issue: `https://github.com/keras-team/keras-tuner/issues/122`.

After the optimization is complete, you can extract the best parameters and save the best model without any need to retrain it:

```
best_hps = tuner.get_best_hyperparameters()[0]
model = tuner.hypermodel.build(best_hps)
print(best_hps.values)
model.summary()
model.save("best_model.h5")
```

In this example, KerasTuner finds a solution that uses:

- A larger embedding layer
- Just plain GRU and LSTM layers (no bi-directional layers)
- Stacking of multiple one-dimensional convolution layers (Conv1D)
- More and larger dense layers

Interestingly, the solution is not only more effective, but also lighter and faster than our previous attempts based on intuition and experience with the problem.

Chollet himself suggests using KerasTuner not just to make your DNNs perform better but also to shrink them to a more manageable size, something that may make the difference in Code competitions. This allows you to put together more models that work together within the limited inference time provided by the sponsors of the competition.

If you would like to examine more examples of using KerasTuner, François Chollet also created a series of Notebooks for Kaggle competitions in order to showcase the workings and functionalities of his optimizer:

- `https://www.kaggle.com/fchollet/keras-kerastuner-best-practices` for the *Digit Recognizer* datasets
- `https://www.kaggle.com/fchollet/titanic-keras-kerastuner-best-practices` for the *Titanic* dataset
- `https://www.kaggle.com/fchollet/moa-keras-kerastuner-best-practices` for the *Mechanisms of Action (MoA) Prediction* competition

The TPE approach in Optuna

We complete our overview of Bayesian optimization with another interesting tool and approach to it. As we have discussed, Scikit-optimize uses Gaussian processes (as well as tree algorithms) and it directly models the surrogate function and the acquisition function.

As a reminder of these topics, the **surrogate function** helps the optimization process to model the potential performance result when you try a set of hyperparameters. The surrogate function is built using the previous experiments and their results; it is just a predictive model applied in order to forecast the behavior of a specific machine learning algorithm on a specific problem. For each parameter input provided to the surrogate function, you get an expected performance output. That's intuitive and also quite hackable, as we have seen.

The **acquisition function** instead points out what set of hyperparameters could be tested in order to improve the ability of the surrogate function to predict the performances of the machine learning algorithm. It is also useful for really testing if we can reach a top-performing result based on the surrogate function's forecasts. These two objectives represent the *explore* part (where you run experiments) and the *exploit* part (where you test the performance) of a Bayesian optimization process.

Instead, optimizers based on **TPE** tackle the problem by estimating the likelihood of success of the values of parameters. In other words, they model the success distribution of the parameters themselves using successive refinements, assigning a higher probability to more successful value combinations.

In this approach, the set of hyperparameters is divided into good and bad ones by these distributions, which take the role of the surrogate and acquisition functions in Bayesian optimization, since the distributions tell you where to sample to get better performances or explore where there is uncertainty.

 To explore the technical details of TPE, we suggest reading Bergstra, J. et al. *Algorithms for hyper-parameter optimization*. Advances in neural information processing systems 24, 2011 (https://proceedings.neurips.cc/paper/2011/file/86e8f7ab32cf d12577bc2619bc635690-Paper.pdf).

Therefore, TPE can model the search space and simultaneously suggest what the algorithm can try next, by sampling from the adjusted probability distribution of parameters.

For a long time, **Hyperopt** was the option for those preferring to use TPE instead of Bayesian optimization based on Gaussian processes. In October 2018, however, Optuna appeared in the open source and it has become the preferred choice for Kagglers due to its versatility (it also works out of the box for neural networks and even for ensembling), speed, and efficiency in finding better solutions compared to previous optimizers.

In this section, we will demonstrate just how easy is to set up a search, which is called a *study* under Optuna terminology. All you need to do is to write an objective function that takes as input the parameters to be tested by Optuna and then returns an evaluation. Validation and other algorithmic aspects can be handled in a straightforward manner inside the objective function, also using references to variables external to the function itself (both global variables or local ones). Optuna also allows **pruning**, that is, signaling that a particular experiment is not going well and that Optuna can stop and forget about it. Optuna provides a list of functions that activate this callback (see https://optuna.readthedocs.io/en/stable/reference/integration.html); the algorithm will run everything efficiently for you after that, which will significantly reduce the time needed for optimization.

All of this is in our next example. We return to optimizing for the *30 Days of ML* competition. This time, we are trying to figure out what parameters make XGBoost work for this competition.

You can find the Notebook for this example at https://www.kaggle.com/ lucamassaron/optuna-bayesian-optimization.

As a first step, we upload the libraries and the data, as before:

```python
import pandas as pd
import numpy as np
from sklearn import preprocessing
from sklearn.metrics import mean_squared_error
from sklearn.model_selection import train_test_split
from sklearn.preprocessing import OrdinalEncoder
from xgboost import XGBRegressor
import optuna
from optuna.integration import XGBoostPruningCallback


# Loading data
X_train = pd.read_csv("../input/30-days-of-ml/train.csv").iloc[:100_000,
:]
X_test = pd.read_csv("../input/30-days-of-ml/test.csv")


# Preparing data as a tabular matrix
y_train = X_train.target
X_train = X_train.set_index('id').drop('target', axis='columns')
X_test = X_test.set_index('id')


# Pointing out categorical features
categoricals = [item for item in X_train.columns if 'cat' in item]


# Dealing with categorical data using OrdinalEncoder
ordinal_encoder = OrdinalEncoder()
X_train[categoricals] = ordinal_encoder.fit_transform(X_
train[categoricals])
X_test[categoricals] = ordinal_encoder.transform(X_test[categoricals])
```

When using Optuna, you just have to define an objective function containing the model, the cross-validation logic, the evaluation measure, and the search space.

Naturally, for data you can refer to objects outside the function itself, rendering the construction of the function much easier. As in KerasTuner, here you need a special input parameter based on a class from Optuna:

```python
def objective(trial):

    params = {
            'learning_rate': trial.suggest_float("learning_rate",
                                        0.01, 1.0, log=True),
            'reg_lambda': trial.suggest_loguniform("reg_lambda",
                                        1e-9, 100.0),
            'reg_alpha': trial.suggest_loguniform("reg_alpha",
                                        1e-9, 100.0),
            'subsample': trial.suggest_float("subsample", 0.1, 1.0),
            'colsample_bytree': trial.suggest_float(
                                "colsample_bytree", 0.1, 1.0),
            'max_depth': trial.suggest_int("max_depth", 1, 7),
            'min_child_weight': trial.suggest_int("min_child_weight",
                                        1, 7),
            'gamma': trial.suggest_float("gamma", 0.1, 1.0, step=0.1)
    }

    model = XGBRegressor(
        random_state=0,
        tree_method="gpu_hist",
        predictor="gpu_predictor",
        n_estimators=10_000,
        **params
    )

    model.fit(x, y, early_stopping_rounds=300,
            eval_set=[(x_val, y_val)], verbose=1000,
            callbacks=[XGBoostPruningCallback(trial, 'validation_0-rmse')])
    preds = model.predict(x_test)
    rmse = mean_squared_error(y_test, preds, squared=False)

    return rmse
```

In this example, for performance reasons, we won't cross-validate but use one fixed dataset for training, one for validation (early stopping), and one for testing purposes. We are using GPU in this example, and we are also subsetting the available data in order to fit the execution of 60 trials into a reasonable length of time. If you don't want to use GPU, just remove the `tree_method` and `predictor` parameters from the `XGBRegressor` instantiation. Also notice how we set a callback in the `fit` method in order to provide Optuna feedback on how the model is performing, so the optimizer can stop an underperforming experiment early to give space to other attempts.

```
x, x_val, y, y_val = train_test_split(X_train, y_train, random_state=0,
                                       test_size=0.2)
x, x_test, y, y_test = train_test_split(x, y, random_state=0, test_size=0.25)
study = optuna.create_study(direction="minimize")
study.optimize(objective, n_trials=100)
```

Another notable aspect is that you can decide to optimize either for minimization or maximization, depending on your problem (Scikit-optimize works only on minimization problems).

```
print(study.best_value)
print(study.best_params)
```

To complete the run, you just have to print or export the best test performance and the best parameters found by the optimization.

Ruchi Bhatia

`https://www.kaggle.com/ruchi798`

As a conclusion to this dense chapter, let's look at one last interview. This time, we're speaking to Ruchi Bhatia, a Grandmaster in Datasets and Notebooks. Ruchi is currently a graduate student at Carnegie Mellon University, a Data Scientist at OpenMined, and a Data Science Global Ambassador at Z by HP.

What's your favorite kind of competition and why? In terms of techniques and solving approaches, what is your specialty on Kaggle?

My favorite kinds of competitions are NLP and Analytics competitions. Being multilingual has played a significant role in my main focus and interest: Natural Language Processing.

As for Analytics competitions, I enjoy making sense out of complex data and backing my answers to questions with the support of data! Every competition on Kaggle is novel and requires different techniques. I mainly follow a data-driven approach to algorithm selection and have no set favorites.

How do you approach a Kaggle competition? How different is this approach to what you do in your day-to-day work?

When a new competition is announced, my priority is to understand the problem statement in depth. Sometimes problem statements can be out of our comfort zone or domain, so it's crucial to ensure we grasp them well before moving on to exploratory data analysis. While performing EDA, my goal is to understand data distribution and focus on getting to know the data at hand. During this, we are likely to come across patterns, and we should make an effort to understand those and form a hypothesis for outliers and exceptional cases.

After this, I spend time understanding the competition metrics. The creation of a leak-free cross-validation strategy is my next step. After this, I choose a baseline model and make my first submission. If the correlation between the local validation and the competition leaderboard is not satisfying, I iterate for as long as needed to understand possible discrepancies and account for them.

Then I move on to improve my modeling approach with time. Apart from this, tweaking parameters and trying new experiments help to gain an understanding of what works best with the data at hand (ensuring that I'm preventing overfitting during the whole process). Finally, in the last few weeks of the competition, I perform model ensembling and check the robustness of my solution.

As for my projects outside of Kaggle, most of my time is spent in data gathering, cleaning, and getting relevant value out of the data.

Has Kaggle helped you in your career? If so, how?

Kaggle has tremendously helped me accelerate my career. Not only did it help me find my passion for data science, but it also motivated me to contribute effectively and stay consistent. It's the perfect place to try hands-on experiments with an enormous amount of data at our fingertips and showcase our work on a global scale. In addition, our work is easily accessible, so we can reach a broader audience as well.

I have used a majority of my Kaggle work on my portfolio to indicate the diversity of work I have done in my journey thus far. Kaggle competitions aim to solve novel and real-world problems, and I feel employers look for our ability and aptitude to solve such problems. I've also curated a broad range of datasets that helped me highlight my acumen in working with raw data. These projects helped me secure multiple job opportunities.

In your experience, what do inexperienced Kagglers often overlook? What do you know now that you wish you'd known when you first started?

In my experience, I've noticed that many Kagglers get disheartened when their ranking in competitions isn't what they expected it to be. After weeks and months of hard work, I can see why they might give up early, but winning Kaggle competitions is no easy feat. There are several people of different educational backgrounds and work experience competing, and having the courage to try is all that's important. We should focus on our individualistic growth and see how far we've come in our journey.

Are there any particular tools or libraries that you would recommend using for data analysis or machine learning?

Comprehensive exploratory data analysis combined with relevant visualizations help us spot data trends and context that can improve our methodology. Since I believe in the power of visualizations, my favorite data science libraries would be Seaborn and TensorBoard. Seaborn for EDA and TensorBoard for visualizations needed during the machine learning workflow. I occasionally use Tableau too.

What's the most important thing someone should keep in mind or do when they're entering a competition?

When people enter a competition, I believe they should prepare themselves for deep diving into the problem statement and researching. Competitions on Kaggle are particularly challenging and help solve real-life problems in many cases. People should have a positive mindset and not get disheartened. Kaggle competitions provide the perfect opportunity to learn and grow!

Summary

In this chapter, we discussed hyperparameter optimization at length as a way to increase your model's performance and score higher on the leaderboard. We started by explaining the code functionalities of Scikit-learn, such as grid search and random search, as well as the newer halving algorithms.

Then, we progressed to Bayesian optimization and explored Scikit-optimize, KerasTuner, and finally Optuna. We spent more time discussing the direct modeling of the surrogate function by Gaussian processes and how to hack it, because it can allow you greater intuition and a more ad hoc solution. We recognize that, at the moment, Optuna has become a gold standard among Kagglers, for tabular competitions as well as for deep neural network ones, because of its speedier convergence to optimal parameters in the time allowed in a Kaggle Notebook.

However, if you want to stand out among the competition, you should strive to test solutions from other optimizers as well.

In the next chapter, we will move on to discuss another way to improve your performance in Kaggle competitions: ensembling models. By discovering the workings of averaging, blending, and stacking, we will illustrate how you can boost your results beyond what you can obtain by tuning hyperparameters alone.

Join our book's Discord space

Join the book's Discord workspace for a monthly *Ask me Anything* session with the authors:

https://packt.link/KaggleDiscord

9

Ensembling with Blending and Stacking Solutions

When you start competing on Kaggle, it doesn't take long to realize that you cannot win with a single, well-devised model; you need to ensemble multiple models. Next, you will immediately wonder how to set up a working ensemble. There are few guides around, and more is left to Kaggle's lore than to scientific papers.

The point here is that if ensembling is the key to winning in Kaggle competitions, in the real world it is associated with complexity, poor maintainability, difficult reproducibility, and hidden technical costs for little advantage. Often, the small boost that can move you from the lower ranks to the top of the leaderboard really doesn't matter for real-world applications because the costs overshadow the advantages. However, that doesn't mean that ensembling is not being used at all in the real world. In a limited form, such as averaging and mixing a few diverse models, ensembling allows us to create models that can solve many data science problems in a more effective and efficient way.

Ensembling in Kaggle is not only a way to gain extra predictive performance, but it is also a teaming strategy. When you are working with other teammates, putting together everyone's contributions produces a result that often performs better than individual efforts, and can also help to organize the work of the team by structuring everyone's efforts toward a clear goal. In fact, when work is performed in different time zones and under different constraints for each participant, collaborative techniques like pair coding are clearly not feasible. One team member may be subject to constraints due to office hours, another due to studying and examinations, and so on.

Teams in a competition often don't have the chance to, and do not necessarily have to, synchronize and align all participants on the same tasks. Moreover, the skills within a team may also differ.

A good ensembling strategy shared among a team means that individuals can keep working based on their own routines and styles, yet still contribute to the success of the group. Therefore, even different skills may become an advantage when using ensembling techniques based on diversity of predictions.

In this chapter, we will start from the ensembling techniques that you already know, because they are embedded in algorithms such as random forests and gradient boosting, and then progress to ensembling techniques for multiple models such as averaging, blending, and stacking. We will provide you with some theory, some practice, and also some code examples you can use as templates when building your own solutions on Kaggle.

We will cover these topics:

- A brief introduction to ensemble algorithms
- Averaging models into an ensemble
- Blending models using a meta-model
- Stacking models
- Creating complex stacking and blending solutions

 Before leaving you to read this chapter and try all the techniques, we have to mention a great reference on ensembling for us and for all practitioners when competing on Kaggle: the blog post written in 2015 by *Triskelion* (*Hendrik Jacob van Veen*) and by a few collaborators (*Le Nguyen The Dat, Armando Segnini*). The *Kaggle Ensembling Guide* was originally found on the *mlwave* blog (https://mlwave.com/kaggle-ensembling-guide), which is no longer up, but you can retrieve the contents of the guide from https://usermanual.wiki/Document/Kaggle20ensembling20guide.685545114.pdf. The post arranged most of the implicit and explicit knowledge about ensembling from Kaggle forums at the time.

A brief introduction to ensemble algorithms

The idea that ensembles of models can outperform single ones is not a recent one. We can trace it back to *Sir Francis Galton*, who was alive in Victorian Britain. He figured out that, in order to guess the weight of an ox at a county fair, it was more useful to take an average from a host of more or less educated estimates from a crowd than having a single carefully devised estimate from an expert.

In 1996, *Leo Breiman* formalized the idea of using multiple models combined into a more predictive one by illustrating the **bagging** technique (also called the "bootstrap aggregating" procedure) that later led to the development of the even more effective **random forests** algorithms. In the period that followed, other ensembling techniques such as **gradient boosting** and **stacking** were also presented, thus completing the range of ensemble methods that we use today.

You can refer to a few articles to figure out how these ensembling algorithms were initially devised:

- For random forests, read Breiman, L. *Bagging predictors.* Machine learning 24.2 – 1996: 123-140.

- If you want to know how boosting originally worked in more detail, read Freund, Y. and Schapire, R.E. *Experiments with a new boosting algorithm. icml. Vol. 96 – 1996,* and *Friedman, J. H. Greedy function approximation: a gradient boosting machine. Annals of Statistics* (2001): 1189-1232.

- As for stacking, refer to Ting, K. M. and Witten, *I. H. Stacking bagged and dagged models,* 1997, for a first formal draft of the technique.

The first basic strategies for ensembling predictors in Kaggle competitions were taken directly from bagging and random forest strategies for classification and regression. They involved making an average of various predictions and were thus named **averaging** techniques. These approaches quickly emerged from the very first Kaggle competitions held over 11 years ago also because of the pre-Kaggle Netflix competition, where strategies based on the average of the results of different models dominated the scene. Given their success, basic ensembling techniques based on averaging set a standard for many competitions to come, and they are still quite useful and valid even today for scoring more highly on the leaderboard.

Stacking, which is more complex and computationally demanding, emerged a bit later, when problems in competitions become more complex and the struggle between participants fiercer. Just as the random forest approach has inspired averaging different predictions, boosting heavily inspired stacking approaches. In boosting, by sequentially re-processing information, your learning algorithm can model problems in a better and more complete way. In fact, in gradient boosting, sequential decision trees are built in order to model the part of data that previous iterations are unable to grasp. This idea is reprised in stacking ensembles, where you stack the results of previous models and re-process them in order to gain an increase in predictive performance.

Rob Mulla

https://www.kaggle.com/robikscube

Rob spoke to us about his views on ensembling and what he has learned from Kaggle. A Grandmaster in Competitions, Notebooks, and Discussion, and Senior Data Scientist at Biocore LLC, there is a lot we can learn from his experiences.

What's your favorite kind of competition and why? In terms of techniques and solving approaches, what is your specialty on Kaggle?

My favorite type of competitions are ones that involve unique datasets requiring novel solutions that incorporate different types of modeling approaches. I enjoy when a competition isn't just training large models on the dataset, but actually requires understanding the data very well and implementing ideas that leverage architectures specific to the tasks. I don't try to specialize in any particular approach. When I first started Kaggle, I mainly stuck to gradient boosted models, but in order to be competitive in recent years I've grown in my understanding of deep learning, computer vision, NLP, and optimization. My favorite competitions require using more than just one technique.

How do you approach a Kaggle competition? How different is this approach to what you do in your day-to-day work?

I approach Kaggle competitions in some ways very similar to work projects. First comes data understanding. In real-world projects, you may need to work on defining the problem and developing a good metric. In Kaggle, that is already done for you. Next is understanding how the data and metric relate to each other – and developing and testing modeling techniques that you believe will best solve the problem. The biggest difference in Kaggle compared to real-life data science is the final bit of ensembling and tuning of models to get a slight edge – in many real-world applications, these types of large ensembles are not necessary because the computational expense to performance gain can be small.

Tell us about a particularly challenging competition you entered, and what insights you used to tackle the task.

A very challenging competition that I entered was the NFL Helmet Impact Detection competition. It involved video data, which I had no prior experience with. It also required researching common approaches and reading existing papers on the topic. I had to work on a two-stage approach, which added to the complexity of the solution. A different competition that I found challenging was the Indoor Location Navigation competition. It involved modeling, optimization, and really understanding the data well. I didn't end up doing very well in the competition, but I learned a lot.

Has Kaggle helped you in your career? If so, how?

Yes. Kaggle has played a big part in helping me gain notoriety in the data science space. I've also grown in my knowledge and understanding of new techniques and have met and worked with many brilliant people who have helped me grow in my skills and understanding of machine learning.

My team placed second for the NFL Helmet Impact Detection Competition. I also participated in a number of NFL competitions prior to that competition. The hosts of the competition reached out to me and eventually it helped me land my current role.

In your experience, what do inexperienced Kagglers often overlook? What do you know now that you wish you'd known when you first started?

I think inexperienced Kagglers sometimes worry too much about the ensembling and hyperparameter tuning of models. These are important towards the end of a competition, but they are not important unless you've already built a good base model. I also think that fully understanding the competition metric is extremely important. Many Kagglers overlook how important it is to understand how to optimize your solution to the evaluation metric.

What mistakes have you made in competitions in the past?

A lot. I've overfit models and spent time working on things that didn't end up being beneficial in the end. However, I feel like this was necessary for me to learn how to better tackle future competitions. The mistakes may have hurt me in the specific competition I was working in, but helped me to be better in later competitions.

Are there any particular tools or libraries that you would recommend using for data analysis or machine learning?

For EDA, know how to manipulate data using NumPy, Pandas, and Matplotlib or another plotting library. For modeling, know how set up a proper cross validation scheme with Scikit-learn. The standard models like XGBoost/LightGBM are good to know how to baseline with. Deep learning libraries are mainly TensorFlow/Keras or PyTorch. Getting to know one of the two main deep learning libraries is important.

Averaging models into an ensemble

In order to introduce the averaging ensembling technique better, let's quickly revise all the strategies devised by Leo Breiman for ensembling. His work represented a milestone for ensembling strategies, and what he found out at the time still works fairly well in a wide range of problems.

Breiman explored all these possibilities in order to figure out if there was a way to reduce the variance of error in powerful models that tended to overfit the training data too much, such as decision trees.

Conceptually, he discovered that ensembling effectiveness was based on three elements: how we deal with the **sampling of training cases**, how we **build the models**, and, finally, how we **combine the different models** obtained.

As for the sampling, the approaches tested and found were:

- **Pasting**, where a number of models are built using subsamples (sampling without replacements) of the examples (the data rows)
- **Bagging**, where a number of models are built using random selections of bootstrapped examples (sampling with replacement)
- **Random subspaces**, where a number of models are built using subsamples (sampling without replacements) of the features (the data columns)
- **Random patches**, an approach similar to bagging, except features are also sampled when each model is selected, as in random subspaces

The reason we sample instead of using the same information is because, by subsampling cases and features, we create models that are all relevant to the same problem while each being different from the others. This difference also applies to the way each model overfits the sample; we expect all the models to grasp the useful, generalizable information from the data *in the same way*, and deal with the noise that is not useful for making predictions *in a different way*. Hence, variation in modeling reduces the variation in predictions, because errors tend to cancel each other out.

If this variation is so useful, then the next step should not just be to modify the *data* the model learns from, but also *the model itself*. We have two main approaches for the models:

- Ensembles of the same type of models
- Ensembles of different models

Interestingly, ensembling in one way or the other doesn't help too much if the models that we are putting together are too different in predictive power. The point here is that you get an advantage if you put together models that are able to correctly guess the same type of predictions, so they can smooth out their errors when averaging the predictions that they get wrong. If you are ensembling models with performances that are too different, you will soon find out that there is no point because the net effect will be negative: as you are not smoothing your incorrect predictions, you are also degrading the correct ones.

This is an important limit of averaging: it can use a set of different models (for instance, because they are trained using different samples and features) only if they are similar in predictive power. To take an example, a linear regression and a k-nearest neighbor algorithm have different ways of modeling a problem and capturing signals from data; thanks to the (distinct) characteristic functional forms at their cores, these algorithms can grasp different predictive nuances from the data and perform better on specific parts of their predictive tasks, but you cannot really take advantage of that when using averaging. By contrast, the different ways algorithms have to capture signals is something that stacking actually can leverage, because it can take the best results from each algorithm.

Based on this, we can summarize that, for an ensemble based on averaging (averaging the results of multiple models) to be effective, it should be:

- Built on models that are trained on different samples
- Built on models that use different subsamples from the available features
- Composed of models similar in predictive power

Technically, this implies that the models' predictions should be as uncorrelated as possible while performing at the same level of accuracy on prediction tasks.

Now that we have discussed the opportunities and limitations of averaging multiple machine learning models, we are finally going to delve into the technical details. There are three ways to average multiple classification or regression models:

- Majority voting, using the most frequent classification among multiple models (only for classification models)
- Averaging values or probabilities
- Using a weighted average of values or probabilities

In the next few sections, we will discuss each approach in detail in the context of Kaggle competitions.

Majority voting

Producing different models by varying the examples, features, and models we use in the ensemble (if they are comparable in predictive power, as we discussed before) requires a certain computational effort, but it doesn't require you to build a data processing pipeline that is all that different from what you would set up when using a single model.

In this pipeline, you just need to collect different test predictions, keeping track of the models used, how you sampled examples or features when training, the hyperparameters that you used, and the resulting cross-validation performance.

If the competition requires you to predict a class, you can use **majority voting**; that is, for each prediction, you take the class most frequently predicted by your models. This works for both binary predictions and multi-class predictions, because it presumes that there are sometimes errors in your models, but that they can guess correctly most of the time. Majority voting is used as an "error correction procedure," discarding noise and keeping meaningful signals.

In our first simple example, we demonstrate how majority voting works. We start by creating our example dataset. Using the `make_classification` function from Scikit-learn, we generate a *Madelon*-like dataset.

The original Madelon was an artificial dataset containing data points grouped in clusters placed on the vertices of some dimensional hypercube and randomly labeled. It comprised a few informative features, mixed with irrelevant and repeated ones (to create multicollinearity between features) and it has a certain amount of injected random noise. Ideated by *Isabelle Guyon* (one of the creators of the SVM algorithm) for the *NIPS 2003 Feature Selection Challenge*, the Madelon dataset is the model example of a challenging artificial dataset for a competition. Even some Kaggle competitions were inspired by it: `https://www.kaggle.com/c/overfitting` and the more recent `https://www.kaggle.com/c/dont-overfit-ii`.

We will use this recreation of the Madelon dataset throughout this chapter as a basis for testing ensembling techniques:

```
from sklearn.datasets import make_classification
from sklearn.model_selection import train_test_split

X, y = make_classification(n_samples=5000, n_features=50,
                           n_informative=10,
                           n_redundant=25, n_repeated=15,
                           n_clusters_per_class=5,
                           flip_y=0.05, class_sep=0.5,
                           random_state=0)
```

```
X_train, X_test, y_train, y_test = train_test_split(X, y,
                            test_size=0.33, random_state=0)
```

After splitting it into a training and a test set, we proceed by instantiating our learning algorithms. We will just use three base algorithms: SVMs, random forests, and *k*-nearest neighbors classifiers, with default hyperparameters for demonstration purposes. You can try changing them or increasing their number:

```
from sklearn.svm import SVC
from sklearn.ensemble import RandomForestClassifier
from sklearn.neighbors import KNeighborsClassifier
from sklearn.metrics import log_loss, roc_auc_score, accuracy_score

model_1 = SVC(probability=True, random_state=0)
model_2 = RandomForestClassifier(random_state=0)
model_3 = KNeighborsClassifier()
```

The following step is just to train each model on the training set:

```
model_1.fit(X_train, y_train)
model_2.fit(X_train, y_train)
model_3.fit(X_train, y_train)
```

At this point, we need to predict on the test set for each model and ensemble all these predictions using majority voting. To do this, we will be using the mode function from SciPy:

```
import numpy as np
from scipy.stats import mode

preds = np.stack([model_1.predict(X_test),
                  model_2.predict(X_test),
                  model_3.predict(X_test)]).T

max_voting = np.apply_along_axis(mode, 1, preds)[:,0]
```

First, we check the accuracy for each single model:

```
for i, model in enumerate(['SVC', 'RF ', 'KNN']):
    acc = accuracy_score(y_true=y_test, y_pred=preds[:, i])
    print(f"Accuracy for model {model} is: {acc:0.3f}")
```

We see that the three models have similar performance, around **0.8**. Now it is time to check the majority voting ensemble:

```
max_voting_accuray = accuracy_score(y_true=y_test, y_pred=max_voting)
print(f"Accuracy for majority voting is: {max_voting_accuray:0.3f}")
```

The voting ensemble is actually more accurate: **0.817**, because it managed to put together the correct signals from the majority.

For multilabel problems (when you can predict multiple classes), you can just pick the classes that are predicted above a certain number of times, assuming a relevance threshold that indicates that a prediction for a class is signal, not noise. For instance, if you have five models, you could set this threshold to 3, which means if a class is predicted by at least three models, then the prediction should be considered correct.

In regression problems, as well as when you are predicting probabilities, you cannot actually use majority voting. Majority voting works exclusively with class ownership. Instead, when you have to predict numbers, you need to combine the results numerically. In this case, resorting to an **average** or a **weighted average** will provide you the right way to combine predictions.

Averaging of model predictions

When averaging your predictions from different models in a competition, you can consider all your predictions as having potentially the same predictive power and use the arithmetic mean to derive an average value.

Aside from the arithmetic mean, we have also found it quite effective to use:

- The **geometric mean**: This is where you multiply the n submissions, then you take the $1/n^{th}$ power of the resulting product.

- The **logarithmic mean**: Analogous to the geometric mean, you take the logarithm of your submission, average them together, and take the exponentiation of the resulting mean.

- The **harmonic mean**: Where you take the arithmetic mean of the reciprocals of your submissions, then you take the reciprocal of the resulting mean.

- The **mean of powers**: Where you take the average of the nth power of the submissions, then you take the $1/n^{th}$ power of the resulting average.

The simple arithmetic average is always quite effective and basically a no-brainer that works more often than expected. Sometimes, variants such as the geometric mean or the harmonic mean may work better.

Continuing with the previous example, we will now try to figure out what kind of mean works best when we switch to **ROC-AUC** as our evaluation metric. To begin with, we evaluate the performances of each single model:

```
proba = np.stack([model_1.predict_proba(X_test)[:, 1],
                  model_2.predict_proba(X_test)[:, 1],
                  model_3.predict_proba(X_test)[:, 1]]).T

for i, model in enumerate(['SVC', 'RF ', 'KNN']):
    ras = roc_auc_score(y_true=y_test, y_score=proba[:, i])
    print(f"ROC-AUC for model {model} is: {ras:0.5f}")
```

The results give us a range from **0.875** to **0.881**.

Our first test is performed using the arithmetic mean:

```
arithmetic = proba.mean(axis=1)
ras = roc_auc_score(y_true=y_test, y_score=arithmetic)
print(f"Mean averaging ROC-AUC is: {ras:0.5f}")
```

The resulting ROC-AUC score is decisively better than the single performances: **0.90192**. We also test if the geometric, harmonic, or logarithmic mean, or the mean of powers, can outperform the plain mean:

```
geometric = proba.prod(axis=1)**(1/3)
ras = roc_auc_score(y_true=y_test, y_score=geometric)
print(f"Geometric averaging ROC-AUC is: {ras:0.5f}")


harmonic = 1 / np.mean(1. / (proba + 0.00001), axis=1)
ras = roc_auc_score(y_true=y_test, y_score=harmonic)
print(f"Geometric averaging ROC-AUC is: {ras:0.5f}")


n = 3
mean_of_powers = np.mean(proba**n, axis=1)**(1/n)
ras = roc_auc_score(y_true=y_test, y_score=mean_of_powers)
print(f"Mean of powers averaging ROC-AUC is: {ras:0.5f}")


logarithmic = np.expm1(np.mean(np.log1p(proba), axis=1))
ras = roc_auc_score(y_true=y_test, y_score=logarithmic)
print(f"Logarithmic averaging ROC-AUC is: {ras:0.5f}")
```

Running the code will tell us that none of them can. In this case, the arithmetic mean is the best choice for ensembling. What actually works better than the simple mean, in almost all cases, is putting some *prior knowledge* into the way you combine the numbers. This happens when you weight your models in the mean calculation.

Weighted averages

When weighting your models, you need to find an empirical way to figure out the right weights. A common method, though very prone to adaptive overfitting, is to test different combinations on the public leaderboard until you find the combination that scores the best. Of course, that won't ensure that you score the same on the private leaderboard. Here, the principle is to weight what works better. However, as we have discussed at length, very often the feedback from the public leaderboard cannot be trusted because of important differences with the private test data. Yet, you *can* use your cross-validation scores or out-of-fold ones (the latter will be discussed along with stacking in a later section). In fact, another viable strategy is to use weights that are **proportional to the models' cross-validation performances**.

Although it is a bit counterintuitive, another very effective method is weighting the submissions **inversely proportionally to their covariances**. In fact, since we are striving to cancel errors by averaging, averaging based on the unique variance of each submission allows us to weight more heavily the predictions that are less correlated and more diverse, more effectively reducing the variance of the estimates.

In the next example, we will first create a **correlation matrix** of our predicted probabilities, and then we proceed by:

1. Removing the one values on the diagonal and replacing them with zeroes
2. Averaging the correlation matrix by row to obtain a vector
3. Taking the reciprocal of each row sum
4. Normalizing their sum to 1.0
5. Using the resulting weighting vector in a matrix multiplication of our predicted probabilities

Here is the code for this:

```
cormat = np.corrcoef(proba.T)
np.fill_diagonal(cormat, 0.0)
W = 1 / np.mean(cormat, axis=1)
W = W / sum(W) # normalizing to sum==1.0
```

```
weighted = proba.dot(W)
ras = roc_auc_score(y_true=y_test, y_score=weighted)
print(f"Weighted averaging ROC-AUC is: {ras:0.5f}")
```

The resulting ROC-AUC of **0.90206** is slightly better than the plain average. Giving more importance to more uncorrelated predictions is an ensembling strategy that is often successful. Even if
it only provides slight improvements, this could suffice to turn the competition to your advantage.

Averaging in your cross-validation strategy

As we have covered, averaging doesn't require you to build any special complex pipelines, only a
certain number of typical data pipelines that create the models you are going to average, either
using the same weights for all predictions or some empirically found weights. The only way to
test it is to run a submission on the public leaderboard, thus risking adaptive fitting because your
evaluation of the averaging will solely be based on the response from Kaggle.

Before testing directly on the leaderboard, though, you may also test at training time by running
the averaging operations on the validation fold (the fold that you are not using for training your
model). This will provide you with less biased feedback than that from the leaderboard. In the
following code, you can find an example of how a cross-validation prediction is arranged:

```
from sklearn.model_selection import KFold

kf = KFold(n_splits=5, shuffle=True, random_state=0)
scores = list()

for k, (train_index, test_index) in enumerate(kf.split(X_train)):
    model_1.fit(X_train[train_index, :], y_train[train_index])
    model_2.fit(X_train[train_index, :], y_train[train_index])
    model_3.fit(X_train[train_index, :], y_train[train_index])

    proba = np.stack(
            [model_1.predict_proba(X_train[test_index, :])[:, 1],
             model_2.predict_proba(X_train[test_index, :])[:, 1],
             model_3.predict_proba(X_train[test_index, :])[:, 1]]).T

    arithmetic = proba.mean(axis=1)
    ras = roc_auc_score(y_true=y_train[test_index],
                        y_score=arithmetic)
```

```
        scores.append(ras)
        print(f"FOLD {k} Mean averaging ROC-AUC is: {ras:0.5f}")


    print(f"CV Mean averaging ROC-AUC is: {np.mean(scores):0.5f}")
```

Relying on the results of a cross-validation as in the code above can help you evaluate which averaging strategy is more promising, without testing directly on the public leaderboard.

Correcting averaging for ROC-AUC evaluations

If your task will be evaluated on the ROC-AUC score, simply averaging your results may not suffice. This is because different models may have adopted different optimization strategies and their outputs may be deeply different. A solution could be to calibrate the models, a type of post-processing we previously discussed in *Chapter 5, Competition Tasks and Metrics*, but this obviously takes further time and computational effort.

In these cases, the straightforward solution would be to convert output probabilities into ranks and just average the ranks (or make a weighted average of them). Using a min-max scaler approach, you simply convert each model's estimates into the range 0-1 and then proceed with averaging the predictions. That will effectively convert your model's probabilistic output into ranks that can be compared:

```
from sklearn.preprocessing import MinMaxScaler


proba = np.stack(
            [model_1.predict_proba(X_train)[:, 1],
             model_2.predict_proba(X_train)[:, 1],
             model_3.predict_proba(X_train)[:, 1]]).T


arithmetic = MinMaxScaler().fit_transform(proba).mean(axis=1)
ras = roc_auc_score(y_true=y_test, y_score=arithmetic)
print(f"Mean averaging ROC-AUC is: {ras:0.5f}")
```

This approach works perfectly when you are directly handling the test predictions. If, instead, you are working and trying to average results during cross-validation, you may encounter problems because the prediction range of your training data may differ from the range of your test predictions. In this case, you can solve the problem by training a calibration model (see **probability calibration** on Scikit-learn (https://scikit-learn.org/stable/modules/calibration.html) and *Chapter 5*), converting predictions into true, comparable probabilities for each of your models.

Blending models using a meta-model

The Netflix competition (which we discussed at length in *Chapter 1*) didn't just demonstrate that averaging would be advantageous for difficult problems in a data science competition; it also brought about the idea that you can use a model to average your models' results more effectively. The winning team, BigChaos, in their paper (Töscher, A., Jahrer, M., and Bell, R.M. *The BigChaos Solution to the Netflix Grand Prize*. Netflix prize documentation – 2009) made many mentions of **blending**, and provided many hints about its effectiveness and the way it works.

In a few words, blending is kind of a weighted averaging procedure where the weights used to combine the predictions are estimated by way of a holdout set and a meta-model trained on it. A **meta-model** is simply a machine learning algorithm that learns from the output of other machine learning models. Usually, a meta-learner is a linear model (but sometimes it can also be a non-linear one; more on that in the next section), but you can actually use whatever you want, with some risks that we will discuss.

The procedure for obtaining a blending is straightforward:

1. Before starting to build all your models, you randomly extract a holdout sample from the training data (in a team, you should all use the same holdout). Usually, the holdout is about 10% of the available data; however, depending on circumstances (for instance, the number of examples in your training data, stratifications), it could be less as well as more. As always in sampling, you may enforce stratification in order to ensure sampling representativeness, and you can test using adversarial validation that the sample really matches the distribution in the rest of the training set.

2. Train all your models on the remaining training data.

3. Predict on the holdout and on the test data.

4. Use the holdout predictions as training data in a meta-learner and reuse the meta-learner model to compute the final test predictions using the test predictions from your models. Alternatively, you can use the meta-learner to figure out the selection of predictors and their weights that should be used in a weighted average.

There a quite a few advantages and disadvantages to such a procedure. Let's start with the advantages. First, it is easy to implement; you just have to figure out what the holdout sample is. In addition, using a meta-learning algorithm ensures you will find the best weights without testing on the public leaderboard.

In terms of weaknesses, sometimes, depending on sample size and the type of models you use, reducing the number of training examples may increase the variance of the predictions of your estimators. Moreover, even if you take great care over how you sample your holdout, you may still fall into adaptive overfitting, that is, finding weights that suit the holdout but are not generalizable, especially if you use a meta-learner that is too complex. Finally, using a holdout for testing purposes has the same limitations as the training and test split we discussed in the chapter on model validation: you won't have a reliable estimate if the sample size of the holdout is too small or if, for some reason, your sampling is not representative.

Best practices for blending

In blending, the kind of meta-learner you use can make a great difference. The most common choices are to use a linear model or a non-linear one. Among linear models, linear or logistic regressions are the preferred ones. Using a regularized model also helps to discard models that are not useful (L1 regularization) or reduce the influence of less useful ones (L2 regularization). One limit to using these kinds of meta-learners is that they may assign some models a negative contribution, as you will be able to see from the value of the coefficient in the model. When you encounter this situation, the model is usually overfitting, since all models should be contributing positively to the building of the ensemble (or, at worst, not contributing at all). The most recent versions of Scikit-learn allow you to impose only positive weights and to remove the intercept. These constraints act as a regularizer and prevent overfitting.

Non-linear models as meta-learners are less common because they tend to overfit in regression and binary classification problems, but they often shine in multiclass and multilabel classification problems since they can model the complex relationships between the classes present. They also generally perform better if, aside from the models' predictions, you also provide them with the *original features*, since they can spot any useful interactions that help them correctly select which models to trust more.

In our next example, we first try blending using a linear model (a logistic regression), then a non-linear approach (a random forest). We start by splitting the training set into a training part for the blend elements and a holdout for the meta-learner. Afterward, we fit the models on the trainable part and predict on the holdout.

```
from sklearn.preprocessing import StandardScaler

X_blend, X_holdout, y_blend, y_holdout = train_test_split(X_train, y_
train, test_size=0.25, random_state=0)
```

```
model_1.fit(X_blend, y_blend)
model_2.fit(X_blend, y_blend)
model_3.fit(X_blend, y_blend)

proba = np.stack([model_1.predict_proba(X_holdout)[:, 1],
                  model_2.predict_proba(X_holdout)[:, 1],
                  model_3.predict_proba(X_holdout)[:, 1]]).T
scaler = StandardScaler()
proba = scaler.fit_transform(proba)
```

We can now train our linear meta-learner using the probabilities predicted on the holdout:

```
from sklearn.linear_model import LogisticRegression

blender = LogisticRegression(solver='liblinear')
blender.fit(proba, y_holdout)

print(blender.coef_)
```

The resulting coefficients are:

```
[[0.78911314 0.47202077 0.75115854]]
```

By looking at the coefficients, we can figure out which model contributes more to the meta-ensemble. However, remember that coefficients also rescale probabilities when they are not well calibrated, so a larger coefficient for a model may not imply that it is the most important one. If you want to figure out the role of each model in the blend by looking at coefficients, you first have to rescale them by standardization (in our code example, this has been done using Scikit-learn's StandardScaler).

Our output shows us that the SVC and *k*-nearest neighbors models are weighted more in the blend than the random forest one; their coefficients are almost equivalent and both are larger than the random forest coefficient.

Once the meta-model is trained, we just predict on our test data and check its performance:

```
test_proba = np.stack([model_1.predict_proba(X_test)[:, 1],
                       model_2.predict_proba(X_test)[:, 1],
                       model_3.predict_proba(X_test)[:, 1]]).T
```

```
blending = blender.predict_proba(test_proba)[:, 1]
ras = roc_auc_score(y_true=y_test, y_score=blending)
print(f"ROC-AUC for linear blending {model} is: {ras:0.5f}")
```

We can try the same thing using a non-linear meta-learner, such as a random forest, for instance:

```
blender = RandomForestClassifier()
blender.fit(proba, y_holdout)

test_proba = np.stack([model_1.predict_proba(X_test)[:, 1],
                       model_2.predict_proba(X_test)[:, 1],
                       model_3.predict_proba(X_test)[:, 1]]).T

blending = blender.predict_proba(test_proba)[:, 1]
ras = roc_auc_score(y_true=y_test, y_score=blending)
print(f"ROC-AUC for non-linear blending {model} is: {ras:0.5f}")
```

An alternative to using a linear or non-linear model as a meta-learner is provided by the **ensemble selection** technique formalized by *Caruana, Niculescu-Mizil, Crew*, and *Ksikes*.

 If you are interested in more details, read their famous paper: Caruana, R., Niculescu-Mizil, A., Crew, G., and Ksikes, A. *Ensemble selection from libraries of models* (Proceedings of the Twenty-First International Conference on Machine Learning, 2004).

The ensemble selection is actually a weighted average, so it could simply be considered analogous to a linear combination. However, it is a constrained linear combination (because it is part of a hill-climbing optimization) that will also make a selection of models and apply only positive weights to the predictions. All this minimizes the risk of overfitting and ensures a more compact solution, because the solution will involve a model selection. From this perspective, ensemble selection is recommended in all problems where the risk of overfitting is high (for instance, because the training cases are few in number or the models are too complex) and in real-world applications because of its simpler yet effective solution.

When using a meta-learner, you are depending on the optimization of its own cost function, which may differ from the metric adopted for the competition. Another great advantage of ensemble selection is that it can be optimized to any evaluation function, so it is mostly suggested when the metric for the competition is different from the canon of those typically optimized in machine learning models.

Implementing ensemble selection requires the following steps, as described in the paper mentioned previously:

1. Start with your trained models and a holdout sample.

2. Test all your models on the holdout sample and, based on the evaluation metric, retain the most effective in a selection (the **ensemble selection**).

3. Then, keep on testing other models that could be added to the one(s) in the ensemble selection so that the average of the proposed selection improves over the previous one. You can either do this with replacement or without. Without replacement, you only put a model into the selection ensemble once; in this case, the procedure is just like a simple average after a forward selection. (In a forward selection, you iteratively add to a solution the model that improves the performance the most, until adding further models no longer improves the performance.) With replacement, you can put a model into the selection multiple times, thus resembling a weighted average.

4. When you cannot get any further improvement, stop and use the ensemble selection.

Here is a simple code example of an ensemble selection. We start by deriving a holdout sample and a training selection from our original training data. We fit the models and obtain the predictions on our holdout, as previously seen when blending with a meta-learner:

```
X_blend, X_holdout, y_blend, y_holdout = train_test_split
    (X_train, y_train, test_size=0.5, random_state=0)

model_1.fit(X_blend, y_blend)
model_2.fit(X_blend, y_blend)
model_3.fit(X_blend, y_blend)

proba = np.stack([model_1.predict_proba(X_holdout)[:, 1],
                  model_2.predict_proba(X_holdout)[:, 1],
                  model_3.predict_proba(X_holdout)[:, 1]]).T
```

In the next code snippet, the ensembling is created through a series of iterations. At each iteration, we try adding all the models in turn to the present ensemble and check if they improve the model. If any of these additions outperforms the previous ensemble on the holdout sample, the ensemble is updated and the bar is raised to the present level of performance.

If no addition can improve the ensemble, the loop is stopped and the composition of the ensemble is reported back:

```python
iterations = 100

proba = np.stack([model_1.predict_proba(X_holdout)[:, 1],
                  model_2.predict_proba(X_holdout)[:, 1],
                  model_3.predict_proba(X_holdout)[:, 1]]).T

baseline = 0.5
print(f"starting baseline is {baseline:0.5f}")


models = []

for i in range(iterations):
    challengers = list()
    for j in range(proba.shape[1]):
        new_proba = np.stack(proba[:, models + [j]])
        score = roc_auc_score(y_true=y_holdout,
                              y_score=np.mean(new_proba, axis=1))
        challengers.append([score, j])

    challengers = sorted(challengers, key=lambda x: x[0],
                         reverse=True)
    best_score, best_model = challengers[0]
    if best_score > baseline:
        print(f"Adding model_{best_model+1} to the ensemble",
              end=': ')
        print(f"ROC-AUC increases score to {best_score:0.5f}")
        models.append(best_model)
        baseline = best_score
    else:
        print("Cannot improve further - Stopping")
```

Finally, we count how many times each model has been inserted into the average and we calculate the weights for our averaging on the test set:

```
from collections import Counter

freqs = Counter(models)
weights = {key: freq/len(models) for key, freq in freqs.items()}
print(weights)
```

You can make the procedure more sophisticated in various ways. Since this approach may overfit, especially at the initial stages, you could start from a randomly initialized ensemble set or, as the authors suggest, you may already be starting with the n best performing models in the set (you decide the value of n, as a hyperparameter). Another variation involves applying sampling to the set of models that can enter the selection at each iteration; in other words, you randomly exclude some models from being picked. Not only will this inject randomness into the process but it will also prevent specific models from dominating the selection.

Stacking models together

Stacking was first mentioned in *David Wolpert*'s paper (*Wolpert, D. H. Stacked generalization.* Neural networks 5.2 – 1992), but it took years before the idea become widely accepted and common (only with release 0.22 in December 2019, for instance, has Scikit-learn implemented a stacking wrapper). This was due principally to the Netflix competition first, and to Kaggle competitions afterward.

In stacking, you always have a meta-learner. This time, however, it is not trained on a holdout, but on the entire training set, thanks to the **out-of-fold (OOF)** prediction strategy. We already discussed this strategy in *Chapter 6, Designing Good Validation*. In OOF prediction, you start from a replicable k-fold cross-validation split. *Replicable* means that, by recording the cases in each training and testing sets at each round or by reproducibility assured by a random seed, you can replicate the same validation scheme for each model you need to be part of the stacking ensemble.

 In the Netflix competition, stacking and blending were often used interchangeably, though the actual method devised by Wolpert originally implied leveraging a scheme based on k-fold cross-validation, not a holdout set. In fact, the core idea in stacking is not to reduce the variance, as in averaging; it is mostly to reduce the bias, because it is expected that each model involved in the stacking will grasp a part of the information present in the data, to be recomposed in the final meta-learner.

Let's remind ourselves of how OOF predictions on the training data work. When testing a model, at each round of the validation you train a model on part of the training data and you validate on another part that is held out from the training.

By recording the validation predictions and then reordering them to reconstruct the ordering of the original training cases, you will obtain a prediction of your model on the very same training set that you have used. However, as you have used multiple models and each model has predicted on cases it didn't use for training, you should not have any overfitting effects on your training set predictions.

Having obtained OOF predictions for all your models, you can proceed to build a meta-learner that predicts your target based on the OOF predictions (first-level predictions), or you can keep on producing further OOF predictions on top of your previous OOF predictions (second- or higher-level predictions), thus creating multiple stacking layers. This is compatible with an idea presented by Wolpert himself: by using multiple meta-learners, you are actually imitating the structure of a fully connected feedforward neural network without backpropagation, where the weights are optimally calculated in order to maximize the predictive performance at the level of each layer separately. From a practical point of view, stacking multiple layers has proven very effective and works very well for complex problems where single algorithms are unable to obtain the best results.

Moreover, one interesting aspect of stacking is that you don't need models of comparable predictive power, as in averaging and often in blending. In fact, even worse-performing models may be effective as part of a stacking ensemble. A k-nearest neighbors model may not be comparable to a gradient boosting solution, but when you use its OOF predictions for stacking it may contribute positively and increase the predictive performance of the ensemble.

When you have trained all the stacking layers, it is time to predict. As far as producing the predictions used at various stacking stages, it is important to note that you have two ways to do this. The original Wolpert paper suggests re-training your models on all your training data and then using those re-trained models for predicting on the test set. In practice, many Kagglers don't retrain, but directly use the models created for each fold and make multiple predictions on the test set that are averaged at the end.

In our experience, stacking is generally more effective with complete re-training on all available data before predicting on the test set when you are using a low number of k-folds. In these cases, the sample consistency may really make a difference in the quality of the prediction because training on less data means getting more variance in the estimates. As we discussed in *Chapter 6*, when creating OOF predictions it is always better to use a high number of folds, between 10 to 20. This limits the number of examples that are held out, and, without re-training on all the data, you can simply use the average of predictions obtained from the cross-validation trained models for obtaining your prediction on the test set.

In our next example, for illustrative purposes, we only have five CV folds and the results are stacked twice. In the diagram below, you can follow how the data and the models move between different stages of the stacking process:

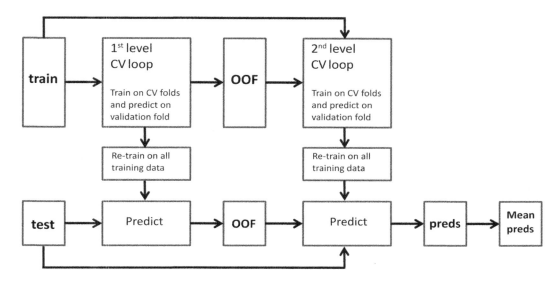

Figure 9.1: Diagram of a two-layer stacking process with final averaging of predictions

Notice that:

- Training data is fed to both levels of the stacking (OOF predictions at the second level of the stacking are joined with the training data)
- After obtaining OOF predictions from the CV loops, models are re-trained on the entire training dataset
- The final predictions are a simple average of all the predictions obtained by the stacked predictors

Let's now take a look at the code to understand how this diagram translates into Python commands, starting with the first level of training:

```
from sklearn.model_selection import KFold

kf = KFold(n_splits=5, shuffle=True, random_state=0)
scores = list()

first_lvl_oof = np.zeros((len(X_train), 3))
```

```
fist_lvl_preds = np.zeros((len(X_test), 3))

for k, (train_index, val_index) in enumerate(kf.split(X_train)):
    model_1.fit(X_train[train_index, :], y_train[train_index])
    first_lvl_oof[val_index, 0] = model_1.predict_proba(
                                    X_train[val_index, :])[:, 1]

    model_2.fit(X_train[train_index, :], y_train[train_index])
    first_lvl_oof[val_index, 1] = model_2.predict_proba(
                                    X_train[val_index, :])[:, 1]

    model_3.fit(X_train[train_index, :], y_train[train_index])
    first_lvl_oof[val_index, 2] = model_3.predict_proba(
                                    X_train[val_index, :])[:, 1]
```

After the first layer, we retrain on the full dataset:

```
model_1.fit(X_train, y_train)
fist_lvl_preds[:, 0] = model_1.predict_proba(X_test)[:, 1]

model_2.fit(X_train, y_train)
fist_lvl_preds[:, 1] = model_2.predict_proba(X_test)[:, 1]

model_3.fit(X_train, y_train)
fist_lvl_preds[:, 2] = model_3.predict_proba(X_test)[:, 1]
```

In the second stacking, we will reuse the same models as those in the first layer, adding the stacked OOF predictions to the existing variables:

```
second_lvl_oof = np.zeros((len(X_train), 3))
second_lvl_preds = np.zeros((len(X_test), 3))

for k, (train_index, val_index) in enumerate(kf.split(X_train)):
    skip_X_train = np.hstack([X_train, first_lvl_oof])

    model_1.fit(skip_X_train[train_index, :],
                y_train[train_index])
    second_lvl_oof[val_index, 0] = model_1.predict_proba(
                        skip_X_train[val_index, :])[:, 1]
```

```
    model_2.fit(skip_X_train[train_index, :],
                y_train[train_index])
    second_lvl_oof[val_index, 1] = model_2.predict_proba(
                        skip_X_train[val_index, :])[:, 1]


    model_3.fit(skip_X_train[train_index, :],
                y_train[train_index])
    second_lvl_oof[val_index, 2] = model_3.predict_proba(
                        skip_X_train[val_index, :])[:, 1]
```

Again, we retrain on the full data for the second layer:

```
skip_X_test = np.hstack([X_test, fist_lvl_preds])

model_1.fit(skip_X_train, y_train)
second_lvl_preds[:, 0] = model_1.predict_proba(skip_X_test)[:, 1]

model_2.fit(skip_X_train, y_train)
second_lvl_preds[:, 1] = model_2.predict_proba(skip_X_test)[:, 1]

model_3.fit(skip_X_train, y_train)
second_lvl_preds[:, 2] = model_3.predict_proba(skip_X_test)[:, 1]
```

The stacking is concluded by averaging all the stacked OOF results from the second layer:

```
arithmetic = second_lvl_preds.mean(axis=1)
ras = roc_auc_score(y_true=y_test, y_score=arithmetic)
scores.append(ras)
print(f"Stacking ROC-AUC is: {ras:0.5f}")
```

The resulting ROC-AUC score is about **0.90424**, which is better than previous blending and averaging attempts on the same data and models.

Stacking variations

The main variations on stacking involve changing how test data is processed across the layers, whether to use only stacked OOF predictions or also the original features in all the stacking layers, what model to use as the last one, and various tricks in order to prevent overfitting.

We discuss some of the most effective here that we have personally experimented with:

- **Optimization may or may not be used.** Some solutions do not care too much about optimizing single models; others optimize only the last layers; others optimize on the first layers. Based on our experiences, optimization of single models is important and we prefer to do it as early as possible in our stacking ensemble.

- **Models can differ at the different stacking layers, or the same sequence of models can be repeated at every stacking layer.** Here we don't have a general rule, as it really depends on the problem. The kind of models that are more effective may vary according to the problem. As a general suggestion, putting together gradient boosting solutions and neural networks has never disappointed us.

- **At the first level of the stacking procedure, just create as many models are possible.** For instance, you can try a regression model if your problem is a classification one, and vice versa. You can also use different models with different hyperparameter settings, thus avoiding too much extensive optimization because the stacking will decide for you. If you are using neural networks, just changing the random initialization seed could suffice to create a diverse bag of models. You can also try models using different feature engineering and even use unsupervised learning (like *Mike Kim* did when he used t-SNE dimensions in a solution of his: `https://www.kaggle.com/c/otto-group-product-classification-challenge/discussion/14295`). The idea is that the selection of all such contributions is done during the second level of the stacking. This means that, at that point, you do not have to experiment any further and you just need to focus on a narrower set of better-performing models. By applying stacking, you can re-use all your experiments and let the stacking decide for you to what degree you should use something in your modeling pipeline.

- Some stacking implementations take on all the features or a selection of them to further stages, reminiscent of skip layers in neural networks. We have noticed that bringing in features at later stages in the stacking can improve your results, but be careful: it also brings in more noise and risk of overfitting.

- Ideally, your OOF predictions should be made from cross-validation schemes with a high number of folds, in other words, between 10 to 20, but we have also seen solutions working with a lower number, such as 5 folds.

- For each fold, bagging the data (resampling with repetition) multiple times for the same model and then averaging all the results from the model (OOF predictions and test predictions) helps to avoid overfitting and produces better results in the end.

- **Beware of early stopping in stacking.** Using it directly on the validation fold may cause a certain degree of overfitting, which may or may not be mitigated in the end by the stacking procedure. We suggest you play it safe and always apply early stopping based on a validation sample from your training folds, not your validation one.

The possibilities are endless. Once you have grasped the basic concept of this ensembling technique, all you need is to apply your creativity to the problem at hand. We will discuss this key concept in the final section of this chapter, where we will look at a stacking solution for a Kaggle competition.

Creating complex stacking and blending solutions

At this point in the chapter, you may be wondering to what extent you should apply the techniques we have been discussing. In theory, you could use all the ensembling techniques we have presented in any competition on Kaggle, not just tabular ones, but you have to consider a few limiting factors:

- Sometimes, datasets are massive, and training a single model takes a long time.
- In image recognition competitions, you are limited to using deep learning methods.
- Even if you can manage to stack models in a deep learning competition, you have a limited choice for stacking different models. Since you are restricted to deep learning solutions, you can only vary small design aspects of the networks and some hyperparameters (or sometimes just the initialization seed) without degrading the performance. In the end, given the same type of models and more similarities than differences in the architectures, the predictions will tend to be too similar and more correlated than they should be, limiting the effectiveness of ensembling.

Under these conditions, complex stacking regimes are usually not feasible. By contrast, averaging and blending are usually possible when you have large datasets.

In earlier competitions, as well as in all recent tabular competitions, complex stacking and blending solutions ruled the day. To give you an idea of the complexity and creativity that needs to be put into stacking for a competition, in this last section we will discuss the solution provided by *Gilberto Titericz* (https://www.kaggle.com/titericz) and *Stanislav Semenov* (https://www.kaggle.com/stasg7) to the *Otto Group Product Classification Challenge* (https://www.kaggle.com/c/otto-group-product-classification-challenge). The competition was held in 2015 and its task required classifying over 200,000 products into 9 distinct classes based on 93 features.

The solution proposed by Gilberto and Stanislav comprised three levels:

1. On the first level, there were 33 models. All the models used quite different algorithms, apart from a cluster of k-nearest neighbors where only the k parameter varied. They also used unsupervised t-SNE. In addition, they engineered eight features based on dimensionality manipulation (computations performed on distances from nearest neighbors and clusters) and on row statistics (the number of non-zero elements in each row). All the OOF predictions and features were passed to the second level.

2. On the second level, they started optimizing hyperparameters and doing model selection and bagging (they created multiple versions of the same model by resampling and averaged the results for each model). In the end, they had only three models that they re-trained on all the data: an XGBoost, an AdaBoost, and a neural network.

3. On the third level, they prepared a weighted average of the results by first doing a geometric mean of XGBoost and the neural network and then averaging it with the AdaBoost.

We can learn a lot from this solution, and not just limited to this competition. Aside from the complexity (on the second level, the number of times they resampled was in the order of hundreds for each model), it is noticeable that there are multiple variations on the schemes we discussed in this chapter. Creativity and trial and error clearly dominate the solution. This is quite typical of many Kaggle competitions, where the problems are seldom the same from one competition to another and each solution is unique and not easily repeatable.

Many AutoML engines, such as **AutoGluon**, more or less explicitly try to take inspiration from such procedures in order to offer a predefined series of automated steps that can ensure you a top result by stacking and blending.

 See https://arxiv.org/abs/2003.06505 for a list of the algorithms used by AutoGluon to build its stacked models. The list is quite long and you will find many ideas for your own stacking solutions.

However, despite the fact they implement some of the best practices around, their results are always subpar compared to what can be achieved by a good team of Kagglers, because creativity in the way you experiment and compose the ensemble is the key to success. The same goes for this chapter of ours. We have shown you the best practices for ensembling; take them as a starting point and create your own by mixing ideas and innovating based on the Kaggle competition or the real-world problem that you are dealing with.

Xavier Conort

`https://www.kaggle.com/xavierconort`

To conclude the chapter, we caught up with Xavier Conort, a Competitions Grandmaster who ranked #1 in 2012-2013. An inspiration for many Kagglers at the beginning of Kaggle history, he is now the founder and CEO of his own company, Data Mapping and Engineering. He spoke to us about his experiences with Kaggle, his career, and more.

What's your favourite kind of competition and why? In terms of techniques and solving approaches, what is your speciality on Kaggle?

I really enjoyed competitions where feature engineering from multiple tables was required to get good results. I liked to mine for good features, especially for business problems that were new to me. This gave me a lot of confidence in my capacity to tackle new problems. In addition to good feature engineering, stacking helped me get good results. I used it to blend multiple models or transform text or high categorical variables into numeric features. My favorite algorithm was GBM, but I tested many other algorithms to add diversity to my blends.

How do you approach a Kaggle competition? How different is this approach to what you do in your day-to-day work?

My primary goal was to learn as much as possible from each competition. Before entering a competition, I tried to assess which skills I would develop. I was not afraid to go beyond my comfort zone. Thanks to the leaderboard feedback, I knew I could learn rapidly from my mistakes. Day-to-day work rarely offers this opportunity. It is difficult to assess the actual quality of the solution we are working on. So, we just play safe and tend to repeat past recipes. I don't think I could have learnt as much as I did without Kaggle.

Tell us about a particularly challenging competition you entered, and what insights you used to tackle the task.

My favorite competition is GE Flight Quest, a competition organised by GE where competitors had to predict arrival time of domestic flights in the US. I especially liked the way the competition's private leaderboard was designed. It tested our capacity to predict future events by scoring our predictions on flights that happened after the competition deadline.

As we had only a few months of history (3 or 4, if my memory is correct), I knew there was a strong risk of overfitting. To mitigate this risk, I decided to build only features that had an obvious causal relation with flight delays, such as features measuring weather conditions and traffic. And I was very careful to exclude the name of the airport from my primary feature lists. Indeed, some airports hadn't experienced bad weather conditions during the few months of history. So, I was very concerned that my favorite ML algorithm, GBM, would use the name of the airport as a proxy for good weather and then fail to predict well for those airports in the private leaderboard. To capture the fact that some airports are better managed than others and improve my leaderboard score slightly, I eventually did use the name of the airport, but as a residual effect only. It was a feature of my second layer of models that used as an offset the predictions of my first layer of models. This approach can be considered a two-step boosting, where you censor some information during the first step. I learnt it from actuaries applying this approach in insurance to capture geospatial residual effects.

Has Kaggle helped you in your career? If so, how?

It definitely helped me in my career as a data scientist. Before converting into data science, I was an actuary in the insurance industry, didn't know anything about machine learning, and didn't know any data scientists. Thanks to Kaggle's diversity of competitions, I boosted my learning curve. Thanks to my good results, I could show a track record and convince employers that a 39-year-old actuary could successfully develop new skills on his own. And thanks to Kaggle's community, I connected with many passionate data scientists across the world. I first had a lot of fun competing with or against them. Finally, I had the chance to work with some of them. Jeremy Achin and Tom De Godoy, the DataRobot founders, were my competition teammates before they asked me to join DataRobot. Without Kaggle's help, I think I would still be working as an actuary in the insurance industry.

Have you ever used something you have done in Kaggle competitions in order to build your portfolio to show to potential employers?

I have to confess that I did enter a few competitions with the goal to impress my employer or potential clients. It worked well, but it was much less fun and much more pressure.

In your experience, what do inexperienced Kagglers often overlook? What do you know now that you wish you'd known when you first started?

I would advise inexperienced Kagglers not to look at the solutions posted during the competition but to try to find good solutions on their own. I am happy that competitors didn't share code during the early days of Kaggle. It forced me to learn the hard way.

What mistakes have you made in competitions in the past?

One mistake is to keep on competing in competitions that are badly designed with leaks. It is just a waste of time. You don't learn much from those competitions.

Are there any particular tools or libraries that you would recommend using for data analysis or machine learning?

Gradient Boosting Machine is my favorite algorithm. I first used R's gbm, then Scikit-learn GBM, then XGBoost, and finally LightGBM. Most of the time, it has been the principal ingredient of my winning solution. To get some insight into what GBM learns, I would recommend the SHAP package.

What's the most important thing someone should keep in mind or do when they're entering a competition?

Compete to learn. Compete to connect with other passionate data scientists. Don't compete only to win.

Summary

In this chapter, we discussed how ensembling multiple solutions works and proposed some basic code examples you can use to start building your own solutions. We started from the ideas that power model ensembles such as random forests and gradient boosting. Then, we moved on to explore the different ensembling approaches, from the simple averaging of test submissions to meta-modeling across multiple layers of stacked models.

As we discussed at the end, ensembling is more an art form based on some shared common practices. When we explored a successful complex stacking regime that won a Kaggle competition, we were amazed by how the combinations were tailored to the data and the problem itself. You cannot just take a stacking, replicate it on another problem, and hope that it will be the best solution. You can only follow guidelines and find the best solution consisting of averaging/stacking/blending of diverse models yourself, through lots of experimentation and computational effort.

In the next chapter, we will start delving into deep learning competitions, beginning with computer vision ones for classification and segmentation tasks.

Join our book's Discord space

Join the book's Discord workspace for a monthly *Ask me Anything* session with the authors:

https://packt.link/KaggleDiscord

10

Modeling for Computer Vision

Computer vision tasks are among the most popular problems in practical applications of machine learning; they were the gateway into deep learning for many Kagglers, including yours truly (Konrad, that is). Over the last few years, there has been tremendous progress in the field and new SOTA libraries continue to be released. In this chapter, we will give you an overview of the most popular competition types in computer vision:

- Image classification
- Object detection
- Image segmentation

We will begin with a short section on image augmentation, a group of task-agnostic techniques that can be applied to different problems to increase the generalization capability of our models.

Augmentation strategies

While deep learning techniques have been extremely successful in computer vision tasks like image recognition, segmentation, or object detection, the underlying algorithms are typically extremely data-intensive: they require large amounts of data to avoid overfitting. However, not all domains of interest satisfy that requirement, which is where **data augmentation** comes in. This is the name for a group of image processing techniques that create modified versions of images, thus enhancing the size and quality of training datasets, leading to better performance of deep learning models. The augmented data will typically represent a more comprehensive set of possible data points, thereby minimizing the distance between the training and validation set, as well as any future test sets.

In this section, we will review some of the more common augmentation techniques, along with choices for their software implementations. The most frequently used transformations include:

- **Flipping**: Flipping the image (along the horizontal or vertical axis)
- **Rotation**: Rotating the image by a given angle (clockwise or anti-clockwise)
- **Cropping**: A random subsection of the image is selected
- **Brightness**: Modifying the brightness of the image
- **Scaling**: The image is increased or decreased to a higher (outward) or lower (inward) size

Below, we demonstrate how those transformations work in practice using the image of an American acting legend and comedian, Betty White:

Figure 10.1: Betty White image

We can flip the image along the vertical or horizontal axes:

Figure 10.2: Betty White image – flipped vertically (left) and horizontally (right)

Rotations are fairly self-explanatory; notice the automatic padding of the image in the background:

Figure 10.3: Betty White image – rotated clockwise

We can also crop an image to the region of interest:

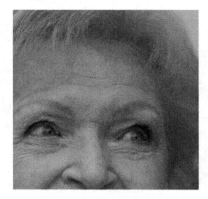

Figure 10.4: Betty White image – cropped

On a high level, we can say that augmentations can be applied in one of two ways:

- **Offline:** These are usually applied for smaller datasets (fewer images or smaller sizes, although the definition of "small" depends on the available hardware). The idea is to generate modified versions of the original images as a preprocessing step for your dataset, and then use those alongside the "original" ones.

- **Online:** These are used for bigger datasets. The augmented images are not saved on disk; the augmentations are applied in mini-batches and fed to the model.

In the next few sections, we will give you an overview of two of the most common methods for augmenting your image dataset: the built-in Keras functionality and the albumentations package. There are several other options available out there (skimage, OpenCV, imgaug, Augmentor, SOLT), but we will focus on the most popular ones.

The methods discussed in this chapter focus on image analysis powered by GPU. The use of **tensor processing units (TPUs)** is an emerging, but still somewhat niche, application. Readers interested in image augmentation in combination with TPU-powered analysis are encouraged to check out the excellent work of *Chris Deotte* (**@cdeotte**):

```
https://www.kaggle.com/cdeotte/triple-stratified-kfold-with-
tfrecords
```

Chris is a quadruple Kaggle Grandmaster and a fantastic educator through the Notebooks he creates and discussions he participates in; overall, a person definitely worth following for any Kaggler, irrespective of your level of experience.

We will be using data from the *Cassava Leaf Disease Classification* competition (`https://www.kaggle.com/c/cassava-leaf-disease-classification`). As usual, we begin with the groundwork: first, loading the necessary packages:

```python
import os
import glob
import numpy as np
import scipy as sp
import pandas as pd

import cv2
from skimage.io import imshow, imread, imsave

# imgaug
import imageio
import imgaug as ia
import imgaug.augmenters as iaa

# Albumentations
import albumentations as A

# Keras
# from keras.preprocessing.image import ImageDataGenerator, array_to_img,
img_to_array, load_img

# Visualization
import matplotlib.pyplot as plt
import matplotlib.image as mpimg
%matplotlib inline
import seaborn as sns
from IPython.display import HTML, Image

# Warnings
import warnings
warnings.filterwarnings("ignore")
```

Next, we define some helper functions that will streamline the presentation later. We need a way to load images into arrays:

```
def load_image(image_id):
    file_path = image_id
    image = imread(Image_Data_Path + file_path)
    return image
```

We would like to display multiple images in a gallery style, so we create a function that takes as input an array containing the images along with the desired number of columns, and outputs the array reshaped into a grid with a given number of columns:

```
def gallery(array, ncols=3):

    nindex, height, width, intensity = array.shape
    nrows = nindex//ncols
    assert nindex == nrows*ncols
    result = (array.reshape(nrows, ncols, height, width, intensity)
             .swapaxes(1,2)
             .reshape(height*nrows, width*ncols, intensity))
    return result
```

With the boilerplate taken care of, we can load the images for augmentation:

```
data_dir = '../input/cassava-leaf-disease-classification/'
Image_Data_Path = data_dir + '/train_images/'
train_data = pd.read_csv(data_dir + '/train.csv')

# We load and store the first 10 images in memory for faster access
train_images = train_data["image_id"][:10].apply(load_image)
```

Let's load a single image so we know what our reference is:

```
curr_img = train_images[7]
plt.figure(figsize = (15,15))
plt.imshow(curr_img)
plt.axis('off')
```

Here it is:

Figure 10.5: Reference image

In the following sections, we will demonstrate how to generate augmented images from this reference image using both built-in Keras functionality and the albumentations library.

Keras built-in augmentations

The Keras library has a built-in functionality for augmentations. While not as extensive as dedicated packages, it has the advantage of easy integration with your code. We do not need a separate code block for defining the augmentation transformations but can incorporate them inside ImageDataGenerator, a functionality we are likely to be using anyway.

The first Keras approach we examine is based upon the ImageDataGenerator class. As the name suggests, it can be used to generate batches of image data with real-time data augmentations.

ImageDataGenerator approach

We begin by instantiating an object of class ImageDataGenerator in the following manner:

```
import tensorflow as tf
from tensorflow.keras.preprocessing.image import ImageDataGenerator,
array_to_img, img_to_array, load_img
```

```
datagen = ImageDataGenerator(
        rotation_range = 40,
        shear_range = 0.2,
        zoom_range = 0.2,
        horizontal_flip = True,
        brightness_range = (0.5, 1.5))

curr_img_array = img_to_array(curr_img)
curr_img_array = curr_img_array.reshape((1,) + curr_img_array.shape)
```

We define the desired augmentations as arguments to `ImageDataGenerator`. The official documentation does not seem to address the topic, but practical results indicate that the augmentations are applied in the order in which they are defined as arguments.

 In the above example, we utilize only a limited subset of possible options; for a full list, the reader is encouraged to consult the official documentation: `https://keras.io/api/preprocessing/image/`.

Next, we iterate through the images with the `.flow` method of the `ImageDataGenerator` object. The class provides three different functions to load the image dataset in memory and generate batches of augmented data:

- `flow`
- `flow_from_directory`
- `flow_from_dataframe`

They all achieve the same objective, but differ in the way the locations of the files are specified. In our example, the images are already in memory, so we can iterate using the simplest method:

```
i = 0
for batch in datagen.flow(
    curr_img_array,
    batch_size=1,
    save_to_dir='.',
    save_prefix='Augmented_image',
    save_format='jpeg'):
    i += 1
    # Hard-coded stop - without it, the generator enters an infinite loop
```

```
    if i > 9:
        break
```

We can examine the augmented images using the helper functions we defined earlier:

```
aug_images = []
for img_path in glob.glob("*.jpeg"):
    aug_images.append(mpimg.imread(img_path))
plt.figure(figsize=(20,20))
plt.axis('off')
plt.imshow(gallery(np.array(aug_images[0:9]), ncols = 3))
plt.title('Augmentation examples')
```

Here is the result:

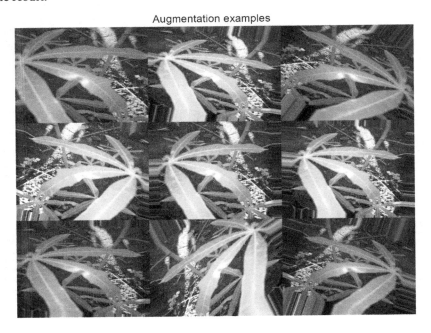

Figure 10.6: A collection of augmented images

Augmentations are a very useful tool, but using them efficiently requires a judgment call. First, it is obviously a good idea to visualize them to get a feeling for the impact on the data. On the one hand, we want to introduce some variation in the data to increase the generalization of our model; on the other, if we change the images too radically, the input data will be less informative and the model performance is likely to suffer. In addition, the choice of which augmentations to use can also be problem-specific, as we can see by comparing different competitions.

If you look at *Figure 10.6* above (the reference image from the *Cassava Leaf Disease Classification* competition), the leaves on which we are supposed to identify the disease can be of different sizes, pointing at different angles, and so on, due both to the shapes of the plants and differences in how the images are taken. This means transformations such as vertical or horizontal flips, cropping, and rotations all make sense in this context.

By contrast, we can look at a sample image from the *Severstal: Steel Defect Detection* competition (`https://www.kaggle.com/c/severstal-steel-defect-detection`). In this competition, participants had to localize and classify defects on a steel sheet. All the images had the same size and orientation, which means that rotations or crops would have produced unrealistic images, adding to the noise and having an adverse impact on the generalization capabilities of an algorithm.

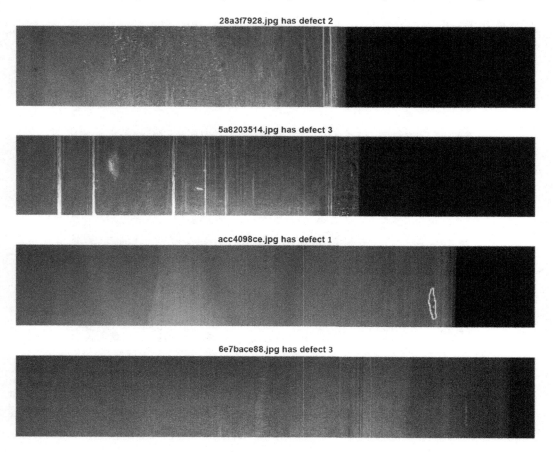

Figure 10.7: Sample images from the Severstal competition

Preprocessing layers

An alternative approach to data augmentation as a preprocessing step in a native Keras manner is to use the preprocessing layers API. The functionality is remarkably flexible: these pipelines can be used either in combination with Keras models or independently, in a manner similar to ImageDataGenerator.

Below we show briefly how a preprocessing layer can be set up. First, the imports:

```
from tensorflow.keras.layers.experimental import preprocessing
from tensorflow.keras import layers
```

We load a pretrained model in the standard Keras manner:

```
pretrained_base = tf.keras.models.load_model(
    '../input/cv-course-models/cv-course-models/vgg16-pretrained-base',
)
pretrained_base.trainable = False
```

The preprocessing layers can be used in the same way as other layers are used inside the Sequential constructor; the only requirement is that they need to be specified before any others, at the beginning of our model definition:

```
model = tf.keras.Sequential([
    # Preprocessing Layers
    preprocessing.RandomFlip('horizontal'), # Flip left-to-right
    preprocessing.RandomContrast(0.5), # Contrast change by up to 50%
    # Base model
    pretrained_base,
    # model head definition
    layers.Flatten(),
    layers.Dense(6, activation='relu'),
    layers.Dense(1, activation='sigmoid'),
])
```

albumentations

The `albumentations` package is a fast image augmentation library that is built as a wrapper of sorts around other libraries.

The package is the result of intensive coding in quite a few Kaggle competitions (see `https://medium.com/@iglovikov/the-birth-of-albumentations-fe38c1411cb3`), and claims among its core developers and contributors quite a few notable Kagglers, including *Eugene Khvedchenya* (`https://www.kaggle.com/bloodaxe`), *Vladimir Iglovikov* (`https://www.kaggle.com/iglovikov`), *Alex Parinov* (`https://www.kaggle.com/creafz`), and *ZFTurbo* (`https://www.kaggle.com/zfturbo`).

The full documentation can be found at `https://albumentations.readthedocs.io/en/latest/`.

Below we list the important characteristics:

- A unified API for different data types
- Support for all common computer vision tasks
- Integration both with TensorFlow and PyTorch

Using `albumentations` functionality to transform an image is straightforward. We begin by initializing the required transformations:

```
import albumentations as A
horizontal_flip = A.HorizontalFlip(p=1)
rotate = A.ShiftScaleRotate(p=1)
gaus_noise = A.GaussNoise()
bright_contrast = A.RandomBrightnessContrast(p=1)
gamma = A.RandomGamma(p=1)
blur = A.Blur()
```

Next, we apply the transformations to our reference image:

```
img_flip = horizontal_flip(image = curr_img)
img_gaus = gaus_noise(image = curr_img)
img_rotate = rotate(image = curr_img)
img_bc = bright_contrast(image = curr_img)
img_gamma = gamma(image = curr_img)
img_blur = blur(image = curr_img)
```

We can access the augmented images with the `'image'` key and visualize the results:

```
img_list = [img_flip['image'],img_gaus['image'], img_rotate['image'],
            img_bc['image'], img_gamma['image'], img_blur['image']]


plt.figure(figsize=(20,20))
plt.axis('off')
plt.imshow(gallery(np.array(img_list), ncols = 3))
plt.title('Augmentation examples')
```

Here are our results:

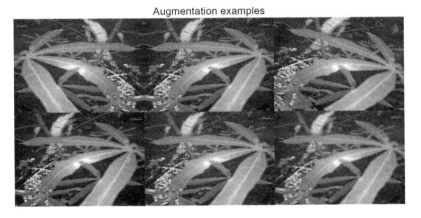

Figure 10.8: Image augmented using the albumentations library

Having discussed augmentation as a crucial preprocessing step in approaching a computer vision problem, we are now in a position to apply this knowledge in the following sections, beginning with a very common task: image classification.

Chris Deotte

`https://www.kaggle.com/cdeotte`

Before we proceed, let's look at a brief conversation we had with Chris Deotte, who we've mentioned quite a few times in this book (including earlier in this chapter), and for good reason. He is a quadruple Kaggle Grandmaster and Senior Data Scientist & Researcher at NVIDIA, who joined Kaggle in 2019.

What's your favorite kind of competition and why? In terms of techniques and solving approaches, what is your specialty on Kaggle?

I enjoy competitions with fascinating data and competitions that require building creative novel models. My specialty is analyzing trained models to determine their strengths and weaknesses. Afterward, I enjoy improving the models and/or developing post-processing to boost CV LB.

How do you approach a Kaggle competition? How different is this approach to what you do in your day-to-day work?

I begin each competition by performing EDA (exploratory data analysis), creating a local validation, building some simple models, and submitting to Kaggle for leaderboard scores. This fosters an intuition of what needs to be done in order to build an accurate and competitive model.

Tell us about a particularly challenging competition you entered, and what insights you used to tackle the task.

Kaggle's Shopee – Price Match Guarantee *was a challenging competition that required both image models and natural language models. A key insight was extracting embeddings from the two types of models and then determining how to use both image and language information together to find product matches.*

Has Kaggle helped you in your career? If so, how?

Yes. Kaggle helped me become a senior data scientist at NVIDIA by improving my skills and boosting my resume's marketability.

Many employers peruse the work on Kaggle to find employees with specific skills to help solve their specific projects. In this way, I have been solicited about many job opportunities.

In your experience, what do inexperienced Kagglers often overlook? What do you know now that you wish you'd known when you first started?

In my opinion, inexperienced Kagglers often overlook the importance of local validation. Seeing your name on the leaderboard is exciting. And it's easy to focus on improving our leaderboard scores instead of our cross-validation scores.

What mistakes have you made in competitions in the past?

Many times, I have made the mistake of trusting my leaderboard score over my cross-validation score and selecting the wrong final submission.

Are there any particular tools or libraries that you would recommend using for data analysis or machine learning?

Absolutely. Feature engineering and quick experimentation are important when optimizing tabular data models. In order to accelerate the cycle of experimentation and validation, using NVIDIA RAPIDS cuDF and cuML on GPU are essential.

What's the most important thing someone should keep in mind or do when they're entering a competition?

The most important thing is to have fun and learn. Don't worry about your final placement. If you focus on learning and having fun, then over time your final placements will become better and better.

Do you use other competition platforms? How do they compare to Kaggle?

Yes, I have entered competitions outside of Kaggle. Individual companies like Booking.com or Twitter.com will occasionally host a competition. These competitions are fun and involve high-quality, real-life data.

Classification

In this section, we will demonstrate an end-to-end pipeline that can be used as a template for handling image classification problems. We will walk through the necessary steps, from data preparation, to model setup and estimation, to results visualization. Apart from being informative (and cool), this last step can also be very useful if you need to examine your code in-depth to get a better understanding of the performance.

We will continue using the data from the *Cassava Leaf Disease Classification* contest (`https://www.kaggle.com/c/cassava-leaf-disease-classification`).

As usual, we begin by loading the necessary libraries:

```
import numpy as np
import pandas as pd
import matplotlib.pyplot as plt
import datetime

from sklearn.model_selection import train_test_split
from sklearn.metrics import accuracy_score
import tensorflow as tf
```

```
from tensorflow.keras import models, layers
from tensorflow.keras.preprocessing import image
from tensorflow.keras.preprocessing.image import ImageDataGenerator
from tensorflow.keras.callbacks import ModelCheckpoint, EarlyStopping,
ReduceLROnPlateau
from tensorflow.keras.applications import EfficientNetB0
from tensorflow.keras.optimizers import Adam

import os, cv2, json
from PIL import Image
```

It is usually a good idea to define a few helper functions; it makes for code that is easier to both read and debug. If you are approaching a general image classification problem, a good starting point can be provided by a model from the **EfficientNet** family, introduced in 2019 in a paper from the Google Research Brain Team (`https://arxiv.org/abs/1905.11946`). The basic idea is to balance network depth, width, and resolution to enable more efficient scaling across all dimensions and subsequently better performance. For our solution, we will use the simplest member of the family, **EfficientNet B0**, which is a mobile-sized network with 11 million trainable parameters.

 For a properly detailed explanation of the EfficientNet networks, you are encouraged to explore `https://ai.googleblog.com/2019/05/efficientnet-improving-accuracy-and.html` as a starting point.

We construct our model with B0 as the basis, followed by a pooling layer for improved translation invariance and a dense layer with an activation function suitable for our multiclass classification problem:

```
class CFG:
    # config
    WORK_DIR = '../input/cassava-leaf-disease-classification'
    BATCH_SIZE = 8
    EPOCHS = 5
    TARGET_SIZE = 512

def create_model():
    conv_base = EfficientNetB0(include_top = False, weights = None,
                               input_shape = (CFG.TARGET_SIZE,
                               CFG.TARGET_SIZE, 3))
```

```
model = conv_base.output
model = layers.GlobalAveragePooling2D()(model)
model = layers.Dense(5, activation = "softmax")(model)
model = models.Model(conv_base.input, model)

model.compile(optimizer = Adam(lr = 0.001),
              loss = "sparse_categorical_crossentropy",
              metrics = ["acc"])
return model
```

Some brief remarks on the parameters we pass to the `EfficientNetB0` function:

- The `include_top` parameter allows you to decide whether to include the final dense layers. As we want to use the pre-trained model as a feature extractor, a default strategy would be to skip them and then define the head ourselves.

- `weights` can be set to None if we want to train the model from scratch, or to `'imagenet'` or `'noisy-student'` if we instead prefer to utilize the weights pre-trained on large image collections.

The helper function below allows us to visualize the activation layer, so we can examine the network performance from a visual angle. This is frequently helpful in developing an intuition in a field notorious for its opacity:

```
def activation_layer_vis(img, activation_layer = 0, layers = 10):
    layer_outputs = [layer.output for layer in model.layers[:layers]]
    activation_model = models.Model(inputs = model.input,
                                    outputs = layer_outputs)
    activations = activation_model.predict(img)

    rows = int(activations[activation_layer].shape[3] / 3)
    cols = int(activations[activation_layer].shape[3] / rows)
    fig, axes = plt.subplots(rows, cols, figsize = (15, 15 * cols))
    axes = axes.flatten()

    for i, ax in zip(range(activations[activation_layer].shape[3]), axes):
        ax.matshow(activations[activation_layer][0, :, :, i],
                   cmap = 'viridis')
        ax.axis('off')
    plt.tight_layout()
    plt.show()
```

We generate the activations by creating predictions for a given model based on a "restricted" model, in other words, using the entire architecture up until the penultimate layer; this is the code up to the `activations` variable. The rest of the function ensures we show the right layout of activations, corresponding to the shape of the filter in the appropriate convolution layer.

Next, we process the labels and set up the validation scheme; there is no special structure in the data (for example, a time dimension or overlap across classes), so we can use a simple random split:

```
train_labels = pd.read_csv(os.path.join(CFG.WORK_DIR, "train.csv"))

STEPS_PER_EPOCH = len(train_labels)*0.8 / CFG.BATCH_SIZE
VALIDATION_STEPS = len(train_labels)*0.2 / CFG.BATCH_SIZE
```

 For a refresher on more elaborate validation schemes, refer to *Chapter 6, Designing Good Validation*.

We are now able to set up the data generators, which are necessary for our TF-based algorithm to loop through the image data.

First, we instantiate two `ImageDataGenerator` objects; this is when we incorporate the image augmentations. For the purpose of this demonstration, we will go with the Keras built-in ones. After that, we create the generator using a `flow_from_dataframe()` method, which is used to generate batches of tensor image data with real-time data augmentation:

```
train_labels.label = train_labels.label.astype('str')

train_datagen = ImageDataGenerator(
    validation_split = 0.2, preprocessing_function = None,
        rotation_range = 45, zoom_range = 0.2,
        horizontal_flip = True, vertical_flip = True,
        fill_mode = 'nearest', shear_range = 0.1,
        height_shift_range = 0.1, width_shift_range = 0.1)

train_generator = train_datagen.flow_from_dataframe(
    train_labels,
    directory = os.path.join(CFG.WORK_DIR, "train_images"),
    subset = "training",
    x_col = "image_id",y_col = "label",
```

```
        target_size = (CFG.TARGET_SIZE, CFG.TARGET_SIZE),
        batch_size = CFG.BATCH_SIZE,
        class_mode = "sparse")

validation_datagen = ImageDataGenerator(validation_split = 0.2)

validation_generator = validation_datagen.flow_from_dataframe(
        train_labels,
        directory = os.path.join(CFG.WORK_DIR, "train_images"),
        subset = "validation",
        x_col = "image_id",y_col = "label",
        target_size = (CFG.TARGET_SIZE, CFG.TARGET_SIZE),
        batch_size = CFG.BATCH_SIZE, class_mode = "sparse")
```

With the data structures specified, we can create the model:

```
model = create_model()
model.summary()
```

Once our model is created, we can quickly examine a summary. This is mostly useful for sanity checks, because unless you have a photographic memory, chances are you are not going to remember the layer composition batches of a sophisticated model like EffNetB0. In practice, you can use the summary to check whether the dimensions of output filters are correct or whether the parameter counts (trainable on non-trainable) are in line with expectations. For the sake of compactness, we only demonstrate the first few lines of the output below; inspecting the architecture diagram for B0 will give you an idea of how long the complete output would be.

```
Model: "functional_1"

Layer (type)                     Output Shape            Param # Connected to
================================================================================
input_1 (InputLayer)             [(None, 512, 512, 3) 0

rescaling (Rescaling)            (None, 512, 512, 3)  0           input_1[0][0]

normalization (Normalization) (None, 512, 512, 3)  7           rescaling[0][0]

stem_conv_pad (ZeroPadding2D) (None, 513, 513, 3)  0           normalization[0]
[0]
```

```
stem_conv (Conv2D)              (None, 256, 256, 32) 864    stem_conv_
pad[0][0]

stem_bn (BatchNormalization)    (None, 256, 256, 32) 128    stem_conv[0][0]

stem_activation (Activation)    (None, 256, 256, 32) 0      stem_bn[0][0]

block1a_dwconv (DepthwiseConv2D (None, 256, 256, 32) 288    stem_
activation[0][0]

block1a_bn (BatchNormalization) (None, 256, 256, 32) 128    block1a_
dwconv[0][0]
```

With the above steps taken care of, we can proceed to fitting the model. In this step, we can also very conveniently define callbacks. The first one is ModelCheckpoint:

```
model_save = ModelCheckpoint('./EffNetB0_512_8_best_weights.h5',
                             save_best_only = True,
                             save_weights_only = True,
                             monitor = 'val_loss',
                             mode = 'min', verbose = 1)
```

The checkpoint uses a few parameters worth elaborating on:

- We can preserve the best set of model weights by setting save_best_only = True.
- We reduce the size of the model by only keeping the weights, instead of the complete set of optimizer state.
- We decide on which model is optimal by locating a minimum for validation loss.

Next, we use one of the popular methods for preventing overfitting, **early stopping**. We monitor the performance of the model on the holdout set and stop the algorithm if the metric stops improving for a given number of epochs, in this case 5:

```
early_stop = EarlyStopping(monitor = 'val_loss', min_delta = 0.001,
                           patience = 5, mode = 'min',
                           verbose = 1, restore_best_weights = True)
```

The ReduceLROnPlateau callback monitors the loss on the holdout set and if no improvement is seen for a patience number of epochs, the learning rate is reduced, in this case by a factor of 0.3. While not a universal solution, it can frequently help with convergence:

```
reduce_lr = ReduceLROnPlateau(monitor = 'val_loss', factor = 0.3,
                              patience = 2, min_delta = 0.001,
                              mode = 'min', verbose = 1)
```

We are now ready to fit the model:

```
history = model.fit(
    train_generator,
    steps_per_epoch = STEPS_PER_EPOCH,
    epochs = CFG.EPOCHS,
    validation_data = validation_generator,
    validation_steps = VALIDATION_STEPS,
    callbacks = [model_save, early_stop, reduce_lr]
)
```

We will briefly explain the two parameters we have not encountered before:

- The training generator yields steps_per_epoch batches per training epoch.
- When the epoch is finished, the validation generator produces validation_steps batches.

An example output after calling model.fit() is given below:

```
Epoch 00001: val_loss improved from inf to 0.57514, saving model to ./
EffNetB0_512_8_best_weights.h5
```

Once a model is fitted, we can examine the activations on a sample image using the helper function we wrote at the start. While this is not necessary for successful model execution, it can help determine what sort of features our model is extracting before applying the classification layer at the top:

```
activation_layer_vis(img_tensor, 0)
```

Here is what we might see:

Figure 10.9: Sample activations from a fitted model

We can generate the predictions with `model.predict()`:

```
ss = pd.read_csv(os.path.join(CFG.WORK_DIR, "sample_submission.csv"))

preds = []

for image_id in ss.image_id:
    image = Image.open(os.path.join(CFG.WORK_DIR,  "test_images",
                                    image_id))
    image = image.resize((CFG.TARGET_SIZE, CFG.TARGET_SIZE))
    image = np.expand_dims(image, axis = 0)
    preds.append(np.argmax(model.predict(image)))

ss['label'] = preds
```

We build the predictions by iterating through the list of images. For each of them, we reshape the image to the required dimensions and pick the channel with the strongest signal (the model predicts class probabilities, of which we pick the largest one with `argmax`). The final predictions are class numbers, in line with the metric utilized in the competition.

We have now demonstrated a minimal end-to-end pipeline for image classification. Numerous improvements are, of course, possible – for instance, more augmentations, bigger architecture, callback customization – but the basic underlying template should provide you with a good starting point going forward.

We move on now to a second popular problem in computer vision: object detection.

Object detection

Object detection is a computer vision/image processing task where we need to identify instances of semantic objects of a certain class in an image or video. In classification problems like those discussed in the previous section, we simply need to assign a class to each image, whereas in object detection tasks, we want to draw a **bounding box** around an object of interest to locate it within an image.

In this section, we will use data from the *Global Wheat Detection* competition (`https://www.kaggle.com/c/global-wheat-detection`). In this competition, participants had to detect wheat heads, which are spikes atop plants containing grain. Detection of these in plant images is used to estimate the size and density of wheat heads across crop varieties. We will demonstrate how to train a model for solving this using **Yolov5**, a well-established model in object detection, and state-of-the-art until late 2021 when it was (based on preliminary results) surpassed by the YoloX architecture. Yolov5 gave rise to extremely competitive results in the competition and although it was eventually disallowed by the organizers due to licensing issues, it is very well suited for the purpose of this demonstration.

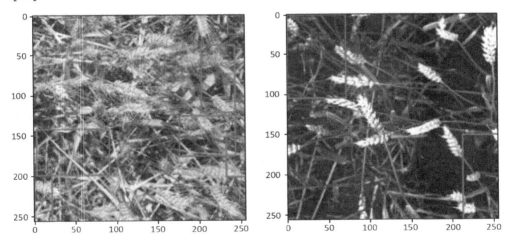

Figure 10.10: Sample image visualizations of detected wheat heads

An important point worth mentioning before we begin is the different formats for bounding box annotations; there are different (but mathematically equivalent) ways of describing the coordinates of a rectangle.

The most common types are coco, voc-pascal, and yolo. The differences between them are clear from the figure below:

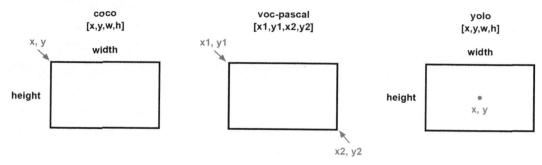

Figure 10.11: Annotation formats for bounding boxes

One more part we need to define is the grid structure: Yolo detects objects by placing a grid over an image and checking for the presence of an object of interest (wheat head, in our case) in any of the cells. The bounding boxes are reshaped to be offset within the relevant cells of the image and the *(x, y, w, h)* parameters are scaled to the unit interval:

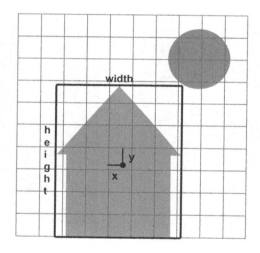

Figure 10.12: Yolo annotation positioning

We start by loading the annotations for our training data:

```
df = pd.read_csv('../input/global-wheat-detection/train.csv')
df.head(3)
```

Let's inspect a few:

	image_id	width	height	bbox	source
0	b6ab77fd7	1024	1024	[834.0, 222.0, 56.0, 36.0]	usask_1
1	b6ab77fd7	1024	1024	[226.0, 548.0, 130.0, 58.0]	usask_1
2	b6ab77fd7	1024	1024	[377.0, 504.0, 74.0, 160.0]	usask_1

Figure 10.13: Training data with annotations

We extract the actual coordinates of the bounding boxes from the bbox column:

```
bboxs = np.stack(df['bbox'].apply(lambda x: np.fromstring(x[1:-1],
                                  sep=',')))

bboxs
```

Let's look at the array:

```
array([[834., 222.,  56.,  36.],
       [226., 548., 130.,  58.],
       [377., 504.,  74., 160.],
       ...,
       [134., 228., 141.,  71.],
       [430.,  13., 184.,  79.],
       [875., 740.,  94.,  61.]])
```

The next step is to extract the coordinates in Yolo format into separate columns:

```
for i, column in enumerate(['x', 'y', 'w', 'h']):
    df[column] = bboxs[:,i]
df.drop(columns=['bbox'], inplace=True)
df['x_center'] = df['x'] + df['w']/2
df['y_center'] = df['y'] + df['h']/2
df['classes'] = 0

df = df[['image_id','x', 'y', 'w', 'h','x_center','y_center','classes']]
df.head(3)
```

The implementation from Ultralytics has some requirements on the structure of the dataset, specifically, where the annotations are stored and the folders for training/validation data.

The creation of the folders in the code below is fairly straightforward, but a more inquisitive reader is encouraged to consult the official documentation (https://github.com/ultralytics/yolov5/wiki/Train-Custom-Data):

```python
# stratify on source
source = 'train'


# Pick a single fold for demonstration's sake
fold = 0


val_index = set(df[df['fold'] == fold]['image_id'])


# Loop through the bounding boxes per image
for name,mini in tqdm(df.groupby('image_id')):
    # Where to save the files
    if name in val_index:
        path2save = 'valid/'
    else:
        path2save = 'train/'
    # Storage path for labels
    if not os.path.exists('convertor/fold{}/labels/'.
                        format(fold)+path2save):
        os.makedirs('convertor/fold{}/labels/'.format(fold)+path2save)
    with open('convertor/fold{}/labels/'.format(fold)+path2save+name+".
            txt", 'w+') as f:
    # Normalize the coordinates in accordance with the Yolo format requirements
        row = mini[['classes','x_center','y_center','w','h']].
        astype(float).values
        row = row/1024
        row = row.astype(str)
        for j in range(len(row)):
            text = ' '.join(row[j])
            f.write(text)
            f.write("\n")
    if not os.path.exists('convertor/fold{}/images/{}'.
                        format(fold,path2save)):
        os.makedirs('convertor/fold{}/images/{}'.format(fold,path2save))
    # No preprocessing needed for images => copy them as a batch
```

```
sh.copy("../input/global-wheat-detection/{}/{}.jpg".
        format(source,name),
        'convertor/fold{}/images/{}/{}.jpg'.
        format(fold,path2save,name))
```

The next thing we do is install the Yolo package itself. If you are running this in a Kaggle Notebook or Colab, make sure to double-check GPU is enabled; Yolo installation will actually work without it, but you are likely to run into all sorts of timeouts and memory issues due to CPU versus GPU performance differences.

```
!git clone https://github.com/ultralytics/yolov5  && cd yolov5 &&
pip install -r requirements.txt
```

We omit the output, as it is rather extensive. The last bit of preparation needed is the YAML configuration file, where we specify the training and validation data locations and the number of classes. We are only interested in detecting wheat heads and not distinguishing between different types, so we have one class (its name is only provided for notational consistency and can be an arbitrary string in this instance):

```
yaml_text = """train: /kaggle/working/convertor/fold0/images/train/
              val: /kaggle/working/convertor/fold0/images/valid/
              nc: 1
              names: ['wheat']"""

with open("wheat.yaml", 'w') as f:
    f.write(yaml_text)
%cat wheat.yaml
```

With that, we can start training our model:

```
!python ./yolov5/train.py --img 512 --batch 2 --epochs 3 --workers 2
--data wheat.yaml --cfg "./yolov5/models/yolov5s.yaml" --name yolov5x_
fold0 --cache
```

Unless you are used to launching things from the command line, the incantation above is positively cryptic, so let's discuss its composition in some detail:

- `train.py` is the workhorse script for training a YoloV5 model, starting from pre-trained weights.

- `--img 512` means we want the original images (which, as you can see, we did not pre-process in any way) to be rescaled to 512x512. For a competitive result, you should use a higher resolution, but this code was executed in a Kaggle Notebook, which has certain limitations on resources.

- `--batch` refers to the batch size in the training process.

- `--epochs 3` means we want to train the model for three epochs.

- `--workers 2` specifies the number of workers in the data loader. Increasing this number might help performance, but there is a known bug in version 6.0 (the most recent one available in the Kaggle Docker image, as of the time of this writing) when the number of workers is too high, even on a machine where more might be available.

- `--data wheat.yaml` is the file pointing to our data specification YAML file, defined above.

- `--cfg "./yolov5/models/yolov5s.yaml"` specifies the model architecture and the corresponding set of weights to be used for initialization. You can use the ones provided with the installation (check the official documentation for details), or you can customize your own and keep them in the same `.yaml` format.

- `--name` specifies where the resulting model is to be stored.

We break down the output of the training command below. First, the groundwork:

```
Downloading the pretrained weights, setting up Weights&Biases https://
wandb.ai/site integration, GitHub sanity check.
Downloading https://ultralytics.com/assets/Arial.ttf to /root/.config/
Ultralytics/Arial.ttf...
wandb: (1) Create a W&B account
wandb: (2) Use an existing W&B account
wandb: (3) Don't visualize my results
wandb: Enter your choice: (30 second timeout)
wandb: W&B disabled due to login timeout.
train: weights=yolov5/yolov5s.pt, cfg=./yolov5/models/yolov5s.yaml,
data=wheat.yaml, hyp=yolov5/data/hyps/hyp.scratch-low.yaml, epochs=3,
batch_size=2, imgsz=512, rect=False, resume=False, nosave=False,
noval=False, noautoanchor=False, evolve=None, bucket=, cache=ram,
image_weights=False, device=, multi_scale=False, single_cls=False,
optimizer=SGD, sync_bn=False, workers=2, project=yolov5/runs/train,
name=yolov5x_fold0, exist_ok=False, quad=False, cos_lr=False, label_
smoothing=0.0, patience=100, freeze=[0], save_period=-1, local_rank=-1,
entity=None, upload_dataset=False, bbox_interval=-1, artifact_alias=latest
```

```
github: up to date with https://github.com/ultralytics/yolov5 ☑
YOLOv5 🚀 v6.1-76-gc94736a torch 1.9.1 CUDA:0 (Tesla P100-PCIE-16GB,
16281MiB)


hyperparameters: lr0=0.01, lrf=0.01, momentum=0.937, weight_decay=0.0005,
warmup_epochs=3.0, warmup_momentum=0.8, warmup_bias_lr=0.1, box=0.05,
cls=0.5, cls_pw=1.0, obj=1.0, obj_pw=1.0, iou_t=0.2, anchor_t=4.0, fl_
gamma=0.0, hsv_h=0.015, hsv_s=0.7, hsv_v=0.4, degrees=0.0, translate=0.1,
scale=0.5, shear=0.0, perspective=0.0, flipud=0.0, fliplr=0.5, mosaic=1.0,
mixup=0.0, copy_paste=0.0
Weights & Biases: run 'pip install wandb' to automatically track and
visualize YOLOv5 🚀 runs (RECOMMENDED)
TensorBoard: Start with 'tensorboard --logdir yolov5/runs/train', view at
http://localhost:6006/
Downloading https://github.com/ultralytics/yolov5/releases/download/v6.1/
yolov5s.pt to yolov5/yolov5s.pt...
100%|████████████████████████| 14.1M/14.1M [00:00<00:00,
40.7MB/s]
```

Then comes the model. We see a summary of the architecture, the optimizer setup, and the augmentations used:

```
Overriding model.yaml nc=80 with nc=1


                    from  n   params  module
arguments
  0                 -1    1    3520   models.common.Conv
[3, 32, 6, 2, 2]
  1                 -1    1   18560   models.common.Conv
[32, 64, 3, 2]
  2                 -1    1   18816   models.common.C3
[64, 64, 1]
  3                 -1    1   73984   models.common.Conv
[64, 128, 3, 2]
  4                 -1    2  115712   models.common.C3
[128, 128, 2]
  5                 -1    1  295424   models.common.Conv
[128, 256, 3, 2]
```

```
  6                 -1  3    625152  models.common.C3
[256, 256, 3]
  7                 -1  1   1180672  models.common.Conv
[256, 512, 3, 2]
  8                 -1  1   1182720  models.common.C3
[512, 512, 1]
  9                 -1  1    656896  models.common.SPPF
[512, 512, 5]
 10                 -1  1    131584  models.common.Conv
[512, 256, 1, 1]
 11                 -1  1         0  torch.nn.modules.upsampling.Upsample
[None, 2, 'nearest']
 12            [-1, 6]  1         0  models.common.Concat
[1]
 13                 -1  1    361984  models.common.C3
[512, 256, 1, False]
 14                 -1  1     33024  models.common.Conv
[256, 128, 1, 1]
 15                 -1  1         0  torch.nn.modules.upsampling.Upsample
[None, 2, 'nearest']
 16            [-1, 4]  1         0  models.common.Concat
[1]
 17                 -1  1     90880  models.common.C3
[256, 128, 1, False]
 18                 -1  1    147712  models.common.Conv
[128, 128, 3, 2]
 19           [-1, 14]  1         0  models.common.Concat
[1]
 20                 -1  1    296448  models.common.C3
[256, 256, 1, False]
 21                 -1  1    590336  models.common.Conv
[256, 256, 3, 2]
 22           [-1, 10]  1         0  models.common.Concat
[1]
 23                 -1  1   1182720  models.common.C3
[512, 512, 1, False]
 24       [17, 20, 23]  1     16182  models.yolo.Detect
[1, [[10, 13, 16, 30, 33, 23], [30, 61, 62, 45, 59, 119], [116, 90, 156,
198, 373, 326]], [128, 256, 512]]
```

```
YOLOv5s summary: 270 layers, 7022326 parameters, 7022326 gradients, 15.8
GFLOPs


Transferred 342/349 items from yolov5/yolov5s.pt
Scaled weight_decay = 0.0005
optimizer: SGD with parameter groups 57 weight (no decay), 60 weight, 60
bias
albumentations: Blur(always_apply=False, p=0.01, blur_limit=(3, 7)),
MedianBlur(always_apply=False, p=0.01, blur_limit=(3, 7)), ToGray(always_
apply=False, p=0.01), CLAHE(always_apply=False, p=0.01, clip_limit=(1,
4.0), tile_grid_size=(8, 8))
train: Scanning '/kaggle/working/convertor/fold0/labels/train' images and
labels
train: New cache created: /kaggle/working/convertor/fold0/labels/train.
cache
train: Caching images (0.0GB ram): 100%|        | 51/51 [00:00<00:00,
76.00it/
val: Scanning '/kaggle/working/convertor/fold0/labels/valid' images and
labels..
val: New cache created: /kaggle/working/convertor/fold0/labels/valid.cache
val: Caching images (2.6GB ram): 100%|        | 3322/3322 [00:47<00:00,
70.51i
Plotting labels to yolov5/runs/train/yolov5x_fold0/labels.jpg...


AutoAnchor: 6.00 anchors/target, 0.997 Best Possible Recall (BPR). Current
anchors are a good fit to dataset ✓
Image sizes 512 train, 512 val
Using 2 dataloader workers
```

This is followed by the actual training log:

```
Starting training for 3 epochs...

     Epoch    gpu_mem        box        obj        cls     labels   img_size
       0/2     0.371G     0.1196    0.05478          0         14        512:
100%|  |
               Class     Images     Labels          P          R
mAP@.5 mAP@WARNING: NMS time limit 0.120s exceeded
               Class     Images     Labels          P          R
mAP@.5 mAP@
```

```
                 all        3322        147409       0.00774       0.0523
0.00437    0.000952


        Epoch    gpu_mem       box        obj        cls     labels   img_size
         1/2      0.474G     0.1176     0.05625        0          5        512:
100%|    |
                Class       Images      Labels          P           R
mAP@.5 mAP@WARNING: NMS time limit 0.120s exceeded
                Class       Images      Labels          P           R
mAP@.5 mAP@WARNING: NMS time limit 0.120s exceeded
                Class       Images      Labels          P           R
mAP@.5 mAP@
                 all        3322        147409       0.00914       0.0618
0.00493    0.00108


        Epoch    gpu_mem       box        obj        cls     labels   img_size
         2/2      0.474G     0.1146     0.06308        0         12        512:
100%|    |
                Class       Images      Labels          P           R
mAP@.5 mAP@
                 all        3322        147409       0.00997       0.0674
0.00558    0.00123


3 epochs completed in 0.073 hours.
Optimizer stripped from yolov5/runs/train/yolov5x_fold0/weights/last.pt,
14.4MB
Optimizer stripped from yolov5/runs/train/yolov5x_fold0/weights/best.pt,
14.4MB
```

```
Validating yolov5/runs/train/yolov5x_fold0/weights/best.pt...
Fusing layers...
YOLOv5s summary: 213 layers, 7012822 parameters, 0 gradients, 15.8 GFLOPs
                Class     Images     Labels        P          R
mAP@.5 mAP@WARNING: NMS time limit 0.120s exceeded
                Class     Images     Labels        P          R
mAP@.5 mAP@WARNING: NMS time limit 0.120s exceeded
                Class     Images     Labels        P          R
mAP@.5 mAP@WARNING: NMS time limit 0.120s exceeded
                Class     Images     Labels        P          R
mAP@.5 mAP@WARNING: NMS time limit 0.120s exceeded
                Class     Images     Labels        P          R
mAP@.5 mAP@WARNING: NMS time limit 0.120s exceeded
                Class     Images     Labels        P          R
mAP@.5 mAP@WARNING: NMS time limit 0.120s exceeded
                Class     Images     Labels        P          R
mAP@.5 mAP@WARNING: NMS time limit 0.120s exceeded
                Class     Images     Labels        P          R
mAP@.5 mAP@WARNING: NMS time limit 0.120s exceeded
                Class     Images     Labels        P          R
mAP@.5 mAP@WARNING: NMS time limit 0.120s exceeded
                Class     Images     Labels        P          R
mAP@.5 mAP@WARNING: NMS time limit 0.120s exceeded
                Class     Images     Labels        P          R
mAP@.5 mAP@
                  all       3322     147409     0.00997    0.0673
0.00556    0.00122
Results saved to yolov5/runs/train/yolov5x_fold0
```

The results from both training and validation stages can be examined; they are stored in the yolov5 folder under `./yolov5/runs/train/yolov5x_fold0`:

Figure 10.14: Validation data with annotations

Once we have trained the model, we can use the weights from the best performing model (Yolov5 has a neat functionality of automatically keeping both the best and last epoch model, storing them as `best.pt` and `last.pt`) to generate predictions on the test data:

```
!python ./yolov5/detect.py --weights ./yolov5/runs/train/yolov5x_fold0/
weights/best.pt --img 512 --conf 0.1 --source /kaggle/input/global-wheat-
detection/test --save-txt --save-conf --exist-ok
```

We will discuss the parameters that are specific to the inference stage:

- `--weights` points to the location of the best weights from our model trained above.

- --conf 0.1 specifies which candidate bounding boxes generated by the model should be kept. As usual, it is a compromise between precision and recall (too low a threshold gives a high number of false positives, while moving the threshold too high means we might not find any wheat heads at all).

- --source is the location of the test data.

The labels created for our test images can be inspected locally:

```
!ls ./yolov5/runs/detect/exp/labels/
```

This is what we might see:

```
2fd875eaa.txt   53f253011.txt   aac893a91.txt   f5a1f0358.txt
348a992bb.txt   796707dd7.txt   cc3532ff6.txt
```

Let's look at an individual prediction:

```
!cat 2fd875eaa.txt
```

It has the following format:

```
0 0.527832 0.580566 0.202148 0.838867 0.101574
0 0.894531 0.587891 0.210938 0.316406 0.113519
```

This means that in image 2fd875eaa, our trained model detected two bounding boxes (their coordinates are entries 2-5 in the row), with confidence scores above 0.1 given at the end of the row.

How do we go about combining the predictions into a submission in the required format? We start by defining a helper function that helps us convert the coordinates from the yolo format to coco (as required in this competition): it is a matter of simple rearrangement of the order and normalizing to the original range of values by multiplying the fractions by the image size:

```
def convert(s):
    x = int(1024 * (s[1] - s[3]/2))
    y = int(1024 * (s[2] - s[4]/2))
    w = int(1024 * s[3])
    h = int(1024 * s[4])

    return(str(s[5]) + ' ' + str(x) + ' ' + str(y) + ' ' + str(w)
           + ' ' + str(h))
```

We then proceed to generate a submission file:

1. We loop over the files listed above.

2. For each file, all rows are converted into strings in the required format (one row represents one bounding box detected).

3. The rows are then concatenated into a single string corresponding to this file.

The code is as follows:

```python
with open('submission.csv', 'w') as myfile:

    # Prepare submission
    wfolder = './yolov5/runs/detect/exp/labels/'
    for f in os.listdir(wfolder):
        fname = wfolder + f
        xdat = pd.read_csv(fname, sep = ' ', header = None)
        outline = f[:-4] + ' ' + ' '.join(list(xdat.apply(lambda s:
                                    convert(s), axis = 1)))
        myfile.write(outline + '\n')

myfile.close()
```

Let's see what it looks like:

```
!cat submission.csv
```

```
53f253011 0.100472 61 669 961 57 0.106223 0 125 234 183 0.1082 96 696 928
126 0.108863 515 393 86 161 0.11459 31 0 167 209 0.120246 517 466 89 147
aac893a91 0.108037 376 435 325 188
796707dd7 0.235373 684 128 234 113
cc3532ff6 0.100443 406 752 144 108 0.102479 405 87 4 89 0.107173 576 537
138 94 0.113459 256 498 179 211 0.114847 836 618 186 65 0.121121 154 544
248 115 0.125105 40 567 483 199
2fd875eaa 0.101398 439 163 204 860 0.112546 807 440 216 323
348a992bb 0.100572 0 10 440 298 0.101236 344 445 401 211
f5a1f0358 0.102549 398 424 295 96
```

The generated submission.csv file completes our pipeline.

In this section, we have demonstrated how to use a YoloV5 to solve the problem of object detection: how to handle annotations in different formats, how to customize a model for a specific task, train it, and evaluate the results.

Based on this knowledge, you should be able to start working with object detection problems.

We now move on to the third popular class of computer vision tasks: semantic segmentation.

Semantic segmentation

The easiest way to think about **segmentation** is that it classifies each pixel in an image, assigning it to a corresponding class; combined, those pixels form areas of interest, such as regions with disease on an organ in medical images. By contrast, object detection (discussed in the previous section) classifies patches of an image into different object classes and creates bounding boxes around them.

We will demonstrate the modeling approach using data from the *Sartorius – Cell Instance Segmentation* competition (https://www.kaggle.com/c/sartorius-cell-instance-segmentation). In this one, the participants were tasked to train models for instance segmentation of neural cells using a set of microscopy images.

Our solution will be built around **Detectron2**, a library created by Facebook AI Research that supports multiple detection and segmentation algorithms.

 Detectron2 is a successor to the original Detectron library (https://github.com/facebookresearch/Detectron/) and the Mask R-CNN project (https://github.com/facebookresearch/maskrcnn-benchmark/).

We begin by installing the extra packages:

```
!pip install pycocotools
!pip install 'git+https://github.com/facebookresearch/detectron2.git'
```

We install pycocotools (https://github.com/cocodataset/cocoapi/tree/master/PythonAPI/pycocotools), which we will need to format the annotations, and Detectron2 (https://github.com/facebookresearch/detectron2), our workhorse in this task.

Before we can train our model, we need a bit of preparation: the annotations need to be converted from the **run-length encoding** (**RLE**) format provided by the organizers to the COCO format required as input for Detectron2. The basic idea behind RLE is saving space: creating a segmentation means marking a group of pixels in a certain manner. Since an image can be thought of as an array, this area can be denoted by a series of straight lines (row- or column-wise).

You can encode each of those lines by listing the indices, or by specifying a starting position and the length of the subsequent contiguous block. A visual example is given below:

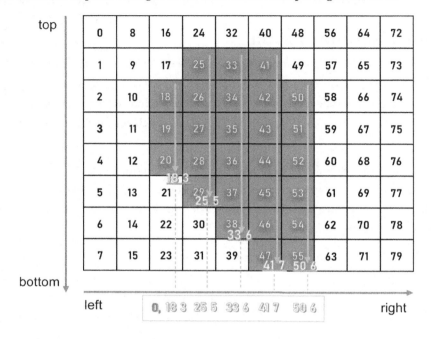

Figure 10.15: Visual representation of RLE

Microsoft's **Common Objects in Context (COCO)** format is a specific JSON structure dictating how labels and metadata are saved for an image dataset. Below, we demonstrate how to convert RLE to COCO and combine it with a k-fold validation split, so we get the required train/validation pair of JSON files for each fold.

Let's begin:

```
# from pycocotools.coco import COCO
import skimage.io as io
import matplotlib.pyplot as plt
from pathlib import Path
from PIL import Image

import pandas as pd
import numpy as np
from tqdm.notebook import tqdm
import json,itertools
```

```
from sklearn.model_selection import GroupKFold

# Config
class CFG:
    data_path = '../input/sartorius-cell-instance-segmentation/'
    nfolds = 5
```

We need three functions to go from RLE to COCO. First, we need to convert from RLE to a binary mask:

```
# From https://www.kaggle.com/stainsby/fast-tested-rle
def rle_decode(mask_rle, shape):
    '''
    mask_rle: run-length as string formatted (start length)
    shape: (height,width) of array to return
    Returns numpy array, 1 - mask, 0 - background

    '''
    s = mask_rle.split()
    starts, lengths = [np.asarray(x, dtype=int)
                        for x in (s[0:][::2], s[1:][::2])]
    starts -= 1
    ends = starts + lengths
    img = np.zeros(shape[0]*shape[1], dtype=np.uint8)
    for lo, hi in zip(starts, ends):
        img[lo:hi] = 1
    return img.reshape(shape)  # Needed to align to RLE direction
```

The second one converts a binary mask to RLE:

```
# From https://newbedev.com/encode-numpy-array-using-uncompressed-rle-for-
# coco-dataset
def binary_mask_to_rle(binary_mask):
    rle = {'counts': [], 'size': list(binary_mask.shape)}
    counts = rle.get('counts')
    for i, (value, elements) in enumerate(
            itertools.groupby(binary_mask.ravel(order='F'))):
        if i == 0 and value == 1:
            counts.append(0)
```

```
            counts.append(len(list(elements)))
        return rle
```

Finally, we combine the two in order to produce the COCO output:

```
def coco_structure(train_df):
    cat_ids = {name: id+1 for id, name in enumerate(
        train_df.cell_type.unique())}
    cats = [{'name': name, 'id': id} for name, id in cat_ids.items()]
    images = [{'id': id, 'width': row.width, 'height': row.height,
                'file_name':f'train/{id}.png'} for id,
                row in train_df.groupby('id').agg('first').iterrows()]
    annotations = []
    for idx, row in tqdm(train_df.iterrows()):
        mk = rle_decode(row.annotation, (row.height, row.width))
        ys, xs = np.where(mk)
        x1, x2 = min(xs), max(xs)
        y1, y2 = min(ys), max(ys)
        enc =binary_mask_to_rle(mk)
        seg = {
            'segmentation':enc,
            'bbox': [int(x1), int(y1), int(x2-x1+1), int(y2-y1+1)],
            'area': int(np.sum(mk)),
            'image_id':row.id,
            'category_id':cat_ids[row.cell_type],
            'iscrowd':0,
            'id':idx
        }
        annotations.append(seg)
    return {'categories':cats, 'images':images,'annotations':annotations}
```

We split our data into non-overlapping folds:

```
train_df = pd.read_csv(CFG.data_path + 'train.csv')


gkf = GroupKFold(n_splits = CFG.nfolds)


train_df["fold"] = -1
y = train_df.width.values
```

```
for f, (t_, v_) in enumerate(gkf.split(X=train_df, y=y,
                               groups=train_df.id.values)):
    train_df.loc[v_, "fold"] = f

fold_id = train_df.fold.copy()
```

We can now loop over the folds:

```
all_ids = train_df.id.unique()
# For fold in range(CFG.nfolds):
for fold in range(4,5):
    train_sample = train_df.loc[fold_id != fold]
    root = coco_structure(train_sample)

    with open('annotations_train_f' + str(fold) +
              '.json', 'w', encoding='utf-8') as f:
        json.dump(root, f, ensure_ascii=True, indent=4)

    valid_sample = train_df.loc[fold_id == fold]

    print('fold ' + str(fold) + ': produced')

for fold in range(4,5):
    train_sample = train_df.loc[fold_id == fold]
    root = coco_structure(train_sample)

    with open('annotations_valid_f' + str(fold) +
              '.json', 'w', encoding='utf-8') as f:
        json.dump(root, f, ensure_ascii=True, indent=4)

    valid_sample = train_df.loc[fold_id == fold]

    print('fold ' + str(fold) + ': produced')
```

The reason why the loop has to be executed in pieces is the size limit of the Kaggle environment: the maximum size of Notebook output is limited to 20 GB, and 5 folds with 2 files (training/validation) for each fold meant a total of 10 JSON files, exceeding that limit.

Such practical considerations are worth keeping in mind when running code in a Kaggle Notebook, although for such "preparatory" work, you can, of course, produce the results elsewhere, and upload them as Kaggle Datasets afterward.

With the splits produced, we can move toward training a Detectron2 model for our dataset. As usual, we start by loading the necessary packages:

```python
from datetime import datetime
import os

import pandas as pd
import numpy as np
import pycocotools.mask as mask_util
import detectron2
from pathlib import Path
import random, cv2, os
import matplotlib.pyplot as plt
# Import some common detectron2 utilities
from detectron2 import model_zoo
from detectron2.engine import DefaultPredictor, DefaultTrainer
from detectron2.config import get_cfg
from detectron2.utils.visualizer import Visualizer, ColorMode
from detectron2.data import MetadataCatalog, DatasetCatalog
from detectron2.data.datasets import register_coco_instances
from detectron2.utils.logger import setup_logger
from detectron2.evaluation.evaluator import DatasetEvaluator
from detectron2.engine import BestCheckpointer
from detectron2.checkpoint import DetectionCheckpointer
setup_logger()

import torch
```

While the number of imports from Detectron2 can seem intimidating at first, their function will become clear as we progress with the task definition; we start by specifying paths to the input data folder, annotations folder, and a YAML file defining our preferred model architecture:

```python
class CFG:
    wfold = 4
    data_folder = '../input/sartorius-cell-instance-segmentation/'
```

```
anno_folder = '../input/sartoriusannotations/'
model_arch = 'mask_rcnn_R_50_FPN_3x.yaml'
nof_iters = 10000
seed = 45
```

One point worth mentioning here is the iterations parameter (nof_iters above). Usually, model training is parametrized in terms of the number of epochs, in other words, complete passes through the training data. Detectron2 is engineered differently: one iteration refers to one mini-batch and different mini-batch sizes are used in different parts of the model.

In order to ensure the results are reproducible, we fix random seeds used by different components of the model:

```
def seed_everything(seed):
    random.seed(seed)
    os.environ['PYTHONHASHSEED'] = str(seed)
    np.random.seed(seed)
    torch.manual_seed(seed)
    torch.cuda.manual_seed(seed)
    torch.backends.cudnn.deterministic = True


seed_everything(CFG.seed)
```

The competition metric was the mean average precision at different **intersection over union (IoU)** thresholds. As a refresher from *Chapter 5, Competition Tasks and Metrics*, the IoU of a proposed set of object pixels and a set of true object pixels is calculated as:

$$IoU(A, B) = A \cap B \ / \ A \cup B$$

The metric sweeps over a range of IoU thresholds, at each point calculating an average precision value. The threshold values range from 0.5 to 0.95, with increments of 0.05.

At each threshold value, a precision value is calculated based on the number of **true positives (TP)**, **false negatives (FN)**, and **false positives (FP)** resulting from comparing the predicted object with all ground truth objects. Lastly, the score returned by the competition metric is the mean taken over the individual average precisions of each image in the test dataset.

Below, we define the functions necessary to calculate the metric and use it directly inside the model as the objective function:

```python
# Taken from https://www.kaggle.com/theoviel/competition-metric-map-iou
def precision_at(threshold, iou):
    matches = iou > threshold
    true_positives = np.sum(matches, axis=1) == 1  # Correct objects
    false_positives = np.sum(matches, axis=0) == 0  # Missed objects
    false_negatives = np.sum(matches, axis=1) == 0  # Extra objects
    return np.sum(true_positives), np.sum(false_positives),
    np.sum(false_negatives)


def score(pred, targ):
    pred_masks = pred['instances'].pred_masks.cpu().numpy()
    enc_preds = [mask_util.encode(np.asarray(p, order='F'))
                    for p in pred_masks]
    enc_targs = list(map(lambda x:x['segmentation'], targ))
    ious = mask_util.iou(enc_preds, enc_targs, [0]*len(enc_targs))
    prec = []
    for t in np.arange(0.5, 1.0, 0.05):
        tp, fp, fn = precision_at(t, ious)
        p = tp / (tp + fp + fn)
        prec.append(p)
    return np.mean(prec)
```

With the metric defined, we can use it in the model:

```python
class MAPIOUEvaluator(DatasetEvaluator):
    def __init__(self, dataset_name):
        dataset_dicts = DatasetCatalog.get(dataset_name)
        self.annotations_cache = {item['image_id']:item['annotations']
                                    for item in dataset_dicts}

    def reset(self):
        self.scores = []

    def process(self, inputs, outputs):
        for inp, out in zip(inputs, outputs):
            if len(out['instances']) == 0:
```

```
                        self.scores.append(0)
                    else:
                        targ = self.annotations_cache[inp['image_id']]
                        self.scores.append(score(out, targ))

    def evaluate(self):
        return {"MaP IoU": np.mean(self.scores)}
```

This gives us the basis for creating a `Trainer` object, which is the workhorse of our solution built around Detectron2:

```
class Trainer(DefaultTrainer):
    @classmethod
    def build_evaluator(cls, cfg, dataset_name, output_folder=None):
        return MAPIOUEvaluator(dataset_name)

    def build_hooks(self):

        # copy of cfg
        cfg = self.cfg.clone()

        # build the original model hooks
        hooks = super().build_hooks()

        # add the best checkpointer hook
        hooks.insert(-1, BestCheckpointer(cfg.TEST.EVAL_PERIOD,
                                          DetectionCheckpointer(self.model,
                                          cfg.OUTPUT_DIR),
                                          "MaP IoU",
                                          "max",
                                          ))
        return hooks
```

We now proceed to load the training/validation data in Detectron2 style:

```
dataDir=Path(CFG.data_folder)
register_coco_instances('sartorius_train',{}, CFG.anno_folder +
                        'annotations_train_f' + str(CFG.wfold) +
                        '.json', dataDir)
```

```
register_coco_instances('sartorius_val',{}, CFG.anno_folder +
                        'annotations_valid_f' + str(CFG.wfold) +
                        '.json', dataDir)

metadata = MetadataCatalog.get('sartorius_train')

train_ds = DatasetCatalog.get('sartorius_train')
```

Before we instantiate a Detectron2 model, we need to take care of configuring it. Most of the values can be left at default values (at least, in a first pass); if you decide to tinker a bit more, start with BATCH_SIZE_PER_IMAGE (for increased generalization performance) and SCORE_THRESH_TEST (to limit false negatives):

```
cfg = get_cfg()
cfg.INPUT.MASK_FORMAT='bitmask'
cfg.merge_from_file(model_zoo.get_config_file('COCO-InstanceSegmentation/' +
                    CFG.model_arch))
cfg.DATASETS.TRAIN = ("sartorius_train",)
cfg.DATASETS.TEST = ("sartorius_val",)
cfg.DATALOADER.NUM_WORKERS = 2
cfg.MODEL.WEIGHTS = model_zoo.get_checkpoint_url('COCO-InstanceSegmentation/'
                    + CFG.model_arch)
cfg.SOLVER.IMS_PER_BATCH = 2
cfg.SOLVER.BASE_LR = 0.001
cfg.SOLVER.MAX_ITER = CFG.nof_iters
cfg.SOLVER.STEPS = []
cfg.MODEL.ROI_HEADS.BATCH_SIZE_PER_IMAGE = 512
cfg.MODEL.ROI_HEADS.NUM_CLASSES = 3
cfg.MODEL.ROI_HEADS.SCORE_THRESH_TEST = .4
cfg.TEST.EVAL_PERIOD = len(DatasetCatalog.get('sartorius_train'))
                       // cfg.SOLVER.IMS_PER_BATCH
```

Training a model is straightforward:

```
os.makedirs(cfg.OUTPUT_DIR, exist_ok=True)
trainer = Trainer(cfg)
trainer.resume_or_load(resume=False)
trainer.train()
```

You will notice that the output during training is rich in information about the progress of the procedure:

```
[01/06 22:26:36 d2.data.datasets.coco]: Loading ../input/sartorius-annotations/annotations_t
rain_f4.json takes 1.16 seconds.
[01/06 22:26:36 d2.data.datasets.coco]: Loaded 485 images in COCO format from ../input/sarto
rius-annotations/annotations_train_f4.json
[01/06 22:26:38 d2.data.build]: Removed 0 images with no usable annotations. 485 images lef
t.
[01/06 22:26:38 d2.data.build]: Distribution of instances among all 3 categories:
|  category  | #instances  | category | #instances  | category | #instances  |
|:----------:|:-----------:|:--------:|:-----------:|:--------:|:-----------:|
|   shsy5y   | 41952       |  astro   | 8360        |   cort   | 8556        |
|            |             |          |             |          |             |
|   total    | 58868       |          |             |          |             |
[01/06 22:26:38 d2.data.dataset_mapper]: [DatasetMapper] Augmentations used in training: [Re
sizeShortestEdge(short_edge_length=(640, 672, 704, 736, 768, 800), max_size=1333, sample_sty
le='choice'), RandomFlip()]
[01/06 22:26:38 d2.data.build]: Using training sampler TrainingSampler
[01/06 22:26:38 d2.data.common]: Serializing 485 elements to byte tensors and concatenating
them all ...
[01/06 22:26:38 d2.data.common]: Serialized dataset takes 6.79 MiB


model_final_f10217.pkl: 178MB [00:04, 35.8MB/s]
```

Figure 10.16: Training output from Detectron2

Once the model is trained, we can save the weights and use them for inference (potentially in a separate Notebook – see the discussion earlier in this chapter) and submission preparation. We start by adding new parameters that allow us to regularize the prediction, setting confidence thresholds and minimal mask sizes:

```
THRESHOLDS = [.18, .35, .58]
MIN_PIXELS = [75, 150, 75]
```

We need a helper function for encoding a single mask into RLE format:

```
def rle_encode(img):
    '''
    img: numpy array, 1 - mask, 0 - background
    Returns run length as string formatted
    '''
    pixels = img.flatten()
```

```
    pixels = np.concatenate([[0], pixels, [0]])
    runs = np.where(pixels[1:] != pixels[:-1])[0] + 1
    runs[1::2] -= runs[::2]
    return ' '.join(str(x) for x in runs)
```

Below is the main function for producing all masks per image, filtering out the dubious ones (with confidence scores below THRESHOLDS) with small areas (containing fewer pixels than MIN_PIXELS):

```
def get_masks(fn, predictor):
    im = cv2.imread(str(fn))
    pred = predictor(im)
    pred_class = torch.mode(pred['instances'].pred_classes)[0]
    take = pred['instances'].scores >= THRESHOLDS[pred_class]
    pred_masks = pred['instances'].pred_masks[take]
    pred_masks = pred_masks.cpu().numpy()
    res = []
    used = np.zeros(im.shape[:2], dtype=int)
    for mask in pred_masks:
        mask = mask * (1-used)
        # Skip predictions with small area
        if mask.sum() >= MIN_PIXELS[pred_class]:
            used += mask
            res.append(rle_encode(mask))
    return res
```

We then prepare the lists where image IDs and masks will be stored:

```
dataDir=Path(CFG.data_folder)


ids, masks=[],[]
test_names = (dataDir/'test').ls()
```

Competitions with large image sets – like the ones discussed in this section – often require training models for longer than 9 hours, which is the time limit imposed in Code competitions (see https://www.kaggle.com/docs/competitions). This means that training a model and running inference within the same Notebook becomes impossible. A typical workaround is to run a training Notebook/script first as a standalone Notebook in Kaggle, Google Colab, GCP, or locally. The output of this first Notebook (the trained weights) is used as input to the second one, in other words, to define the model used for predictions.

We proceed in that manner by loading the weights of our trained model:

```
cfg = get_cfg()
cfg.merge_from_file(model_zoo.get_config_file("COCO-InstanceSegmentation/"+
                    CFG.arch+".yaml"))
cfg.INPUT.MASK_FORMAT = 'bitmask'
cfg.MODEL.ROI_HEADS.NUM_CLASSES = 3
cfg.MODEL.WEIGHTS = CFG.model_folder + 'model_best_f' +
                    str(CFG.wfold)+'.pth'
cfg.MODEL.ROI_HEADS.SCORE_THRESH_TEST = 0.5
cfg.TEST.DETECTIONS_PER_IMAGE = 1000
predictor = DefaultPredictor(cfg)
```

We can visualize some of the predictions:

```
encoded_masks = get_masks(test_names[0], predictor)

_, axs = plt.subplots(1,2, figsize = (40, 15))
axs[1].imshow(cv2.imread(str(test_names[0])))
for enc in encoded_masks:
    dec = rle_decode(enc)
axs[0].imshow(np.ma.masked_where(dec == 0, dec))
```

Here is an example:

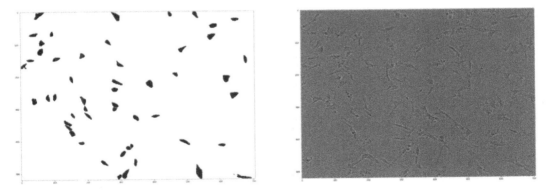

Figure 10.17: Visualizing a sample prediction from Detectron2 alongside the source image

With the helper functions defined above, producing the masks in RLE format for submission is straightforward:

```
for fn in test_names:
    encoded_masks = get_masks(fn, predictor)
    for enc in encoded_masks:
        ids.append(fn.stem)
        masks.append(enc)


pd.DataFrame({'id':ids, 'predicted':masks}).to_csv('submission.csv',
                                            index=False)

pd.read_csv('submission.csv').head()
```

Here are the first few rows of the final submission:

	id	predicted
0	7ae19de7bc2a	139541 4 140244 7 140948 8 141652 8 142356 9 1...
1	7ae19de7bc2a	96418 4 97121 6 97825 7 98529 8 99233 8 99937...
2	7ae19de7bc2a	26627 14 27329 17 28031 19 28733 21 29435 23 3...
3	7ae19de7bc2a	148230 2 148931 6 149633 9 150336 11 151039 13...
4	7ae19de7bc2a	224918 2 225620 7 226324 9 227027 12 227731 13...

Figure 10.18: Formatted submission from a trained Detectron2 model

We have reached the end of the section. The pipeline above demonstrates how to set up a semantic segmentation model and train it. We have used a small number of iterations, but in order to achieve competitive results, longer training is necessary.

Laura Fink

https://www.kaggle.com/allunia

To wrap up this chapter, let's see what Kaggler Laura Fink has to say about her time on the platform. As well as being a Notebooks Grandmaster and producing many masterful Notebooks, she is also Head of Data Science at MicroMata.

What's your favorite kind of competition and why? In terms of techniques and solving approaches, what is your specialty on Kaggle?

My favorite competitions are those that want to yield something good to humanity. I especially like all healthcare-related challenges. Nonetheless, each competition feels like an adventure for me with its own puzzles to be solved. I really enjoy learning new skills and exploring new kinds of datasets or problems. Consequently, I'm not focused on specific techniques but rather on learning something new. I think I'm known for my strengths in exploratory data analysis (EDA).

How do you approach a Kaggle competition? How different is this approach to what you do in your day-to-day work?

When entering a competition, I start by reading the problem statement and the data description. After browsing through the forum and public Notebooks for collecting ideas, I usually start by developing my own solutions. In the initial phase, I spend some time on EDA to search for hidden groups and get some intuition. This helps quite a lot in setting up a proper validation strategy, which I believe is the foundation of all remaining steps. Then, I start to iterate through different parts of the machine learning pipeline like feature engineering or preprocessing, improving the model architecture, asking questions about the data collection, searching for leakages, doing more EDA, or building ensembles. I try to improve my solution in a greedy fashion. Kaggle competitions are very dynamic and one needs to try out diverse ideas and different solutions to survive in the end.

This is definitely different from my day-to-day work, where the focus is more on gaining insights from data and finding simple but effective solutions to improve business processes. Here, the task is often more complex than the models used. The problem to be solved has to be defined very clearly, which means that one has to discuss with experts of different backgrounds which goals should be reached, which processes are involved, and how the data needs to be collected or fused. Compared to Kaggle competitions, my daily work needs much more communication than machine learning skills.

Tell us about a particularly challenging competition you entered, and what insights you used to tackle the task.

The G2Net Gravitational Wave Detection competition was one of my favorites. The goal was to detect simulated gravitational wave signals that were hidden in noise originating from detector components and terrestrial forces. An important insight during this competition was that you should have a critical look at standard ways to analyze data and try out your own ideas. In the papers I read, the data was prepared mainly by using the Fourier or Constant-Q transform after whitening the data and applying a bandpass filter.

It came out very quickly that whitening was not helpful, as it used spline interpolation of the Power Spectral Density, which was itself very noisy. Fitting polynomials to small subsets of noisy data adds another source of errors because of overfitting.

After dropping the whitening, I tried out different hyperparameters of the Constant-Q transform, which turned out to be the leading method in the forum and public Notebooks for a long time. As there were two sources of gravitational waves that can be covered by different ranges of Q-values, I tried out an ensemble of models that differed in these hyperparameters. This turned out to be helpful in improving my score, but then I reached a limit. The Constant-Q transform applies a series of filters to time series and transforms them into the frequency domain. I started to ask myself if there was a method that does these filtering tasks in a better, more flexible way. It was at the same time that the idea of using 1 dim CNNs came up in the community, and I loved it. We all know that filters of 2 dim CNNs are able to detect edges, lines, and textures given image data. The same could be done with "classical" filters like the Laplace or Sobel filter. For this reason, I asked myself: can't we use the 1dCNN to learn the most important filters on its own, instead of applying transformations that are already fixed somehow?

I was not able to get my 1 dim CNN solution to work, but it turned out that many top teams managed it well. The G2Net competition was one of my favorites even though I missed out on the goal of winning a medal. However, the knowledge I gained along the way and the lesson I learned about so-called standard approaches were very valuable.

Has Kaggle helped you in your career? If so, how?

I started my first job after university as a Java software developer even though I already had my first contact with machine learning during my master's thesis. I was interested in doing more data analytics, but at that time, there were almost no data science jobs, or they were not named this way. When I heard about Kaggle the first time, I was trapped right from the start. Since then, I often found myself on Kaggle during the evenings to have some fun. It was not my intent to change my position at that time, but then a research project came up that needed machine learning skills. I was able to show that I was a suitable candidate for this project because of the knowledge I gained by participating on Kaggle. This turned out to be the entry point for my data science career.

Kaggle has always been a great place for me to try out ideas, learn new methods and tools, and gain practical experience. The skills I obtained this way have been quite helpful for data science projects at work. It's like a boost of knowledge, as Kaggle provides a sandbox for you to try out different ideas and to be creative without risk. Failing in a competition means that there was at least one lesson to learn, but failing in a project can have a huge negative impact on yourself and other people.

Besides taking part in competitions, another great way to build up your portfolio is to write Notebooks. In doing so, you can show the world how you approach problems and how to communicate insights and conclusions. The latter is very important when you have to work with management, clients, and experts from different backgrounds.

In your experience, what do inexperienced Kagglers often overlook? What do you know now that you wish you'd known when you first started?

I think many beginners that enter competitions are seduced by the public leaderboard and build their models without having a good validation strategy. While measuring their success on the leaderboard, they are likely overfitting to the public test data. After the end of the competition, their models are not able to generalize to the unseen private test data, and they often fall down hundreds of places. I still remember how frustrated I was during the Mercedes-Benz Greener Manufacturing *competition as I was not able to climb up the public leaderboard. But when the final standings came out, it was a big surprise how many people were shuffled up and down the leaderboard. Since then, I always have in mind that a proper validation scheme is very important for managing the challenges of under- and overfitting.*

What mistakes have you made in competitions in the past?

My biggest mistake so far was to spend too much time and effort on the details of my solution at the beginning of a competition. Indeed, it's much better to iterate fast through diverse and different ideas after building a proper validation strategy. That way, it's easier and faster to find promising directions for improvements and the danger of getting stuck somewhere is much smaller.

Are there any particular tools or libraries that you would recommend using for data analysis or machine learning?

There are a lot of common tools and libraries you can learn and practice when becoming active in the Kaggle community and I can only recommend them all. It's important to stay flexible and to learn about their advantages and disadvantages. This way, your solutions don't depend on your tools, but rather on your ideas and creativity.

What's the most important thing someone should keep in mind or do when they're entering a competition?

Data science is not about building models, but rather about understanding the data and the way it was collected. Many competitions I have entered so far showed leakages or had hidden groups in the test data that one could find with exploratory data analysis.

Summary

In this chapter, we gave you an overview of the most important topics related to computer vision from a Kaggle competition angle. We introduced augmentations, an important class of techniques used for extending the generalization capabilities of an algorithm, and followed by demonstrating end-to-end pipelines for three of the most frequent problems: image classification, object detection, and semantic segmentation.

In the next chapter, we switch our attention to natural language processing, another extremely broad and popular category of problems.

Join our book's Discord space

Join the book's Discord workspace for a monthly *Ask me Anything* session with the authors:

`https://packt.link/KaggleDiscord`

11

Modeling for NLP

Natural language processing (NLP) is a field operating at the intersection of linguistics, computer science, and AI. Its primary focus is algorithms to process and analyze large amounts of natural language data. Over the last few years, it has become an increasingly popular topic of Kaggle competitions. While the domain itself is very broad and encompasses very popular topics such as chatbots and machine translation, in this chapter we will focus on specific subsets that Kaggle contests frequently deal with.

Sentiment analysis as a simple classification problem is extremely popular and discussed all over, so we'll begin with a somewhat more interesting variation on the problem: identifying sentiment-supporting phrases in a tweet. We'll proceed to describe an example solution to the problem of open domain question answering and conclude with a section on augmentation for NLP problems, which is a topic that receives significantly less attention than its computer vision counterpart.

To summarize, we will cover:

- Sentiment analysis
- Open domain Q&A
- Text augmentation strategies

Sentiment analysis

Twitter is one of the most popular social media platforms and an important communication tool for many, individuals and companies alike.

Capturing sentiment in language is particularly important in the latter context: a positive tweet can go viral and spread the word, while a particularly negative one can be harmful. Since human language is complicated, it is important not to just decide on the sentiment, but also to be able to investigate the *how*: which words actually led to the sentiment description?

We will demonstrate an approach to this problem by using data from the *Tweet Sentiment Extraction* competition (`https://www.kaggle.com/c/tweet-sentiment-extraction`). For brevity, we have omitted the imports from the following code, but you can find them in the corresponding Notebook in the GitHub repo for this chapter.

To get a better feel for the problem, let's start by looking at the data:

```
df = pd.read_csv('/kaggle/input/tweet-sentiment-extraction/train.csv')
df.head()
```

Here are the first few rows:

	textID	text	selected_text	sentiment
0	cb774db0d1	I'd have responded, if I were going	I'd have responded, if I were going	neutral
1	549e992a42	Sooo SAD I will miss you here in San Diego!!!	Sooo SAD	negative
2	088c60f138	my boss is bullying me...	bullying me	negative
3	9642c003ef	what interview! leave me alone	leave me alone	negative
4	358bd9e861	Sons of ****, why couldn't they put them on t...	Sons of ****,	negative

Figure 11.1: Sample rows from the training data

The actual tweets are stored in the `text` column. Each of them has an associated `sentiment`, along with the **support phrase** stored in the `selected_text` column (the part of the tweet that was the basis for the decision on sentiment assignment).

We start by defining basic cleanup functions. First, we want to get rid of website URLs and non-characters and replace the stars people use in place of swear words with a single token, `"swear"`. We use some regular expressions to help us do this:

```
def basic_cleaning(text):
    text=re.sub(r'https?://www\.\S+\.com','',text)
    text=re.sub(r'[^A-Za-z|\s]','',text)
    text=re.sub(r'\*+','swear',text) # Capture swear words that are **** out
    return text
```

Next, we remove HTML from the content of the tweets, as well as emojis:

```python
def remove_html(text):
    html=re.compile(r'<.*?>')
    return html.sub(r'',text)


def remove_emoji(text):
    emoji_pattern = re.compile("["
                               u"\U0001F600-\U0001F64F" #emoticons
                               u"\U0001F300-\U0001F5FF" #symbols & pictographs
                               u"\U0001F680-\U0001F6FF" #transport & map symbols
                               u"\U0001F1E0-\U0001F1FF" #flags (iOS)
                               u"\U00002702-\U000027B0"
                               u"\U000024C2-\U0001F251"
                               "]+", flags=re.UNICODE)
    return emoji_pattern.sub(r'', text)
```

Lastly, we want to be able to remove repeated characters (for example, so we have "way" instead of "waaaayyyyy"):

```python
def remove_multiplechars(text):
    text = re.sub(r'(.)\1{3,}',r'\1', text)
    return text
```

For convenience, we combine the four functions into a single cleanup function:

```python
def clean(df):
    for col in ['text']:#,'selected_text']:
        df[col]=df[col].astype(str).apply(lambda x:basic_cleaning(x))
        df[col]=df[col].astype(str).apply(lambda x:remove_emoji(x))
        df[col]=df[col].astype(str).apply(lambda x:remove_html(x))
        df[col]=df[col].astype(str).apply(lambda x:remove_multiplechars(x))

    return df
```

The last bit of preparation involves writing functions for creating the embeddings based on a pre-trained model (the `tokenizer` argument):

```python
def fast_encode(texts, tokenizer, chunk_size=256, maxlen=128):
    tokenizer.enable_truncation(max_length=maxlen)
    tokenizer.enable_padding(max_length=maxlen)
```

```
    all_ids = []

    for i in range(0, len(texts), chunk_size):
        text_chunk = texts[i:i+chunk_size].tolist()
        encs = tokenizer.encode_batch(text_chunk)
        all_ids.extend([enc.ids for enc in encs])

    return np.array(all_ids)
```

Next, we create a pre-processing function enabling us to work with the entire corpus:

```
def preprocess_news(df,stop=stop,n=1,col='text'):
    '''Function to preprocess and create corpus'''
    new_corpus=[]
    stem=PorterStemmer()
    lem=WordNetLemmatizer()
    for text in df[col]:
        words=[w for w in word_tokenize(text) if (w not in stop)]

        words=[lem.lemmatize(w) for w in words if(len(w)>n)]

        new_corpus.append(words)

    new_corpus=[word for l in new_corpus for word in l]
    return new_corpus
```

Using our previously prepared functions, we can clean and prepare the training data. The sentiment column is our target, and we convert it to dummy variables (one-hot encoding) for performance:

```
df.dropna(inplace=True)
df_clean = clean(df)

df_clean_selection = df_clean.sample(frac=1)
X = df_clean_selection.text.values
y = pd.get_dummies(df_clean_selection.sentiment)
```

A necessary next step is **tokenization** of the input texts, as well as conversion into sequences (along with padding, to ensure equal lengths across the dataset):

```
tokenizer = text.Tokenizer(num_words=20000)
tokenizer.fit_on_texts(list(X))
```

```
list_tokenized_train = tokenizer.texts_to_sequences(X)
X_t = sequence.pad_sequences(list_tokenized_train, maxlen=128)
```

We will create the embeddings for our model using **DistilBERT** and use them as-is. DistilBERT is a lightweight version of BERT: the tradeoff is 3% performance loss at 40% fewer parameters. We could train the embedding layer and gain performance – at the cost of massively increased training time.

```
tokenizer = transformers.AutoTokenizer.from_pretrained("distilbert-base-
uncased")

# Save the loaded tokenizer locally
save_path = '/kaggle/working/distilbert_base_uncased/'
if not os.path.exists(save_path):
    os.makedirs(save_path)
tokenizer.save_pretrained(save_path)

# Reload it with the huggingface tokenizers library
fast_tokenizer = BertWordPieceTokenizer(
                 'distilbert_base_uncased/vocab.txt', lowercase=True)
fast_tokenizer
```

We can use the previously defined `fast_encode` function, along with the `fast_tokenizer` defined above, to encode the tweets:

```
X = fast_encode(df_clean_selection.text.astype(str),
                fast_tokenizer,
                maxlen=128)
```

With the data prepared, we can construct the model. For the sake of this demonstration, we will go with a fairly standard architecture for these applications: a combination of LSTM layers, normalized by global pooling and dropout, and a dense layer on top. In order to achieve a truly competitive solution, some tweaking of the architecture would be needed: a "heavier" model, bigger embeddings, more units in the LSTM layers, and so on.

```
transformer_layer = transformers.TFDistilBertModel.from_
pretrained('distilbert-base-uncased')

embedding_size = 128
input_ = Input(shape=(100,))
```

```
inp = Input(shape=(128, ))

embedding_matrix=transformer_layer.weights[0].numpy()

x = Embedding(embedding_matrix.shape[0],
              embedding_matrix.shape[1],
              embeddings_initializer=Constant(embedding_matrix),
              trainable=False)(inp)
x = Bidirectional(LSTM(50, return_sequences=True))(x)
x = Bidirectional(LSTM(25, return_sequences=True))(x)
x = GlobalMaxPool1D()(x)
x = Dropout(0.5)(x)
x = Dense(50, activation='relu', kernel_regularizer='L1L2')(x)
x = Dropout(0.5)(x)
x = Dense(3, activation='softmax')(x)

model_DistilBert = Model(inputs=[inp], outputs=x)

model_DistilBert.compile(loss='categorical_crossentropy',
                         optimizer='adam',
                         metrics=['accuracy'])
```

There is no special need to pay attention to a temporal dimension of the data, so we are fine with a random split into training and validation, which can be achieved inside a call to the `fit` method:

```
model_DistilBert.fit(X,y,batch_size=32,epochs=10,validation_split=0.1)
```

Below is some sample output:

```
Epoch 1/10
27480/27480 [==============================] - 480s 17ms/step - loss:
0.5100 - accuracy: 0.7994
Epoch 2/10
27480/27480 [==============================] - 479s 17ms/step - loss:
0.4956 - accuracy: 0.8100
Epoch 3/10
27480/27480 [==============================] - 475s 17ms/step - loss:
0.4740 - accuracy: 0.8158
Epoch 4/10
```

```
27480/27480 [==============================] - 475s 17ms/step - loss:
0.4528 - accuracy: 0.8275
Epoch 5/10
27480/27480 [==============================] - 475s 17ms/step - loss:
0.4318 - accuracy: 0.8364
Epoch 6/10
27480/27480 [==============================] - 475s 17ms/step - loss:
0.4069 - accuracy: 0.8441
Epoch 7/10
27480/27480 [==============================] - 477s 17ms/step - loss:
0.3839 - accuracy: 0.8572
```

Generating a prediction from the fitted model proceeds in a straightforward manner. In order to utilize all the available data, we begin by re-training our model on all available data (so no validation):

```
df_clean_final = df_clean.sample(frac=1)
X_train = fast_encode(df_clean_selection.text.astype(str),
                      fast_tokenizer,
                      maxlen=128)
y_train = y
```

We refit the model on the entire dataset before generating the predictions:

```
Adam_name = adam(lr=0.001)
model_DistilBert.compile(loss='categorical_crossentropy',optimizer=Adam_
name,metrics=['accuracy'])
history = model_DistilBert.fit(X_train,y_train,batch_size=32,epochs=10)
```

Our next step is to process the test data into the same format we are using for training data fed into the model:

```
df_test = pd.read_csv('/kaggle/input/tweet-sentiment-extraction/test.csv')
df_test.dropna(inplace=True)
df_clean_test = clean(df_test)

X_test = fast_encode(df_clean_test.text.values.astype(str),
                     fast_tokenizer,
                     maxlen=128)
y_test = df_clean_test.sentiment
```

Finally, we generate the predictions:

```
y_preds = model_DistilBert.predict(X_test)
y_predictions = pd.DataFrame(y_preds,
                            columns=['negative','neutral','positive'])
y_predictions_final = y_predictions.idxmax(axis=1)
accuracy = accuracy_score(y_test,y_predictions_final)
print(f"The final model shows {accuracy:.2f} accuracy on the test set.")
```

The final model shows **0.74** accuracy on the test set. Below we show a sample of what the output looks like; as you can see already from these few rows, there are some instances where the sentiment is obvious to a human reader, but the model fails to capture it:

	textID	text	sentiment	predicted_negative	predicted_neutral	predicted_positive
0	f87dea47db	Last session of the day httptwitpiccomezh	neutral	0.022949	0.967165	0.009886
1	96d74cb729	Shanghai is also really exciting precisely s...	positive	0.000075	0.012165	0.987760
2	eee518ae67	Recession hit Veronique Branquinho she has to ...	negative	0.993622	0.006364	0.000014
3	01082688c6	happy bday	positive	0.000020	0.005859	0.994122
4	33987a8ee5	httptwitpiccomwp I like it	positive	0.006184	0.119946	0.873870
5	726e501993	thats great weee visitors	positive	0.000165	0.019434	0.980401
6	261932614e	I THINK EVERYONE HATES ME ON HERE lol	negative	0.916203	0.081649	0.002148
7	afa11da83f	so wish i could but im in school and myspace ...	negative	0.877504	0.116624	0.005871
8	e64208b4ef	and within a short time of the last clue all ...	neutral	0.116272	0.859304	0.024424
9	37bcad24ca	What did you get My day is alright havent do...	neutral	0.223977	0.756474	0.019550

Figure 11.2: Example rows from the predicted results

We have now demonstrated a sample pipeline for solving sentiment attribution problems (identifying parts of the text that lead to annotator decisions on sentiment classification). There are some improvements that can be made if you want to achieve competitive performance, given below in order of likely impact:

- **Larger embeddings:** This allows us to capture more information already at the (processed) input data level
- **Bigger model:** More units in the LSTM layers
- **Longer training:** In other words, more epochs

While the improvements listed above will undoubtedly boost the performance of the model, the core elements of our pipeline are reusable:

- Data cleaning and pre-processing
- Creating text embeddings
- Incorporating recurrent layers and regularization in the target model architecture

We'll now move on to a discussion of open domain question answering, a frequent problem encountered in NLP competitions.

Abhishek Thakur

`https://www.kaggle.com/abhishek`

We caught up with Abhishek Thakur, the world's first quadruple Kaggle Grandmaster. He currently works at Hugging Face, where he is building AutoNLP; he also wrote pretty much the only book on Kaggle in English (aside from this one!), *Approaching (Almost) Any Machine Learning Problem*.

What's your specialty on Kaggle?

None. Every competition is different and there is so much to learn from each one of them. If I were to have a specialty, I would win all competitions in that domain.

How do you approach a Kaggle competition? How different is this approach to what you do in your day-to-day work?

The first thing I do is to take a look at the data and try to understand it a bit. If I'm late to the competition, I take the help of public EDA kernels.

The first thing I do when approaching a problem on (or off) Kaggle is to build a benchmark. Building a benchmark is very important as it provides you with a baseline you can compare your future models to. If I'm late to the game, for building the baseline, I try not to take the help of public Notebooks. If we do that, we think only in a single direction. At least, that's what I feel.

When I am done with a benchmark, I try to squeeze as much as possible without doing anything complicated like stacking or blending. Then I go over the data and models again and try to improve on the baseline, one step at a time.

Day-to-day work sometimes has a lot of similarities. Most of the time there is a benchmark and then you have to come up with techniques, features, models that beat the benchmark.

What was the most interesting competition you entered? Did you have any special insights?

Every competition is interesting.

Has Kaggle helped you in your career?

Sure, it has helped. In the last few years, Kaggle has gained a very good reputation when it comes to hiring data scientists and machine learning engineers. Kaggle rank and experience with many datasets is something that surely helps in the industry in one way or another. The more experienced you are with approaching different types of problems, the faster you will be able to iterate. And that's something very useful in industries. No one wants to spend several months doing something that doesn't bring any value to the business.

In your experience, what do inexperienced Kagglers often overlook? What do you know now that you wish you'd known when you first started?

Most beginners give up quite easily. It's very easy to join a Kaggle competition and get intimidated by top scorers. If beginners want to succeed on Kaggle, they have to have perseverance. In my opinion, perseverance is the key. Many beginners also fail to start on their own and stick to public kernels. This makes them think like the authors of public kernels. My advice would be to start with competitions on your own, look at data, build features, build models, and then dive into kernels and discussions to see what others might be doing differently. Then incorporate what you have learned into your own solution.

Open domain Q&A

In this section, we will be looking at the *Google QUEST Q&A Labeling* competition (`https://www.kaggle.com/c/google-quest-challenge/overview/description`). In this competition, question-answer pairs were evaluated by human raters on a diverse set of criteria, such as "question conversational," "question fact-seeking," or "answer helpful." The task was to predict a numeric value for each of the target columns (corresponding to the criteria); since the labels were aggregated across multiple raters, the objective was effectively a multivariate regression output, with target columns normalized to the unit range.

Before engaging in modeling with advanced techniques (like transformer-based models for NLP), it is frequently a good idea to establish a baseline with simpler methods. As with the previous section, we will omit the imports for brevity, but you can find them in the Notebook in the GitHub repo.

We begin by defining several helper functions, which can help us extract different aspects of the text. First, a function that will output a word count given a string:

```
def word_count(xstring):
    return xstring.split().str.len()
```

The metric used in the competition was **Spearman correlation** (linear correlation computed on ranks: https://en.wikipedia.org/wiki/Spearman%27s_rank_correlation_coefficient).

Since we intend to build a Scikit-learn pipeline, it is useful to define the metric as a scorer (the make_scorer method is a wrapper in Scikit-learn that takes a scoring function – like accuracy or MSE – and returns a callable that scores an output of the estimator):

```
def spearman_corr(y_true, y_pred):
        if np.ndim(y_pred) == 2:
            corr = np.mean([stats.spearmanr(y_true[:, i],
                                        y_pred[:, i])[0]
for i in range(y_true.shape[1])])
        else:
            corr = stats.spearmanr(y_true, y_pred)[0]
        return corr

custom_scorer = make_scorer(spearman_corr, greater_is_better=True)
```

Next, a small helper function to extract successive chunks of size n from 1. This will help us later with generating embeddings for our body of text without running into memory problems:

```
def chunks(l, n):
    for i in range(0, len(l), n):
        yield l[i:i + n]
```

Part of the feature set we will use is embeddings from pre-trained models. Recall that the idea of this section is the construction of a baseline without training elaborate models, but this need not prevent us from using existing ones.

We begin by importing the tokenizer and model, and then we process the corpus in chunks, encoding each question/answer into a fixed-size embedding:

```
def fetch_vectors(string_list, batch_size=64):
    # Inspired by https://jalammar.github.io/a-visual-guide-to-using-bert-
    for-the-first-time/
    DEVICE = torch.device("cuda")
    tokenizer = transformers.DistilBertTokenizer.from_pretrained
                  ("../input/distilbertbaseuncased/")
    model = transformers.DistilBertModel.from_pretrained
              ("../input/distilbertbaseuncased/")
    model.to(DEVICE)

    fin_features = []
    for data in chunks(string_list, batch_size):
        tokenized = []
        for x in data:
            x = " ".join(x.strip().split()[:300])
            tok = tokenizer.encode(x, add_special_tokens=True)
            tokenized.append(tok[:512])

        max_len = 512
        padded = np.array([i + [0] * (max_len - len(i)) for i in tokenized])
        attention_mask = np.where(padded != 0, 1, 0)
        input_ids = torch.tensor(padded).to(DEVICE)
        attention_mask = torch.tensor(attention_mask).to(DEVICE)

        with torch.no_grad():
            last_hidden_states = model(input_ids,
                                       attention_mask=attention_mask)

        features = last_hidden_states[0][:, 0, :].cpu().numpy()
        fin_features.append(features)

    fin_features = np.vstack(fin_features)
    return fin_features
```

We can now proceed to load the data:

```
xtrain = pd.read_csv(data_dir + 'train.csv')
xtest = pd.read_csv(data_dir + 'test.csv')

xtrain.head(4)
```

Here are the first few rows:

question_title	question_body	question_user_name	question_user_page	answer
What am I losing when using extension tubes in...	After playing around with macro photography on...	ysap	https://photo.stackexchange.com/users/1024	I just got extension tubes, so here's the skin...
What is the distinction between a city and a s...	I am trying to understand what kinds of places...	russellpierce	https://rpg.stackexchange.com/users/8774	It might be helpful to look into the definitio...
Maximum protusion length for through-hole comp...	I'm working on a PCB that has through-hole com...	Joe Baker	https://electronics.stackexchange.com/users/10157	Do you even need grooves? We make several pro...
Can an affidavit be used in Beit Din?	An affidavit, from what i understand, is basic...	Scimonster	https://judaism.stackexchange.com/users/5151	Sending an "affidavit" it is a dispute between...

Figure 11.3: Sample rows from the training data

We specify our 30 target columns of interest:

```
target_cols = ['question_asker_intent_understanding',
               'question_body_critical',
               'question_conversational', 'question_expect_short_answer',
               'question_fact_seeking',
               'question_has_commonly_accepted_answer',
               'question_interestingness_others',
               'question_interestingness_self',
               'question_multi_intent', 'question_not_really_a_question',
               'question_opinion_seeking', 'question_type_choice',
               'question_type_compare', 'question_type_consequence',
               'question_type_definition', 'question_type_entity',
```

```
                    'question_type_instructions', 'question_type_procedure',
                    'question_type_reason_explanation',
                    'question_type_spelling',
                    'question_well_written', 'answer_helpful',
                    'answer_level_of_information', 'answer_plausible',
                    'answer_relevance', 'answer_satisfaction',
                    'answer_type_instructions', 'answer_type_procedure',
                    'answer_type_reason_explanation', 'answer_well_written']
```

For a discussion of their meaning and interpretation, the reader is referred to the competition's **Data** page, at https://www.kaggle.com/c/google-quest-challenge/data.

Next, we proceed with **feature engineering**. We start by counting the words in the title and body of the question, as well as the answer. This is a simple yet surprisingly useful feature in many applications:

```
for colname in ['question_title', 'question_body', 'answer']:
    newname = colname + '_word_len'

    xtrain[newname] = xtrain[colname].str.split().str.len()
    xtest[newname] = xtest[colname].str.split().str.len()
```

The next feature we create is **lexical diversity**, counting the proportion of unique words in a chunk of text:

```
colname = 'answer'
xtrain[colname+'_div'] = xtrain[colname].apply
                         (lambda s: len(set(s.split())) / len(s.split()) )
xtest[colname+'_div'] = xtest[colname].apply
                        (lambda s: len(set(s.split())) / len(s.split()) )
```

When dealing with information sourced from online, we can extract potentially informative features by examining the components of a website address (where we define components as elements of the address separated by dots); we count the number of components, and store individual ones as features:

```
for df in [xtrain, xtest]:

    df['domcom'] = df['question_user_page'].apply
                   (lambda s: s.split('://')[1].split('/')[0].split('.'))
```

```
    # Count components
    df['dom_cnt'] = df['domcom'].apply(lambda s: len(s))


    # Pad the length in case some domains have fewer components in the name
    df['domcom'] = df['domcom'].apply(lambda s: s + ['none', 'none'])


    # Components
    for ii in range(0,4):
        df['dom_'+str(ii)] = df['domcom'].apply(lambda s: s[ii])
```

Numerous target columns deal with how relevant the answer is for a given question. One possible way of quantifying this relationship is evaluating **shared words** within a pair of strings:

```
# Shared elements
for df in [xtrain, xtest]:
    df['q_words'] = df['question_body'].apply(lambda s: [f for f in
s.split() if f not in eng_stopwords] )
    df['a_words'] = df['answer'].apply(lambda s: [f for f in s.split() if
f not in eng_stopwords] )
    df['qa_word_overlap'] = df.apply(lambda s: len(np.intersect1d(s['q_
words'], s['a_words'])), axis = 1)
    df['qa_word_overlap_norm1'] = df.apply(lambda s: s['qa_word_overlap']/
(1 + len(s['a_words'])), axis = 1)
    df['qa_word_overlap_norm2'] = df.apply(lambda s: s['qa_word_overlap']/
(1 + len(s['q_words'])), axis = 1)
    df.drop(['q_words', 'a_words'], axis = 1, inplace = True)
```

Stopwords and punctuation occurrence patterns can tell us something about the style and intent:

```
for df in [xtrain, xtest]:

    ## Number of characters in the text ##
    df["question_title_num_chars"] = df["question_title"].apply(lambda x:
len(str(x)))
    df["question_body_num_chars"] = df["question_body"].apply(lambda x:
len(str(x)))
    df["answer_num_chars"] = df["answer"].apply(lambda x: len(str(x)))


    ## Number of stopwords in the text ##
```

```
    df["question_title_num_stopwords"] = df["question_title"].apply(lambda
x: len([w for w in str(x).lower().split() if w in eng_stopwords]))
    df["question_body_num_stopwords"] = df["question_body"].apply(lambda
x: len([w for w in str(x).lower().split() if w in eng_stopwords]))
    df["answer_num_stopwords"] = df["answer"].apply(lambda x: len([w for w
in str(x).lower().split() if w in eng_stopwords]))


    ## Number of punctuations in the text ##
    df["question_title_num_punctuations"] =df['question_title'].
apply(lambda x: len([c for c in str(x) if c in string.punctuation]) )
    df["question_body_num_punctuations"] =df['question_body'].apply(lambda
x: len([c for c in str(x) if c in string.punctuation]) )
    df["answer_num_punctuations"] =df['answer'].apply(lambda x: len([c for
c in str(x) if c in string.punctuation]) )


    ## Number of title case words in the text ##
    df["question_title_num_words_upper"] = df["question_title"].
apply(lambda x: len([w for w in str(x).split() if w.isupper()]))
    df["question_body_num_words_upper"] = df["question_body"].apply(lambda
x: len([w for w in str(x).split() if w.isupper()]))
    df["answer_num_words_upper"] = df["answer"].apply(lambda x: len([w for
w in str(x).split() if w.isupper()]))
```

With the "vintage" features prepared – where our focus is on simple summary statistics of the text, without paying heed to semantic structure – we can move on to creating **embeddings** for the questions and answers. We could theoretically train a separate word2vec-type model on our data (or fine-tune an existing one), but for the sake of this presentation we will use a pre-trained model as-is. A useful choice is the **Universal Sentence Encoder** from Google (https://tfhub. dev/google/universal-sentence-encoder/4). This model is trained on a variety of data sources. It takes as input a piece of text in English and outputs a 512-dimensional vector.

```
module_url = "../input/universalsentenceencoderlarge4/"
embed = hub.load(module_url)
```

The code for turning the text fields into embeddings is presented below: we loop through the entries in the training/test sets in batches, embed each batch (for memory efficiency reasons), and then append them to the original list.

The final data frames are constructed by stacking each list of batch-level embeddings vertically:

```
embeddings_train = {}
embeddings_test = {}
for text in ['question_title', 'question_body', 'answer']:
    train_text = xtrain[text].str.replace('?', '.').str.replace('!', '.').
tolist()
    test_text = xtest[text].str.replace('?', '.').str.replace('!', '.').
tolist()

    curr_train_emb = []
    curr_test_emb = []
    batch_size = 4
    ind = 0
    while ind*batch_size < len(train_text):
        curr_train_emb.append(embed(train_text[ind*batch_size: (ind +
1)*batch_size])["outputs"].numpy())
        ind += 1

    ind = 0
    while ind*batch_size < len(test_text):
        curr_test_emb.append(embed(test_text[ind*batch_size: (ind +
1)*batch_size])["outputs"].numpy())
        ind += 1

    embeddings_train[text + '_embedding'] = np.vstack(curr_train_emb)
    embeddings_test[text + '_embedding'] = np.vstack(curr_test_emb)

    print(text)
```

Given the vector representations for both questions and answers, we can calculate the semantic similarity between the fields by using different distance metrics on the pairs of vectors. The idea behind trying different metrics is the desire to capture diverse types of characteristics; an analogy in the context of classification would be to use both accuracy and entropy to get a complete picture of the situation:

```
l2_dist = lambda x, y: np.power(x - y, 2).sum(axis=1)

cos_dist = lambda x, y: (x*y).sum(axis=1)
```

```
dist_features_train = np.array([
    l2_dist(embeddings_train['question_title_embedding'], embeddings_
train['answer_embedding']),
    l2_dist(embeddings_train['question_body_embedding'], embeddings_
train['answer_embedding']),
    l2_dist(embeddings_train['question_body_embedding'], embeddings_
train['question_title_embedding']),
    cos_dist(embeddings_train['question_title_embedding'], embeddings_
train['answer_embedding']),
    cos_dist(embeddings_train['question_body_embedding'], embeddings_
train['answer_embedding']),
    cos_dist(embeddings_train['question_body_embedding'], embeddings_
train['question_title_embedding'])
]).T

dist_features_test = np.array([
    l2_dist(embeddings_test['question_title_embedding'], embeddings_
test['answer_embedding']),
    l2_dist(embeddings_test['question_body_embedding'], embeddings_
test['answer_embedding']),
    l2_dist(embeddings_test['question_body_embedding'], embeddings_
test['question_title_embedding']),
    cos_dist(embeddings_test['question_title_embedding'], embeddings_
test['answer_embedding']),
    cos_dist(embeddings_test['question_body_embedding'], embeddings_
test['answer_embedding']),
    cos_dist(embeddings_test['question_body_embedding'], embeddings_
test['question_title_embedding'])
]).T
```

Let's gather the distance features in separate columns:

```
for ii in range(0,6):
    xtrain['dist'+str(ii)] = dist_features_train[:,ii]
    xtest['dist'+str(ii)] = dist_features_test[:,ii]
```

Finally, we can also create **TF-IDF** representations of the text fields; the general idea is to create multiple features based on diverse transformations of the input text, and then feed them to a relatively simple model.

This way, we can capture the characteristics of the data without the need to fit a sophisticated deep learning model.

We can achieve it by analyzing the text at the word as well as the character level. To limit the memory consumption, we put an upper bound on the maximum number of both kinds of features (your mileage might vary; with more memory, these limits can be upped):

```
limit_char = 5000
limit_word = 25000
```

We instantiate character- and word-level vectorizers. The setup of our problem lends itself to a convenient usage of the Pipeline functionality from Scikit-learn, allowing a combination of multiple steps in the model fitting procedure. We begin by creating two separate transformers for the title column (word- and character-level):

```
title_col = 'question_title'
title_transformer = Pipeline([
    ('tfidf', TfidfVectorizer(lowercase = False, max_df = 0.3, min_df = 1,
                              binary = False, use_idf = True, smooth_idf =
False,
                              ngram_range = (1,2), stop_words = 'english',
                              token_pattern = '(?u)\\b\\w+\\b' , max_
features = limit_word ))
])

title_transformer2 = Pipeline([
  ('tfidf2',  TfidfVectorizer(sublinear_tf=True,
     strip_accents='unicode', analyzer='char',
     stop_words='english', ngram_range=(1, 4), max_features= limit_char))
])
```

We use the same logic (two different pipelined transformers) for the body:

```
body_col = 'question_body'
body_transformer = Pipeline([
    ('tfidf',TfidfVectorizer(lowercase = False, max_df = 0.3, min_df = 1,
                              binary = False, use_idf = True, smooth_idf =
False,
                              ngram_range = (1,2), stop_words = 'english',
```

```
                                    token_pattern = '(?u)\\b\\w+\\b' , max_
features = limit_word ))
])


body_transformer2 = Pipeline([
 ('tfidf2',  TfidfVectorizer( sublinear_tf=True,
    strip_accents='unicode', analyzer='char',
    stop_words='english', ngram_range=(1, 4), max_features= limit_char))
])
```

And finally for the answer column:

```
answer_col = 'answer'

answer_transformer = Pipeline([
    ('tfidf', TfidfVectorizer(lowercase = False, max_df = 0.3, min_df = 1,
                              binary = False, use_idf = True, smooth_idf =
False,
                              ngram_range = (1,2), stop_words = 'english',
                              token_pattern = '(?u)\\b\\w+\\b' , max_
features = limit_word ))
])

answer_transformer2 = Pipeline([
 ('tfidf2',  TfidfVectorizer( sublinear_tf=True,
    strip_accents='unicode', analyzer='char',
    stop_words='english', ngram_range=(1, 4), max_features= limit_char))
])
```

We wrap up the feature engineering part by processing the numerical features. We use simple methods only: missing value imputation to take care of N/A values and a power transformer to stabilize the distribution and make it closer to Gaussian (which is frequently helpful if you are using a numerical feature inside a neural network):

```
num_cols = [
    'question_title_word_len', 'question_body_word_len',
    'answer_word_len', 'answer_div',
    'question_title_num_chars','question_body_num_chars',
    'answer_num_chars',
```

```
        'question_title_num_stopwords','question_body_num_stopwords',
        'answer_num_stopwords',
        'question_title_num_punctuations',
        'question_body_num_punctuations','answer_num_punctuations',
        'question_title_num_words_upper',
        'question_body_num_words_upper','answer_num_words_upper',
        'dist0', 'dist1', 'dist2', 'dist3', 'dist4',          'dist5'
    ]

num_transformer = Pipeline([
    ('impute', SimpleImputer(strategy='constant', fill_value=0)),
    ('scale', PowerTransformer(method='yeo-johnson'))
])
```

A useful feature of Pipelines is they can be combined and nested. Next, we add functionality to handle categorical variables, and then put it all together in a `ColumnTransformer` object to streamline the data pre-processing and feature engineering logic. Each part of the input can be handled in its own appropriate manner:

```
cat_cols = [ 'dom_0',  'dom_1', 'dom_2',
    'dom_3', 'category','is_question_no_name_user',
    'is_answer_no_name_user','dom_cnt'
]

cat_transformer = Pipeline([
    ('impute', SimpleImputer(strategy='constant', fill_value='')),
    ('encode', OneHotEncoder(handle_unknown='ignore'))
])

preprocessor = ColumnTransformer(
    transformers = [
        ('title', title_transformer, title_col),
        ('title2', title_transformer2, title_col),
        ('body', body_transformer, body_col),
        ('body2', body_transformer2, body_col),
        ('answer', answer_transformer, answer_col),
        ('answer2', answer_transformer2, answer_col),
        ('num', num_transformer, num_cols),
```

```
        ('cat', cat_transformer, cat_cols)
    ]
)
```

Finally, we are ready to use a `Pipeline` object combining pre-processing and model fitting:

```
pipeline = Pipeline([
    ('preprocessor', preprocessor),
    ('estimator',Ridge(random_state=RANDOM_STATE))
])
```

It is always a good idea to evaluate the performance of your model out of sample: a convenient way to go about this is to create **out-of-fold predictions**, which we discussed in *Chapter 6*. The procedure involves the following steps:

1. Split the data into folds. In our case we use `GroupKFold`, since one question can have multiple answers (in separate rows of the data frame). In order to prevent information leakage, we want to ensure each question only appears in one fold.

2. For each fold, train the model using the data in the other folds, and generate the predictions for the fold of choice, as well as the test set.

3. Average the predictions on the test set.

We start with preparing the "storage" matrices in which we will store the predictions. `mvalid` will contain the out-of-fold predictions, while `mfull` is a placeholder for the predictions on the entire test set, averaged across folds. Since several questions contain more than one candidate answer, we stratify our `KFold` split on `question_body`:

```
nfolds = 5
mvalid = np.zeros((xtrain.shape[0], len(target_cols)))
mfull = np.zeros((xtest.shape[0], len(target_cols)))

kf = GroupKFold(n_splits= nfolds).split(X=xtrain.question_body,
groups=xtrain.question_body)
```

We loop through the folds and build the separate models:

```
for ind, (train_index, test_index) in enumerate(kf):

    # Split the data into training and validation
    x0, x1 = xtrain.loc[train_index], xtrain.loc[test_index]
```

```
        y0, y1 = ytrain.loc[train_index], ytrain.loc[test_index]

    for ii in range(0, ytrain.shape[1]):

        # Fit model
        be = clone(pipeline)
        be.fit(x0, np.array(y0)[:,ii])

        filename = 'ridge_f' + str(ind) + '_c' + str(ii) + '.pkl'
        pickle.dump(be, open(filename, 'wb'))

        # Storage matrices for the OOF and test predictions, respectively
        mvalid[test_index, ii] = be.predict(x1)
        mfull[:,ii] += be.predict(xtest)/nfolds

    print('---')
```

Once the fitting part is done, we can evaluate the performance in accordance with the metric specified in the competition:

```
corvec = np.zeros((ytrain.shape[1],1))
for ii in range(0, ytrain.shape[1]):
    mvalid[:,ii] = rankdata(mvalid[:,ii])/mvalid.shape[0]
    mfull[:,ii] = rankdata(mfull[:,ii])/mfull.shape[0]

    corvec[ii] = stats.spearmanr(ytrain[ytrain.columns[ii]], mvalid[:,ii])
[0]

print(corvec.mean())
```

The final score is **0.34**, which is fairly acceptable as a starting point.

In this section, we have demonstrated how to build descriptive features on a body of text. While this is not a winning formula for an NLP competition (the score is OK, but not a guarantee for landing in the medal zone), it is a useful tool to keep in your toolbox. We close this chapter with a section providing an overview of text augmentation techniques.

Shotaro Ishihara

`https://www.kaggle.com/sishihara`

Our second interview of the chapter is with Shotaro Ishihara, aka u++, a Competitions and Notebooks Master who was a member of the winning team in the *PetFinder.my Adoption Prediction* competition. He is currently a Data Scientist and Researcher at a Japanese news media company, and has also published books in Japanese on Kaggle, including a translation of Abhishek Thakur's book. He maintains a weekly newsletter in Japanese on Kaggle initiatives (`https://www.getrevue.co/profile/upura`).

Where can we find the Kaggle books you've written/translated?

`https://www.kspub.co.jp/book/detail/5190067.html` *is a Kaggle primer for beginners based on the* Titanic *GettingStarted competition.*

`https://book.mynavi.jp/ec/products/detail/id=123641` *is the Japanese translation of Abhishek Thakur's* Approaching (Almost) Any Machine Learning Problem.

What's your favorite kind of competition and why? In terms of techniques and solving approaches, what is your specialty on Kaggle?

In Kaggle, I love joining competitions with tabular or text datasets. These types of datasets are familiar to me because they are widely used in news media companies. I have a good knowledge of the approaches used to handle these datasets.

How do you approach a Kaggle competition? How different is this approach to what you do in your day-to-day work?

The first process is the same: thinking about how to tackle the problem through exploratory data analysis. Kaggle assumes the use of advanced machine learning, but this is not the case in business. In practice, I try to find ways to avoid using machine learning. Even when I do use it, I prefer working with classical methods such as TF-IDF and linear regression rather than advanced methods such as BERT.

We are interested in learning more about how to avoid using machine learning in real-world problems. Can you give us some examples?

When working on automated article summaries at work, we adopt a more straightforward extractive approach (`https://www.jstage.jst.go.jp/article/pjsai/JSAI2021/0/JSAI2021_1D2OS3a03/_article/-char/en`*) rather than a neural network-based method (*`https://www.jstage.jst.go.jp/article/pjsai/JSAI2021/0/JSAI2021_1D4OS3c02/_article/-char/en`*).*

It is difficult to guarantee 100% performance with machine learning, and simple methods that are easy for humans to understand and engage with are sometimes preferred.

Tell us about a particularly challenging competition you entered, and what insights you used to tackle the task.

In the PetFinder.my Adoption Prediction *competition, a multi-modal dataset was provided. Many participants tried to explore and use all types of data, and the main approach was to extract features from images and texts, concatenate them, and train LightGBM. I also employed the same approach. Surprisingly, one of my teammates, takuoko (*https://www.kaggle.com/takuok*), developed a great neural network that handles all datasets end to end. Well-designed neural networks have the potential to outperform LightGBM in multi-modal competitions. This is a lesson I learned in 2019.*

Is that lesson still valid today?

I think the answer is yes. Compared to 2019, neural networks are getting better and better at handling multimodal data.

Has Kaggle helped you in your career? If so, how?

Yes. Kaggle gave me a lot of experience in data analysis. The machine learning knowledge I've gained from Kaggle has significantly helped me to work more successfully. My achievements in Kaggle and business work were one of the main reasons why I received the 30 Under 30 Awards and Grand Prize in 2020 from the International News Media Association. Kaggle has also allowed me to get to know a lot of people. These relationships have definitely contributed to my career development.

How have you built up your portfolio thanks to Kaggle?

Learned skills, achieved competition results, and published Notebooks, books, newsletters, and so on.

How do you promote your publishing?

I have various communication channels and I use the appropriate tools for promotion. For example, Twitter, personal blogs, and YouTube.

In your experience, what do inexperienced Kagglers often overlook? What do you know now that you wish you'd known when you first started?

The importance of exploratory data analysis. In the field of machine learning, there is a concept of the No Free Lunch theorem. We should not only learn algorithms, but also learn how to address challenges. The No Free Lunch theorem is a statement that there is no universal model that performs well on all problems.

In machine learning competitions, it is essential to find a model that is appropriate to the characteristics of the dataset and the task in order to improve your score.

What mistakes have you made in competitions in the past?

Overfitting to the public leaderboard. In the LANL Earthquake Prediction *competition, I scored pretty well on the public leaderboard and finished the competition at the rank of fifth. However, my final ranking was 211st, which means I believed too much in a limited dataset. Overfitting is a very popular concept in machine learning, and I realized the importance of this with pain through Kaggle.*

Do you suggest any particular way to avoid overfitting?

It is important to observe carefully how the training and evaluation datasets are divided. I try to build a validation set that reproduces this partitioning.

Are there any particular tools or libraries that you would recommend using for data analysis or machine learning?

I love Pandas, which is an essential library for handling tabular datasets. I use it for exploratory data analysis by extracting, aggregating, and visualizing.

What do you suggest readers do to master Pandas?

You can look at some community tutorials. Kaggle also provides some learning tutorial courses on Pandas and feature engineering.

Do you use other competition platforms? How do they compare to Kaggle?

I sometimes use Japanese platforms like Signate, Nishika, etc. (`https://upura.github.io/projects/data_science_competitions/`*). These are obviously inferior to Kaggle in terms of functionality and UX/UX, but it's interesting to see familiar subjects like the Japanese language.*

Text augmentation strategies

We discussed augmentation strategies for computer vision problems extensively in the previous chapter. By contrast, similar approaches for textual data are a less well-explored topic (as evidenced by the fact there is no single package like `albumentations`). In this section, we demonstrate some of the possible approaches to addressing the problem.

Basic techniques

As usual, it is informative to examine the basic approaches first, focusing on random changes and synonym handling. A systematic study of the basic approaches is provided in *Wei* and *Zou* (2019) at `https://arxiv.org/abs/1901.11196`.

We begin with **synonym replacement**. Replacing certain words with their synonyms produces text that is close in meaning to the original, but slightly perturbed (see the project page at `https://wordnet.princeton.edu/` if you are interested in more details, like where the synonyms are actually coming from):

```python
def get_synonyms(word):

    synonyms = set()

    for syn in wordnet.synsets(word):
        for l in syn.lemmas():
            synonym = l.name().replace("_", " ").replace("-", " ").lower()
            synonym = "".join([char for char in synonym if char in '
qwertyuiopasdfghjklzxcvbnm'])
            synonyms.add(synonym)
    if word in synonyms:
        synonyms.remove(word)

    return list(synonyms)
```

We create a simple wrapper around the workhorse function defined above, specifying a chunk of text (a string containing multiple words) and replace at most *n* of the words:

```python
def synonym_replacement(words, n):
    words = words.split()
    new_words = words.copy()
    random_word_list = list(set([word for word in words if word not in
stop_words]))
    random.shuffle(random_word_list)
    num_replaced = 0

    for random_word in random_word_list:
```

```
        synonyms = get_synonyms(random_word)

        if len(synonyms) >= 1:
            synonym = random.choice(list(synonyms))
            new_words = [synonym if word == random_word else word for word
    in new_words]
            num_replaced += 1

        if num_replaced >= n: # Only replace up to n words
            break
    sentence = ' '.join(new_words)
    return sentence
```

Let's see how the function works in practice:

```
print(f" Example of Synonym Replacement: {synonym_replacement('The quick
brown fox jumps over the lazy dog',4)}")
```

```
Example of Synonym Replacement: The spry brown university fox jumpstart
over the lazy detent
```

Not quite what you would call Shakespearean, but it does convey the same message while changing the style markedly. We can extend this approach by creating multiple new sentences per tweet:

```
trial_sent = data['text'][25]
print(trial_sent)
the free fillin' app on my ipod is fun, im addicted
for n in range(3):
    print(f" Example of Synonym Replacement: {synonym_replacement(trial_
sent,n)}")
```

```
Example of Synonym Replacement: the free fillin' app on my ipod    fun, im
addict
Example of Synonym Replacement: the innocent fillin' app on my ipod
fun, im addicted
Example of Synonym Replacement: the relinquish fillin' app on my ipod
fun, im addict
```

As you can see, generating variations of a text chunk using synonyms is quite straightforward.

Next, **swapping** is a simple and efficient method; we create a modified sentence by randomly swapping the order of words in the text.

Carefully applied, this can be viewed as a potentially useful form of **regularization**, as it disturbs the sequential nature of the data that models like LSTM rely on. The first step is to define a function swapping words:

```
def swap_word(new_words):
    random_idx_1 = random.randint(0, len(new_words)-1)
    random_idx_2 = random_idx_1
    counter = 0
    while random_idx_2 == random_idx_1:
        random_idx_2 = random.randint(0, len(new_words)-1)
        counter += 1
        if counter > 3:
            return new_words

    new_words[random_idx_1], new_words[random_idx_2] = new_words[random_
idx_2], new_words[random_idx_1]
    return new_words
```

Then, we write a wrapper around this function:

```
# n is the number of words to be swapped
def random_swap(words, n):
    words = words.split()
    new_words = words.copy()

    for _ in range(n):
        new_words = swap_word(new_words)

    sentence = ' '.join(new_words)
    return sentence
```

Synonyms and swapping do not affect the length of the sentence we are modifying. If in a given application it is useful to modify that attribute, we can remove or add words to the sentence.

The most common way to implement the former is to delete words at random:

```python
def random_deletion(words, p):

    words = words.split()

    # Obviously, if there's only one word, don't delete it
    if len(words) == 1:
        return words

    # Randomly delete words with probability p
    new_words = []
    for word in words:
        r = random.uniform(0, 1)
        if r > p:
            new_words.append(word)

    # If you end up deleting all words, just return a random word
    if len(new_words) == 0:
        rand_int = random.randint(0, len(words)-1)
        return [words[rand_int]]

    sentence = ' '.join(new_words)

    return sentence
```

Let's look at some examples:

```python
print(random_deletion(trial_sent,0.2))
print(random_deletion(trial_sent,0.3))
print(random_deletion(trial_sent,0.4))
```

```
the free fillin' app on my     fun, addicted
free fillin' app on my ipod      im addicted
the free on my ipod      fun, im
```

If we can remove, we can also add, of course. Random insertion of words to a sentence can be viewed as the NLP equivalent of adding noise or blur to an image:

```python
def random_insertion(words, n):
    words = words.split()
    new_words = words.copy()
    for _ in range(n):
        add_word(new_words)
    sentence = ' '.join(new_words)
    return sentence


def add_word(new_words):
    synonyms = []
    counter = 0

    while len(synonyms) < 1:
        random_word = new_words[random.randint(0, len(new_words)-1)]
        synonyms = get_synonyms(random_word)
        counter += 1
        if counter >= 10:
            return
    random_synonym = synonyms[0]
    random_idx = random.randint(0, len(new_words)-1)
    new_words.insert(random_idx, random_synonym)
```

Here is the function in action:

```python
print(random_insertion(trial_sent,1))
print(random_insertion(trial_sent,2))
print(random_insertion(trial_sent,3))
```

```
the free fillin' app on my addict ipod    fun, im addicted
the complimentary free fillin' app on my ipod along    fun, im addicted
the free along fillin' app addict on my ipod along    fun, im addicted
```

We can combine all the transformations discussed above into a single function, producing four variants of the same sentence:

```
def aug(sent,n,p):
    print(f" Original Sentence : {sent}")
    print(f" SR Augmented Sentence : {synonym_replacement(sent,n)}")
    print(f" RD Augmented Sentence : {random_deletion(sent,p)}")
    print(f" RS Augmented Sentence : {random_swap(sent,n)}")
    print(f" RI Augmented Sentence : {random_insertion(sent,n)}")

aug(trial_sent,4,0.3)
```

```
Original Sentence : the free fillin' app on my ipod is fun, im addicted
SR Augmented Sentence : the disembarrass fillin' app on my ipod is fun, im
hook
RD Augmented Sentence : the free app on my ipod fun, im addicted
RS Augmented Sentence : on free fillin' ipod is my the app fun, im
addicted
RI Augmented Sentence : the free fillin' app on gratis addict my ipod is
complimentary make up fun, im addicted
```

The augmentation methods discussed above do not exploit the structure of text data - to give one example, even analyzing a simple characteristic like "part of speech" can help us construct more useful transformations of the original text. This is the approach we will now focus on.

nlpaug

We conclude this section by demonstrating the capabilities provided by the `nlpaug` package (`https://github.com/makcedward/nlpaug`). It aggregates different methods for text augmentation and is designed to be lightweight and easy to incorporate into a workflow. We demonstrate some examples of the functionality contained therein below.

```
! pip install nlpaug
```

We import the character- and word-level augmenters, which we will use to plug in specific methods:

```
import nlpaug.augmenter.char as nac
import nlpaug.augmenter.word as naw
```

```
test_sentence = "I genuinely have no idea what the output of this sequence
of words will be - it will be interesting to find out what nlpaug can do
with this!"
```

What happens when we apply a **simulated typo** to our test sentence? This transformation can be parametrized in a number of ways; for a full list of parameters and their explanations, the reader is encouraged to examine the official documentation: `https://nlpaug.readthedocs.io/en/latest/augmenter/char/keyboard.html`.

```
aug = nac.KeyboardAug(name='Keyboard_Aug', aug_char_min=1,
                      aug_char_max=10, aug_char_p=0.3, aug_word_p=0.3,
                      aug_word_min=1, aug_word_max=10, stopwords=None,
                      tokenizer=None, reverse_tokenizer=None,
                      include_special_char=True, include_numeric=True,
                      include_upper_case=True, lang='en', verbose=0,
                      stopwords_regex=None, model_path=None, min_char=4)

test_sentence_aug = aug.augment(test_sentence)
print(test_sentence)
print(test_sentence_aug)
```

This is the output:

```
I genuinely have no idea what the output of this sequence of words will be
- it will be interesting to find out what nlpaug can do with this!
I geb&ine:y have no kdeZ qhQt the 8uYput of tTid sequsnDr of aorVs will be
- it wi,k be jnterewtlHg to find out what nlpaug can do with this!
```

We can simulate an **OCR error** creeping into our input:

```
aug = nac.OcrAug(name='OCR_Aug', aug_char_min=1, aug_char_max=10,
                 aug_char_p=0.3, aug_word_p=0.3, aug_word_min=1,
                 aug_word_max=10, stopwords=None, tokenizer=None,
                 reverse_tokenizer=None, verbose=0,
                 stopwords_regex=None, min_char=1)

test_sentence_aug = aug.augment(test_sentence)
print(test_sentence)
print(test_sentence_aug)
```

We get:

```
I genuinely have no idea what the output of this sequence of words will be
- it will be interesting to find out what nlpaug can do with this!
I 9enoine1y have no idea what the ootpot of this sequence of wokd8 will be
- it will be inteke8tin9 to find out what nlpaug can du with this!
```

While useful, character-level transformations have a limited scope when it comes to creative changes in the data. Let us examine what possibilities nlpaug offers when it comes to word-level modifications. Our first example is replacing a fixed percentage of words with their antonyms:

```
aug = naw.AntonymAug(name='Antonym_Aug', aug_min=1, aug_max=10, aug_p=0.3,
                     lang='eng', stopwords=None, tokenizer=None,
                     reverse_tokenizer=None, stopwords_regex=None,
                     verbose=0)


test_sentence_aug = aug.augment(test_sentence)
print(test_sentence)
print(test_sentence_aug)
```

We get:

```
I genuinely have no idea what the output of this sequence of words will be
- it will be interesting to find out what nlpaug can do with this!
I genuinely lack no idea what the output of this sequence of words will
differ - it will differ uninteresting to lose out what nlpaug can unmake
with this!
```

nlpaug also offers us a possibility for, for example, replacing synonyms; such transformations can also be achieved with the more basic techniques discussed above. For completeness' sake, we demonstrate a small sample below, which uses a BERT architecture under the hood:

```
aug = naw.ContextualWordEmbsAug(model_path='bert-base-uncased',
                                model_type='', action='substitute',
                                # temperature=1.0,
                                top_k=100,
                                # top_p=None,
                                name='ContextualWordEmbs_Aug', aug_min=1,
                                aug_max=10, aug_p=0.3,
                                stopwords=None, device='cpu',
                                force_reload=False,
```

```
                                    # optimize=None,
                                    stopwords_regex=None,
                                    verbose=0, silence=True)


test_sentence_aug = aug.augment(test_sentence)
print(test_sentence)
print(test_sentence_aug)
```

Here is the result:

```
I genuinely have no idea what the output of this sequence of words will be
- it will be interesting to find out what nlpaug can do with this!
i genuinely have no clue what his rest of this series of words will say -
its will seemed impossible to find just what we can do with this!
```

As you can see, nlpaug offers a broad range of options for modifying your textual input to generate augmentations. Which ones should actually be chosen is very much context-dependent and the decision requires a little bit of domain knowledge, suited to a particular application.

> Some places for further exploration would be beginner competitions such as *Natural Language Processing with Disaster Tweets* (https://www.kaggle.com/c/nlp-getting-started), as well as more intermediate or advanced ones like *Jigsaw Rate Severity of Toxic Comments* (https://www.kaggle.com/c/jigsaw-toxic-severity-rating) or *Google QUEST Q&A Labeling* (https://www.kaggle.com/c/google-quest-challenge). In all of these cases, nlpaug has been widely used – including in the winning solutions.

Summary

In this chapter, we discussed modeling for NLP competitions. We demonstrate both vintage and state-of-the-art methods applicable to a diverse range of problems appearing in Kaggle competitions. In addition, we touched upon the frequently ignored topic of text augmentation.

In the next chapter, we will discuss simulation competitions, a new class of contests that has been gaining popularity over the last few years.

Join our book's Discord space

Join the book's Discord workspace for a monthly *Ask me Anything* session with the authors:

https://packt.link/KaggleDiscord

12

Simulation and Optimization Competitions

Reinforcement learning (RL) is an interesting case among the different branches of machine learning. On the one hand, it is quite demanding from a technical standpoint: various intuitions from supervised learning do not hold, and the associated mathematical apparatus is quite a bit more advanced; on the other hand, it is the easiest one to explain to an outsider or layperson. A simple analogy is teaching your pet (I am very intentionally trying to steer clear of the dogs versus cats debate) to perform tricks: you provide a treat for a trick well done, and refuse it otherwise.

Reinforcement learning was a latecomer to the competition party on Kaggle, but the situation has changed in the last few years with the introduction of simulation competitions. In this chapter, we will describe this new and exciting part of the Kaggle universe. So far – at the time of writing – there have been four **Featured** competitions and two **Playground** ones; this list, while admittedly not extensive, allows us to give a broad overview.

In this chapter, we will demonstrate solutions to the problems presented in several simulation competitions:

- We begin with *Connect X.*
- We follow with *Rock, Paper, Scissors*, where a dual approach to building a competitive agent is shown.
- Next, we demonstrate a solution based on multi-armed bandits to the *Santa* competition.
- We conclude with an overview of the remaining competitions, which are slightly outside the scope of this chapter.

If reinforcement learning is a completely new concept for you, it is probably a good idea to get some basic understanding first. A very good way to start on the RL adventure is the Kaggle Learning course dedicated to this very topic in the context of Game AI (`https://www.kaggle.com/learn/intro-to-game-ai-and-reinforcement-learning`). The course introduces basic concepts such as agents and policies, also providing a (crash) introduction to deep reinforcement learning. All the examples in the course use the data from the Playground competition *Connect X*, in which the objective is to train an agent capable of playing a game of connecting checkers in a line (`https://www.kaggle.com/c/connectx/overview`).

On a more general level, it is worth pointing out that an important aspect of simulation and optimization competitions is the **environment**: due to the very nature of the problem, your solution needs to exhibit more dynamic characteristics than just submitting a set of numbers (as would be the case for "regular" supervised learning contests). A very informative and detailed description of the environment used in the simulation competitions can be found at `https://github.com/Kaggle/kaggle-environments/blob/master/README.md`.

Connect X

In this section, we demonstrate how to approach the simple problem of playing checkers using heuristics. While not a deep learning solution, it is our view that this bare-bones presentation of the concepts is much more useful for people without significant prior exposure to RL.

If you are new to the concept of using AI for board games, the presentation by *Tom van de Wiele* (`https://www.kaggle.com/tvdwiele`) is a resource worth exploring: `https://tinyurl.com/36rdv5sa`.

The objective of *Connect X* is to get a number (X) of your checkers in a row – horizontally, vertically, or diagonally – on the game board before your opponent. Players take turns dropping their checkers into one of the columns at the top of the board. This means each move may have the purpose of trying to win for you or trying to stop your opponent from winning.

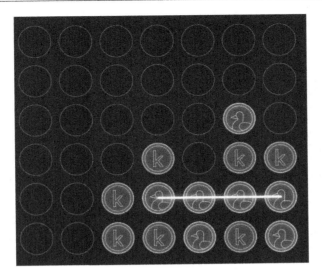

Figure 12.1: Connect X board

Connect X was the first competition that introduced **agents**: instead of a static submission (or a Notebook that was evaluated against an unseen dataset), participants had to submit agents capable of playing the game against others. The evaluation proceeded in steps:

1. Upon uploading, a submission plays against itself to ensure it works properly.
2. If this validation episode is successful, a skill rating is assigned, and the submission joins the ranks of all competitors.
3. Each day, several episodes are played for each submission, and subsequently rankings are adjusted.

With that setup in mind, let us proceed toward demonstrating how to build a submission for the *Connect X* competition. The code we present is for *X=4*, but can be easily adapted for other values or variable *X*.

First, we install the Kaggle environments package:

```
!pip install kaggle-environments --upgrade
```

We define an environment in which our agent will be evaluated:

```
from kaggle_environments import evaluate, make


env = make("connectx", debug=True)
env.render()
```

While a frequent impulse you might have is to try sophisticated methods, it is useful to start simple – as we will do here, by using simple heuristics. These are combined into a single function in the accompanying code, but for the sake of presentation, we describe them one at a time here.

The first rule is checking whether either of the players has a chance to connect four checkers vertically and, if so, returning the position at which it is possible. We can achieve this by using a simple variable as our input argument, which can take on two possible values indicating which player opportunities are being analyzed:

```
def my_agent(observation, configuration):
    from random import choice

    # me:me_or_enemy=1, enemy:me_or_enemy=2
    def check_vertical_chance(me_or_enemy):
        for i in range(0, 7):
            if observation.board[i+7*5] == me_or_enemy \
            and observation.board[i+7*4] == me_or_enemy \
            and observation.board[i+7*3] == me_or_enemy \
            and observation.board[i+7*2] == 0:
                return i
            elif observation.board[i+7*4] == me_or_enemy \
            and observation.board[i+7*3] == me_or_enemy \
            and observation.board[i+7*2] == me_or_enemy \
            and observation.board[i+7*1] == 0:
                return i
            elif observation.board[i+7*3] == me_or_enemy \
            and observation.board[i+7*2] == me_or_enemy \
            and observation.board[i+7*1] == me_or_enemy \
            and observation.board[i+7*0] == 0:
                return i
        # no chance
        return -99
```

We can define an analogous method for horizontal chances:

```python
def check_horizontal_chance(me_or_enemy):
    chance_cell_num = -99
    for i in [0,7,14,21,28,35]:
        for j in range(0, 4):
            val_1 = i+j+0
            val_2 = i+j+1
            val_3 = i+j+2
            val_4 = i+j+3
            if sum([observation.board[val_1] == me_or_enemy, \
                    observation.board[val_2] == me_or_enemy, \
                    observation.board[val_3] == me_or_enemy, \
                    observation.board[val_4] == me_or_enemy]) == 3:
                for k in [val_1,val_2,val_3,val_4]:
                    if observation.board[k] == 0:
                        chance_cell_num = k
                        # bottom line
                        for l in range(35, 42):
                            if chance_cell_num == l:
                                return l - 35
                        # others
                        if observation.board[chance_cell_num+7] != 0:
                            return chance_cell_num % 7
    # no chance
    return -99
```

We repeat the same approach for the diagonal combinations:

```python
# me:me_or_enemy=1, enemy:me_or_enemy=2
def check_slanting_chance(me_or_enemy, lag, cell_list):
    chance_cell_num = -99
    for i in cell_list:
        val_1 = i+lag*0
        val_2 = i+lag*1
        val_3 = i+lag*2
        val_4 = i+lag*3
        if sum([observation.board[val_1] == me_or_enemy, \
```

```
                    observation.board[val_2] == me_or_enemy, \
                    observation.board[val_3] == me_or_enemy, \
                    observation.board[val_4] == me_or_enemy]) == 3:
                for j in [val_1,val_2,val_3,val_4]:
                    if observation.board[j] == 0:
                        chance_cell_num = j
                        # bottom line
                        for k in range(35, 42):
                            if chance_cell_num == k:
                                return k - 35
                        # others
                        if chance_cell_num != -99 \
                        and observation.board[chance_cell_num+7] != 0:
                            return chance_cell_num % 7
        # no chance
        return -99
```

We can combine the logic into a single function checking the opportunities (playing the game against an opponent):

```
def check_my_chances():
    # check my vertical chance
    result = check_vertical_chance(my_num)
    if result != -99:
        return result
    # check my horizontal chance
    result = check_horizontal_chance(my_num)
    if result != -99:
        return result
    # check my slanting chance 1 (up-right to down-left)
    result = check_slanting_chance(my_num, 6, [3,4,5,6,10,11,12,13,17,
18,19,20])
    if result != -99:
        return result
    # check my slanting chance 2 (up-left to down-right)
    result = check_slanting_chance(my_num, 8, [0,1,2,3,7,8,9,10,14,15,
16,17])
    if result != -99:
        return result
```

```
    # no chance
    return -99
```

Those blocks constitute the basics of the logic. While a bit cumbersome to formulate, they are a useful exercise in converting an intuition into heuristics that can be used in an agent competing in a game.

 Please see the accompanying code in the repository for a complete definition of the agent in this example.

The performance of our newly defined agent can be evaluated against a pre-defined agent, for example, a random one:

```
env.reset()
env.run([my_agent, "random"])
env.render(mode="ipython", width=500, height=450)
```

The code above shows you how to set up a solution from scratch for a relatively simple problem (there is a reason why *Connect X* is a Playground and not a Featured competition). Interestingly, this simple problem can be handled with (almost) state-of-the-art methods like AlphaZero: https://www.kaggle.com/connect4alphazero/alphazero-baseline-connectx.

With the introductory example behind us, you should be ready to dive into the more elaborate (or in any case, not toy example-based) contests.

Rock-paper-scissors

It is no coincidence that several problems in simulation competitions refer to playing games: at varying levels of complexity, games offer an environment with clearly defined rules, naturally lending itself to the agent-action-reward framework. Aside from Tic-Tac-Toe, connecting checkers is one of the simplest examples of a competitive game. Moving up the difficulty ladder (of games), let's have a look at **rock-paper-scissors** and how a Kaggle contest centered around this game could be approached.

The idea of the *Rock, Paper, Scissors* competition (https://www.kaggle.com/c/rock-paper-scissors/code) was an extension of the basic rock-paper-scissors game (known as *roshambo* in some parts of the world): instead of the usual "best of 3" score, we use "best of 1,000."

We will describe two possible approaches to the problem: one rooted in the game-theoretic approach, and the other more focused on the algorithmic side.

We begin with the **Nash equilibrium**. Wikipedia gives the definition of this as the solution to a non-cooperative game involving two or more players, where each player is assumed to know the equilibrium strategies of the others, and no player can obtain an advantage by changing only their own strategy.

 An excellent introduction to rock-paper-scissors in a game-theoretic framework can be found at https://www.youtube.com/watch?v=-1GDMXoMdaY.

Denoting our players as red and blue, each cell in the matrix of outcomes shows the result of a given combination of moves:

	Rock	Paper	Scissors
Rock	0, 0	-1, 1	1, -1
Paper	1, -1	0, 0	-1, 1
Scissors	-1, 1	1, -1	0, 0

Figure 12.2: Payoff matrix for rock-paper-scissors

As an example, if both play Rock (the top-left cell), both gain 0 points; if blue plays Rock and red plays Paper (the cell in the second column of the first row), red wins – so red gains +1 point and blue has -1 point as a result.

If we played each action with an equal probability of 1/3, then the opponent must do the same; otherwise, if they play Rock all the time, they will tie against Rock, lose against Paper, and win against Scissors – each with a probability of 1/3 (or one-third of the time). The expected reward, in this case, is 0, in which case we can change our strategy to Paper and win all the time. The same reasoning can be conducted for the strategy of Paper versus Scissors and Scissors versus Rock, for which we will not show you the matrix of outcomes due to redundancy.

The remaining option in order to be in equilibrium is that both players need to play a random strategy – which is the Nash equilibrium. We can build a simple agent around this idea:

```
%%writefile submission.py

import random

def nash_equilibrium_agent(observation, configuration):
    return random.randint(0, 2)
```

 The magic at the start (writing from a Notebook directly to a file) is necessary to satisfy the submission constraints of this particular competition.

How does our Nash agent perform against others? We can find out by evaluating the performance:

```
!pip install -q -U kaggle_environments

from kaggle_environments import make
```

 At the time of writing, there is an error that pops up after this import (**Failure to load a module named 'gfootball'**); the official advice from Kaggle is to ignore it. In practice, it does not seem to have any impact on executing the code.

We start by creating the rock-paper-scissors environment and setting the limit to 1,000 episodes per simulation:

```
env = make(
    "rps",
    configuration={"episodeSteps": 1000}
)
```

We will make use of a Notebook created in this competition that implemented numerous agents based on deterministic heuristics (https://www.kaggle.com/ilialar/multi-armed-bandit-vs-deterministic-agents) and import the code for the agents we compete against from there:

```
%%writefile submission_copy_opponent.py
def copy_opponent_agent(observation, configuration):
    if observation.step > 0:
```

```
        return observation.lastOpponentAction
    else:
        return 0

# nash_equilibrium_agent vs copy_opponent_agent
env.run(
    ["submission.py", "submission_copy_opponent.py"]
)

env.render(mode="ipython", width=500, height=400)
```

When we execute the preceding block and run the environment, we can watch an animated board for the 1,000 epochs. A snapshot looks like this:

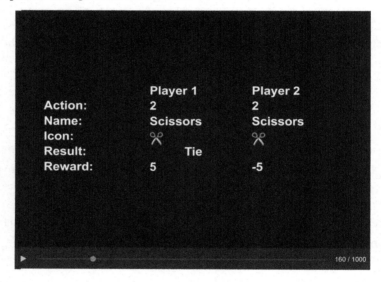

Figure 12.3: A snapshot from a rendered environment evaluating agent performance

In supervised learning – both classification and regression – it is frequently useful to start approaching any problem with a simple benchmark, usually a linear model. Even though not state of the art, it can provide a useful expectation and a measure of performance. In reinforcement learning, a similar idea holds; an approach worth trying in this capacity is the multi-armed bandit, the simplest algorithm we can honestly call RL. In the next section, we demonstrate how this approach can be used in a simulation competition.

Santa competition 2020

Over the last few years, a sort of tradition has emerged on Kaggle: in early December, there is a Santa-themed competition. The actual algorithmic side varies from year to year, but for our purposes, the 2020 competition is an interesting case: `https://www.kaggle.com/c/santa-2020`.

The setup was a classical **multi-armed bandit (MAB)** trying to maximize reward by taking repeated action on a vending machine, but with two extras:

- **Reward decay:** At each step, the probability of obtaining a reward from a machine decreases by 3 percent.

- **Competition:** You are constrained not only by time (a limited number of attempts) but also by another player attempting to achieve the same objective. We mention this constraint mostly for the sake of completeness, as it is not crucial to incorporate explicitly in our demonstrated solution.

 For a good explanation of the methods for approaching the general MAB problem, the reader is referred to `https://lilianweng.github.io/lil-log/2018/01/23/the-multi-armed-bandit-problem-and-its-solutions.html`.

The solution we demonstrate is adapted from `https://www.kaggle.com/ilialar/simple-multi-armed-bandit`, code from *Ilia Larchenko* (`https://www.kaggle.com/ilialar`). Our approach is based on successive updates to the distribution of reward: at each step, we generate a random number from a Beta distribution with parameters (*a+1*, *b+1*) where:

- *a* is the total reward from this arm (number of wins)

- *b* is the number of historical losses

When we need to decide which arm to pull, we select the arm with the highest generated number and use it to generate the next step; our posterior distribution becomes a prior for the next step.

The graph below shows the shape of a Beta distribution for different pairs of (a, b) values:

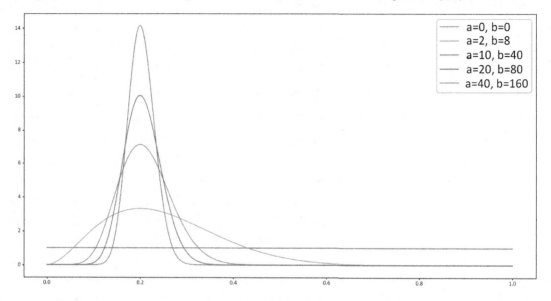

Figure 12.4: Shape of the beta distribution density for different combinations of (a,b) parameters

As you can see, initially, the distribution is flat (Beta(0,0) is uniform), but as we gather more information, it concentrates the probability mass around the mode, which means there is less uncertainty and we are more confident about our judgment. We can incorporate the competition-specific reward decay by decreasing the a parameter every time an arm is used.

We begin the creation of our agent by writing a submission file. First, the necessary imports and variable initialization:

```
%%writefile submission.py

import json
import numpy as np
import pandas as pd

bandit_state = None
total_reward = 0
last_step = None
```

We define the class specifying an MAB agent. For the sake of reading coherence, we reproduce the entire code and include the explanations in comments within it:

```python
def multi_armed_bandit_agent (observation, configuration):
    global history, history_bandit

    step = 1.0           # balance exploration / exploitation
    decay_rate = 0.97  # how much do we decay the win count after each call

    global bandit_state,total_reward,last_step

    if observation.step == 0:
        # initial bandit state
        bandit_state = [[1,1] for i in range(configuration["banditCount"])]
    else:
        # updating bandit_state using the result of the previous step
        last_reward = observation["reward"] - total_reward
        total_reward = observation["reward"]

        # we need to understand who we are Player 1 or 2
        player = int(last_step == observation.lastActions[1])

        if last_reward > 0:
            bandit_state[observation.lastActions[player]][0] += last_
reward * step
        else:
            bandit_state[observation.lastActions[player]][1] += step

        bandit_state[observation.lastActions[0]][0] = (bandit_
state[observation.lastActions[0]][0] - 1) * decay_rate + 1
        bandit_state[observation.lastActions[1]][0] = (bandit_
state[observation.lastActions[1]][0] - 1) * decay_rate + 1

    # generate random number from Beta distribution for each agent and
    select the most lucky one
    best_proba = -1
```

```
    best_agent = None
    for k in range(configuration["banditCount"]):
        proba = np.random.beta(bandit_state[k][0],bandit_state[k][1])
        if proba > best_proba:
            best_proba = proba
            best_agent = k

    last_step = best_agent
    return best_agent
```

As you can see, the core logic of the function is a straightforward implementation of the MAB algorithm. An adjustment specific to our contest occurs with the bandit_state variable, where we apply the decay multiplier.

Similar to the previous case, we are now ready to evaluate the performance of our agent in the contest environment. The code snippet below demonstrates how this can be implemented:

```
%%writefile random_agent.py

import random

def random_agent(observation, configuration):
    return random.randrange(configuration.banditCount)

from kaggle_environments import make

env = make("mab", debug=True)

env.reset()
env.run(["random_agent.py", "submission.py"])
env.render(mode="ipython", width=800, height=700)
```

We see something like this:

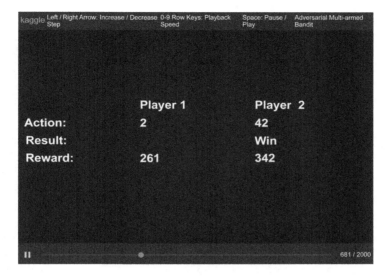

Figure 12.5: Snapshot from a rendered environment evaluating agent performance

In this section, we demonstrated how a vintage multi-armed bandit algorithm can be utilized in a simulation competition on Kaggle. While useful as a starting point, this was not sufficient to qualify for the medal zone, where deep reinforcement learning approaches were more popular.

We will follow up with a discussion of approaches based on other methods, in a diverse range of competitions.

The name of the game

Beyond the relatively elementary games discussed above, simulation competitions involve more elaborate setups. In this section, we will briefly discuss those. The first example is *Halite*, defined on the competition page (`https://www.kaggle.com/c/halite`) in the following manner:

> *Halite [...] is a resource management game where you build and control a small armada of ships. Your algorithms determine their movements to collect halite, a luminous energy source. The most halite at the end of the match wins, but it's up to you to figure out how to make effective and efficient moves. You control your fleet, build new ships, create shipyards, and mine the regenerating halite on the game board.*

This is what the game looks like:

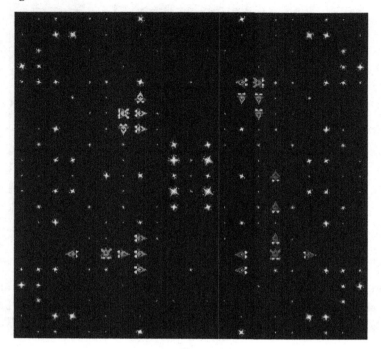

Figure 12.6: Halite game board

Kaggle organized two competitions around the game: a Playground edition (`https://www.kaggle.com/c/halite-iv-playground-edition`) as well as a regular Featured edition (`https://www.kaggle.com/c/halite`). The classic reinforcement learning approach was less useful in this instance since, with an arbitrary number of units (ships/bases) and a dynamic opponent pool, the problem of credit assignment was becoming intractable for people with access to a "normal" level of computing resources.

Explaining the problem of credit assignment in full generality is beyond the scope of this book, but an interested reader is encouraged to start with the Wikipedia entry (`https://en.wikipedia.org/wiki/Assignment_problem`) and follow up with this excellent introductory article by Mesnard et al.: `https://proceedings.mlr.press/v139/mesnard21a.html`.

A description of the winning solution by *Tom van de Wiele* (`https://www.kaggle.com/c/halite/discussion/183543`) provides an excellent overview of the modified approach that proved successful in this instance (deep RL with independent credit assignment per unit).

Another competition involving a relatively sophisticated game was *Lux AI* (https://www.kaggle.com/c/lux-ai-2021). In this competition, participants were tasked with designing agents to tackle a multi-variable optimization problem combining resource gathering and allocation, competing against other players. In addition, successful agents had to analyze the moves of their opponents and react accordingly. An interesting feature of this contest was the popularity of a "meta" approach: **imitation learning** (https://paperswithcode.com/task/imitation-learning). This is a fairly novel approach in RL, focused on learning a behavior policy from demonstration – without a specific model to describe the generation of state-action pairs. A competitive implementation of this idea (at the time of writing) is given by Kaggle user Ironbar (https://www.kaggle.com/c/lux-ai-2021/discussion/293911).

Finally, no discussion of simulation competitions in Kaggle would be complete without the *Google Research Football with Manchester City F.C.* competition (https://www.kaggle.com/c/google-football/overview). The motivation behind this contest was for researchers to explore AI agents' ability to play in complex settings like football. The competition **Overview** section formulates the problem thus:

> *The sport requires a balance of short-term control, learned concepts such as passing, and high-level strategy, which can be difficult to teach agents. A current environment exists to train and test agents, but other solutions may offer better results.*

Unlike some examples given above, this competition was dominated by reinforcement learning approaches:

- Team Raw Beast (3rd) followed a methodology inspired by *AlphaStar*: https://www.kaggle.com/c/google-football/discussion/200709
- Salty Fish (2nd) utilized a form of self-play: https://www.kaggle.com/c/google-football/discussion/202977
- The winners, WeKick, used a deep learning-based solution with creative feature engineering and reward structure adjustment: https://www.kaggle.com/c/google-football/discussion/202232

Studying the solutions listed above is an excellent starting point to learn how RL can be utilized to solve this class of problems.

Firat Gonen

https://www.kaggle.com/frtgnn

For this chapter's interview, we spoke to Firat Gonen, a Triple Grandmaster in Datasets, Notebooks, and Discussion, and an HP Data Science Global Ambassador. He gives us his take on his Kaggle approach, and how his attitude has evolved over time.

What's your favorite kind of competition and why? In terms of technique and solving approaches, what is your specialty on Kaggle?

My favorite kind evolved over time. I used to prefer very generic tabular competitions where a nice laptop and some patience would suffice to master the trends. I felt like I used to be able to see the outlying trends between training and test sets pretty good. Over time, with being awarded the ambassadorship by Z by HP and my workstation equipment, I kind of converted myself towards more computer vision competitions, though I still have a lot to learn.

How do you approach a Kaggle competition? How different is this approach to what you do in your day-to-day work?

I usually prefer to delay the modeling part for as long as I can. I like to use that time on EDAs, outliers, reading the forum, etc., trying to be patient. After I feel like I'm done with feature engineering, I try to form only benchmark models to get a grip on different architecture results. My technique is very similar when it comes to professional work as well. I find it useless to try to do the best in a huge amount of time; there has to be a balance between time and success.

Tell us about a particularly challenging competition you entered, and what insights you used to tackle the task.

The competition hosted by François Chollet was extremely challenging; the very first competition to force us into AGI. I remember I felt pretty powerless in that competition, where I learned several new techniques. I think everybody did that while remembering data science is not just machine learning. Several other techniques like mixed integer programming resurfaced at Kaggle.

Has Kaggle helped you in your career? If so, how?

Of course: I learned a lot of new techniques and stayed up to date thanks to Kaggle. I'm in a place in my career where my main responsibility lies mostly in management. That's why Kaggle is very important to me for staying up to date in several things.

How have you built up your portfolio thanks to Kaggle?

I believe the advantage was in a more indirect way, where people saw both practical skills (thanks to Kaggle) and more theoretical skills in my more conventional education qualifications.

In your experience, what do inexperienced Kagglers often overlook? What do you know now that you wish you'd known when you first started?

I think there are two things newcomers do wrong. The first one is having fear in entering a new competition, thinking that they will get bad scores and it will be registered. This is nonsense. Everybody has bad scores; it's all about how much you devote to a new competition. The second one is that they want to get to the model-building stage ASAP, which is very wrong; they want to see their benchmark scores and then they get frustrated. I advise them to take their time in feature generation and selection, and also in EDA stages.

What mistakes have you made in competitions in the past?

My mistakes are, unfortunately, very similar to new rookies. I got impatient in several competitions where I didn't pay enough attention to early stages, and after some time you feel like you don't have enough time to go back.

Are there any particular tools or libraries that you would recommend using for data analysis or machine learning?

I would recommend PyCaret for benchmarking to get you speed, and PyTorch for a model-building framework.

What's the most important thing someone should keep in mind or do when they're entering a competition?

Exploratory data analysis and previous similar competition discussions.

Do you use other competition platforms? How do they compare to Kaggle?

To be honest, I haven't rolled the dice outside Kaggle, but I have had my share of them from a tourist perspective. It takes time to adjust to other platforms.

Summary

In this chapter, we discussed simulation competitions, a new type of contest that is increasing in popularity. Compared to vision or NLP-centered ones, simulation contests involve a much broader range of methods (with somewhat higher mathematical content), which reflects the difference between supervised learning and reinforcement learning.

This chapter concludes the technical part of the book. In the remainder, we will talk about turning your Kaggle Notebooks into a portfolio of projects and capitalizing on it to find new professional opportunities.

Join our book's Discord space

Join the book's Discord workspace for a monthly *Ask me Anything* session with the authors:

https://packt.link/KaggleDiscord

Part III

Leveraging Competitions for Your Career

13

Creating Your Portfolio of Projects and Ideas

Participation on Kaggle has its benefits: scoring well in the four areas and consequently ranking high in the esteem of other Kagglers certainly brings satisfaction and a sense of accomplishment. However, your experience on Kaggle also has an impact beyond Kaggle and can help advance your career. It is not just the experience you gain from participating in competitions, experimenting on data you have never worked on before, or repeating experiments with new techniques; it is also the connections you create with other data scientists and the attention you may get from companies.

Although Kaggle is not fully recognized as a qualification by many companies, the work you do in competitions can demonstrate a lot about your capabilities and help you to stand out from the crowd. In this chapter, we will explore ways you can stand out by showcasing your work on Kaggle itself and other sites in an appropriate way. We will cover the following topics:

- Building your portfolio with Kaggle
- Arranging your online presence beyond Kaggle
- Monitoring competition updates and newsletters

In the next chapter, we will conclude the book by exploring how Kaggle can directly affect your career by enhancing your professional network and providing you with career opportunities.

Building your portfolio with Kaggle

Kaggle's claim to be the *"home of data science"* has to be taken into perspective. As we have discussed at length, Kaggle is open to everyone willing to compete to figure out the best models in predictive tasks according to a given evaluation metric.

There are no restrictions based on where you are in the world, your education, or your proficiency in predictive modeling. Sometimes there are also competitions that are not predictive in nature, for instance, reinforcement learning competitions, algorithmic challenges, and analytical contests that accommodate a larger audience than just data scientists. However, making the best predictions from data according to a metric is the core purpose of Kaggle competitions.

Real-world data science, instead, has many facets. First, your priority is to solve problems, and the metric for scoring your model is simply a more or less exact measurement of how well it solves the problem. You may not only be dealing with a single metric but have to take into account multiple ones. In addition, problems are open to being solved in different ways and much depends on how you formulate them.

As for data, you seldom get specifications about the data you have to use, and you can modify any existing dataset to fit your needs. Sometimes you can even create your own dataset from scratch if you need to. There are no indications about how to put data together or process it. When solving a problem, you also have to consider:

- Technical debt
- Maintainability of the solution over time
- Time and computational costs for running the solution
- Explainability of the workings of the model
- Impact on the operating income (if the real-world project is a business one, increasing profits and/or reducing costs is the leitmotif)
- Communication of the results at different levels of complexity and abstraction

Often, all these aspects count more than raw performance against evaluation metrics.

 Technical debt is a term more common in software development than data science, though it is a relevant one. For technical debt, you should consider whatever you have to do in order to deliver your project faster but that you will have to redo again later at a higher cost. The classic paper *Hidden Technical Debt in Machine Learning Systems* by *David Sculley* and other Google researchers should enlighten you on the relevance of the problem for data science: https://proceedings.neurips.cc/paper/2015/file/86df7dcfd896fcaf2674f757a2463eba-Paper.pdf

Not all this expertise can be supplemented by Kaggle competitions. Most of this should be gained by direct practice and experience-building in an enterprise environment. Yet, the knowledge and skills attached to Kaggle competitions are not completely separate from many of the considerations we discussed above, and they are a good complement to many of the enterprise-level data science processes. By competing on Kaggle, you are being exposed to different types of data and problems; you need to execute extensive feature engineering and fast iterations of model hypotheses; you also have to devise methods of putting together state-of-the-art solutions using common open-source packages. This is a set of valuable skills, and it should be promoted on your side. The best way to do so is to build a **portfolio**, a collection of your solutions and work based on Kaggle competitions and other resources from Kaggle.

In order to build a portfolio from Kaggle competitions, you can take multiple approaches. The easiest is to leverage the facilities offered by Kaggle, especially the Datasets, Notebooks, and Discussions.

Gilberto Titericz

https://www.kaggle.com/titericz

Before we proceed, we present a discussion on career opportunities derived from Kaggle in our interview with *Gilberto Titericz*. He is a Grandmaster in Competitions and Discussions, the former number 1 in rankings, and the current number 1 in total gold medals from Kaggle competitions. He is also a Senior Data Scientist at NVIDIA and was featured not long ago in an article on Wired on the topic (https://www.wired.com/story/solve-these-tough-data-problems-and-watch-job-offers-roll-in/).

What's your favourite kind of competition and why? In terms of techniques and solving approaches, what is your specialty on Kaggle?

Since I started to compete on Kaggle in 2011, the types of competitions that I prefer are the ones with structured tabular data. The techniques that I use more in Kaggle are target encoding of categorical features (there are infinite ways to do it wrong) and stacking ensembles.

How do you approach a Kaggle competition? How different is this approach to what you do in your day-to-day work?

Kaggle is a great playground for machine learning. The main difference from real-life projects is that in Kaggle we already have the problem very well defined and formatted, the dataset created, the target variable built, and the metric chosen. So, I always start a Kaggle competition playing with EDA. Understanding the problem and knowing the dataset is one of the keys to an advantage over other players. After that, I spend some time defining a proper validation strategy. This is very important to validate your model correctly and in line with the way that Kaggle scores the private test set. Besides the fact that using a stratified Kfold is something that works for most binary classification problems, we must evaluate if a grouped Kfold or a time-based split must be used in order to validate correctly, avoid overfitting, and mimic, as much as possible, the private test set. After that, it is important to spend some time running experiments on feature engineering and hyperparameter optimization. Also, I always end a competition with at least one Gradient Boosted Tree model and one deep learning-based approach. A blend of such diverse approaches is very important to increase diversity in the predictions and boost the competition metric.

Has Kaggle helped you in your career? If so, how?

Yes, Kaggle was the main reason I changed the direction of my career. Up to 2016 I worked as an electronic engineer, and due to everything that I learned competing since 2011 I was able to switch to the data science area. Kaggle helped me to understand the concepts of machine learning and apply everything I learned from the theory. In addition, Kaggle is an excellent place for experimentation, where you can download a dataset and play with it to extract the maximum information possible from the data. That, combined with the competition environment, makes it perfect to learn coding and machine learning, and at the same time, it gets addictive and makes you want to learn more and more. Winning a few competitions puts your name at the top of the leaderboard and this is priceless for anyone's career. Headhunters all around the world look at Kaggle to find good matches for their positions and the knowledge and experience gained from competitions can boost any career.

How have you built up your portfolio thanks to Kaggle?

Once I joined Kaggle, I spent some years learning all the techniques, algorithms, and tricks to extract more information from data and boost the metrics as much as possible. High accuracy is the main goal of most of the competitions, but to do that relying on luck alone is almost impossible; knowledge and experience play a big role when the goal is to win or at least finish in the gold medal zone. The number of medals I have in Kaggle competitions is my portfolio; up to now (11/2021) it's 58 gold and 47 silver, which summarizes well the ML experience I got from Kaggle. Taking into account that each competition runs for at least 1 month, this is more than 105 consecutive months of experience doing competitive ML.

In your experience, what do inexperienced Kagglers often overlook? What do you know now that you wish you'd known when you first started?

Novices often overlook a proper validation strategy. That doesn't just happen in Kaggle; I've seen data scientists all around the world building models and neglecting one of the most important things in the experimentation theory. There is no general rule when setting a proper validation strategy, but the data scientist must take into account how the model is going to be used in the future, and make the validation as close as possible to that.

What mistakes have you made in competitions in the past?

Several mistakes; it is impossible to list them all. I have probably made all the possible combinations of mistakes. The good thing about mistakes is that you can learn from them. Once you make a mistake and you detect it, it is very likely that you won't make it again. The main mistake people make in Kaggle is to trust in the leaderboard score and not in their local validation score. Overfitting to the leaderboard is a constant in Kaggle and this is the main difference from the real world. In a real project, we must build a strong validation strategy that we can trust, because in the real world the models will be tested on real data and you have only one chance to hit the mark, not multiple submissions per day.

Are there any particular tools or libraries that you would recommend using for data analysis and machine learning?

Some years ago I would have recommended R, but taking into account how fast Python is growing in the ML space and how generic and easy it is to use in production, I recommend to anyone starting ML that they learn it. In terms of libraries for tabular data, I recommend pandas for manipulation, and if you want speed then go with cuDF (the RAPIDS.ai GPU version of pandas). For EDA, I recommend using DataFrame with the Seaborn or Matplotlib libraries, and for machine learning Scikit-learn, SciPy, cuML (GPU), XGBoost, LightGBM, CatBoost, and PyTorch. Keep in mind that building a simple XGBoost model using the raw features is fast and can give you a good benchmark to compare with further models.

What's the most important thing someone should keep in mind or do when they're entering a competition?

Entering a Kaggle competition and submitting a public Notebook is easy, but finishing a competition in the gold zone can be extremely challenging. So the most important thing, at least for me, is to keep in mind that independent of the final ranking, we should use Kaggle to have fun and learn as much as possible from the discussion forums, from the public Notebooks, and even from the post-deadline winners' posts describing their ideas and what worked.

Also keep in mind that what makes a competition winner is not just replicating what everyone else is doing, but thinking out of the box and coming up with novel ideas, strategies, architectures, and approaches.

Do you use other competition platforms? How do they compare to Kaggle?

I have won a couple of competitions on other competition platforms, but the main difference compared to Kaggle is the number of users. Kaggle has 171k active users as of November 2021, which makes the forums, Notebooks, and dataset interactions much richer in terms of content. Also, Kaggle offers something unique: Notebooks where you can write and run code for free using Google servers, which can be priceless if you don't have access to good hardware.

Leveraging Notebooks and discussions

Besides rankings themselves, Notebooks are the way to get you noticed on Kaggle because they simultaneously demonstrate how you solve problems, how you present ideas, and how you code them. Conceived as a way to easily and openly share solutions and ideas among participants, Notebooks are the most important tool (after rankings) for demonstrating abilities that are appreciated by employers.

In fact, one of the most important changes in the world of data science in recent years has been its transition from a game of outstanding talents (unicorn data scientists) to a team game, where data scientists have to collaborate with each other and with other departments to ensure the success of a project. Consequently, in their hiring processes, companies often care more about you being able to communicate ideas and results, as well as coding in a clean and effective way.

In the previous section, we discussed how real-world projects require a wider range of skills, ranging from dealing with technical debt to designing cost-effective solutions. You can still demonstrate these skills on Kaggle, even if they are not the ones that will make you win a competition. Notebooks are the best tools for doing this.

Refer to *Chapter 3, Working and Learning with Kaggle Notebooks,* for an introduction to Kaggle Notebooks.

You will find different types of Notebooks on Kaggle. As a good approximation, we can group them into four categories:

- Solutions and ideas for ranking in a competition
- **Exploratory data analysis (EDA)** on the data
- Tutorials explaining machine learning models or data science principles
- Fresh implementations of models derived from papers or other original solutions

Each of these can provide you with an edge by means of an interesting set of skills. If solutions and ideas for competitions are the classic way to demonstrate that you know how to tackle a complex problem in data science, the other three can show the world that you can:

- Manipulate, represent, and extract visual and non-visual insights from data (EDA), which is a skill deemed very important in every setting, from scientific research to business
- Educate on data science, opening the door to roles in education, mentorship, and developer advocacy
- Translate research into practice, a key skill at a time when innovations in data science (especially in deep learning) appear daily and need to be translated into working solutions quickly

Even if you don't rank highly in Kaggle competitions or have astonishing solutions to present, these other three kinds of Notebooks (EDA, tutorials, and paper implementations) can provide you opportunities in the real world if you can promote them in the best way. To do so, you need to understand how to code readable and interesting Notebooks, which is something that you learn from practice and experience. Since it is an art, our suggestion is to learn from others, especially from the Notebooks Grandmasters who place high in the Notebooks user ranking (https://www.kaggle.com/rankings?group=notebooks&page=1&pageSize=20).

We recommend you look at what kind of Notebooks they have developed, how they have arranged their work using figures, how they have structured their code, and then, finally, based on your skills and interests, try to imitate one of their Notebooks. We also suggest that you do not bet your chances for success only on code and charts, but also on the **narrative** that you present. No matter whether you are showing off a solution, teaching, or implementing a neural architecture in TensorFlow, how you explain the Notebook's cells with words is very important in terms of leaving a lasting positive impression.

Aside from browsing the Notebooks of high rankers, there is also a way to be notified about less mainstream – yet still finely crafted – Notebooks that have recently appeared on Kaggle. The astrophysicist and passionate Kaggle user Heads or Tails, *Martin Henze* (`https://www.kaggle.com/headsortails`), publishes on the discussion forums a weekly *Notebooks of the Week: Hidden Gems* post, a collection of the most interesting Notebooks around. At the moment, there are already over 100 volumes and the author continues to search Kaggle for anything that could prove interesting. If you would like to be updated about cool Notebooks, just follow Martin Henze's profile on Kaggle or check if he has published something new under his discussions from time to time.

If you love digging through Notebooks looking for ideas and learning from them, we never tire of stressing that you should not brainlessly copy other people's work. There are many Notebooks on Kaggle, and often someone copies one, makes some small changes, and re-presents the Notebook to other Kagglers as if it were their own original idea. It is also customary to cherry-pick a function, or part of the code from a Notebook, and insert it into your own. In both these cases, please remember always to quote the source and the author. If you cannot retrace something to the original author, even referring to the last Notebook where you found the code you used is enough. While the main purpose of a showcase is to display your own efforts and skills, it is very important to recognize that some parts of your code or some ideas are taken from elsewhere. Aside from being a sign of respect toward your fellow Kagglers, a source attribution highlights that you are knowledgeable enough to recognize other people's efforts and inventions, and that you know how to employ them in your own work.

In a minor way, discussions on Kaggle's forums can help you get noticed for specific roles in data science and software development. Initially, discussions on Kaggle were just for communicating with organizers or for asking pressing questions about the competition itself. At the end of competitions, participants seldom felt compelled to present or discuss their solutions. However, since discussions obtained their own user rankings and mastery grades, you have been able to find much more information on forums.

Refer to *Chapter 4*, *Leveraging Discussion Forums*, for an introduction to discussions on Kaggle.

In our experience, discussions on Kaggle can be split into four categories:

- Competition solutions that explain in detail (sometimes with the help of an associated Notebook) how a team managed to reach a certain position on the private leaderboard

- Help with and an explanation of requirements during a competition
- Thanks, compliments, and chit-chat
- Posts that help and tutor other competitors, explaining things to them

We have observed that excelling in the last type of post and being widely noticed for it can help you achieve the role of developer advocate, especially if you also have other active channels where you interact with your fellow data scientists (for instance, a Twitch or YouTube channel, a Twitter account, or a Medium blog).

With the growth of developer advocate roles in both large companies and start-ups, there is an important demand for experts skilled at helping other data scientists and developers in their projects. If you want to learn more about this role, the following article on `draft.dev` is quite explanatory and exhaustive: `https://draft.dev/learn/what-is-a-developer-advocate`.

Leveraging Datasets

Kaggle competitions are often criticized for presenting data that is already cleaned, well arranged, and far from representative of data found in the real world. Our point of view is slightly different; we find the data that Kaggle presents in competitions can also be quite messy or noisy. Sometimes the data presented will not actually suffice in terms of quality and quantity for getting a top score, and you will need to look around for additional data on the internet.

What Kaggle does miss out with regard to data in a data science project is the process of collecting and gathering data in organized repositories and files, a process that, in real-world settings, is not possible to standardize because it differs from company to company and problem to problem. Data handling in the real world should mostly be learned on the field.

The introduction of datasets into Kaggle was aimed at mitigating the idea that Kaggle was just focused on modeling problems. Kaggle Datasets are very helpful in this sense because they allow you to create and upload your own data and document the features and their values; they also require you to manage your data over time by planning the frequency with which you are going to update or completely replace it.

 Refer to *Chapter 2, Organizing Data with Datasets*, for an introduction to Kaggle Datasets.

More interestingly, in Kaggle Datasets, you are also given the opportunity to attach different analyses and models built using Kaggle Notebooks, uploaded from your data or a competition. These models could be work you came up with during a competition, or something you devised because you studied the uploaded data attentively and found a set of interesting problems you could solve with it.

In addition, Kaggle Datasets offer you a template to check for the completeness of the meta-information accompanying your data. A description, tags, a license, sources, and the frequency of updates: these are only a few of the required pieces of information (used to calculate a usability score) that will help anyone using your data to understand how to use it. You may even point out (in the description or in discussions) tasks for the dataset that relate to pending work you would like to do with it. This is a good way to communicate your full understanding of the potential value of the data you have uploaded.

 Previously, Tasks were part of the Kaggle Dataset functionality, but they have recently been removed: `https://www.kaggle.com/product-feedback/292674`. Nevertheless, you can use the data description and discussions to point out what you expect your data could be used for.

All these characteristics make Kaggle Datasets a very good way to show off your experience with problems on Kaggle and, in general, your ability with data and machine learning algorithms, because they allow you to:

- Publish and maintain a dataset
- Demonstrate that you have understood the value of the data with a tasks roadmap
- Show coded and fully working solutions (since Kaggle Notebooks can immediately work on the same data, without any preparation), ranging from data preparation to explanatory data analysis to predictive modeling

We strongly recommend using Kaggle Datasets for showing off the work you have done during Kaggle competitions or on any other project, because they separate your work from others' and integrate data and Notebooks. In short, Kaggle Datasets can demonstrate to anyone a working solution that you have implemented. There is a downside, though: you are mostly tied to a Notebook environment (even when you use scripting), which is not perfectly transparent in terms of the package and version requirements necessary for someone to know to run the code in other environments.

In fact, Kaggle Notebooks depend on a Docker environment (`https://www.docker.com/`) set by a configuration file, a **Dockerfile**, that determines which versions have been installed. When browsing a Notebook, it is not immediately evident what version of packages are being used until you inspect this configuration file. For this purpose, as well as for replicating the settings, the Dockerfile can be found on the Kaggle repository on GitHub (`https://github.com/Kaggle/docker-python/blob/main/Dockerfile.tmpl`), though it changes over time and you may need to keep track of the one used in your work.

Finally, in addition to this aspect, don't forget that getting even a glimpse of a Dataset and its related Notebooks requires access to the Kaggle community.

Gabriel Preda

`https://www.kaggle.com/gpreda`

We had an inspiring career-oriented talk with *Gabriel Preda*, a Kaggle Grandmaster in Datasets, Notebooks, and Discussions, and Principal Data Scientist at Endava. Gabriel has a PhD in Computational Electromagnetics and had a long career in software development before devoting himself completely to data science. When he discovered Kaggle, he felt at home on the platform and invested a lot of time and effort into it, which paid dividends for him professionally.

Has Kaggle helped you in your career? How?

Kaggle helped me to accelerate my learning curve in data science. Before Kaggle, I was looking all around for sources of information or problems to solve, but it was not very methodical or effective. On Kaggle, I found a community of people interested in the same things as me. I was able to see the work of top experts in the field, learn from their published Notebooks with analyses or models, get insights from them, ask them questions, and even compete against them. I was mostly in data analysis at the time I joined Kaggle, but very quickly I started to compete; that means learning how to build, validate, and iteratively improve models. After around two years on Kaggle, I switched my career; I went from managing software projects to a full-time data science job. Kaggle also gave me some visibility, and during interviews with candidates at my present company they mentioned that they wanted to join because they saw that I worked there.

Have you ever used something you have done on Kaggle as part of your portfolio to show potential employers?

I use my Kaggle portfolio as the main source of information for potential employers; my LinkedIn profile points to my Kaggle profile. Also, in recent years, employers have become more aware about Kaggle, and some of them ask specifically about your Kaggle profile. There are also potential employers that make very clear that they do not consider Kaggle relevant. I disagree with this view; personally, before interviewing candidates, I normally check their GitHub and Kaggle profiles. I find them extremely relevant. A good Kaggle profile will demonstrate not only technical skills and experience with certain languages, tools, techniques, or problem-solving skills, but also how well someone is able to communicate through discussions and Notebooks. This is a very important quality for a data scientist.

You reached Grandmaster in Notebooks (Kernels) first, then in Discussions, and finally in Datasets. Can you tell us about your journey?

I became the seventh Kernels Grandmaster and I got as high as the third rank. For maybe two years I think I was in the top 10 in the Kernels hierarchy as well. I started writing Kernels primarily to improve my knowledge of the R language while analyzing datasets I found more interesting. I also experimented with all kinds of techniques, including polygon clips, building dual meshes of Voronoi polygons, and 2D Delaunay tessellation. I gradually started to focus on exploratory data analysis, followed by building models for datasets and then for competitions. Also, once I started to compete more, I started to write Kernels for competing in Python. About the same time, I began to notice that some of my Kernels attracted attention from Kagglers, primarily upvotes and forks but also favorable comments. Some of my Kernels written for exploration of data in active competitions reached a very wide audience and brought me many gold medals; therefore, I reached the Master and then Grandmaster tier. Currently, I do not publish many Kernels related to competitions; mostly I create starting Kernels related to datasets that I publish.

Next, I also obtained the Discussions Grandmaster level. I never anticipated that I would reach this tier in discussions. First, I started commenting on other people's Kernels. Then, gradually, as I got more involved in competitions, most of my comments were in the discussion sections of active competitions, either asking questions about topics of interest in these competitions or starting new topics, for example, suggesting solutions for one problem in a competition or collections of resources to address various open issues related to the competition. I want to mention a special set of comments that I added. As a Kaggle Kernels Grandmaster (one of the first), I frequently upvoted new Kagglers' Notebooks when I discovered very good content.

In such cases, I try to find a few moments to also praise (especially if the content is of good quality) the achievement of the author. Especially to beginners, giving not only the expression of your appreciation by upvoting their work, but also adding some positive feedback about their contribution, might give them a boost of confidence so that they will invest more in learning and contributing even more on Kaggle. I like to do this, and I hope it helps. I once also compiled a list of recommendations about how to comment on Kaggle. This is the list: be short (but not too short); be specific; provide information, not opinions; praise other people's work when you have the opportunity; keep calm and try to be helpful; do not tag people in your comments unless it makes sense (for example, if it is a discussion, and you need to direct your comment to someone that addressed you in that thread).

The last Grandmaster tier I reached is in Datasets. This is also the tier where I reached the highest ranking, second. My progress through the ranks was slow. I started with something I liked. Getting a high profile in Datasets requires investment in curating, cleaning, and documenting the data. If it is not something that you really like, you most probably will not keep going. I pursued things that were important to me but also to a wider community: to my country, my continent, or the whole world. I published datasets about elections in my country, and about various social, demographic, and economic topics in Europe. I focused on subjects of actuality, that were both relevant and of high importance for the community. For example, during the pandemic, I published datasets on COVID-19 cases, about vaccinations, tests, and virus variants both from my country and worldwide. I captured data that went beyond simple numerical, tabular values. Text data, especially originating from direct contributions from people, provided important insights for many people. One of my most upvoted datasets consists of collections of Reddit posts and comments or Twitter posts (tweets) on subjects as diverse as vaccine myths, cricket, pandemics, sports events, and political personalities. I invested significantly in automating data collection, data cleaning, and data processing scripts. This saved me precious time (especially for datasets updated frequently – some of them were collected continuously, with scripts triggered every hour) but also made it possible to have better control of the process. Every time I publish a new dataset, I also write one or more starting Kernels. These Kernels are not intended to reach a large audience. I create them as helper Kernels for potential users of my Datasets, so that they find it easier to use the data. In many cases, I prefer to keep the original data (as I collected it, or downloaded from an alternative source) and include a Kernel for data cleaning, transformation, and preliminary analysis as well as the result of this process, the data in a more accessible format. In this way, I try to capture in the dataset more than the data itself; I also provide information about techniques for data transformation.

Arranging your online presence beyond Kaggle

Since Kaggle Datasets and Notebooks require a Kaggle account, you have to take into account that not everyone may already have one or want to create one just to look at your work. You also have to consider alternatives that are more accessible. More frequently, Kagglers choose to use a project on GitHub (https://github.com/), write an article on Medium (https://medium.com/) as well as other publishing platforms, or post on their own blog. There are other opportunities to promote your work and skills, however, such as:

- Publishing code relevant to Kaggle competitions that can be executed from the browser on https://deepnote.com/

- Setting up a Discord community that gathers Kagglers, such as *Abhishek Thakur*'s MLSpace (https://discord.com/invite/4RMwz64gdH), or running a YouTube channel (also from Abhishek Thakur: https://www.youtube.com/channel/UCBPRJjIWfyNG4X-CRbnv78A)

- Setting up a Twitch channel like *Rob Mulla*'s, where he demonstrates coding relevant to Kaggle competitions: https://www.twitch.tv/medallionstallion (also on GitHub: https://github.com/RobMulla/twitch-stream-projects)

- Delivering a weekly newsletter on Kaggle news, like *Shotaro Ishihara*: https://www.getrevue.co/profile/upura

- Interviewing Kagglers and other data science experts as *Sanyam Bhutani* is doing, and broadcasting the interviews using videos, podcasts, and blog posts: https://chaitimedatascience.com/ (you can browse the dataset containing all the data about the interviews held so far, prepared by *Rohan Rao*: https://www.kaggle.com/rohanrao/chai-time-data-science)

As you can deduce, there are really quite a lot of opportunities and media through which you can diffuse your work and skills on Kaggle, depending on what you want to achieve. In this chapter, our focus is on just blogs and a GitHub presence (which are the most common choices and quite effective), but you are free to decide on any different approach you deem suitable for your purposes.

Blogs and publications

Writing can be a way both to refine your knowledge – because you need to read up on a topic in order to write about it – and to let others know about you and your skills. Getting famous for your writing helps you in various ways, from being spotted by recruiters and companies to building your connections for both Kaggle competitions and your wider professional life.

Social media (LinkedIn, Twitter, and Facebook) allows you to post ideas and short pieces of text, and this is something that we do suggest you leverage. Given that data science and Kaggle competition topics require discussion and reasoning at length, the best approach, however, is to write **long articles** and publish them by means of a blog or a website that publishes writing. Ideally, we suggest you coordinate your communication between social media and your articles in order to promote them, with dedicated posts announcing them or discussing key points in your writing.

Let's first discuss how and where you could publish your articles.

An article on Medium, especially on **Medium publications** such as Towards Data Science (https://towardsdatascience.com/), can get a lot of attention. Medium publications are shared spaces for stories written around a common theme or topic, usually by multiple authors. As a website, Medium can reach a wide audience of readers and some publications have a very good reputation in the data science community for the quality of their articles. A publication can have one or more editors who select the pieces and assure that their contents are consistent with the policies of the publication and its quality level. Medium publications where you could post your articles are:

- **Towards Data Science**, as mentioned (https://towardsdatascience.com/questions-96667b06af5)
- **Better Programming** (https://betterprogramming.pub/write-for-us-5c4bcba59397)
- **Mlearning.ai** (https://medium.com/mlearning-ai/mlearning-ai-submission-suggestions-b51e2b130bfb)
- **Becoming Human** (https://becominghuman.ai/write-for-us-48270209de63)
- **Towards AI** (https://pub.towardsai.net/submit-your-medium-story-to-towards-ai-a4fa7e8b141d)

Each of these publications has the great advantage of already having a large audience, probably larger than your following on social media. You will get more readers than you would probably expect, reaching people at companies as well as other professionals you can network with.

Besides Medium, these other websites might also accept your publications:

- **Hacker Noon** (https://www.publish.hackernoon.com/): Quite popular among tech bloggers and contains anything tech-related (it is quite generalist). With a monthly audience of four million people, it is the right place if you want to reach many tech lovers with anything tech-related. Being featured on the top pages is extremely difficult and a double-edged sword: you will get a lot of attention, as well as many critics.

- **Dev.to** (https://dev.to/): Mainly has an audience of developers (almost eight hundred thousand) and features articles and tutorials on coding. Your posts should be more focused on the quality and efficacy of your code (modeling is in the background).

- **FreeCodeCamp** (https://www.freecodecamp.org/news/developer-news-style-guide/): More focused on tutorials; people go there to learn how to code. It is ideal for promoting courses on machine learning and promoting new packages.

- **Analytics Vidhya** (https://www.analyticsvidhya.com/about/write/): Quite popular in India; it is more centered around articles explaining machine learning and deep learning building blocks.

- **KDnuggets** (https://www.kdnuggets.com/news/submissions.html): One of the oldest publications in data mining. It still has quite a lot of followers (one million unique visitors in March 2021) among the old guard of data scientists and academics.

Each publication has strong and weak points and differs in the audience it reaches, so you have to decide which one better suits your content. Start by browsing the publications they offer in order to understand how your writing could fit in.

Of course, if you would prefer, you can instead use your own blog. Having your own blog has its advantages, such as no advertising or editorial scrutiny over what you write. On the other hand, you cannot leverage a pre-existing audience and you will have to work to create one by promoting your articles on social media. You can set up your own website from scratch on a web domain of your choice or you could create your own blog on GitHub, too.

 If you decide to use GitHub (since it is free and you may already use it as a repository for your code), here is a simple and fast guide to creating GitHub blog posts: http://jmcglone.com/guides/github-pages/

If you need something even more automated, using a platform such as *Jeremy Howard*'s **fastpages** (https://github.com/fastai/fastpages) can simplify the way you deal with writing content together with code examples, because it automatically converts notebooks and Word documents into blog pages and publishes them for you.

If you prefer to be completely independent and set up your own website, this will require more effort and some expense; domain names and web space are not free. In this case, self-promotion of your content becomes critical.

The main advantage of writing about your solutions is the storytelling element, because you have to accompany your code snippets with descriptions and explanations and you need to write in a more verbose way than you could do in a Notebook. In a sense, how you describe your work becomes as important as the code you write. By adjusting the tone of your writing, you can reach different types of audiences. Writing concepts in an accessible way means you will enlarge your audience and connect with more professionals. Writing in a highly technical way instead could impress more potential companies that may consider hiring you, though limiting the number of readers you get.

Since writing is a very personal act and our hints and suggestions won't apply to every scenario, our general suggestion is to decide beforehand the purpose of your writing and who you would like to reach with it.

GitHub

Aside from writing articles and having a code repository you can direct readers to, having your code on GitHub will also help you not to reinvent the wheel in every competition you enter. You can store the code you want to reuse in a project or in **Gists** (`https://docs.github.com/en/github/writing-on-github/editing-and-sharing-content-with-gists`), which are small snippets of code that can be accessed individually.

Even if it may appeal to you to leave all your code on Kaggle, with time you will find it difficult to access and you may even have trouble finding it altogether. This is because you cannot arrange your Kaggle Notebooks into separate projects; they will just be presented as a long list that you can order by a few attributes such as the number of votes or when you last ran the Notebook. GitHub makes it much easier to find what you need and reuse it. For instance, you can create scripts containing all your code and then download and import them into a Kaggle Notebook without needing to copy anything.

In the following example, we download and reuse helper functions for a tabular neural network:

```
!wget https://raw.githubusercontent.com/lmassaron/deep_learning_for_
tabular_data/master/tabular.py

# Importing from Tabular
from tabular import gelu, Mish, mish
from tabular import TabularTransformer, DataGenerator
```

A wget command will directly access code on GitHub and download it onto the disk of the Notebook; afterward, you can just import the functions and classes that you need from it. To obtain the link providing direct access to your code, you just need to look for the file containing it on the GitHub repository and then click on the **Raw** button on the header of the page:

Figure 13.1: The header of a visualized file on GitHub. Notice the Raw button on the upper right part of the header bar.

After clicking on the **Raw** button, you will be taken to the web address where the file is stored on GitHub. You can use that web address to refer to the file from outside of GitHub.

GitHub is also useful also for storing images that you can use on Kaggle discussions (since you can no longer upload images on the Kaggle forums). In the case of images, you won't have a **Raw** button to click, but you can instead right-click on the image and open the file in another tab; this will have the same effect.

GitHub is another great way to showcase your work, but given the nature of the website (it is targeted at developers) and the content you can put on it (files containing code), you should expect a very technical audience. In companies, human resources probably won't look too deeply at your GitHub account, instead stopping at the README.md, which should therefore be well written and visually appealing. Recruiting managers, on the other hand, will be more interested in the code in your projects. You should put some effort into having well-structured code in your files, procedures, and classes, also including the instructions necessary for the installation and replication of your results.

You will have to use tools such as conda (https://docs.conda.io/en/latest/) or poetry (https://python-poetry.org/) to ensure the correct packages are installed for your code to work. In order to give the best structure to your project, you'll probably need something like CookieCutter (https://drivendata.github.io/cookiecutter-data-science/). Using a template for your projects, like the ones CookieCutter provides, enables your code to be arranged into specific directories easily and will provide the files that allow its usage and understanding. A CookieCutter template will make your project easier to read, understand, and maintain.

Finally, for managing your experiments and data sources, you will also need some **version control system** for the data being used, not just for your code, for instance using **Data Version Control (DVC:** `https://dvc.org/`). All these resources and the skills you need to run them properly (creating your environment, structuring your project, versioning data and models) are closer to software engineering than data science competencies. They are not so relevant on Kaggle – or can be done in simple ways – and will require effort and learning. Yet, they will become part of the capabilities that you will present with your projects on GitHub, improving your chances of making a good impression on job interviewers.

If you want to put in live demonstrations of your models, you have a few different options. The easiest is having the code running on the original Notebooks (just by putting a link to your Kaggle Notebook in the `README.md` file of your GitHub project) or on **Google Colab**. To have the Notebook you stored on GitHub run automatically in Google Colab, just post its link with the domain changed from `github.com` to `githubtocolab.com`: the link will open your Notebook in Colab.

The most impressive showcase you can prepare, however, is using **HuggingFace Spaces** (`https://huggingface.co/spaces`) to demonstrate how your Kaggle model could be used in an online application. Spaces are a simple way to host machine learning demonstrations and create online portfolios of your work, as explained in the documentation (`https://huggingface.co/docs/hub/spaces`). They are limited to 16GB of RAM and 8 CPU cores, but they are free and sufficient for demonstrating how your model can run in a dedicated application. You can install your dependencies on the HuggingFace remote machine, sync code and models with GitHub, or build an app using `Streamlit` (`https://streamlit.io/`) or `Gradio` (`https://gradio.app/`).

As an example, *Rashmi Banthia*, a Kaggle Expert and a Teaching Fellow at Harvard University (`https://www.kaggle.com/rashmibanthia`), has posted a demonstration of her model from the *Sartorious Cell Instance Segmentation* competition: `https://huggingface.co/spaces/rashmi/Cell-Instance-Segmentation-MMDetection`. By presenting your model together with a few examples in a real-time demonstration, you can immediately convey its effectiveness even to a non-machine learning audience.

Monitoring competition updates and newsletters

By now, you can see that it is important to showcase your work on Kaggle so you can communicate to the world your interest in certain types of models and data problems. From this perspective, it is important that you are always aware of the opportunities offered by competitions.

The main way to do this is to visit the Kaggle website frequently and agree to receive emails from them. You can set this option from your profile, on the **Notification and e-mail settings** page, where you can agree to receive notifications both on the site and by email. You can also choose to receive emails containing tips on new features and initiatives on Kaggle, along with news about recently launched competitions:

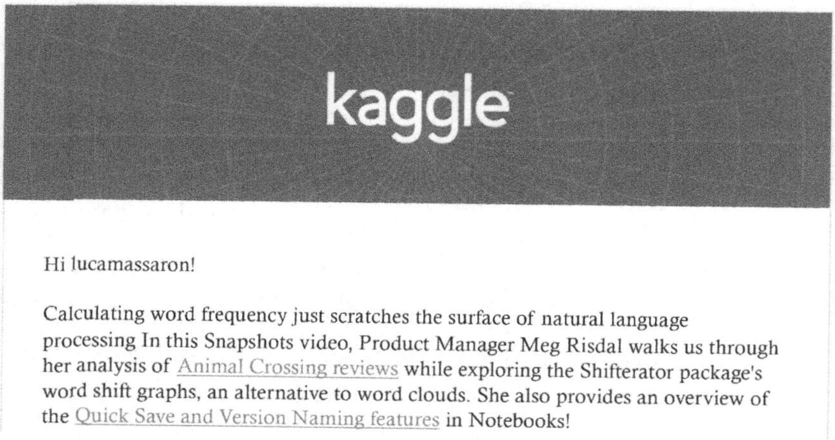

Hi lucamassaron!

Calculating word frequency just scratches the surface of natural language processing In this Snapshots video, Product Manager Meg Risdal walks us through her analysis of Animal Crossing reviews while exploring the Shifterator package's word shift graphs, an alternative to word clouds. She also provides an overview of the Quick Save and Version Naming features in Notebooks!

Figure 13.2: A Kaggle email announcing a series of videos from the Kaggle Team

If you are a Twitter user, you'll find it useful to follow a couple of profiles to keep you updated about new stuff on Kaggle. **Kagoole** (`https://twitter.com/kagoole`) is a web application that can inform you about new competitions and also, in its Heroku app form (`https://kagoole.herokuapp.com/`), provides you with solutions for past competitions. It was created by Doarakko (`https://github.com/Doarakko/`). The other Twitter profile you could follow is **Is he Kerneler?** (`https://twitter.com/HKerneler`), created by Regonn (`https://github.com/regonn/`), which tells you how much time is left before each active Kaggle competition closes.

As we know from *Chapter 1*, Kaggle is not the only organization that holds data science competitions. In order to keep better track of what is actually happening both on Kaggle and other data science competition websites, we suggest using websites such as `https://mlcontests.com/` or `https://ods.ai/competitions` that monitor all ongoing competitions on Kaggle, as well as on other platforms such as AICrowd and DrivenData. For instance, `mlcontests.com` provides you with information on prizes, deadlines, and useful links for each competition.

It also gives you cloud GPU comparisons in terms of performance, machines, and prices. You can register your email and receive much of this information directly to your inbox.

Summary

In this chapter, we discussed how to showcase your work and how this can be valuable for progressing your career. It helps you to demonstrate capabilities that, while (of course) not covering the entire span of your data science knowledge and experience, still represent a great asset.

In order to display your work, you can either use Kaggle resources or external resources. Kaggle resources offer you an integrated environment and, provided you have everything at hand, are quite accessible and quick to set up. External resources (Medium publications, GitHub, HuggingFace Spaces, and so on) are more widely known and accessible for the majority of recruiters, human resource officers, and hiring managers because they use them routinely.

In the next chapter, we will complete our discussion of the opportunities that Kaggle competitions offer you by talking about network building and how to use your Kaggle efforts to get an interview.

Join our book's Discord space

Join the book's Discord workspace for a monthly *Ask me Anything* session with the authors:

```
https://packt.link/KaggleDiscord
```

14

Finding New Professional Opportunities

After introducing how to better highlight your work and achievements in competitions in the previous chapter, we will now conclude our overview of how Kaggle can positively affect your career. This last chapter discusses the best ways to leverage all your efforts to find new professional opportunities. We expect you now have all the previously described instruments (your Kaggle Discussions, Notebooks, and Datasets, and a GitHub account presenting quite a few projects derived from Kaggle), so this chapter will move to softer aspects: how to network and how to present your Kaggle experience to recruiters and companies.

It is common knowledge that networking opens up many possibilities, from being contacted about new job opportunities that do not appear on public boards to having someone to rely on for data science problems you are not an expert in. Networking on Kaggle is principally related to team collaboration during competitions and connections built during meetups and other events organized by Kagglers.

 When it comes to job opportunities, as we have often repeated previously, Kaggle is not a widely recognized source used by human resources and hiring managers for selecting candidates. Some companies do take your Kaggle rankings and achievements into good consideration, but that's a special case, not the general rule. Typically, you should expect your Kaggle experience to be ignored or sometimes even criticized. Our experience tells us, however, that what you learn and practice on Kaggle is highly valuable and it can be promoted by showcasing your coding and modeling efforts, and also by being able to talk about your experiences working alone or in a team.

Here, we will cover:

- Building connections with other competition data scientists
- Participating in Kaggle Days and other Kaggle meetups
- Getting spotted and other job opportunities

Building connections with other competition data scientists

Connections are essential for finding a job, as they help you get into contact with people who may know about an opportunity before it becomes public and the search for potential candidates begins. In recent years, Kaggle has increasingly become a place where you can connect with other data scientists, collaborate, and make friends. In the past, competitions did not give rise to many exchanges on forums, and teams were heavily penalized in the global rankings because competition points were split equally among the team members. Improved rankings (see https://www.kaggle.com/general/14196) helped many Kagglers see teaming up in a more favorable light.

Teaming up in a Kaggle competition works fine if you already know the other team members and you already have an established approach to assigning tasks and collaborating remotely. In these situations, each team member already knows how to collaborate by:

- Taking on part of the experimentation agreed by the team members
- Collaborating with another team member to build a solution
- Exploring new solutions based on their skills and experience
- Preparing models and submissions so they are easily stacked or blended

If you are new to teaming, however, you will find it difficult either to enter a team or to organize one yourself. Unless you have contacts, it will be hard to get in touch with other people on the leaderboard. Firstly, not all of them will want to team up because they prefer to compete alone. Furthermore, some of the other competitors might be interested in teaming but will be too wary to accept your proposal. When forming a team with Kagglers you don't know, there are a few concerns:

- The person entering the team won't bring any value to the team
- The person entering the team won't actually collaborate but just be a freeloader
- The person entering the team has infringed (or will infringe) Kaggle rules, which will lead to the disqualification of the entire team

- The person entering the team is actually interested in spying and leaking information to other teams

Most of these situations are pathological in a competition, and you should be aware that these are common considerations that many make when evaluating whether or not to team up with another Kaggler for the first time. You can only dispel these perceived potential problems by presenting yourself as someone with a strong background in Kaggle; that is, someone who has taken part in some competitions alone and, in particular, published Notebooks and participated in discussions. This will add great credibility to your proposal and more likely bring you acceptance into a team.

When you have finally joined a team, it is important to establish **efficient and dedicated forms of communication** between the team members (for instance, by creating a channel on Slack or Discord). It is also essential to agree on daily operations that involve both:

- Deciding how to divide your experimentation efforts.
- Deciding how to use the daily submissions, which are limited in number (often a cause of conflict in the team). In the end, only the team leader chooses the final two submissions, but the process of getting there naturally involves discussion and disagreement. Be prepared to demonstrate to your teammates why you have decided on certain submissions as final by showing them your local cross-validation strategy and results.

After you have experienced working together in a team in a positive manner, you will surely have gained the respect and trust of other team members. In future competitions, you will probably find it easier to team up again with the same people, or join a different team that they are part of with their help.

The people you will meet and get to work with on Kaggle include data scientists, data enthusiasts, students, domain specialists, and more. Below, we speak to a diverse cross-section of Kagglers, who describe their day jobs and how Kaggle fits into their lives.

Yirun Zhang

https://www.kaggle.com/gogo827jz

Yirun Zhang is a **final-year PhD student** at King's College London. A Notebooks and Discussion Grandmaster, he was a member of the winning team in the *Jane Street Market Prediction* competition (https://www.kaggle.com/c/jane-street-market-prediction).

Can you tell us about yourself?

My research area lies in the field of applying machine learning algorithms to solving challenging problems in modern wireless communication networks such as time series forecasting, resource allocation, and optimization. I have also been involved in projects that study AI privacy, federated learning, and data compression and transmission.

Apart from daily PhD research, I have been active on Kaggle for almost two years, since the second year of my PhD. The first competition I took part in on Kaggle was Instant Gratification, *in which I utilized a diversity of machine learning and statistical methods from the* sklearn *library. This competition helped me develop a general sense of what a machine learning modeling pipeline is for Kaggle competitions.*

I have been actively sharing my knowledge with the community in terms of Notebooks and discussion posts on Kaggle, and am now a Kaggle Notebooks and Discussion Grandmaster. Through sharing and discussing with others on the forum, I have gained precious feedback and new knowledge, which has also helped me finally become the winner of a Kaggle competition recently.

Tell us a bit about the competition you won.

Jane Street Market Prediction *was a really tough one. The reason is that it was hard to build a robust cross-validation (CV) strategy and lots of people were just using the public leaderboard as the validation set. They were training a neural network for hundreds of epochs without using a validation strategy to overfit the public leaderboard. Our team tried hard to maintain our own CV strategy, and survived in the shake-up.*

How different is your approach to Kaggle from what you do in your day-to-day work?

Kaggle competitions are very different from my daily PhD research. The former is very tense and contains instant feedback, while the latter is a long-term process. However, I have found that the new knowledge and methodology I learn from Kaggle competitions is also very useful in my PhD research.

Osamu Akiyama

https://www.kaggle.com/osciiart

Osamu Akiyama, aka OsciiArt, is a Kaggler whose day job does not involve data science. He's a **medical doctor** at Osaka University Hospital and a Competitions Master.

Can you tell us about yourself?

I'm a second-year resident working at Osaka University Hospital. I received my master's degree in Life Science from Kyoto University. After I worked in an R&D job for a pharmaceutical company, I transferred to the Faculty of Medicine of Osaka University and I obtained a medical license for Japan.

I started to learn data science and AI on my own because I was shocked by AlphaGo. I started participating on Kaggle in order to learn and test my skills in data science and AI. My first competition was NOAA Fisheries Steller Sea Lion Population Count in 2017. I participate in Kaggle competitions constantly and I've got three gold medals.

Has Kaggle helped you in your career?

Because I'm not educated in information science, I used my results in Kaggle to demonstrate my skill when I applied for an internship at an AI company and when I applied to be a short-term student in an AI laboratory. As I'm just a medical doctor, I've never used my data science skills in my main job. However, thanks to my Kaggle results, I sometimes have the opportunity to participate in medical data research.

What is your favorite type of competition and why?

My favorite kind of competition is medical data competitions. I love to try finding some insight from the medical data using my knowledge of medicine.

How do you approach a Kaggle competition?

I love to find a secret characteristic of competition data that most other competitors are not aware of or to try a unique approach customized to the characteristics of competition data. Actually, such an approach is not successful in most cases, but still, it's fun to try.

Tell us about a particularly challenging competition you entered, and what insights you used to tackle the task.

I'd like to mention Freesound Audio Tagging 2019, which was a multi-label classification task for sound data. The training data was composed of a small amount of reliably labeled data (clean data) and a larger amount of data with unreliable labels (noisy data). Additionally, there was a difference between data distribution in the curated data and the noisy data. To tackle this difficulty, we used two strategies. The first was multitask learning, in which training on noisy data was treated as a different task from clean data. The second was pseudo-labeling (a kind of semi-supervised learning), in which noisy data was relabeled by predicted labels from a model trained with the clean data.

Do you use other competition platforms? How do they compare to Kaggle?

*I use Signate (*https://signate.jp/*) and guruguru (*https://www.guruguru.science/*). These are Japanese data science competition platforms. They are not as big as platforms like Kaggle; competitions on these platforms use smaller datasets than Kaggle in general, so it is easier to participate. Also, sometimes there are interesting competitions that are different from the ones on Kaggle.*

Mikel Bober-Irizar

https://www.kaggle.com/anokas

Mikel Bober-Irizar, aka Anokas, is a Competitions Grandmaster, a Master in Notebooks and Discussion, and a **machine learning scientist** at ForecomAI. He is also a **student of Computer Science** at the University of Cambridge and the youngest ever Grandmaster on Kaggle.

Can you tell us about yourself?

I joined Kaggle in 2016, back when I was 14 and I had no idea what I was doing – I had just read about machine learning online and it seemed cool. I started in my first few competitions by copying other people's public code from the forums and making small tweaks to them. Throughout a few competitions, I slowly gained an understanding of how things worked, motivated by trying to climb the leaderboard – until I started making good progress, which culminated in coming second in the Avito Duplicate Ads Competition later that year.

Since then, I have participated in 75 competitions, in 2018 becoming the youngest competition Grandmaster and the first ever Triple Master. I was since a Visiting Research Fellow at Surrey University, and I'm now studying Computer Science at the University of Cambridge, where I'm also doing research in machine learning and security.

What's your favorite kind of competition and why? In terms of techniques and solving approaches, what is your speciality on Kaggle?

I really enjoy competitions with lots of opportunity for feature engineering, and those with lots of different types of data, which allow you to be really creative in the approach you take to solving it – it's a lot more fun than a competition where everyone has to take the same approach and you're fighting over the last decimal place.

I wouldn't say I have a specialty in terms of approach, but enjoy trying different things.

Tell us about a particularly challenging competition you entered, and what insights you used to tackle the task.

A couple of years ago, Google ran a competition for detecting objects within images and the relationships between them (e.g., "chair at table"). Other teams spent ages taking a conventional approach and training large neural networks to tackle the tasks, which I didn't have the knowledge or compute to compete with. I chose to attack the problem from a different angle, and using some neat heuristics and tree models I ended up in seventh place with just a few hours of work.

Has Kaggle helped you in your career?

Kaggle has led to lots of opportunities for me and has been a really great community to get to know. I've met lots of people and learned a lot throughout all the competitions I've participated in. But Kaggle is also how I got into machine learning in the first place – and I don't think I would be in this field otherwise. So yes, it's helped a lot.

What mistakes have you made in competitions in the past?

It's quite easy to end up with a complicated solution that you can't replicate from scratch, since chances are you'll be using various versions of code and intermediate datasets in your final solution. Then, if you're lucky enough to win, it can be very stressful to deliver working code to the host! If you're doing well, it's a good idea to pin down what your solution is and clean up your code.

It's also easy to get into a situation where you use different validation sets for different models, or don't retain validation predictions, which can make it hard to compare them or do meta-learning later on in the competition.

Are there any particular tools or libraries that you would recommend using for data analysis or machine learning?

I really like XGBoost, which still tends to beat neural networks on tabular data (as well as its newer cousin, LightGBM). SHAP is really nice for explaining models (even complex ones), which can give you more insights into what to try next.

What's the most important thing someone should keep in mind or do when they're entering a competition?

I think it's important to try not to get bogged down in implementing ultra-complicated solutions, and instead try to make incremental solutions.

Competitions now are a lot harder than when I first started out, so it's a good idea to look at other people's code (lots of people make this public during the competition) and try to learn from them. You might want to consider joining a team with some other Kagglers: competitions in teams have been the most fun competitions for me, and have always been a fantastic learning experience.

And finally: most ideas tend to not work – if you want to win a competition, you need to persevere and keep experimenting!

Kaggle has certainly been influential in the previous three interviewees' rich lives and careers, and they are only just getting started. Below we speak to two Kagglers who now hold senior roles in their respective companies, and who have had long and fruitful journeys also thanks to Kaggle.

Dan Becker

https://www.kaggle.com/dansbecker

First, we have Dan Becker, a Notebooks Grandmaster and Vice President of Product, Decision Intelligence, at DataRobot. Kaggle has played a significant part in Dan's career.

Can you tell us about yourself?

I first tried using machine learning at a 3-person start-up in 2000 where we tried to use neural networks to help retailers optimize the reserve prices they set for items on eBay. We had no clue what we were doing, and we failed miserably.

By 2002, I was confident that machine learning could never work. I got a PhD in economics and took a job as an economist for the US government. I wanted to move to Colorado, but there weren't many jobs there looking for economics PhDs. So I was looking for a less academic credential.

In 2010, I saw a newspaper article about the Heritage Health Prize. *It was an early Kaggle competition with a $3 million prize. I still believed that simpler models like what I used as an economist would give better predictions than fancy machine learning models. So I started competing, thinking that a good score in this competition would be the credential I needed to find an interesting job in Colorado. My first submission to that competition was not last place, but it was pretty close. My heart sank when I watched my model get scored, and then saw everyone else was so far ahead of me. I briefly gave up any hope of doing well in the competition, but I was frustrated not even to be average.*

I spent all my nights and weekends working on the competition to climb up the leaderboard. I relearned machine learning, which had progressed a lot in the 10 years since I'd first tried it. I'd learn more and upload a new model each day. It took a lot of time, but it was rewarding to march up the leaderboard each day. By the time my score was in the middle of the leaderboard, I thought continued work might get me in the top 10%. So I kept working. Soon I was in the top 10%, thinking I might get in the top 10 competitors.

When I was in the top 10, an analytics consulting company reached out to me to ask if I wanted to be hired and compete under their company name, which they would use for marketing. I told them I would do it if I could work from Colorado. So the Kaggle competition helped me achieve my original goal.

We finished in 2nd place. There was no prize for 2nd place, but everything I've done in my career since then has been enabled by this one Kaggle competition. It was a bigger success than I ever could have imagined.

How else has Kaggle helped you in your career?

Kaggle has almost entirely made my career. My first job as a data scientist came when someone recruited me off the leaderboard. My next job after that was working for Kaggle. Then I worked at DataRobot, whose recruiting strategy at the time was to hire people who had done well in Kaggle competitions. Then I went back to Kaggle to start Kaggle Learn, which is Kaggle's data science education platform. The list goes on. Every job I've had in the last decade is clearly attributable to my initial Kaggle success.

As I switched from economics to data science, my Kaggle achievements were at the heart of why I was hired. Being further in my career now, I don't think in terms of portfolios... and I'm fortunate that I'm recruited more than I look for work.

What's your favorite kind of competition and why? In terms of techniques and solving approaches, what is your specialty on Kaggle?

I've been around the community for a long time, but I haven't intensely dedicated myself to a competition in 7 or 8 years. I enjoy new types of competitions. For example, I was first exposed to deep learning in 2013 as part of Kaggle's first competitions where deep learning was competitive. This was before Keras, TensorFlow, PyTorch, or any of the deep learning frameworks that exist today. No one in the community really knew how to do deep learning, so everyone was learning something new for the first time.

Kaggle also ran an adversarial modeling competition, where some people built models that tried to manipulate images slightly to fool other models. That was very experimental, and I don't know if they'll ever run anything like that again. But I really like the experimental stuff, when everyone in the community is figuring things out together in the forums.

How do you approach a Kaggle competition? How different is this approach to what you do in your day-to-day work?

The last few times I've done competitions, I focused on "what tooling can I build for this competition that would automate my work across projects?". That hasn't been especially successful, but it's an interesting challenge. It's very different from how I approach everything else professionally.

Outside of competitions, I LOVE analytics and just looking at data on interesting topics. I sometimes say that my strength as a data scientist is that I just look at the data (in ways that aren't filtered by ML models).

I also spend a lot of time thinking about how we go from an ML model's prediction to what decision we make. For example, if a machine learning model predicts that a grocery store will sell 1,000 mangos before the next shipment comes, how many should that grocery store hold in stock? Some people assume it's 1,000... exactly what you forecast you can sell. That's wrong.

You need to think about trade-offs between the cost of spoiling mangos if you buy too many vs the cost of running out. And what's their shelf life? Can you carry extra stock until after your next shipment comes? There's a lot of optimization to be done there that's part of my day-to-day work, and it's stuff that doesn't show up in Kaggle competitions.

Tell us about a particularly challenging competition you entered, and what insights you used to tackle the task.

I tried to build an automated system that did joins and feature engineering for the Practice Fusion Diabetes Classification *challenge. The main thing I learned was that if you have more than a few files, you still needed a person to look at the data and understand what feature engineering makes sense.*

In your experience, what do inexperienced Kagglers often overlook? What do you know now that you wish you'd known when you first started?

New participants don't realize how high the bar is to do well in Kaggle competitions. They think they can jump in and score in the top 50% with a pretty generic approach... and that's usually not true. The thing I was most surprised by was the value of using leaderboard scores for different models in assigning weights when ensembling previous submissions.

What mistakes have you made in competitions in the past?

I've screwed up last-minute details of submissions in multi-stage competitions several times (and ended up in last place or near last place as a result).

Are there any particular tools or libraries that you would recommend using for data analysis or machine learning?

Mostly the standard stuff.

Outside of Kaggle competitions, I personally like Altair for visualization... and I write a lot of SQL. SQL is designed for looking at simple aggregations or trends rather than building complex models, but I think that's a feature rather than a bug.

Jeong-Yoon Lee

`https://www.kaggle.com/jeongyoonlee`

Finally, we have Jeong-Yoon Lee, a multiple-medal-winning Competitions Master and Senior Research Scientist in the Rankers and Search Algorithm Engineering team at Netflix Research.

Can you tell us about yourself?

My name is Jeong, and I'm a Senior Research Scientist at Netflix. I started Kaggle back in 2011 when I finished my PhD and joined an analytic consulting start-up, Opera Solutions. There, I met avid Kaggle competitors including Michael Jahrer, and we participated in KDD Cups and Kaggle competitions together. Since then, even after leaving the company, I continue working on competitions both as a competitor and an organizer. Lately, I don't spend as much time as I did before on Kaggle, but still check it out from time to time to learn the latest tools and approaches in ML.

Has Kaggle helped you in your career?

Tremendously. First, it provides credentials in ML. Many hiring managers (when I was an interviewee) as well as candidates (when I was an interviewer) mentioned that my Kaggle track records had caught their attention. Second, it provides learning in state-of-the-art approaches in ML. By working on over 100 competitions across different domains, I'm familiar with more approaches to almost any ML problem than my peers. Third, it provides a network of top-class data scientists across the world. I've met so many talented data scientists at Kaggle and enjoy working with them. I translated Abhishek Thakur's book, organized a panel at KDD with Mario, Giba, and Abhishek, and am interviewing for Luca's book. ;)

In 2012, I used Factorization Machine, which was introduced by Steffen Rendle at KDD Cup 2012, and improved on prediction performance by 30% over an existing SVM model in a month after I joined a new company. At a start-up I co-founded, our main pitch was the ensemble algorithm to beat the market-standard linear regression. At Uber, I introduced adversarial validation to address covariate shifts in features in the machine learning pipelines.

What's your favorite kind of competition and why? In terms of techniques and solving approaches, what is your specialty on Kaggle?

I like competitions with small to medium-size datasets, which are mostly tabular data competitions, because I can quickly iterate different approaches even on my laptop anytime anywhere. During my peak time at Kaggle in 2015, I often built my solutions on the airplane or in between my babysitting shifts. My triplets were born in late 2014 and I was working at a new start-up I'd co-founded.

I don't think I have any special modeling techniques, but my specialty is more around competition management, which includes recruiting team members, setting up a collaboration framework (e.g., Git, S3, Messenger, Wiki, internal leaderboard, cross-validation splits), helping the team work effectively throughout the competition, etc. So I'm not a competition Grandmaster myself, but was able to reach the top 10 because other Grandmasters liked to work with me.

How do you approach a Kaggle competition? How different is this approach to what you do in your day-to-day work?

I try to build a pipeline that enables fast iterations and incremental improvements. The more ideas you try, the better chance you have to do well in a competition. The principle applies to my day-to-day work as well. The scope is different, though. At work, we start by defining problems and identifying the data, while at Kaggle, both are given, and we start from EDA.

In your experience, what do inexperienced Kagglers often overlook? What do you know now that you wish you'd known when you first started?

Recently, I noticed that many users simply fork a Notebook shared by other users and fine-tune it to get better scores. Eventually what matters is learning, not the Kaggle ranking or points. I recommend that new Kagglers spend more time building their own solutions.

What's the most important thing someone should keep in mind or do when they're entering a competition?

It's about learning, not about winning.

> ## Do you use other competition platforms? How do they compare to Kaggle?
>
> *I'm advising Dacon AI, a Korean ML competition platform company. It started in 2018 and has hosted 96 competitions so far. It's still in an early stage compared to Kaggle, but provides similar experiences to Korean users.*

Participating in Kaggle Days and other Kaggle meetups

A good way to build connections with other Kagglers (and also be more easily accepted into a team) is simply to meet them. Meetups and conferences have always been a good way to do so, even if they do not specifically deal with Kaggle competitions, because the speakers talk about their experiences on Kaggle or because the topics have been dealt with in Kaggle competitions. For instance, many Research competitions require successful competitors to write papers on their experience, and the paper could be presented or quoted during a conference speech.

There were no special events directly connected with Kaggle until 2018, when LogicAI, a company created by *Maria Parysz* and *Paweł Jankiewicz*, arranged the first Kaggle Days event in Warsaw, Poland, in collaboration with Kaggle. They gathered over 100 participants and 8 Kaggle Grandmasters as speakers.

More Kaggle Days events followed. Here are the events that were arranged, along with the links to the materials and talks:

- Warsaw, May 2018 (`https://kaggledays.com/events/warsaw2018`)
- Paris, January 2019 (`https://kaggledays.com/events/paris2019`)
- San Francisco, April 2019 (`https://kaggledays.com/event/sanfrancisco2019`)
- Dubai, April 2019 (`https://kaggledays.com/events/dubai2019`)
- Beijing, October 2019 (`https://kaggledays.com/events/beijing2019`)
- Tokyo, December 2019 (`https://kaggledays.com/events/tokyo2019`)

Starting from the second event in Paris, smaller events in the form of meetups were held in various cities (over 50 meetups in 30 different locations). Participating in a major event or in a meetup is a very good opportunity to meet other Kagglers and make friends, and could be helpful both for career purposes or for teaming up for future Kaggle competitions.

In fact, one of the authors found their next job in just this way.

Getting spotted and other job opportunities

For some time, Kaggle was a hotspot where employers could find rare competencies in data analysis and machine learning modeling. Kaggle itself offered a job board among the discussion forums and many recruiters roamed the leaderboard looking for profiles to contact. Companies themselves held contests explicitly to find candidates (Facebook, Intel, and Yelp arranged recruiting competitions for this purpose) or conveniently pick up the best competitors after seeing them perform excellently on certain kinds of problems (such as the insurance company AXA did after its telematics competitions). The peak of all this was marked by a Wired interview with *Gilberto Titericz*, where it was stated that *"highly ranked solvers are flooded with job offers"* (https://www.wired.com/story/solve-these-tough-data-problems-and-watch-job-offers-roll-in/).

Recently, things have changed somewhat and many Kagglers report that the best that you can expect when you win or score well in a competition is some contact from recruiters for a couple of months. Let's look at how things have changed and why.

Nowadays, you seldom find job offers requiring Kaggle experience, since companies most often require previous experience in the field (even better, in the same industry or knowledge domain), an academic background in math-heavy disciplines, or certifications from Google, Amazon, or Microsoft. Your presence on Kaggle will still have some effect because it will allow you to:

- Be spotted by recruiters that monitor Kaggle rankings and competitions
- Be spotted by companies themselves, since many managers and human resource departments keep an eye on Kaggle profiles
- Have some proof of your coding and machine learning ability that could help companies select you, perhaps not requiring you to take any further tests
- Have specific experience of problems highly relevant to certain companies that you cannot acquire otherwise because data is not easily accessible to everyone (for instance, telematics, fraud detection, or deepfakes, which have all been topics of Kaggle competitions)

Seldom will your results and rankings be taken into account at face value, though, because it is difficult to distinguish the parts that are actually due to your skill from other factors affecting the results that are of less interest to a company thinking of hiring you (for instance, the time you have available to devote to competitions, hardware availability, or some luck).

Your Kaggle rankings and results will more likely be noticed in the following cases:

- You have scored well in a competition whose problem is particularly important for the company.

- You have systematically scored well in multiple competitions around topics of interest for the company, a sign of real competency that means you are not simply labeling yourself a "data scientist" or a "machine learning engineer" without a solid basis.

- Through your Kaggle participation, you are showing a true passion for data analysis to the point where you are investing your free time for free. This is a positive, but may also turn into a double-edged sword and bring lower monetary offers unless you show that you recognize your value.

While they might not make the difference alone, your Kaggle rankings and results can act as **differentiators**. Recruiters and companies may use Kaggle rankings to make lists of potential candidates. The two most noticed rankings are in Competitions and Notebooks (hence, they also have the more intense competition and larger numbers of Grandmasters out of the four ranked areas), but sometimes they also watch the rankings for a *specific* competition. When certain rare competencies (for instance, in NLP or computer vision) are sought after, it is easier to find them in competitions that require you to use them skillfully in order to be successful.

Another great differentiator comes at interview time. You can quote your competitions to show how you solved problems, how you coded solutions, and how you interacted and collaborated with teammates. On these occasions, more than the ranking or medal you got from Kaggle, it is important to talk about the specifics of the Kaggle competition, such as the industry it referred to, the type of data you had to deal with and why it interested you, and also to present your actions during the competition using the **STAR approach**, often used in job interviews.

The STAR approach

In the STAR approach, you should structure what you did in a competition based on the framework **Situation**, **Task**, **Action**, and **Result**. This method aims to have you talk more about behaviors than techniques, thus putting more emphasis on your capacities than the capabilities of the algorithm you have chosen; anyone else could have used the same algorithm, but it was you who managed to use it so successfully.

 The method works principally when dealing with success stories, but you can also apply it to unsuccessful ones, especially for situations where you gained important insights about the reasons for your failure that stopped you from failing in the same way again.

To apply the method, you break down your story into four components:

- **Situation**: Describe the context and the details of the situation so the interviewer can understand, at a glance, the problems and opportunities
- **Task**: Describe your specific role and responsibilities in the situation, helping to frame your individual contribution in terms of skills and behaviors
- **Action**: Explain what action you took in order to handle the task
- **Result**: Illustrate the results of your actions as well as the overall result

Some companies do explicitly ask for the STAR approach (or its relative, the **Goal-Impact-Challenges-Finding** method, where more emphasis is put on the results); others do not, but expect something similar.

 The best answers are those that suit the values and objectives of the company you are interviewing for.

Since just reporting the rankings and medals you got in a competition may not be enough to impress your interviewer, reformulating your successful experience in a Kaggle competition is paramount. The approach can work either when you have competed solo or in a team; in the latter case, an important aspect to describe is how you interacted with and positively influenced the other teammates. Let's discuss some ways you could do that.

First, you describe the situation that arose in the competition. This could be in the initial phases, in the experimentation phases, or in the final wrap-up. It is important you provide clear context in order for the listener to evaluate whether your behavior was correct for the situation. Be very detailed and explain the situation and why it required your attention and action.

Then, you should explain the task that you took on. For instance, it could be cleaning your data, doing explorative analysis, creating a benchmark model, or continuously improving your solution.

Next, you describe how you executed the task. Here, it would be quite handy if you could present a Medium article or a GitHub project in support of your description (as we discussed in the previous chapter). Systematically presenting your experience and competence through well-written documentation and good coding will enforce your value proposition in front of the interviewer.

Finally, you have to explain the result obtained, which could be either qualitative (for instance, how you coordinated the work of a team competing on Kaggle) or quantitative (for instance, how much your contribution affected the final result).

Summary (and some parting words)

In this chapter, we have discussed how competing on Kaggle can help improve your career prospects. We have touched on building connections, both by teaming up on competitions and participating in events related to past competitions, and also on using your Kaggle experience in order to find a new job. We have discussed how, based on our experience and the experience of other Kagglers, results on Kaggle alone cannot ensure that you get a position. However, they can help you get attention from recruiters and human resource departments and then reinforce how you present competencies in data science (if they are supported by a carefully-built portfolio, as we described in the previous chapter).

This chapter also marks the conclusion of the book. Through fourteen chapters, we have discussed Kaggle competitions, Datasets, Notebooks, and discussions. We covered technical topics in machine learning and deep learning (from evaluation metrics to simulation competitions) with the aim of helping you achieve more both on Kaggle and after Kaggle.

Having been involved in Kaggle competitions for ten years, we know very well that you can find everything you may need to know on Kaggle – but everything is dispersed across hundreds of competitions and thousands of Notebooks, discussions, and Datasets. Finding what you need, when you need it, can prove daunting for anyone starting off on Kaggle. We compiled what we think is essential, indispensable knowledge to guide you through all the competitions you may want to take part in. That is why this has not been a book on data science in a strict sense, but a book specifically on data science on Kaggle.

Aside from technical and practical hints, we also wanted to convey that, in over ten years, we have always found a way to turn our experiences on Kaggle into positive ones. You can re-read this work as a book that describes our endless journey through the world of data science competitions. A journey on Kaggle does not end when you get all the Grandmaster titles and rank first worldwide. It actually never ends, because you can re-invent how you participate and leverage your experience in competitions in endless ways. As this book ends, so your journey on Kaggle starts, and we wish for you a long, rich, and fruitful experience – as it has been for us. Have a great journey!

Join our book's Discord space

Join the book's Discord workspace for a monthly *Ask me Anything* session with the authors:

https://packt.link/KaggleDiscord

packt.com

Subscribe to our online digital library for full access to over 7,000 books and videos, as well as industry leading tools to help you plan your personal development and advance your career. For more information, please visit our website.

Why subscribe?

- Spend less time learning and more time coding with practical eBooks and Videos from over 4,000 industry professionals
- Improve your learning with Skill Plans built especially for you
- Get a free eBook or video every month
- Fully searchable for easy access to vital information
- Copy and paste, print, and bookmark content

At www.packt.com, you can also read a collection of free technical articles, sign up for a range of free newsletters, and receive exclusive discounts and offers on Packt books and eBooks.

Other Books
You May Enjoy

If you enjoyed this book, you may be interested in these other books by Packt:

Machine Learning with PyTorch and Scikit-Learn

Sebastian Raschka

Yuxi (Hayden) Liu

Vahid Mirjalili

ISBN: 9781801819312

- Explore frameworks, models, and techniques for machines to 'learn' from data
- Use scikit-learn for machine learning and PyTorch for deep learning
- Train machine learning classifiers on images, text, and more

- Build and train neural networks, transformers, and boosting algorithms
- Discover best practices for evaluating and tuning models
- Predict continuous target outcomes using regression analysis
- Dig deeper into textual and social media data using sentiment analysis

Transformers for Natural Language Processing – Second Edition

Denis Rothman

ISBN: 9781803247335

- Discover new ways of performing NLP techniques with the latest pretrained transformers

- Grasp the workings of the original Transformer, GPT-3, BERT, T5, DeBERTa, and Reformer

- Find out how ViT and CLIP label images (including blurry ones!) and reconstruct images using DALL-E

- Carry out sentiment analysis, text summarization, casual language analysis, machine translations, and more using TensorFlow, PyTorch, and GPT-3

- Measure the productivity of key transformers to define their scope, potential, and limits in production

Machine Learning for Time-Series with Python

Ben Auffarth

ISBN: 9781801819626

- Understand the main classes of time-series and learn how to detect outliers and patterns
- Choose the right method to solve time-series problems
- Characterize seasonal and correlation patterns through autocorrelation and statistical techniques
- Get to grips with time-series data visualization
- Understand classical time-series models like ARMA and ARIMA
- Implement deep learning models, like Gaussian processes, transformers, and state-of-the-art machine learning models
- Become familiar with many libraries like Prophet, XGboost, and TensorFlow

Packt is searching for authors like you

If you're interested in becoming an author for Packt, please visit authors.packtpub.com and apply today. We have worked with thousands of developers and tech professionals, just like you, to help them share their insight with the global tech community. You can make a general application, apply for a specific hot topic that we are recruiting an author for, or submit your own idea.

Share your thoughts

Now you've finished *The Kaggle Book*, we'd love to hear your thoughts! Scan the QR code below to go straight to the Amazon review page for this book and share your feedback or leave a review on the site that you purchased it from.

https://packt.link/r/1-801-81747-2

Your review is important to us and the tech community and will help us make sure we're delivering excellent quality content.

Index

Download a free PDF copy of this book

Thanks for purchasing this book!

Do you like to read on the go but are unable to carry your print books everywhere? Is your eBook purchase not compatible with the device of your choice?

Don't worry, now with every Packt book you get a DRM-free PDF version of that book at no cost.

Read anywhere, any place, on any device. Search, copy, and paste code from your favorite technical books directly into your application.

The perks don't stop there, you can get exclusive access to discounts, newsletters, and great free content in your inbox daily

Follow these simple steps to get the benefits:

1. Scan the QR code or visit the link below

https://packt.link/free-ebook/9781801817479

2. Submit your proof of purchase
3. That's it! We'll send your free PDF and other benefits to your email directly

Made in United States
North Haven, CT
19 February 2023

32832008R00291